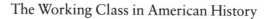

The Working Class in American History

Editorial Advisors

David Brody
Alice Kessler-Harris
David Montgomery
Sean Wilentz

A list of books in the series
appears at the end of this volume.

Southern Labor
and Black Civil Rights

Southern Labor
and Black Civil Rights

Organizing Memphis Workers

MICHAEL K. HONEY

University of Illinois Press
Urbana and Chicago

© 1993 by the Board of Trustees of the University of Illinois
Manufactured in the United States of America
1 2 3 4 5 C P 5 4 3 2 1
This book is printed on acid-free paper.

Library of Congress Cataloging-in-Publication Data
Honey, Michael K.
  Southern labor and black civil rights : organizing Memphis
workers / Michael K. Honey
      p. cm. — (Working class in American history)
  Includes bibliographical references and index.
  ISBN 0-252-02000-6. — ISBN 0-252-06305-8 (pbk.)
    1. Trade-unions—Tennessee—Memphis—History—20th century.
  2. Trade-unions—Tennessee—Memphis—Afro-American membership.
  3. Labor movement—Tennessee—Memphis—History—20th century.
  I. Title.   II. Series.
  HD6519.M45H66 1993
  331.6'396073076819—dc20
                                                      92-28735
                                                        CIP

Dr. Martin Luther King, Jr., died on 4 April 1968
in Memphis, Tennessee.
For twenty-five years and more,
people committed to his memory
have been trying to learn the meaning of that death.
This book tells something
of that meaning.

To Keith Honey and Betty Miner Honey,
who made the historian,
and to the working people of Memphis,
who made the history.

Contents

Acknowledgments

I began this history as a dissertation in the fall of 1982. It has been a project for nearly ten years. My interest in the topic resulted partly from my own experience as a community and civil liberties organizer in Memphis and around the South in the early 1970s. My first career came in trying to change history; my second, in trying to record it (and change it).

Many people and institutions led to this book. Parents and family taught me to care and to back up my beliefs with action. Anne and Carl Braden, Frank Wilkinson, Pete Seeger, Candy and Guy Carawan, David Sawyer, Jimmy Collier, and other important friends and colleagues taught me about organizing and about the power of music. The Howard University History Department first opened my mind to the worlds of African-American and southern history. The history faculty at Northern Illinois University exposed me to yet other worlds. Otto Olsen taught me about writing, about humility, about how to be a historian. I owe a great deal to his friendship and teaching. He gave the closest attention to the many crude drafts of this manuscript from its earliest days.

I owe a special debt to David Montgomery for his careful readings and his trenchant comments. As a book, this volume has fewer faults due to the attention he has given it, despite his many pressing obligations. As author and editor, he has helped me to try to understand labor history and to say what needed to be said in this study.

I would like to thank August Meier also for his early and painstaking attention to the manuscript. In addition, numerous colleagues and friends have read all or parts of the manuscript. Although I did not always follow their advice, in many ways their comments helped me to improve it. Readers include Joe William Trotter, Mark Naison, Robert Korstad, Nell

Irvin Painter, Robert Zieger, Nelson Lichtenstein, Russ Allen, Jacquelyn Dowd Hall, Stuart Kaufman, John Harkins, David Tucker, David Smith, Roger Biles, Pete Daniel, Gavin Wright, J. Carroll Moody, Morton Sosna, Dan Perlstein, Patti Krueger, William Minter, Mark Allen, Pamela Wilson, and Gary Fink. A number of people in other ways have helped me to think about my work in history, including Henry Rosemont, Arnold Taylor, Rick Halpern, Ira Berlin, Robin Kelley, Joe Reidy, and Susan and Clayborne Carson. I am grateful to all of these people for sharing their time, energy, and encouragement.

The people who enabled me to do research, often on a shoestring, are too numerous to mention. The gracious and candid working people I interviewed provided much of the inspiration for this book. A number of these people fed me and put me up while they took hours or days to tell me about their lives. I will always regret that I did not locate Thomas Watkins in time to hear his life story. Among others who helped an itinerant scholar, Mark Allen and Joy Tremewin and Steve Lockwood and Mary Durham graciously hosted me many times in Memphis; Leon Fink and Susan Levine and Lou Paul gave me early refuge in Chapel Hill, as did Mary Green Britting in Atlanta. Martha and Donna Allen gave me constant encouragement and advice in Washington, D.C. I especially thank them for their solidarity and love.

The National Endowment for the Humanities gave me a one-year fellowship to complete this book. The Stanford Humanities Center gave me a fellowship that made it possible for me to use my NEH grant in residence at Stanford in 1989–90. The American Council of Learned Societies gave me an earlier grant to transcribe many of the interviews I have used portions of in this book. W. H. and Carol Ferry and the Marion Davis Scholarship Fund both helped at critical times during the completion of the early manuscript as a dissertation, as did the Northern Illinois University Graduate School. The University of Washington–Tacoma provided me with critical time off from teaching to complete this work.

During an era of cutbacks and sometimes drastic staff reductions and reorganizations, the continued commitment of librarians and research specialists has been the key to my study of southern labor history. Thanks to the precious people who make research happen at the Walter Reuther Archives of Labor and Urban Affairs; the Special Collections Department at the Perkins Library, Duke University; the Mississippi Valley Collection of Memphis State University; the Memphis Public Library; the Wisconsin Historical Society in Madison; the Southern Labor Archives at Georgia State University in Atlanta; the Library of Congress; the National Archives and Records Administration; and the Highlander Research and Education Center in Tennessee.

Finally, I thank my parents, Keith and Betty Honey, siblings Maureen and Charles, and companion and partner Patti Krueger for encouraging and supporting me during years of difficulty, hard work, and, finally, reward.

Labor and Civil Rights

Thomas Watkins rolled over with a groan. His muscles ached from the previous day's work, loading cotton onto Mississippi River barges. Those cotton bales could weigh nearly five hundred pounds. The workers, all of them black, did the loading with primitive two-wheeled hand trucks. It was 26 May 1939.

He looked at the clock; it was 2:30 in the morning. The pounding on the door grew louder, and Watkins scrambled to his feet and turned on the light. His wife, Arlene, partially deaf and nearly blind, didn't hear a thing. It was the police, and he knew what they wanted. Watkins's children began to cry. There was nothing to do but open the door.

Two heavy-set officers entered. They walked through his house, a small wooden frame building at 69 West De Soto Street in an old part of Memphis inhabited by poor black and white river workers. Another officer entered through the back door. "We have some people want to look at you," they told him.[1]

The city's all-white police force had a well-known reputation for brutality in the African-American community of Memphis. Although the officers at the Watkinses' home appeared strangely calm, the police often seemed to be in a rage, especially around black people. They could be perfectly courteous when they felt like it; Watkins had witnessed their mild, almost obsequious behavior around well-dressed cotton brokers and their jocularity and good-ol'-boy humor around rough-and-tumble riverboat owners. But because of his color, Watkins also knew a different side of the police. He knew police, and whites, in ways they didn't even know themselves. If he grinned, and acted as witless as the police sometimes acted themselves, they might let him live.

But Watkins was not the grinning type. The police had already beaten him severely one night on President's Island. Earlier, they had arrested Watkins and a white union organizer on the nebulous charge of "communism." In another run-in, Memphis police chief Will Lee told Watkins, "I'll get you if it takes me twenty years, you son of a bitch." He wondered what they would charge him with this time.[2]

Heavily muscled black dockworkers had begun to guard Watkins to protect him against police and the agents of Memphis riverboat owners. But he was alone now. The officers snapped a pair of handcuffs on him. At the insistence of the police, Tom got Arlene out of bed, and within minutes the couple found themselves locked in an unmarked car, speeding toward the riverfront. Despite their pleadings, the police had left two children, one five and the other eighteen months, at home alone in the middle of the night, with the door unlocked.

Tom Watkins had met up with southern "justice" before he came to Memphis. For a period during his childhood, his parents had lived as sharecroppers. Their white landlord forced them to leave when Tom insisted on going to school instead of working in the fields. His parents moved about from Texas, where Tom was born, to Massachusetts, Kansas City, and Indianapolis, looking for work. For reasons he never discussed, Watkins left them at an early age to begin his own odyssey. In 1925, he joined the military looking for a vocation, hoping he would be treated like a man. Instead, white officers consigned him to cleaning latrines and ditch-digging, constantly insulting him. One enlisted man attempted to kick Watkins in the behind, but instead of grinning, Tom knocked the man down. Not long after this incident, white officers charged Tom with stealing, a charge he denied for the rest of his life, and had him court-martialed. After he had served eight months of a prison term at hard labor in Fort Leavenworth, the military dishonorably discharged him.[3]

For years after this, Watkins had been part of the army of the wandering unemployed, riding in boxcars and living in jungle camps, periodically arrested by police for vagrancy and "train riding." He worked a variety of jobs in the western states and then moved south and east. He learned to be a plumber, a brickmason, and worked for a time in the Pittsburgh steel mills. The depression struck, and he continued to wander from job to job. But he never learned how to say "sir" to a white man with the proper enthusiasm or to keep his eyes down, to stoop and shuffle around whites. Despite his hard knocks, when he arrived in Memphis in 1934, Watkins still believed that he had a right to improve himself, to make a decent living, and to carry himself with pride. He was thirty-nine years old.[4]

In Memphis, Watkins became a natural leader among the black dock-workers. Like them, Watkins rippled with muscles and knew how to handle a heavy load. He also knew how to say no to a white man. He carried a whistle around his neck, and whenever he blew it, every dockworker stopped work. If the bosses pushed them too hard or abused them too much, Watkins blew the whistle. Years later, white riverboat worker W. E. "Red" Davis still stood in awe of Watkins. "He was like the slave revolt leader Denmark Vesey, absolutely fearless," said Davis. "He figured he would not live long, but he decided to fight for the union anyway." His intense, fiery demeanor easily marked him as an enemy of the South's system of white supremacy.[5]

As the police led him handcuffed to the riverfront, Tom may have considered why so few others took on the leadership role he had accepted. Blacks who tried to unionize the Warner-Tamble Transportation Company in the 1930s were known to "disappear" from Memphis. Several months after Watkins's own arrest, one worker by the name of Willie Cotton, after being taken across the Mississippi by the company's owners, appeared floating face down in the river. Others disappeared, never to be found.[6] Besides the employers, the police themselves posed a continual threat to upstarts such as Watkins. They regularly beat, shot, and killed enough blacks in Memphis that everyone knew the penalty for not living within the etiquette of Jim Crow. Black workers had few allies: even the white leaders of the American Federation of Labor (AFL) had threatened Watkins with physical harm in order to silence his militance on behalf of longshore workers.[7]

The police took Watkins into a darkened warehouse on the docks at the foot of Beale Street. They placed Arlene on a pile of lumber. "We'll take care of the Nigger woman later, and we'll take care of this bastard first," one of the men commented. When Frank Tamble jerked Watkins's head back and his partner, Russell Warner, shined a flashlight in his face, the union leader knew his life was in peril. Both employers had gotten their start illegally running liquor into Memphis; they had killed a number of men and had a reputation for being violently anti-union.[8] Tamble first landed a heavy blow to the back of Watkins's head with a capstan bar—a thirty-pound piece of oak timber used to draw barges to the docks. Watkins fell, dazed, while one of the officers urged his partner to tie him up with rope and iron and "drop him overboard quick." Tamble delivered another blow, but missed Watkins's head and hit his shoulder instead.[9]

"What are you trying to do, kill me Captain Frank?" Tom shouted out. Tamble had already aimed his third blow at the union leader, who this time dodged the blow and knocked Tamble's feet from under him. Watkins desperately dashed past Tamble, but ran into a steel door and fell backwards, as the police began firing their pistols at him. With a mad strength born of panic, Watkins bulldozed Tamble, Warner, and one of the police officers and ran out a side door. The two officers still standing fired numerous shots at him as he ran down a gangway to the end of the docks and leaped across the water onto a barge. Watkins jumped to a second barge, then somersaulted into the river while trying to reach a third barge, breaking his handcuffs as he fell. One bullet grazed his pants cuff, but once he was in the river, the police could no longer follow his movements.

Watkins made his way in the dark along the river's edge until he found a safe spot to climb out. He passed a black night watchman and yelled out for him to call for help, but when the guard realized the police were chasing Watkins, he would do nothing. The union leader followed a number of levees to the railroad tracks near Beale Street, where he collapsed, bleeding from his head wound. After recovering his strength, he ran down the railroad tracks, avoiding the police cars circling the area. He finally went to a woman's house where he once boarded on Front Street and asked her to send for a union member from the Western Kentucky Coal Company. Several hours later, two union men took him to one of their homes near Butler Street. Watkins hid there for a time and then moved to another location.

Meanwhile, Watkins's fellow union members went to the Federal Bureau of Investigation, asking them to give him protection. FBI agents showed up the next morning and took Watkins to their downtown offices. After taking an affidavit from Watkins, the agents brought Police Inspector Clagg Richards over to unlock the broken handcuffs. Richards claimed that the police arrested Watkins merely to question him about a barge set loose by vandals during the recent river strike Watkins had led and had no charges against him. The FBI agents released Watkins to get medical treatment for his scalp and shoulder wounds.

After Watkins left the doctor, he found that the police had his house surrounded. When unionists went to the Greyhound bus station to get him a ticket out of town, they found a number of blacks, unknown to Watkins or his friends, looking for him. "Memphis, like all southern cities," Watkins explained in an FBI affidavit, "has a corps of Negro informants who keep their oppressors up to date on what is being talked about or thought in the Negro community." Fearing to buy the tickets, Watkins's friends kept him hidden for the next two days. Changing houses repeatedly, and at one point going out disguised in women's clothing to check the situation in his neighborhood, Watkins overheard a conversation of building tradespeople, including the head of the AFL Labor Council, who vowed to kill him.

Watkins decided he had to find a way out of Memphis. A group of black women drove him through town to Oseceola, Arkansas. There he finally purchased a bus ticket to East St. Louis. The police eventually released his children, whom they had turned over to juvenile court. Arlene, after enduring further personal threats from the police, left Memphis to join her husband, but the Watkinses could not afford to bring both sons and left their oldest behind with friends. St. Louis police arrested Tom as a suspected fugitive, but the Memphis authorities, responding to national protests from unions and civil liberties groups, decided not to have him extradited.[10]

Watkins never returned to Memphis, for although his supporters called for federal intervention, Watkins had no chance of receiving justice there. Not that federal officials lacked evidence to prosecute; the night guard, Arlene, and three white campers who witnessed his flight verified various parts of Watkins's story. Even more damning, the police offered only a transparent cover-up of their activity. The officers involved in abducting Watkins claimed that he suffered his injuries by falling out of their car when it turned a corner and denied the rest of the events. The FBI agents and the doctor said such injuries could not be the result of a fall. An outraged Memphis citizen asked Attorney General Frank Murphy, "How could a handcuffed man—sitting beside two armed policemen—open a car door, hit the pavement at thirty miles per hour, and be able to run away?"[11]

However much evidence might have existed against the police, the wheels of justice simply did not turn in favor of civil rights or labor activists in Memphis. Local, state, and federal officials remained far more responsive to the whims of local political boss Edward H. Crump than to the U.S. government or the Bill of Rights. In the Watkins case, the local U.S. Attorney, R. G. Draper, dismissed the incident as "merely a scrape between the Memphis police and a negro."[12] Draper quoted city officials, who called Watkins a "vicious agitator, a man who used coercive methods in bringing about strikes among employees who were satisfied and who were entirely at peace with their employers." He told Attorney General Murphy that Watkins did not deserve "any particular consideration, being a recognized criminal, an agitator, a troublemaker, and an altogether bad citizen." White AFL leaders in Memphis likewise condemned Watkins as a violent agitator. Draper refused to bring possible violations of the Wagner Act's labor rights protections or the post–Civil War civil rights statutes before a federal grand jury. Union supporter Lucy Randolph Mason later concluded that "the local FBI and the U.S. District Attorney are completely under Crump's domination," and a local reporter drew the logical conclusion: "They will kill him if he comes back and tries to organize poor people to struggle for a life with human dignity. . . . They will kill all the new Tom Watkins! The people, themselves," she warned, "must stop this thing."[13]

Watkins continued a difficult struggle for the rest of his long life. He became an organizer for the International Longshoremen's Association in St. Louis, but left in 1942 after white barge workers attempted to kill him for helping to elect black officers to the union. He then moved to Portland, Oregon, to work in the shipyards, leaving his family and his old life behind. For the next forty years, he worked at a variety of jobs in Portland, sometimes running his own businesses. He frequently advised black unionists about union politics, but Watkins never regained his place as a natural leader of workers. Sadly, people in Portland did not believe his stories of what had happened in Memphis, and to his close friends he sometimes confessed that he felt like a failure. He never formed a stable family after Memphis, and the FBI continued to investigate him for what they called his alleged "procommunist tendencies" as late as 1973.[14]

His harsh experiences made him a hard man on the outside. "Some would even say he was a mean man," one of his friends commented, "but I know that truly wasn't so." Watkins frequently loaned what money he had to acquaintances, and was renowned for his energy and hard work into his eighties. Despite his great strength and unrelenting years of hard work, however, he died with little money or family, and not even a photograph by which he could be remembered.[15]

Yet, for a short period, Watkins had helped to change the world by standing up to the segregationist South, for the strike he led in 1939 proved to be one of the important turning points for the industrial union movement in Memphis. Many others, women and men, black and white, stood up as well. Like Watkins, many of these people paid a high price for their courage. Thugs beat organizers Norman Smith and George Bass nearly to death in the streets of Memphis; whites attacked African-American activists such as Clarence Coe, George Holloway, and Earl Fisher at work and in their homes; during the cold war years, the news media and the unions themselves hounded union stalwarts like Red Davis, Ed McCrea, Lawrence McGurty, and others out of Memphis. The FBI followed Davis everywhere, repeatedly getting him fired because of his Communist party membership. During his black-listing, Davis had a bout with cancer that almost killed him, and poverty nearly destroyed his family. Yet Davis continued to organize in every job and community of which he became a part, and in the end he felt he had helped in a small way to change the course of history.[16]

The personal commitment and sacrifice of many such working people constituted the life's blood of the southern industrial union movement during the 1930s and 1940s, in the dark days of Jim Crow. Such workers played a major role in the movement away from the racially exclusive craft unionism of the American Federation of Labor (AFL) and toward the biracial industrial unionism of the Congress of Industrial Organizations (CIO). "Biracial" unions included blacks and whites in the same union, rather than segregating blacks and whites into separate locals. But they did not necessarily end segregated seating arrangements, include blacks at top levels of union leadership, or open up the better-paying factory jobs to them. Nonetheless, the participation of African Americans in union elections, picket lines, mass meetings, collective bargaining, and union politics, and of southern whites in biracial forms of organization, profoundly unsettled the segregation system. These developments in the South also raised larger questions about the goals of trade unionism. Were the unions only there to win higher wages and better working conditions? Or did unionism's agenda include larger social goals, such as ending an apartheid system that had helped to lock generations of southern workers into economic squalor and political impotence? And what role should unions play in broad movements for social change?

Southern industrial unions became both a meeting ground for black and white and a battleground over such issues in the 1930s and 1940s. Yet labor histories still provide little documentation of this development in the South or of the significance of biracialism for the CIO as a whole, despite the fact that racial policies often played as significant a role in the ultimate success or failure for unions as their emphasis on industrial or craft style of organization.[17] Only recently have labor historians begun to connect black working-class activism and industrial unionism to the rise of the civil rights movement.[18] Civil rights histories for their part rarely consider the influence that industrial union growth or the experiences of black workers had on the rise of the freedom movements of the 1950s and 1960s.[19] This book, then, seeks to document a missing link in the evolution of the black freedom movement and to analyze labor history with a new perspective. Covering the critical period from the 1930s to the 1950s in detail and with broader references to earlier and later periods, it examines how industrial union organizing affected the system of southern segregation, the workers themselves, and the rise of the black freedom movement. It also considers why the racial system provided such formidable barriers to organizing working people into unions. Memphis, Tennessee, provides the arena for this investigation.

Most people identify Memphis as the home of the blues and a way station for rock and roll. Musicians from Mississippi and West Tennessee converged on the speakeasies and dives of Beale Street to create the distinctive idiom that became urban rhythm and blues. Musicians such as W. C. Handy, B. B. King, Howling Wolf, Memphis Minnie, Elvis Presley, Jerry Lee Lewis, Carl Perkins, and many others reached commercial success via Memphis radio and recording studios. Aretha Franklin and other artists came from Memphis but only gained fame for their enormous talents when they went elsewhere. Songs such as Bessie Smith's "Poor Man's Blues," Maggie Jones's "North Bound Blues," Hattie Burleson's "Sadie's Servant Room Blues," Jimmy Reed's "Big Boss Man," and Big Bill Broonzy's "Black, Brown, and White Blues" all expressed the working-class basis for much of this musical outpouring. As the "capital" of the Mississippi Delta, and the "leader of evil doings in the world," as Sleepy John Estes put it, Memphis became a magnet for rural to urban migrants and a crossroads for the emergence of black and white musical styles that changed the face of American popular culture.[20]

However, Memphis has another, less celebrated but equally important history. First as a bastion of southern slavery, and then as a center for the growth of Delta commerce and industry under a "free" labor system, Memphis became an arena of struggle over the meaning of freedom. Here generations of African Americans fought for the legal due process and voting rights enacted in the Thirteenth, Fourteenth, and Fifteenth Amendments to the Constitution, while radicals and industrial labor organizers at various points fought for political, economic, and social emancipation for workers. While the two struggles were not identical, they remained closely interrelated. The imperatives of the South's racially based class system not only suppressed the civil rights of blacks but practically extinguished the civil liberties guarantees contained in the Bill of Rights for both white and black. Memphis for nearly the first half of the twentieth century became the stronghold of one of the toughest political bosses ever to emerge in the United States, Edward H. Crump. In an atmosphere of pervasive repression, struggles for civil rights, civil liberties, and labor rights became inextricably intertwined. Without the right to organize, neither African Americans nor workers as a group could change their conditions, and that right could not be gained without seriously undermining the segregation system.

Tremendous obstacles to industrial unionism, the greatest of which remained the racial-economic system of southern apartheid, defeated nearly every significant movement for labor or civil rights throughout the 1930s. Yet Memphis in the 1940s witnessed one of the most successful CIO efforts in the South. And just as its music emerged from the singular contributions of African Americans and from the cultural mixture of black and white, its industrial union movement emerged as the result of these influences as well. Both its music and its industrial unions struggled out of the shadows of obscurity during a turning point in the nation's history, in which the United States moved from the disaster of the depression to military and economic dominance of the globe. Curiously, this new era of expansion set off the worst red scare in its history. These national developments had a major impact on the outcome of the local struggle for labor rights, civil liberties, and civil rights.

The history of labor and civil rights struggles in Memphis, placed within the context of regional, national, and international developments, is important for what it tells us about why interracial organizing of any sort has been, and remains, so difficult in the United States. The significance of Memphis history is magnified by the death of Dr. Martin Luther King., Jr., there in 1968 while combining labor and civil rights causes during the "poor people's campaign." The massive confrontation in 1968 between the city government and the African-American community over the right of black sanitation workers to be treated with respect, in a city where nearly half the African-American population lived below the poverty level, indicated that the union gains of a previous era still had not reached into the ranks of many of the poorest and most oppressed citizens of the community.[21] Industrial unionism's organizational expansion had long passed, along with its reform impulse. This study asks what happened to that expansion and that impulse in the South. It concludes that both the successes and limitations of industrial unionism hinged in large measure on how effectively workers and their unions dealt with the issue of racial justice.

The civil rights movement's quest for equality of rights before the law, King insisted, remained hollow without achieving a degree of economic justice. For this reason, he repeatedly turned to the American labor movement as the civil rights movement's greatest potential supporter and ally. But he also emphasized to the union movement that it could not bring about economic justice unless it developed a sustaining social vision that could incorporate the most downtrodden and oppressed into its ranks.[22] Since King's death, concerned people have continued his quest to seek viable movements linking labor rights, civil rights, civil liberties, and economic justice. It is in this context of continuing concern that this study examines the past. Where did the union movement fail, and where did it succeed, and why? What effects did southern industrial unions have on the struggle to end the South's segregation system, and why was that system so hard to kill? What kept blacks and whites so at odds? What did African Americans themselves do to struggle against this system in the lost (to history) decades of the 1930s and 1940s? Does the history of southern unionism offer any hope to future movements for change? How does this history measure up to the vision of King, or for that matter, Tom Watkins or Red Davis? Even an approximate answer to such questions requires a return to an era when organizing a union was worth the price of one's life.

I

Southern Apartheid and the Labor Movement

What was it that made the hate of whites for blacks so steady, seemingly interwoven into the texture of things? What kind of life was possible under that hate? How had this hate come to be?
—Richard Wright

Not logic but a hollow social distinction has separated the races. The economically depressed white accepts his poverty by telling himself that, if in no other respect, at least socially he is above the Negro. For this empty pride in a racial myth he has paid the crushing price of insecurity, hunger, ignorance, and hoplessness for himself and his children.
—Martin Luther King, Jr.

CHAPTER ONE

Segregation and Southern Labor

'Race' is the witchcraft of our time. . . . Man's most dangerous myth.
—Ashley Montague

The slaveholders, by encouraging the enmity of the laboring man against the blacks,
succeeded in making the white man almost as much a slave as the black man himself.
—Frederick Douglass

According to numerous physical anthropologists and biologists, the term *race* has no scientific meaning and should be discarded as a means of categorizing the human species. In this view, there exists only one "race" of people in world history: the human race. Nonetheless, the *belief* in race, specifically the belief in superior and subordinate "races," remains one of the most enduring features of history and culture in the United States. As a source of continual conflict and violence, the history of racism in America demonstrates, as the historian Barbara Fields put it, that "a delusion may be as murderous as a fact." This history has a special meaning in the American South.[1] Here slaveholding and the cotton trade became the surest routes to wealth and power, as enslaved African Americans became the primary source of labor in the fields. Although only a relative handful of white southerners became large plantation owners, many held a few slaves and many more aspired to slave ownership. Nonslaveholding farmers and workers participated in patrolling the slaves and repressing revolts, while planters encouraged them to believe in a "white man's democracy," in which black slaves did much of the field work and menial labor that might have otherwise fallen to poorer whites. An elaborate mythology of inherent white superiority, supported by laws, biblical quotations, and a variety of economic and social sanctions, justified slavery's betrayal of otherwise widely accepted ideals of personal liberty. Both material circumstances and ideology thoroughly racialized southern labor relations.[2]

The city of Memphis arose within this context. Founded as a land specu-
lation in 1819 by Andrew Jackson and associates, who took the land from
the Chickasaws, Memphis owed its very existence to the cotton trade and
slavery. A natural harbor with high river bluffs protecting the area from
floods and surrounded by the rich river bottom lands of the Mississippi
Delta—an area in which slaves made up the majority of the population—
Memphis became the largest slave-trading and cotton-selling market in
the mid-South. As the production of cotton in the South fueled the world
industrial revolution and American economic growth, buyers and sellers
of cotton and slaves made a fortune; many Memphis traders literally sold
Africans "down the river," along with horses and mules. Memphis provided a vital link in a growing grid of river, canal, road, and rail transportation that interlocked industries and markets in the North and the Ohio
River Valley with raw materials and markets in the South and West. As the
city grew, Memphis bankers, merchants, railroad and riverboat owners,
land owners, and manufacturers would continue to associate prosperity
with the cotton trade and cheap black labor, as they had from its inception.[3]

The spread of slavery and the entrenchment of the racial system that
accompanied economic growth produced long-standing problems for the
labor movement. In the city's rough frontier days, poor whites, Native
Americans, and free blacks intermingled, influenced by migrating river
workers and footloose frontier settlers such as Davy Crockett, and by free
labor, anti-slavery advocates such as Frances Wright. But as slavery became
increasingly profitable, city and state leaders outlawed interracial marriage
as well as black education and black civil and political rights, placing
whites of all classes in a position of dominance over blacks. Though the
city's large number of German and Irish immigrants did not particularly
approve of slavery, neither did they organize against it. Rather, the few
existing working men's organizations increasingly tended to blame free
blacks and slaves, rather than slavery or the racial system, for depressing
working-class wages; the city's first unions, of typographers, tailors, and
molders, limited their membership to white males. The city's voting majority of poor and working class white males opposed southern secession in
1860, and yet slavery had involved them in a tangled web of social relations
that made it difficult even to conceive of opposing the racial system.[4]

The social divisions imposed by slavery made it virtually impossible for
free and unfree workers to organize together. Few unions survived in this
climate, but when the Civil War overturned slavery, new possibilities arose.
Railroad construction increasingly linked Memphis industry and trade to

the broader economy after the war, and as it did so the population boomed. The need for new buildings, streets, and commercial and urban services spawned a variety of new industries and new unions as well. During the Reconstruction era, workers engaged in the city's first strikes, and blacks in the Republican party and whites in the Workingman's party joined together briefly to elect a reform mayor, on a platform emphasizing labor rights "irrespective of race or color." By the 1880s, some two thousand workers belonged to unions. Among these, the Knights of Labor organized blacks as well as whites, though typically into separate locals, and stressed the belief that "an injury to one is the concern of all." Construction workers, railroad and iron workers, artisans, and skilled and unskilled workers in woodworking, cigar, cottonseed oil, and furniture factories also organized. During several decades of labor turmoil following the war, attempts to unite workers regardless of race seemed to hold great promise.[5]

However, other forces pushed potential working-class allies apart. The collapse of slavery unleashed a flood of migrants from the countryside, causing the Memphis black population to increase by some 400 percent in ten years. The resulting lower-class competition for housing and jobs in 1866 helped trigger one of the worst white race riots of the post–Civil War era, leaving forty-six blacks and two whites dead and much of the African-American community, including all of its schools, burned to the ground. State imposition of legal segregation and the adoption of the poll tax robbed the freed slaves of upward mobility, civil rights, and political power, as Delta planters imposed new forms of control over black labor to replace the slave system. In the surrounding Delta, the "better elements" organized the Ku Klux Klan and worked with Democratic party "redeemers" to defeat Reconstruction government through a combination of race-baiting, fraud, and terror. In the 1870s, Memphis experienced another kind of terror, as a series of deadly yellow fever plagues cut the city's population in half; Mother Jones, later a heroine of the U.S. labor movement, lost her entire family in the plague. In 1879, the state of Tennessee placed the devastated city, with a population about 70 percent black, into receivership. The legislature appointed a group of business leaders to run the town strictly along business lines, and, although African Americans remained a political force in the 1880s, interracial alliances increasingly faded. The more class-conscious foreign-born element declined from 30 percent of the population in 1860 to almost nothing after the plague. Rural white southerners, with no union traditions and steeped in the white supremacist teachings of the plantation districts, took their place (see table 1.1).[6]

Table 1.1. Population Statistics, 1850–1950

Year	Black	White	Total	Percentage Black
1850	2,486	6,355	8,841	28.1
1860	3,882	18,741	22,623	17.2
1870	15,741	24,485	40,221	39.1
1880	14,896	18,696	33,592	44.3
1890	28,706	35,789	64,495	44.5
1900	49,910	52,410	102,320	48.8
1910	52,441	78,764	131,105	40.0
1920	61,181	101,170	162,351	37.7
1930	93,550	156,603	253,153	37.0
1940	121,498	171,406	292,942	41.5
1950	147,141	248,859	396,000	37.2

Source: Gerald M. Capers, *Biography of a River Town* (Chapel Hill: University of North Carolina Press, 1933), 164; Leigh D. Fraser, "A Demographic Analysis of Memphis and Shelby County, Tennessee, 1820–1970" (M.A. thesis, Memphis State University, 1974), 18; *Sixteenth Census of the United States: 1940* (Washington, D.C.: GPO, 1943), vol. 5, part 2, p. 710; *Census of Population: 1950* (Washington, D.C.: GPO, 1952), vol. 5, part 2, p. 42–57, table 34.

In a climate of accelerating racism, all-white craft unions of the American Federation of Labor displaced the biracial Knights of Labor as the dominant force in the labor movement. And although the national AFL in its 1893 convention unanimously resolved that "working people must unite and organize, irrespective of creed, color, sex, nationality or politics," it rarely if ever enforced principles of biracial solidarity on its constituent unions, in the South or anywhere else. In Memphis, building and commercial growth resumed after the plague, giving rise to a rapid expansion of AFL craft unions. This expansion, as in many parts of the South, came at the expense of African Americans. Whites used unions to bar blacks from direct economic competition, and white workers and employers alike subordinated blacks to the poorest-paying and most menial jobs. In its first Labor Day march, held in 1889, the Memphis Trades and Labor Council excluded blacks, and most of its locals did the same. AFL machinists, railroad unions, and transportation and building trades locals used initiation rituals, denial of apprenticeship training, and occasional violence to exclude blacks from unions and drive them from skilled employment. As the Memphis black population reached a new high point in 1900, becoming the fourth largest African-American community in the United States, blacks continued to work in a variety of trades and even as building contractors. But only a few black locals of carpenters, bricklayers, and letter carriers were among the two dozen or more craft unions that existed at the turn of the century. Among both white and black unskilled workers, unions had virtually disappeared.[7]

The racial polarization of labor in Memphis reflected the consolidation of segregation throughout the South. Jim Crow laws separated whites and blacks in schools and public accommodations, excluded blacks from juries, public office, and other means of exercising civil rights, and took away their right to vote. Jim Crow practices by whites subordinated blacks to the lowest rungs of employment and undermined the economic position of black artisans, while vigilante terror and economic crises destroyed independent black farmers and forced thousands into tenant farming or sharecropping, and, in some cases, into debt peonage.[8] As racial and economic divisions drove a wedge between potential allies among the lower classes, state-imposed restrictions on voting, including the poll tax in Tennessee, along with racial terrorism, eliminated black voters and extinguished interracial voting alliances. Black and poor white disfranchisement undermined potential Populist and southern working-class political mobilization, ultimately allowing the Democratic party to rule the South unchallenged as the party of "white supremacy" throughout the first half of the twentieth century.[9]

In this context, a climate of racial intolerance came to dominate Memphis. The town's major newspaper, the *Commercial Appeal,* once renowned as the "voice of the Confederacy," regularly used terms such as *darkey* and *nigger*, called the conservative Booker T. Washington an "Alabama coon," and printed lurid tales of black criminality and cartoons depicting African Americans as retarded, Sambo-like creatures. A monument to Nathan Bedford Forrest—once the city's largest slave trader, a leader of the Confederate massacre of black and white Union soldiers at Fort Pillow during the Civil War, a founder of the Ku Klux Klan, and a leading businessman—symbolized the city's commitment to white supremacy.[10] This glorification of white rule promoted a climate in which civil liberties counted for little. In 1892, a newspaper-incited mob attack by some of the city's "leading men" against a black grocery store owner resulted in the lynching of three black men and the exile of Memphis journalist and black leader Ida B. Wells. In 1917 lynching returned with the burning and dismemberment of a young black man named Ell Persons at the Wolf River Bridge in the Memphis suburbs by a mob of thousands, an event preannounced in the press. Lynchings were rare in Memphis, but other forms of racial violence were not, and legal authorities often proved to be as much a threat as lynchers—as a Shelby County sheriff in 1919 proved when he dynamited the home of a terrified black man who would not open his door to him. Even the "reforms" enacted by business leaders during the "Progressive" Era only intensified segregation on public conveyances and meeting places, while zoning ordinances restricted the majority of African Americans to ghettoized shanty towns. Although thousands of blacks fled Memphis during the 1890s and the "great migration" prior to World War I, many more came to Memphis, fleeing from even worse conditions in the rural areas. At the end of the war, the Memphis branch of the National Association for the Advancement of Colored People (NAACP),formed in response to the Person's lynching, observed that "the colored people in Memphis feel that they have nothing to celebrate . . . fighting with our backs to the wall." [11]

Lynching ceased in Memphis after 1917, but other features of the racial system increasingly hardened. During the twenties, under the influence of Christian fundamentalism, Memphis became "the buckle of the Bible belt," as the city's white population became increasingly parochial and hostile to all outside influences. The legendary Robert Church, Jr., son of the first black millionaire in the South and a leader in black institution building in Memphis, along with a few others, bravely maintained underground resistance to the racial terrorism of the era, sending messages about lynchings and police brutality throughout the Delta region in code to the national NAACP.[12] But the repressive racial climate soon drove the NAACP out of existence, while the etiquette of Jim Crow increasingly required black subservience to whites in matters small and large. As the novelist Richard Wright related his own experience in Memphis during the midtwenties, "although Memphis had an air of relative urbanity that took some of the sharpness off the attitude of whites toward Negroes," they still expected blacks to grin and shuffle for small tips and rock-bottom wages. Those like Wright, who could not adopt such subservient behavior, frequently found themselves in deep trouble.[13]

African Americans thus experienced the Jim Crow system on an intensely personal level. Black labor leader George Holloway in his final days still bitterly recalled the daily humiliations of Jim Crow during his youth in the thirties. Whites had nine high schools, blacks had one; black students had no football stadium at which to play; blacks could not go to swimming pools or the parks, except for Overton Park one day a week, and at semiprofessional baseball games had to sit at the far end of the field; most movie theaters remained off limits as well, and the few "white" theaters that admitted blacks forced them to sit in the balconies and enter through the side doors. On streetcars, blacks had to move to the back as whites entered, until eventually the whites had all the seats and the blacks had to stand; on some conveyances, a veil separated blacks from whites. Blacks could not even walk through white neighborhoods on the way to school without fear of arrest, and police brutality for the slightest violation of racial etiquette remained common. The news media, he recalled, almost uniformly pictured blacks arrested in such cases as criminals. "We all knew this was wrong," recalled Holloway, "but there was nothing we could do about it."[14]

Far from resisting this racial system, white workers tried to use it to their advantage. One of the problems for white craftworkers during slavery had been the large role played by artisan slaves in the South's economy. In the free labor economy, segregation made it easier for white craft unionists to exclude blacks from such skilled employment. Hence, as the Memphis population multiplied in the early twentieth century, union membership grew in the building trades, in the printing industry and a few other skilled labor markets, and in municipal services—but this membership remained almost entirely white. After World War I, at the peak of its influence, the Trades and Labor Council claimed 16,000 members out of a city population of 162,000, making Memphis one of the most organized and highly paid skilled labor markets in the South. The extent to which many white workers would go to exclude blacks from better-paying jobs became apparent when white members of the railroad unions (known as brotherhoods) placed a bounty of three hundred dollars on the heads of black brake and switch operators, leading to the vigilante kidnapping and assassination of three black Illinois Central railroad workers in 1921.[15]

Under the weight of such pressures, by 1928 African Americans made up only 256 members out of the city's 12,000 organized workers. The Memphis Teachers' Association refused to admit them, as did most other unions. Blacks made up 75 of the 350 members of the bricklayers' union, but many whites would not work on the same jobs with blacks. Blacks made up 100 of the 166 members of a letter carriers' association, in segregated units, a number of them still belonged to black railroad unions, and a handful belonged to small segregated locals of carpenters and painters. Emblematic of the relationship between white and black craftworkers, white AFL members used a big brick building on Beale Street as their headquarters; the few blacks who belonged to AFL unions met in a wooden servants' quarters behind the main building.[16]

However, if white craftworkers gained economically from the exclusion of blacks from skilled labor markets, the economic benefits of the racial system to white industrial workers in Memphis were not so clear. By separating whites and blacks and maintaining racial hierarchies in all areas of life, the segregation system prevented workers from meeting together as equals to change their economic conditions or to organize politically. Most white workers understood very well that those who violated racial codes by organizing interracially faced severe penalties, a fact that stopped most of them from ever making the attempt.[17] Racial division of labor markets and a repressive social climate helped employers to obtain white labor at the same low wages paid to blacks. According to a number of studies, prior to unionization white and black workers in the South classified as unskilled made about the same wages. Racial fragmentation and worker disorganization, as well as the South's poverty and isolation from national labor markets, helped to ensure that white industrial workers—as well as sharecroppers, tenants, and other "unskilled" laborers in the surrounding Delta—shared almost equally bad economic conditions with blacks. Until the forties few Memphis factory workers could support even a modest standard of living. Employer control over black labor thus implied control over white labor, or at least the unskilled portion of it.[18]

Yet, as in South Africa and other white settler societies, southern segregation also offered some distinct advantages to white industrial workers relative to blacks. On the one hand, white supremacy for some, W. E. B. Du Bois observed, served as a kind of "psychological wage." The system offered more concrete advantages, however—what one historian has called the "wages of whiteness." Since the caste relationship ensured that blacks obtained the worst jobs, whatever higher-paying or more highly skilled jobs existed within a factory automatically went to whites. Occupational segregation thus made it possible for whites in the factories to move up and to do marginally better than blacks. During the early twentieth century, as occupational segregation hardened, the southern racial system as a whole undercut black resistance by preventing blacks from protesting, from gaining access to education, skills, political power, or the courts. The increasing subordination of blacks to whites and, ultimately, the worsening of black wages relative to those of whites made the interests of black and white factory workers appear increasingly at odds. This made it possible for southern elites to continue to recruit the support of ill-paid white factory workers for a system that kept both black and white industrial workers powerless and unorganized.[19]

SOUTHERN INDUSTRIALIZATION, SOUTHERN WAGES

While the South's racialized labor system placed many whites in a privileged position relative to blacks, employers, not workers, most clearly benefited from the racial system. Economic power in Memphis overwhelmingly rested in the hands of white male entrepreneurs and property owners. The decisions of these men, not those of white workers, shaped the Memphis economy. Perhaps a score of families connected to the cotton trade dominated the city's culture, economy, and social life. Many of their names, including among them the Brinkleys, Donelsons, Dunavants, Fontaines, Galbreaths, Mallorys, Norfleets, Orgills, Snowdens, Trezevants, and others, still adorn Memphis street signs, and many of their descendants still influence the city's civic affairs. Most of these families made their fortunes in cotton, as well as related investments in real estate, railroads, banking, and insurance. Many of their ancestors played an integral role in the resurrection of the cotton economy after the Civil War, and some traced their lineage back to the planter class of slavery times. These cotton capitalists based much of their wealth on the "free" labor of sharecroppers, tenants, and wage laborers instead of slaves, but their roots went clearly back to the old order. As their family dynasties grew, their influence on the Memphis economy became decisive. "Cotton Row" on Front Street near the river became the city's economic center. Here resided the directors of the Memphis Cotton Exchange and what the sociologist Rupert Vance, in 1932, called the South's "cotton system."[20]

Not all entrepreneurs belonged to this older group of families, but whether they did or did not, most remained tied to the agricultural economy. Grain merchants and dealers in a wide variety of wholesale and retail goods sold to both urban consumers and to farmers, and they made up a sizeable group of mercantile capitalists. Owners and managers of railroad lines, river barges, warehouses, and trucking lines stored and shipped the cotton and farm goods produced in a vast rural area that surrounded the city for hundreds of miles. Some invested heavily in timber companies that devastated Delta area forests with clear-cutting. The figures in table 1.2 give a crude picture of those involved in Memphis trade and commerce.

A more distinct group in the city's ruling economic circles engaged primarily in manufacturing. Like the others, southern manufacturers based their industries on the resources the surrounding countryside had to offer and on the region's low wages, which they saw as an advantage over manufacturers in the more diversified, capitalized, technology-endowed, and industrially advanced North. Manufacturers in Memphis particularly specialized in cotton and hardwood production and processing, both of which utilized unskilled black labor extensively.[21] Under their guidance, Memphis became the "hardwood capital of the world," with dozens of sawmills, lumberyards, and companies making hardwood flooring, barrels, paper, boxes, building supplies, tool handles, and furniture. Local hard-

Table 1.2. Owners/Managers of Commercial and Trade Enterprises, 1930

Occupation	Total Males	Black Males	Percentage Black
Bankers and officials	117	0	0.00
Brokers and commissioners	252	1	0.40
Insurance agents and managers	1,114	84	7.50
Loan brokers and pawnbrokers	87	5	5.70
Manufacturers:			
Owners	376	4	1.06
Managers	1,077	1	.09
Owners and managers, truck/cab	102	20	19.60
Real estate agents	645	22	3.40
Retail dealers	4,151	516	12.40
Stockbrokers	162	13	8.00
Wholesale dealers	393	2	0.50

Source: Fifteenth Census of the United States, 1930 (Washington, D.C.: GPO, 1933), vol. 5, part 4, pp. 1536–37.

wood industries also attracted Fisher Body, a division of General Motors, which employed over one thousand workers, the majority of them black, to make wooden auto bodies, and Ford Motor, which opened a small Memphis plant employing mostly whites. Another group of industrialists plied the cotton economy with factories that extracted cottonseed oil and cotton meal and warehouses that compressed and stored cotton for shipping. Cotton also attracted northern-based firms like Proctor and Gamble's Buckeye cellulose, as well as Cudahy and other cottonseed oil producers. Food-processing, bottling, and meat-packing plants and those that produced fertilizer, animal feed, and snuff tobacco dotted the Memphis landscape, along with chemical plants making paints, drugs, cosmetics, and veneers. Memphis supported foundries, machine shops, steel-fabricating plants, and a variety of smaller manufacturers. Railroad companies, whose lines crisscrossed the city's retail and wholesale districts downtown and tied them to the manufacturing areas in north and south Memphis, freight and passenger terminals, round houses and rail yards, and repair shops also employed large numbers of workers. The railroads, highways, and barge terminals covering four miles of waterfront made Memphis a major transportation center. Except for printing and publishing companies, Ford, and a few others, nearly all manufacturers employed large numbers of blacks (see table 1.3).[22]

Memphis fit into an interlocking and resource-based regional economy

Table 1.3. Largest Industries, 1929–39

Industry	Number of workers	
	1929	1939
Auto bodies and equipment		1,016
Bakery products	803	799
Cottonseed oil products	949	676
Cooperage	219	468
Drugs and medicine		322
Fabricated steel		220
Feeds, animal	278	294
Foundry/machine shops	396	
Furniture and lumber products	2,844	2,456
Ice manufacturing	369	95
Iron and steel products		937
Mattresses and springs		397
Meatpacking		411
Planing mill products	1,232	564
Other wood products	405	1,064
Paper products		591
Printing	343	231
Newspaper industry	456	351
Railroad car shops	1,688	
Rubber products		2,000
Tobacco products		387
Other industry	1,113	1,965

Source: Fifteenth Census of the United States (Washington, D.C.: GPO, 1933), vol. 5, part 3, p. 505; *Sixteenth Census of the United States: 1940* (Washington, D.C.: GPO, 1942), vol. 5, part 3, pp. 973–74. For rubber workers see Final Report of V. C. Finch, 30 Dec. 1940, Mediation and Conciliation Service File 199-6048, RG 280, NARA.

that to a large measure determined the nature of its industrialization. That economy included the cotton and agricultural goods–producing hinterland; the southern timber fields; the river system, which went north and south from New Orleans to Chicago on the Mississippi and east and west from St. Louis on the Ohio River; and the rail and highway systems, which connected Memphis to the east and the trans-Mississippi west. Within this regional framework, Memphis developed a typically southern, largely extractive industrial base. Most industries drew on cheap raw materials from the surrounding region, remained locally owned and poorly capitalized, and relied on intensive use of human labor rather than expensive technology to boost production. Some of these industries, especially in woodworking and cotton processing, probably were little more mecha-

Table 1.4. Average Number of Wage Earners in Manufacturing

Date	Number	Date	Number
1921	10,174	1931	11,086
1923	10,508	1933	10,264
1925	9,988	1935	14,668
		1937	16,741
1929	15,921	1939	13,921

Source: U.S. Bureau of the Census, "Memorandum Report on the Current Housing Situation in Memphis, Tennessee," 25 Oct. 1941, Federal Housing Administration Division of Research and Statistics, Manufacturing and Employment, 1921–39, File, USES, RG 183, NARA.

nized in 1929 than they had been at the turn of the century. Heavy industry such as auto making in the North, which created demand for steel, rubber, glass, machine tools, and other subsidiary industries, eluded Memphis. And although the city experienced a spurt of growth in industrial employment in the late twenties, when the Great Depression struck in 1929 it lost nearly a third of the existing industrial jobs. For the next decade, the city's industrial base remained weak. Indeed, as table 1.4 demonstrates, not a great deal more manufacturing jobs existed in 1939 than in 1921. In rural parts of the state, jobs became so scarce that thousands of workers left to seek work outside of the region. "Not only is Tennessee producing and shipping out raw materials to be processed in other areas but it is also sending a large number of workers to do the processing," commented one state analyst.[23]

Memphis had a stagnant industrial base, with cotton capitalists and commercial interests dominating the city during most of its history. During the depression era, however, the collapse of the world market for cotton swung the interests of the chamber of commerce increasingly toward industrial expansion. Convinced that industrialization offered the only way out of the economic crisis, city leaders called for "more smokestacks and more payrolls" to offset agricultural decline. Their thinking accorded with that of business boosters throughout the South, who crusaded to "balance agriculture with industry" by luring northern capital with low taxes or tax abatements, industrial subsidies (with communities footing the costs of building plants, sewers, and providing fire and police protection), and most of all, guarantees of lower wages through a union-free environment. In their rush to attract industry, some communities in Tennessee not only provided free industrial facilities but they then required workers to donate 10 percent of their wages to pay for them. Others set up "learners" schools in which businesses "trained" workers in production techniques at little or no pay for up to six weeks at a time, but frequently failed to provide them with jobs once the "training" period ended. Tri-State Dress Company operated just such a "school" for some of its female employees in Memphis.[24]

The key to the business campaign to "sell" Memphis to outside investors, however, was the promise of low wages, and Memphis leaders clung to their low-wage theory of growth throughout the thirties. Even during Franklin D. Roosevelt's National Recovery Act, aimed at reviving the economy in part through raising wages (and thus consumer spending), local business leaders did everything possible to hold down southern wages. E. L. Bruce, the largest producer of hardwood flooring in the South, headed the National Recovery Administration (NRA) committee for establishing minimum wage codes in the lumber industry in Memphis, and he and other employers succeeded in keeping wages in that industry exceedingly low. Not surprisingly, blacks comprised most of the workers at E. L. Bruce and other lumber companies.[25] Many such companies ignored the NRA wage codes altogether, but even those who complied often made "no pretense of obeying codes when negroes are concerned," according to one student of the situation.[26]

African Americans had been paid so little that NRA codes did raise their wages in many cases, but employers adopted a variety of means to avoid paying them. At Fisher Body in Memphis, where blacks comprised nearly 60 percent of the 1,800 workers, the company refused to pay the automobile code of forty cents an hour, paying instead the lumber code of twenty-three cents an hour, and threatened to fire black workers if the NRA intervened. Memphis Furniture raised wages for its predominantly black work force by nine cents, to twenty cents an hour, but still kept its wages below the minimum for the furniture industry. Federal Barge Line, Plough Manufacturing, Tri-State Dress Company, and others ignored NRA wage standards altogether and fired those who protested. Lumber plantation owners classified blacks as yard workers or tenants, placing them in the lowest wage category, even though they might be production workers. The Buckeye cottonseed oil company actually lowered its wages under the NRA, claiming they had been paying above the regional rates set for the South.[27]

In some cases when significant wage increases did occur, white employers simply fired their black employees. Most employers only hired blacks to keep wage costs low, and many felt that if they had to raise wages they might as well hire whites. So many employers turned over better-paying jobs formerly occupied by blacks to whites that national civil rights supporters began calling it the "Negro Removal Act." Katie Hurston, a black woman in Memphis, complained to President Roosevelt that "here in the South they think that shorter hour and more money is for white only and therefore they are dismissing the negroes from their jobs and taking white ones their places." Black elevator operator George Isabel wrote that "the colored people of this town are being discharged without any notice . . . and being replaced by white. I am wondering if this is the purpose of the NRA." But the NRA provided no protections against the dismissals of black workers.[28] So it went around the South: in Mississippi, contractors in the Flood Control Project utilized a loophole in the codes to employ some thirty thousand black workers at ten to fifteen cents an hour instead of the NRA standard of forty cents.[29]

The NRA approved a "southern" wage differential, one that allowed lower wages for workers in the South than in the North, based on supposedly lower living standards in the South. In fact, the "southern wage" remained largely a racial wage differential, based on the large number of southern African Americans in the lowest-paid and dirtiest occupations. The NRA allowed employers in Memphis to pay a "southern wage" of fourteen cents an hour in the laundry shops, for example, to an entirely black work force.[30] Allowing employers to continue paying blacks less than whites and southerners less than northerners allowed a few companies in the South to maintain their "competitive advantage" against the North, but it also reinforced the racial segmentation of the southern labor market that made it so difficult to organize southern workers. For this reason, employers and state officials sprang to the defense of the southern wage differential, some explicitly identifying it as a racial differential, throughout the NRA's brief tenure in 1933 and 1934. Some southern employers even demanded that the South's racial wage differential be applied to the whole nation, distributing a pamphlet titled "The Subnormal Negro and the Subnormal Code."[31] Whether identified as a regional or a racial differential, black scholar Robert C. Weaver warned, NRA recognition of such codes would split white and black interests and "destroy any possibility of ever forming a strong and effective labor movement"—precisely what southern employers desired.[32] AFL officials for their part objected to the NRA's North/South differentials but remained silent about its acceptance of wage discrimination against blacks, the very basis of low southern wages.[33]

Not only southern-based industries but migrating northern industries sought the cheap wages of the southern labor market. The chamber of commerce scored its greatest success in drawing industries to Memphis on the basis of cheap labor in 1937, when the Firestone Tire and Rubber

Company established a mass-production subsidiary plant in Memphis in an effort to escape the organizing drives of industrial unions in Akron. The city allowed the company to set up shop outside municipal limits to avoid paying taxes, but at the same time provided water, police, and fire protection at minimal charges. The city also guaranteed Firestone freedom from industrial union organization, a promise it would deliver on during subsequent CIO organizing.[34]

In its quest for profits, Firestone proved itself as willing as any locally based employer to take advantage of the economic benefits of southern segregation, immediately establishing wage and job classifications that split the work force along racial lines and depressed the wage scale for unskilled labor. The company established three wage classifications: "A" rates for adult white males ranging from thirty-two cents up to forty cents an hour, a top wage for Memphis industrial labor; "B" rates for white boys, aged eighteen to twenty-one; and "C" rates for "colored" of all ages, with the latter two groups beginning at twenty-eight cents an hour. While under-aged white males could move out of this lowest wage classification into the "A" rate, blacks could not. To match this wage scale, the company assigned jobs on the basis of race, with blacks doing work classified as unskilled, mixing crude rubber, sweeping, hauling rubber on trucks weighing hundreds of pounds, and doing much of the other heavy lifting and pulling work on the shop floor. Whites worked for the most part as machinists, tire builders, mechanics, and as skilled and semiskilled operatives. The dirty and hot jobs did not in every case go to blacks, but the best-paying jobs always went to whites, according to workers at the plant. Firestone enforced segregation in other ways as well, with separate rest rooms, eating areas, and even separate time clocks and parking lots for blacks and whites. This arrangement fragmented workers socially, economically, and occupationally along race lines, making union organizing difficult at best. Although the company paid high wages compared to many local industries, it paid substantially less in Memphis than it did in the North; its segregation of the labor force almost guaranteed that it could continue to do so long into the future, for few whites would take up the cause of the lowest paid laborers, most of whom had dark skin.[35]

Firestone's move to Memphis only confirmed the belief of Memphis employers that hope for industrial growth rested on the availability of cheap and unorganized labor, which provided southern industry with relative advantages over the more highly organized, skilled, and expensive labor markets in the North. Cheap labor, in turn, rested on the South's racial system. "There is small likelihood of strike disturbances," the chamber of commerce assured potential investors in 1929, "because of Anglo-Saxon stock and the negro . . . [who] is not prone to organize in matters of wages and working conditions." The chamber continued for the next decade to proudly point to the city's absence of white European immigrants with "foreign ideologies" of socialism and unionism, and to the supposed docility of black workers, as signs of potential business prosperity. As a result of such factors, the chamber in 1936 claimed that "almost without a single exception" wages for Memphis industrial workers remained far below those paid elsewhere.[36]

Continued reliance on low wages to sustain profit margins, however, entrapped the city's economy in a cycle of low consumption and continued depression. Other northern-based industries did come to Memphis during the thirties to take advantage of low wages, including major employers such as Continental Can, Armour, and Humko Oil. As a result, by 1937 industrial employment would increase almost 50 percent from its low point in 1933. However, the city's campaign to "sell" Memphis to outside industries based on its low wages and cheap local resources typically attracted companies trying to cut their costs and unwilling to invest in the future of the city or the welfare of its workers. These included poorly capitalized industries, such as textile and garment companies, that had already become famous elsewhere for their exploitation of female and child laborers. Industrialization on these terms, union supporters argued, did not improve the living standards or consuming power of the workers because it failed to create consumer purchasing power capable of supporting significant economic growth. The point was made clearly when Memphis industrial employment collapsed again during the recession in late 1937.[37]

Still, local business leaders measured success primarily on the basis of their own short-term economic gains. Their narrow economic interests, combined with a racialized understanding of labor questions shaped by slavery and sharecropping, as well as their own frequent lack of capital, led them to believe in the absolute necessity of a cheap labor system. But reliance on cheap labor had delayed mechanization and economic diversification, undercut education and the development of human resources, and held down consumption among the mass of the people for generations. The very thing southern leaders claimed would save the region—the existence of a cheap, unorganized, and racially divided industrial labor force—bound the South in a state of underdevelopment matched only by colonized countries and reduced the living standards of a large number of its workers to among the poorest in the United States. By holding down black labor, employers and the segregation system of which they were a part held down white labor as well.[38]

In a sense, however, the segregation system worked for whites. Although it did not improve the wages of unskilled white workers, it did provide a labor system segmented into superiors and subordinates, which placed them in relatively better positions than blacks. White managers, clerical workers, supervisors, and owners with the clean hands and white shirts remained few, while the black and the white poor were many, but all whites could at least aspire to jobs other than manual labor. Blacks, on the other hand, remained almost universally condemned to do the dirty, hot, heavy, or menial work and existed on a lower plane than whites in terms of occupations, tasks, wages, and the exercise of rights. This labor system of superiors and subordinates offered significant numbers of whites privileged positions in comparison with blacks in virtually every sector of the economy. Under this racially based system it often appeared impossible to unite workers. As black Firestone worker Matthew Davis recalled, "segregation was in our system, part of the customs of our people." Industrialization only accentuated that fact.[39]

The racial division of labor rested in part on the belief that blacks existed to serve the personal needs of whites, and a look at the 1930 Census Bureau figures shows how overall occupational divisions in Memphis upheld this belief (see table 1.5). Except for the combined categories of manufacturing and mechanical (craft) work, domestic and personal service employed the largest number of workers in any occupational category, 25 percent of the entire Memphis work force. For the African-American community, domestic and personal service remained by far the largest single source of employment, consuming 46 percent of the work force. Some 75 percent of domestic workers were black women, who often earned three dollars or less per week and often survived by working two or three jobs. Yet because of the city's low wage structure, their labor remained essential to family survival in the African-American community. The fact that so many black women worked in such a dead-end and extremely underpaid occupation is a profound indicator of how economic oppression reinforced the black community's status as a collective servant to white society.

The white South's belief in blacks as servants transferred to the black

Table 1.5. Blacks and Women in the Work Force, 1930

Occupation	Total	Black Men Number	%	Black Women Number	%	White Women Number	%
Clerical	6,065	0	0.0	132	2.0	5,936	98.0
Domestic	27,514	5,511	20.0	17,349	63.0	2,613	10.0
Manufacturing and mechanical	32,769	13,926	42.5	1,600	5.0	1,674	5.0
Professional	7,545	808	11.0	762	10.0	2,985	40.0
Public service	2,146	623	29.0	6	0.2	22	1.0
Trade	21,583	4,046	19.0	245	1.0	2,286	11.0
Transportation and communication	12,093	5,806	48.0	48	0.4	991	8.0
Total	109,715	30,720	28.0	20,142	18.0	16,507	15.0

Source: Fifteenth Census of the United States, 1930 (Washington, D.C.: GPO, 1931), vol. 5, part 4.

male work force as well as to black women. The Census Bureau, which organized its data by male and female occupations, shows black men doing nearly half the work in transportation but for the most part in positions subordinate to whites (see table 1.6). Higher-status, higher-paying jobs as conductors, supervisors, inspectors, or superintendents remained strictly reserved for white males, while black men worked as chauffeurs, teamsters and carriage drivers, laborers on the streets and city railroad, and deckhands on river barges. Considerable numbers of African-American males still held jobs as railroad brake operators, stokers, switch operators, and flaggers in 1930, and as riverboat deckhands and truck and tractor drivers, occupations with higher pay and status than most of those reserved for blacks. But white men during the thirties eventually forced blacks out of most of these positions. By the end of the decade, for example, scarcely a black deckhand could be found on the rivers and very few black stokers or brake operators remained on the railroads. Federal postal delivery jobs remained one of the very few clean-hands occupations, along with jobs as Pullman porters on the railroads, still open to blacks, and as a result both black postal carriers and porters held esteemed positions as part of the black "middle" class.

In the retail and wholesale economy similar racial restrictions within male employment applied (see table 1.7). Hardly a black banker, broker, advertising agent, or wholesaler could be found, but black men did almost all the labor as helpers in stores, as coal and lumberyard workers, and as deliverers for bakeries and grocery stores. Only as salespersons, undertakers, and store owners in the African-American community did

Table 1.6. Men in Selected Transportation Occupations, 1930

Occupation	Total	Black	Percentage Black
Drivers	2,878	2,071	71.9
Laborers, railroad	1,480	1,252	84.6
Railroad porters	432	431	99.9
Teamsters	445	402	90.3
Laborers, road and street	419	359	85.7
Sailors and deckhands	369	281	76.2
Garage laborers	197	174	88.3
Mail carriers	242	171	70.6
Switch operators and signalers	679	135	19.9
Railroad brake operators	175	79	45.2
Locomotive stokers	419	60	14.3
Garage owners and managers	95	6	6.3
Supervisors and inspectors	365	3	0.8
Captains, pilots	67	0	0.0
Railroad conductors	274	0	0.0
Total, all transportation	11,054	5,806	52.5

Source: *Fifteenth Census of the United States, 1930* (Washington, D.C.: GPO, 1933), vol. 5, part 4.

any sizeable number of black managers or owners appear. Memphis in fact had a significant, if mostly poor, black business class, based on the enforced consumer market within the black community created by segregation. These relatively independent people ran churches, funeral homes, grocery stores and other retail outlets, barber and beauty shops, laundries, and other businesses catering to the black community. A few black-owned honky tonks and second-hand shops existed on Beale Street, home of the blues, a district that offered blacks a rare haven from the daily rigors of Jim Crow. And black real estate investor Robert Church, Jr., up until the 1930s the wealthiest black man in the South, and Joseph Walker's Universal Negro Life Insurance Company provided some white-collar employment for blacks. Black business people, as in most southern cities, provided one of the few sources of relatively independent leadership in the African-American community. But they had little control over the city's economy and could produce only a limited number of jobs, given their lack of ownership of factories, banks, or other major assets. Even on Beale Street, whites owned most of the vice establishments frequented by black migrants to the city.[40]

In male public and professional employment, census figures indicate

Table 1.7. Men in Selected Trade Occupations, 1930

Occupation	Total	Black	Percentage Black
Store laborers and helpers	1,921	1,683	87.60
Deliverers	813	672	82.70
Coal mine and lumberyard laborers	569	517	90.90
Retail dealers	4,151	516	12.40
Salespeople	4,838	137	3.00
Insurance agents	1,114	84	7.50
Undertakers	111	54	48.60
Store clerks	694	33	4.70
Real estate agents	645	20	3.00
Newspaper carriers	163	18	11.00
Store floorwalkers	112	3	0.30
Wholesale dealers	393	2	0.50
Bankers, brokers, ad agents	829	1	0.01
Total	18,512	4,046	21.90

Source: Fifteenth Census of the United States, 1930 (Washington, D.C.: GPO, 1933), vol. 5, part 4.

not only the racial divisions in work but the almost total exclusion of black men from positions of influence or power in the government, the media, and college education. Black men held public service laboring jobs and worked as door attendants, while white males worked as fire fighters, guards, sheriffs, and other law enforcement officials. In professional work, white men worked as writers, editors, architects, drafters, lawyers, judges, and engineers, but black men remained almost totally absent from such positions. The extent to which the African-American community remained excluded from public discourse and power is highlighted by an almost total exclusion from reporting, writing, and editing: among the 112 men working in the print media in 1930, only 4 were black, and these worked in black media. Likewise, in higher education out of 75 college presidents and teachers only 6 were black men, all of these employed at LeMoyne, an African-American college established after the Civil War. Black male professionals included over 300 ministers, some 80 teachers, and a slightly larger number of doctors and dentists. These professional people, along with black entertainers, buoyed up the black economy and provided role models other than laborer, servant, or factory worker. But except for a few musicians, black professionals operated strictly within the confines of the African-American community, largely shunned from discourse and contact with white society.[41]

Table 1.8. Men in Selected Skilled and Semiskilled Occupations, 1930

Occupation	Total	Black	Percentage Black
Carpenters	2,556	864	33.8
Plaster and cement finishers	350	270	77.1
Painters, buildings	1,157	262	22.6
Brickmasons	387	224	57.9
Plumbers and steamfitters	622	111	17.8
Sawyers	188	107	56.9
Contractors	474	63	13.3
Painters, factory	294	60	20.4
Paperhangers	105	56	53.3
Mechanics	1,883	29	1.5
Stationary engineers	546	27	5.0
Machinists	1,029	22	2.1
Electricians	556	12	2.2
Millwrights	162	11	6.7
Supervisors	584	10	1.7
Press operators and plate printers	102	2	2.0

Source: *Fifteenth Census of the United States, 1930* (Washington, D.C.: GPO, 1933), vol. 5, part 4.

The fact that white men had access to a range of business, professional, and public service jobs denied to black men reinforced the belief that segregation genuinely served white interests. So did the widespread white use of blacks as servants in domestic and menial occupations. Although black women made up the great majority of the population of domestic workers, many black men did similar work, making up 73 percent of the total of 7,550 men doing domestic and personal service. Black males composed 60 percent of the men cleaning and pressing clothes, 87 percent of the janitors, 67 percent of the elevator operators, 92 percent of the male domestic laborers, 88 percent of the male servants, 74 percent of the waiters, and 99 percent of the red caps at the train and bus stations. In contrast, black men composed only 1 percent of the restaurant and cafe owners and 7 percent of the barbers and manicurists. And, as Richard Wright discovered, whites expected blacks, male and female alike, to not only serve them but behave as servants and observe the southern racial code.

Within this pervasive framework of blacks as servants, one can better comprehend the occupational divisions apparent in industry and the building trades (see table 1.8). According to the 1930 census, manufacturing and craftworkers totaled 29,495, with 13,926 African Americans comprising

47 percent of the total. However, when census takers broke these total numbers down into smaller categories, the pervasive pattern of discrimination became apparent. Out of 14,640 craftworkers, only 3,338, or about 23 percent, were black. Even more revealing, in the highest-paying craft occupations of electricians, railroad and stationary engineers, supervisors, machinists, millwrights, and press operators, African Americans remained almost entirely absent. In the more accessible skilled trades, hundreds of black carpenters, contractors, and plumbers worked in the African-American community, but they remained frozen out of the unionized labor market by their white counterparts, who refused to work with them. Blacks worked in large numbers and sometimes alongside whites in the less-skilled and dirtier jobs—as sawyers, paper hangers, plasterers and cement finishers, painters, locomotive stokers, and brickmasons. In these areas, particularly the trowel trades, black men traditionally had some entry. However, during the depression years white unionists escalated efforts to freeze black semiskilled craftworkers out of the building trades. Black artisans, when they could work at all, usually did so outside the unions, did most of their work in the African-American community, and characteristically received lower wages than those paid to white craftworkers.[42]

Occupational segregation remained even more evident in the factories than in the crafts (see table 1.9). Blacks comprised over 70 percent of the male factory labor force and did 80 percent of the unskilled labor. As at Firestone, in Memphis factories whites worked as machinists, superintendents, inspectors, mechanics, repairers, and in product finishing, while blacks swept floors, lifted and hauled materials, or did semiskilled fabricating and production work. In the sawmills, for example, whites ran the saws and other machinery, while blacks piled cut lumber, pulled logs along conveyor belts, or loaded the final products on pallets and trucks. Under this system, no matter how much seniority a black man might have over a white, he retained a lower skill classification, lower wages, lower status, and might be referred to as a "boy" by whites half his age. Black males comprised some 40 percent of the city's factory operatives, but even when blacks and whites did the same work, employers often classified blacks as "helpers" to whites, a justification for paying them less money for the same work. At Firestone, black worker Fred Higgins explained, "you'd be classified as a 'helper,' but you'd be doing all the work. The white man would get the high wage . . . [but] he'd just be sittin' there watchin'." Firestone worker Matthew Davis similarly recalled that "all you had to do was have your face be white, and you'd move up the ladder," while blacks remained stuck in low-wage classifications.[43]

Table 1.9. Men in Selected Factory Occupations, 1930

Occupation	Total	Black	Percentage Black
Operatives			
Food and allied	276	131	47.5
Iron, steel, auto	932	329	35.3
Sawmills	3,178	1,261	39.7
Other wood and furniture	230	92	40.0
Total operatives	3,454	1,392	40.3
Laborers			
Auto factories	1,684	1,290	76.6
Iron and steel	702	534	76.1
Chemical	351	298	84.9
Light and power	240	202	84.2
Flour and grain	198	195	98.5
Other food and allied	285	194	68.1
General labor	1,769	1,601	90.1
Construction labor	973	821	84.4
Sawmills	2,030	1,885	93.0
Other wood and furniture	303	208	68.6
Other industry	2,099	1,858	88.5
Total laborers	11,401	9,196	80.6
Total	14,855	10,588	71.3

Source: Fifteenth Census of the United States, 1930 (Washington, D.C.: GPO, 1933), vol. 5, part 4.

Production workers ("factory operatives"), however, constituted less than one-fourth of the factory workers in Memphis. Most of the city's extractive industries relied on unskilled hand labor rather than mechanized assembly-line processes, and blacks did most of this work. In factory work as in other sectors of the economy, clean-hands jobs for whites, at better rates of pay, and heavy, dirty work for black laborers, at lower rates of pay, remained the rule. Black lumber workers, for example, made the lowest wages of any group of industrial workers in the entire South, and furniture and cotton warehouse workers were almost as poorly paid. In such industries where blacks played the dominant role in the labor force, wages remained among the lowest of all occupations for whites as well.[44]

In short, as the figures indicate, at the start of the thirties black males made up more than two-thirds of the factory labor force. And yet, as in society generally, white males continued to have considerable advantages over blacks, from the types of tasks assigned to the status given to those tasks. If many white males did not in many cases make a great deal more than black males, whatever wage advantage there was to be gained in a given situation almost always went to a white and almost never went to a black. Such advantages to whites could totally obscure the fact that both white and black workers made far less than enough to live on, that owners could afford to pay more, or that even a white operative and a black laborer at different rates of pay had a common problem that required common action.

A separate set of census figures shows an equally stark segregation of task and occupation among women (see table 1.10). Black and white women remained occupationally segregated not only from male workers but from each other. Employers in most sectors of the economy, and particularly in the factories, denied women access to any employment at all, reserving for them only a few tasks that they regarded as typically female. Women as a whole made up 30 percent of Memphis employment in 1930, but a mere 10 percent of manufacturing workers, concentrated in specific occupations. Yet white women, although virtually excluded from many occupations by men, had far greater access to clean-hands and white-collar jobs outside of the manufacturing sector than black women, who remained largely confined to domestic work and menial occupations. White women made up practically the entire force of telephone operators and worked in stores, offices, and sales departments with white men. Black women remained excluded from such places except as cleaners or as typists or clerks in black-owned insurance companies and stores. In professional work, white women worked as reporters in small numbers and made up practically the entire force of librarians in the city. They made up 80 percent of the school and music teachers in the white community, just as did black women in the African-American community. Women did all of the nursing in the city, but white women held 90 percent of the trained positions, working in institutions, while black women held more than half of the untrained positions, working mostly in people's homes. As in male employment, racial restrictions applied in virtually every occupational category, in work defined by both gender and race.

Both white and black women remained subject to a system in which white males controlled the highest-paying management and skilled labor positions while women worked in lower-paying occupations having to do with communication and nurturing. This gendered division of labor and social authority generally precluded most women from rising above their assigned occupations, accumulating capital, or exercising political power. Yet because wage labor remained much more central to the experience of black women than white women, racial and gender exclusion and sub-

Table 1.10. Women in Selected Occupations, 1930

Occupation	Total	Black	Percentage Black
Selected manufacturing and mechanical			
Dressmakers and garment workers	722	395	54.7
Laborers	824	602	73.1
Operatives:			
Chemical	145	44	30.3
Clothing	306	20	6.5
Food and allied	306	151	49.3
Total manufacturing and mechanical	3,274	1,600	48.9
Selected communication			
Telegraph operators	119	0	0.0
Telephone operators	842	3	0.3
Total communication	1,039	48	4.6
Selected trade			
Store clerks	385	19	4.9
Insurance agents	96	18	18.7
Retail owners and managers	249	60	24.1
Saleswomen	1,916	56	2.9
Total trade	3,071	245	7.9
Selected professional			
Authors, editors, reporters	38	1	2.6
College teachers	38	5	13.2
Librarians	44	2	4.5
Music teachers	227	36	15.9
Social and welfare workers	76	6	7.8
Schoolteachers	1,621	540	33.3
Nurses	1,203	95	7.8
Total professional	3,747	762	20.3
Selected domestic and personal			
Hairdressers	596	273	45.8
Boardinghouse owners	701	212	30.2
Dry cleaners and pressers	189	130	68.8
Housekeepers	410	129	31.5
Launderers	3,345	3,313	99.0
Laundry operatives	1,442	1,281	88.8
Nurses (not trained)	539	314	58.3
Restaurant and cafe owners	209	95	45.5
Servants	11,451	11,092	96.9
Waitresses	806	288	35.7
Total domestic and personal	19,964	17,349	86.9
Clerical	6,088	132	2.2

Source: Fifteenth Census of the United States, 1930 (Washington, D.C.: GPO, 1933), vol. 5, part 4.

ordination in the marketplace had a much greater effect on them. And racial occupational divisions almost uniformly placed white women in a superior position to black women. This superior/subordinate relationship was made glaringly evident by the fact that the city's 17,349 black female domestic workers comprised by far the largest group of female employees—almost half of the combined white and black female labor force of 36,649. At the pittance paid to black women domestics, even lower middle-class white families could often afford to hire black maids, launderers, and "mammies," placing white women as a group in a position of dominance over black women as a group.

Although white women made less, usually far less, than men, black women still remained below them, undermining potential alliances between the two. Even when black and white women worked together, as in the hotel industry, blacks worked as cleaners, while whites worked as linen room attendants with better conditions and wages. Likewise, when white women worked with black women in kitchens, bakeries, restaurants, and (occasionally) in department stores, southern racial etiquette continued to clearly differentiate their roles and separate them socially. Little solidarity between white and black women could be expected, given the social conditions imposed by racism.[45]

Black women, like black men, also had an infinitely more difficult problem relative to factory employment than did white women. Though their numbers were small, the plight of white female factory workers, concentrated in a few garment shops, at the Plough pharmaceutical company, and in a few food-processing companies, would give rise to some of the first industrial labor struggles of the thirties and to a larger concern about the plight of working women. Black women remained almost completely excluded from all but the worst factory employment; they received less attention from unions, and their plight was ignored by white society. In 1930 the largest group of black women in industry, some six hundred of them, worked as factory laborers, doing hot, heavy, dirty, and menial work. Another four hundred of them, along with about an equal number of white women, worked out of the public eye in their own homes or in small shops as stitchers, doing tedious, usually unhealthy, work for hours on end. Beyond these two occupations, only a handful of black females worked as factory operatives, in chemical, clothing, and food-processing industries. Otherwise, black women remained almost entirely excluded from Memphis industry throughout the thirties. As a result of the low value most employers placed on female labor, both white and black women would appear only rarely as actors and leaders in the labor movement.[46]

THE PRICE OF POWERLESSNESS

Deep internal divisions within the industrial labor force kept most factory workers unorganized, and their wages and conditions showed it, especially as the great economic depression of the thirties took its toll; conditions could hardly have been worse. The fact that the city did not rely on one industry partially saved its economy from the worst effects of the Great Depression for a few years after the 1929 stock market crash, but by the time of Franklin D. Roosevelt's election in 1932, the Memphis economy had collapsed. It revived only slowly throughout the remainder of the decade, with industrial and other employment barely working its way back up to 1929 levels. Even when new factories opened their doors, without union organization conditions for Memphis workers improved little. New factories seeking to take advantage of existing wage standards often paid only a little better wages than those paid to cotton pickers and domestic workers.

"As far as unskilled and semi-skilled workers were concerned, wages were pitiful," recalled Memphis Typographical union leader Robert Tillman. In the cooperage (barrel-making) industry, wages remained so low that companies could beat the prices of mechanized factories in the North by using crude hand labor techniques. At Fisher Body, Chickasaw Wood, and other wood products industries, black laborers earned $.10 to $.15 an hour. Wages in sawmills sometimes went as low as $.07 an hour. As late as 1937, average wages among the 450 workers at Memphis Furniture, half of them black, went from a low of $.13 an hour to a high of $.25 an hour. White women in several dress factories made between $5.00 to $8.00 for a fifty-four-hour week. Some 240 white workers at American Bag Company averaged $1.75 to $2.00 per day, while white women at American Snuff averaged $6.00 to $10.00 per week. Black cotton pickers, some fifteen thousand of whom took buses daily into Arkansas, made as little as $.60 a day after working from dawn to dusk. Black women fared the worst in terms of wages. A survey of women workers for Tennessee in 1935 found that black female workers, most of them concentrated in West Tennessee, made a median wage of $5.65 a week in all occupations, less than half the median wage of white women.[47]

In contrast to the pathetic wages in industrial, service, and rural employment, wages of white craft unionists, the majority of them unionized, ranged up to $1.25 an hour in the building trades. In fact, bricklayers, cement finishers, carpenters, and other artisans, when they could get work, made about the same wages as in other cities, North and South, of comparable size. Although the economic crash initially deprived many of these workers of employment and drove down wage scales, New Deal economic programs eventually revived the local construction industry and made it possible for white craftworkers to maintain wage rates far higher than those paid to the mass of common laborers and factory workers. This is not to say that white craftworkers were secure. Nearly all workers lacked any sort of social security or health care coverage, and few if any received vacations, private insurance coverage, or extra pay for overtime work. However, the great wage gap between organized white craftworkers and unorganized laborers and production workers (the majority of them black) effectively divided Memphis workers into haves and have-nots. The have-nots included black female domestics who made as little as three dollars a week; between caring for a white family and their own, their day's work never ended until they slept, but they did not make enough to adequately feed their children. Industrial workers, black or white, fared a little better, but not much. A survey of families in Memphis and eleven other southern cities in the midthirties found that the average family expended almost all its meager income on the basic necessities of life, and many of them could not maintain even a minimally adequate diet.[48]

The have-nots in the Memphis working class not only lived close to hunger but suffered from unsanitary, hot, dangerous, and generally depressing working conditions. Factory environments reflected the undercapitalized conditions of locally owned industries, as well as the fact that as long as factory owners did not have to answer to the organized response of labor they could get away with enforcing abysmal working conditions. Since women and blacks remained the least organized of any group, their conditions remained among the worst in the city. A series of reports on working conditions compiled by a traveling representative of the Women's Bureau of the U.S. Labor Department in 1935 provided graphic descriptions of sweatshop conditions, particularly in shops with predominantly black and female work forces. At the Memphis Pecan and Walnut Company, where 103 black women worked, the Women's Bureau inspector found wet floors, steep stairways with no railings, poor seating (the women had to bring pillows in order to work on cane seats), filthy plumbing, and toilets only partially covered by burlap ("view of seats is open to basement"). One woman, she reported, fell from the upstairs bathroom to a concrete floor below because the stairs were so bad. At Memphis Furniture, where blacks made up most of the work force, black women lacked decent washing facilities to get paint and lacquer off their hands and were put to work running spray guns that filled the air with benzene. At White Rose Laundry, condensation streamed off paintless walls and ceilings in an uninsulated building, floors were slippery and steep, and the management made no effort to clean the "filthy" work area. At this and other laundries, black women lacked chairs to sit on, decent toilet facilities, drinking fountains, and lunch rooms.[49]

Where management exhibited concern for workers, it typically reserved the best facilities for white women and ignored the needs of black women. At Loeb's laundry, for example, white women had enclosed toilets, hot running water, dressing rooms, chairs, benches and lockers, and a well-lighted and ventilated work area. In none of the facilities where black women worked did the Women's Bureau representative find such favorable conditions. At Goldsmith's Department Store the management installed clean lockers and rest rooms with cots, a cafeteria, and even day beds and a sick room for their white female employees. Such conditions, unheard of for black women, were exceptional for white women as well. More typically, at Khun Dress Company white women worked on the second floor of an old building without adequate lighting or ventilation, while at Tri-State Dress Company they ate meals at their machines and made their coffee on a hot plate in the bathroom. Under the laissez-faire governments of the early thirties, rarely would anyone interfere with such unhealthy working conditions. With its high concentration of African Americans and poor factory workers, Memphis led the state in the number of recorded industrial accidents.[50]

Unsafe working conditions for the most part remained hidden behind factory doors, but the effects of poverty-level wages in Memphis could be easily seen. Blacks in the working-class districts of north and south Memphis typically lived in long and narrow "shotgun" shacks (so named because one could shoot through the house without hitting anything). These shacks typically lacked paint and rested on bricks or wood posts in a yard of sand or gravel. Black housing remained situated in the least favorable environments, often in low-lying areas of poor drainage lacking sidewalks, paved streets, indoor plumbing, and access to city services. In south Memphis neighborhoods such as Orange Mound and Person, and in north Memphis neighborhoods such as Klondyke, Hollywood, Jackson Avenue, Chelsea-Cypress Creek, and Binghampton, African Americans suffered from frequent outbreaks of typhoid fever or other diseases.[51] Conditions in white working-class neighborhoods were not much better, except that white workers tended over time to move out of the worst neighborhoods, with their places taken by the expanding black population. The north Memphis neighborhood of Pinchgut, for example, was first occupied by riverboat workers and then poor Irish before the Civil War, then by Jews, and by the thirties, finally, by African Americans. But in some sections of Pinchgut and the Fort Pickering neighborhood, black and white workers lived side by side in poverty. Federal aid would eventually help the city to demolish many such neighborhoods and replace them with low-income housing projects, built separately for blacks and whites, and individual new homes built with FHA loans almost exclusively for whites.[52]

*   *   *

The disruption of the economic system caused by the Great Depression seemed to invite a new period of lower-class alliances across racial boundaries. Yet barriers to change would fall very slowly in a city surrounded not only by cotton fields but by more than a century of racial oppression. For the strength of white supremacy resulted not only from the ideas in people's minds but from the multitude of ways in which social and economic distinctions based on "race" functioned in people's daily lives. Such distinctions caused most white workers to support the racial system. White craft unionists used the racial system to shore up their control over skilled labor markets; white factory workers often lived as poorly as many blacks, but they too identified the specific advantages the system gave to them, such as having a black "helper" who would do the most unpleasant work or having access to jobs or housing denied to blacks. Whites typically failed to recognize that this system that seemed to place them a cut above blacks in the social order also dragged down the region's wage scales by keeping workers as a group, but especially noncraftworkers, politically and economically impotent. Gender divisions, intermingled with racial and caste distinctions, further segmented and fragmented working people, undermining the potential movements of resistance and protest required to fundamentally alter the system.

Only strong unions could counteract the tendencies of employers, both homegrown and imported from the North, to exploit labor to the maximum. In the industrial sphere, where blacks made up a large portion of the work force, unions could be effective only by organizing all the employees, black and white, together. But as long as the social order of segregation remained stable and exclusionary practices prevailed among white workers, employers had little reason to fear labor challenges to the "southern way of life." Furthermore, should any such challenges arise, workers faced the likelihood of repression, since the white community had largely sacrificed the civil liberties protections embodied in the Bill of Rights in the process of imposing a racial dictatorship over blacks. When workers finally did begin to demand change, the repressive exercise of state power, built up during decade after decade of southern segregation, provided the ultimate guarantor of the South's racial and class system.

CHAPTER TWO

No Bill of Rights in Memphis

Mr Rovell . . . i wont to work but it is a shame the way the White Mens doing the Black
Man they put the Black Man on the line and Kick him and Beat him . . . i wont to work
but i dont wont to get Killed   the Police man is going around Pickin the mens up and
hitting and Beating them all over . . . the Pore white class mens Kicks and do us Black
mens Bad . . . it is they time at this time   But some day they will find out Better.
    —W. Groper to President Roosevelt

If you are interested in cleaning a mess that stinks to high heaven come to Memphis. . . .
Boss Crump and his henchman [Senator] McKellar have things in such shape that they
not only control Memphis and Shelby County, but through them they control the entire
State . . . most people are like myself—afraid to make the slightest move. There is
nothing worse in the whole U.S. of that I am sure.
    —"A Memphian"
    to U.S. Attorney General Frank Murphy

Civil liberties had always been weak in the South. The right to speak
against the dominant system had almost ceased to exist during slavery,
and in subsequent eras state and local authorities as well as vigilantes ruthlessly repressed opposition to the dominant order. The racial system had
everything to do with this; the South, as W. E. B. Du Bois put it, became "an armed camp for intimidating black folk." But in the process of
destroying black freedom, the white South surrendered some of its own
freedoms as well. In Memphis, under the political machine of Edward H.
Crump, almost any kind of unorthodox view became suspect; the civil liberties and due process protections of the Bill of Rights and the Fourteenth
Amendment in many ways simply did not apply. And although many liberals hoped that New Deal reforms would "modernize" the South and
undermine such regimes, the New Deal seemed to only strengthen Crump's
political reign. Such conditions made any kind of organizing extremely
difficult.[1]

By the time Franklin Roosevelt gained the presidency in 1932, Crump had already begun moving toward the heights of his power. His origins tied him to both Old South cotton interests and New South industrialists. The son of a Mississippi slaveholder whose plantation had gone to ruin after the Civil War, Crump found his fortune in Memphis early in the century. His marriage into the wealthy McLean family gave him early access to old-line cotton families and his insurance and real estate business gave him economic independence. Red-haired, red-faced, and combative, the "Red Snapper" took over one of Memphis's seamiest political wards in a city known for its gambling dens and for having the highest murder rate in the country. Crump gained attention by raiding gambling parlors as police commissioner in 1908, won a narrow election victory as mayor in 1909, and reelection in 1911 and 1915. He gained wide business support during the "Progressive" Era for improving city services, lowering taxes and utility rates, and implementing a commissioner form of government that placed the city more firmly in the hands of the business class. However, lawyers for the utility companies, which Crump wanted to take over, sued him for failing to enforce state prohibition, gambling, and prostitution laws; in 1916 he resigned, only to take a more lucrative position as county trustee, a combination tax collector and treasurer. For the next eight years he cultivated the city's vice establishment and accumulated a small fortune as citizens found it increasingly advantageous to buy and sell their homes or get mortgages and insurance through Crump and Trezevant. Crump took up ownership of several banks, at least two large plantations in Mississippi, and several bottling plants in upstate New York. His wealth and social position increasingly placed him at the top of the city's elite.[2]

Crump reasserted his political power in 1924 by defeating the mayoral slate of the predominantly white-collar, lower middle-class Ku Klux Klan, which established a membership of nearly ten thousand and threatened to take control from the city's dominant business interests. In this and the pivotal 1927 election, Crump made a tacit alliance with black Republican Robert Church, Jr., and other black business leaders. Although the poll tax provided an easy method for white political bosses to manipulate the black vote, the fact that blacks could vote still made them a power to be reckoned with. During the 1924 campaign black votes had been instrumental in defeating the Klan; again, in 1927, 80 percent of the black community voted with Crump to replace the incumbent mayor Rowlett Paine with Watkins Overton, a member of one of the city's earliest wealthy families. During the campaign, black business leaders organized voting leagues that qualified thousands of new black registrants to vote and pressed for better hospital care, recreational and educational facilities—concerns that, in various ways, the Crump machine sought to address. In a period in which Crump had not totally solidified his control over the white vote, anti-Crump politicians sought to suppress the black vote to undermine him. Clarence Saunders, founder of the innovative Piggly Wiggly chain stores in Memphis, took the lead with newspaper advertisements, one of which began, "Listen, you peaceful and law-abiding niggers, you know your place, you had better get around some of these presumptuous and impudent self-styled leaders of yours and remind them of their place in a white man's country."[3]

While making judicious recognition of the dynamic power of Church and the black vote, Crump also co-opted the Klan's only elected official, city judge Clifford Davis, making him police and fire commissioner and later a member of Congress. In 1928, Crump battled with millionaire and *Commercial Appeal* owner Luke Lea and other local business leaders over election of the state's governor and lost. But in 1930, Crump's overwhelming election to Congress made him a national political figure, and when Lea went to jail bankrupt Crump began to extend his influence over the governorship and the state supreme court as well as city, state, and congressional officeholders in Memphis. After serving two terms in Congress, Crump returned to the business of making money. He continued to gain a strong public following, however, as a "populist" who championed the Tennessee Valley Authority (TVA) and city ownership of the local power company. He held major office only once more: elected as mayor in 1940, he turned the office over to his appointed successor the same day. From 1927 to his death in 1954, no one doubted that, without holding office or even making a speech, "Mister Crump," not the elected leaders, made all the basic decisions about running Memphis and much of Tennessee as well.[4]

Crump's political supremacy rested on a number of factors, most notably his studied manipulation of a notoriously undemocratic political system. Tennessee legislators in 1891 had put the poll tax in place largely to enforce black political subordination, but ironically this proved to be the very method by which blacks did exert some influence with Crump. Other southern states disfranchised black voters outright. But despite the fact that Robert Church, Jr., and other black leaders got some leverage from the black vote, Crump and his machine came to have most of the control over it. Black union organizer George Holloway explained that "if you didn't pay the poll tax, you didn't vote," and since the tax was cumulative, every year a potential voter failed to pay it less and less possibility existed of ever being able to afford to vote. Hence, although Church could organize and lead the black political constituency in Memphis, in most cases someone else paid the bill and pulled the strings. Crump's first mayoral opponent, Joe Williams, paid the poll tax for blacks so they would vote for him, but Crump defeated him at his own game. Subsequently Crump and his supporters collected money from businesses, vice establishments, city employees, and industrialists (a few of whom even instituted a payroll checkoff system to provide funds for the machine). Ward leaders rounded up hundreds of blacks, sometimes bringing them in from Mississippi and Arkansas, and gave them free rides to the polls, money, red-eye whiskey, or barbecue. "A lot of blacks were paid to get receipts," Holloway recalled, "and since many didn't have jobs, they'd mark the ballot the way they were told, to earn some money. Someone would watch them at the polls to make sure it happened that way." The Crump machine also had extensive card files on registered white voters, including several thousand city employees, and made sure that they voted for the Crump candidates. Eventually Crump gained virtual one-man control over much of the white and the black vote.[5]

The 1931 elections illustrated the degree of Crump's local control when he received 90 percent of the vote for the Memphis congressional seat. The only opponent of Crump's mayoral candidate received a minuscule 869 votes. Crump handpicked the mayors for the next three elections with no opponents running against them. By 1936, only 29 percent of the state's depression-struck voters could pay the poll tax; in Memphis, however, the Crump machine turned out so many votes, both white and black, that the city's fraudulent election returns increasingly dominated state politics. Between Shelby County and votes managed by machines in other parts of the state, Crump and his allies could determine about one-third of Tennessee's vote and make or break gubernatorial candidates. By controlling the state's most populous voting district, Crump also exercised considerable control over the state legislature, the governor, and the supreme court. The poll tax, and the fact that Memphis had a large black population with few rights, made it possible for the Crump machine to exercise decisive influence in a state where voter turnout, except in Memphis, remained exceedingly low.[6]

Of course, Crump's rise to power could not have happened without business support. "We had bossism," said Memphis Typographical Union leader (and later city judge) Robert Tillman, "because that was the way the business people wanted it." According to Crump's biographer William Miller, almost the entire business community supported Crump's career "from the time he first entered politics." Crump was one of them. He offered efficiency, quality city services, cheap tax rates, and the stability of one-man rule in a wild river town known far and wide for its speak-

easies and gambling dens. As one cotton merchant stated the case for Boss
Crump, "Somebody has to look after all these things and we are glad
to have Ed Crump do it."[7] But according to Miller, the newer industrial
interests supported Crump perhaps even more than the old-line families.
"No other interest group," he wrote, "put out more effort to get votes for
the organization" than large manufacturers, who "supported Crump with
almost total dedication." It is not difficult to discover why. Crump played
the key role in persuading Firestone to establish one of its major production facilities in Memphis, and Raymond Firestone (son of the company's
owner) quickly became a part of the city's power elite. In return for cheap
city services, an exemption from city taxes, free police and fire protection,
and assurances that his plant would remain nonunion, Firestone, like the
officials at Ford Motor and other industries, became a staunch supporter
of the Crump machine. The company used a checkoff system to make sure
its workers had registered to vote and drove them to the polls.[8]

Obviously, Crump's support from black middle-class leaders also played
an important role in his success. Church and other members of the black
business community had a degree of economic power in the twenties, nurturing two banks, a number of insurance companies, and other businesses;
indeed, Memphis became something of a mecca for black capitalists in the
mid-South. Church and other elites had a potentially large voting block
with which to bargain for small gains for the black community, and in
return for their support at the polls, Crump offered blacks a few parks,
schools, housing and health improvements, and a degree of paternalism.
In contrast to the regimes in Mississippi, "noblesse oblige," Memphis historian John Harkins commented, "was a significant improvement over no
obliges whatsoever."[9] Crump's paternalistic racism viewed blacks as children to be managed rather than as enemies to be exterminated. At the
same time, the interests of the city's small black elite often remained distinctly separate from those of black workers, who frequently had their own
leaders and always comprised the overwhelming bulk of the black population. Civil rights activities by black ministers and the black middle class,
so notable in later years, remained extremely weak. Accommodationism
dominated the thinking of some of the community's most influential ministers, especially in the latter twenties when the black business elite weakened
as the result of economic failures and business scandals.[10]

In this context, Crump developed a number of black "lieutenants," referred to by some as the "brown screws" in the political machine, who
scrupulously avoided confrontations over racial issues. During his consolidation of power in the twenties, Crump allowed Robert Church and a few

other black business leaders and professionals to exercise some degree of independence by organizing the Lincoln League and serving as local leaders of the Republican party. Church even served as a delegate to national Republican party conventions and dispensed considerable patronage to blacks across the nation. Some indeed felt that Memphis provided a kind of haven from the most violent features of the Jim Crow system. "Even though the Memphis Negroes were a cog in a most efficient machine," the journalist Ralph McGill commented, "the very fact that they voted gave them a status above that enjoyed by Negroes in [other] southern cities." [11]

However, the heavy "stick" that Crump carried constituted an equally important factor in his control of black Memphis. The depression nearly wiped out black businesses. Their fortunes dictated the rise and fall of the local branch of the NAACP, as did the repressive atmosphere in which the organization operated. During most of the twenties, the NAACP operated virtually underground and provided no local power base to resist the political machine. Hence, as Crump's power grew, he increasingly eschewed alliances with independent-minded leaders such as Church. In the end, no black leader could survive without the Crump regime's approval, as became evident in 1940 when Crump decided to dispense with Church and other Republicans and ran them out of town. Crump had "his people" in control of black schools, churches, vice establishments, and most civic organizations. These people served as his eyes and ears, reporting on any real or imagined slights to Crump to the police, whose violent rule created a general atmosphere of fear and constraint. [12]

Although Crump contended that black people had no better friend than himself, police power always remained a central component of his rule. KKK leader Clifford Davis served as police commissioner, and one candidate for office in the twenties claimed that 70 percent of the Memphis police belonged to the Klan. The city's policies only encouraged their racist conduct. Police wages during the thirties remained only a little higher than those paid to industrial workers and well below wages paid to police in the three smaller major cities of Tennessee. Instead of a professional police force, the city relied on the willingness of poor whites, many of them migrants from the plantation districts, to accept their low-wage status in exchange for the personal power their position conferred. Their sense of white skin privilege did nothing to shore up wages but provided many of them with a more visceral incentive to serve as defenders of white supremacy. Although the city had once employed a few black police officers, by the thirties, according to Ralph Bunche, "the only connection Negroes have had to the Memphis police force has been Negro heads colliding with nightsticks in the hands of white policemen." Police violence throughout the thirties struck terror into the hearts of labor and civil rights organizers alike.[13]

Aside from the police, political cronies, the vice establishments, the city's middle class, the business community, and most of the city's black leaders, Crump cultivated a strong base of support among the city's craft and railroad unions. Earlier in their careers, these unions had to struggle with employers and the city for recognition and acceptance, but by the twenties they had gained a degree of respectability. They soon became important cogs in the Crump machine, and in return for votes gained considerable advantages. Crump's political machine appointed union electricians, plumbers, and motion picture operators to city licensing boards, which determined who could work on building construction and repair, in the theaters, or in other businesses in which union labor played a role. The licensing system ensured that the family members and associates of union members received work and kept blacks out. In addition, many painters, carpenters, boiler attendants, and other craft union members worked directly for the city, and when work in many of the established trades petered out during the depression, the Crump machine provided a number of AFL members with temporary jobs in the police department. Thus, in city work and the private sector, the ability of white unionists to obtain jobs often depended on cooperation with the Crump machine. New Deal spending programs created even more largesse to be dispensed, tying the interests of the Trades and Labor Council and the Crump machine even more tightly together.[14]

Despite the generally bad economic conditions during the thirties, the pump-priming economics of the New Deal made it possible for many in the craft unions connected to the Crump regime to retain their status as the "middle class" of the laboring population. Public works programs revived the building trades unions, the core of the Memphis AFL, while minimum wage codes adopted by the NRA substantially raised wage rates in the organized sectors of employment. In the construction industry, NRA wage codes increased the earnings of craftworkers to $1.10 an hour and laborers to $.45 an hour, far above the scale of the average industrial worker, while Painters' Local 49 achieved wages of $1.00 an hour and a forty-hour work week under the NRA codes. Blacks of course remained excluded from craft unions in most of these occupations. The New Deal thus enhanced the position of the AFL unions without doing anything to get them to open their ranks to black workers, the best of all possible worlds in the thinking of many white trade unionists.[15]

Politics, via the Crump machine, also cemented the relationship between the city's labor establishment and the upper classes. Crump traditionally delegated at least one slot in the county's state legislative delegation to a trade unionist, and he endorsed Labor Council leaders for local office as well. In the 1934 election, for example, the council endorsed all of the machine candidates as "friends of labor," and in return numerous business leaders endorsed Labor Council president Jake Cohen as a "responsible" labor leader. Cohen's overwhelming election to local office, a foregone conclusion given Crump's support, fostered the illusion that trade unionists in Memphis had real power. The 1934 "campaign," led in large part by officials of the railroad and plumbers' unions, both of which excluded blacks, also signified that conservative white males would continue to dominate the existing unions.[16]

Under these conditions it is not surprising that during the depression few AFL unionists broke from their tradition of harmony with the business class. During annual Trades and Labor Council banquets and Labor Day parades in 1933 and 1934, leading bankers, attorneys, law enforcement officials, elected officials, the *Commercial Appeal* editor, and other members of the city's establishment gladly joined with AFL officials to denounce the various "isms" they considered alien to American labor and to join arm in arm in celebrating cooperation between employers and workers.[17] In these settings, at least, the desperation and grinding poverty suffered by most workers seem to have been forgotten.

New Deal economic development programs, many of them identified with Crump, added to his popularity. Under his tutelage, over $20 million of federal aid funded public works projects that modernized the city's facilities and expanded its industrial infrastructure, built hospitals and public housing, and provided work relief. The city also created an innovative home-buyer's assistance plan with federal funds. These programs modernized the city and made it possible for industry to expand, at the same time producing thousands of jobs. Some of the New Deal projects enriched Crump and Senator Kenneth McKellar, both major investors in the South Memphis Land Company. Crump's economic fortunes had always risen in tandem with his increased political power, and now federal aid built Crump's popularity and wealth to their peak in the thirties.[18]

In a real sense, many people, white and black, were indebted to Crump. He dispensed city jobs, appointments to licensing boards, judgeships, and other official positions that determined day-to-day affairs affecting the common citizen. From his undisputed position as the "father" of Memphis, he became a kind of plantation boss in the city, intervening personally in the lives of "his" people, who came to him to get streetlights and potholes fixed or to get jobs and political favors. Some seventy-five thousand local citizens turned out annually to honor him—and enjoy free food, refreshments, and entertainment—on E. H. Crump Day, and when Crump turned up for the local football games at Crump Stadium the citizens stood up and applauded. Even the mayor wrote to Crump as if he were a sharecropper addressing his plantation lord, while Crump scribbled crude two-sentence letters and postcards telling him how to run the city.[19]

As his popularity grew, so did his arrogance. In 1927, machine thugs beat up reporters and smashed their cameras when they tried to record election fraud; by 1938, even Tennessee governor Gordon Browning could scarcely make his way into Memphis. When Browning, once a Crump protege, went against his patron, facilities for his Memphis speeches were canceled, at least one of his local supporters was fired, and thugs beat up three of his supporters within as many days. When two thugs wielding a lead pipe and a blackjack beat attorney and Browning supporter Ben Kohn in broad daylight, police arrested Kohn on charges of assault and battery. On election day, police arrested Browning poll watchers, and the governor's opponent won by almost the same margin by which Browning had triumphed two years earlier with Crump support. As one journalist wrote, "There is a man in Memphis who can make up 60,000 minds, then change them at will."[20]

Crump's combination of ruthless repression and benign paternalism built a regime that puzzled and astounded outside observers. Investigations in the U.S. Senate probed the Crump machine's electoral frauds, and northern journalists condemned the machine's violations of the most fundamental tenets of civil liberties and representative government. The *Chicago Tribune* even labeled him "the Führer in Memphis." City leaders, on the other hand, preferred to view the city's machine leader as a humane if autocratic man who helped to bring order out of chaos, rather than the acerbic crackpot and dictator he sometimes appeared to be. But the dominant images of Crump as homegrown fascist or paternalistic populist don't entirely convey the true nature of the regime, which reflected not only Crump's personalized power but the needs and ideology of the city's upper classes and, to some degree, the interests of other voting constituents as well.

THE REPRESSION OF SOUTHERN RADICALISM

In Memphis as elsewhere, during the thirties a new generation of southern labor organizers and anticapitalist radicals emerged, seeking to challenge the existing system by building interracial and biracial working-class movements. In some places, their efforts helped to create a new degree of labor unity.[21] But almost everywhere, southern officials unleashed extraordinary violence against even the most minimal efforts of such people to demand economic or social justice. In Birmingham, Alabama, authorities hauled out machine guns when unemployed workers marched on municipal buildings; in "Bloody Harlan" County, Kentucky, in Gastonia, North Carolina, and in Atlanta, hired thugs and police arrested, beat, and shot people for trying to picket, strike, or assemble in demands for union rights. This terror against the exercise of democratic rights made it apparent that neither labor nor civil rights organizing could succeed without establishing a degree of respect for the Constitution among the region's ruling elite.[22]

So it was in Memphis. In the stultifying political conditions in Crump's town, only a few had the nerve to speak out. The Crump machine put considerable efforts into silencing those few, no matter how limited or ineffective their efforts might have been, so that others would remain silent. Marion and Horace Davis, northerners who moved to Memphis in the fall of 1929, later recalled the frightful lack of freedom in the city during the early depression years. Horace, an economics professor, came to teach at Southwestern College, a white, four-year, liberal arts school. He was astounded at the violent racial attitudes of students and faculty alike. When he asked students in one of his classes whether lynching was ever justified, they voted yes by twenty-six to three; opinions split in half over the right to burn a man to death. Marion learned about southern racism through more personal experiences. One night a carload of white men kidnapped and raped their fourteen-year-old black baby-sitter, who refused to go to the authorities with the car's license plate number because she feared even worse trouble from the police.[23]

Other local incidents horrified them as well: a white streetcar conductor shot to death a black man who questioned the change he received; a white female grocery clerk charged a black man with rape when he argued with her in the store; a Southwestern faculty member even called a Davis family friend a "nigger lover" simply because he read a book about African-American history. Astounding insensitivity to blacks underlay pretensions to southern white paternalism: neighbors whose black house cleaner had a stroke on the job put her in the barn for several days until she could walk to a doctor, never even thinking to bring her inside the house or take her to a hospital. Marion also saw a black woman making ten cents an hour carrying wood for ten hours a day at a local lumber mill and witnessed hundreds of people drifting into town looking for work and finding none, but the plight of these people evoked little concern among the white middle class.[24]

The unrelieved brutality and dismal conditions they witnessed during the early depression years increasingly radicalized the Davises, prompting Marion to write to the Communist party for help and advice. It was natural that she should write to the party. In the early depression years, Communists worked to organize interracial labor activity as no other group and called for "full racial, political and social equality" for blacks, insisting that "the white workers cannot do much to improve things so long as the Negroes are in chains." Based on their willingness to act, in Birmingham and Atlanta Communist party activists sparked unprecedented interracial working-class activity. In response, southern authorities made a fetish of "common-ism," as many of them pronounced it, and tied every movement for change to a potential breakdown in the racial system. According to Memphis police chief Will Lee, "The dictatorship of the pro-lat-erate" led directly to "social equality" of the "races." [25]

Hence, when the Davises decided to take on an organizing role, the police and the newspapers quickly silenced them. The Davises sought to help in the regional defense of six Atlanta supporters of the Gastonia textile strikers. The state of Georgia charged the Atlanta Six with inciting insurrection, a capital offense, for merely handing out leaflets, based on a law enacted to suppress slave rebellion (a law next used in the famous case of black Communist Angelo Herndon). The Davises printed up handbills calling a meeting in Confederate Park to protest the Atlanta Six arrests, but only a few clergy and members of the Workmen's Circle, a Jewish fraternal organization, pledged support. A *Commercial Appeal* reporter claimed the Davises planned to use the meeting to organize a local Communist party chapter and demanded to know from Marion whether she thought "the negro and the white man should be placed upon an equal basis." When she said yes, the newspaper emblazoned this "interview" with a startling headline stating "Negro for Governor Is Communists Plan, Social Equality Meeting to Be Held Here Tonight," blasting all hopes of support in Memphis for the Atlanta Six. [26]

The article immediately touched off reprisals by the American Legion, business leaders, and the police. Police picked up Horace Davis and Tom Johnson, a seventeen-year-old Communist organizer from Chattanooga. At the jail, city attorney Walter Chandler and American Legion leader H. O. Beck told them that they would be physically stopped from holding any meeting to speak in favor of racial equality. When the men refused to promise not to hold the meeting, the police arrested them. They picked up Marion as well, leaving the doors to her home wide open and taking what the newspapers called "a ton of Communist documents." The police escorted Johnson to the train station and shipped him back to Chattanooga, where authorities had been warned of his arrival. They also arrested a local grocer named Joe Norvell, who they claimed was an unnaturalized Russian immigrant suspected of Communist leanings.[27]

After this, the Davises had little choice but to leave town. The parents of their son's playmates had already told a Davis child not to come around, and only by secretly placing her children in the hands of a friend before the arrests did she keep them away from the police. She came home from jail to find that the police had strewn books and personal items all over the house. The *Commercial Appeal,* the leading instigator of the arrests, happily declared that "communism and social equality forums in Memphis are dead, at least temporarily." As fair warning to the educational establishment to clean house, the paper carried a J. P. Alley cartoon on the front page titled "Find Them Out, Kick Them Out, and Keep Them Out!" The newspaper pictured a professor with a menacing look on his face carrying a book titled "Revolting Social Propaganda" (subtitled "Seditious Literature") into a classroom. The city's legal establishment would do nothing to defend freedom of speech in Memphis, according to the local American Civil Liberties Union attorney, Robert Keebler, who declared that "the police acted wisely" in making the arrests and that "the matter is closed for good." A friend told Marion that she was lucky: "Honey, down in Mississippi where I was raised, if you'd said aloud what you told that newspaper man they'd have strung you up by your toes." When they left town, Memphis plainclothes police agents followed the Davises all the way to Chicago.[28]

This incident made the point, if it needed making, that Memphis remained closed to outsiders or anyone locally who spoke against the racial system or tried to organize for change. The point would be made repeatedly. In the fall of 1932, Communists held a public meeting in Memphis as part of their presidential campaign, featuring black and white Communists on the same stage (though seated in separate areas). *Daily Worker* editor Clarence Hathaway urged a march of the unemployed on city hall to demand relief, but the *Commercial Appeal* focused on what it called Communist party presidential candidate William Z. Foster's "thick lipped negro running mate from Alabama," James Ford, and ignored whatever else transpired. Even though these and other thoroughly negative accounts of Communist activity pervaded the media, Communist candidate for Mayor Ollie Harrington obtained 495 votes from 123 of Memphis's 126 election districts, a hint that Communists may have been building a significant base. If so, authorities quickly drove it far underground.[29]

Boris Israel, a twenty-three-year-old Ohio State graduate, also tried to make headway in Memphis, to no avail. Israel had faced down shooting and jail to organize support for embattled miners in "Bloody Harlan"; he came to Memphis representing the Communist-led International Labor Defense (ILD), an organization mainly noted for making world famous the case of seven black men condemned to death on bogus charges of raping two white women near Scottsboro, Alabama. Israel saw another Scottsboro in the unprovoked killing of a local black man by six white police officers. The small Memphis NAACP, split by personality and power disputes between two factions, one led by insurance executive Joseph E. Walker and the other by Robert Church, Jr., refused to get involved with a Communist-led organization. Nor could Israel get much support from organized labor some time later when he went to work in a New Deal construction project and led a strike of two thousand Reconstruction Finance Corporation relief workers for higher wages. The Memphis AFL Labor Council and a few liberal white ministers passed a resolution of support, but they went silent when the police invoked the danger of communism and, charging Israel with sedition, held him without bail. During court proceedings police even knocked down and arrested Israel's assertive attorney Herman I. Goldberger, whom Police Commissioner Davis denounced as "one of the most radical influences in the town today." [30]

The arrest of Israel and his attorney produced no outcry of support for civil liberties. Instead, it triggered a barrage of anticommunist rhetoric, with the *Commercial Appeal* claiming that Communist support for political prisoners and the Scottsboro Boys proved their "unvarying support for violence and criminal activities." In a story headlined "Reds Plot Destruction of All Churches in Memphis," the paper claimed that a local Communist organization of ten thousand members had issued leaflets urging workers to "destroy every church in Memphis." With a sedition charge on his head, Israel shortly left Memphis. Attempts by southern Communist party organizers to replace him failed. When in 1934 they sent in Mack Coad, a black veteran of sharecropper battles in Alabama, black business leaders turned him in to the Memphis police. They whipped him nearly to death before putting him on a train back to Birmingham. [31]

One other potential group of activists initially fared better in Boss Crump's town than did the Communists. The Memphis Socialist branch had been in existence since the early years of the twentieth century and had been little threat to the existing order. The Tennessee Socialist party had long held that racism was "only a tactical method used by the capitalist class to keep workers divided on the economic field" and saw no necessity for mounting a struggle against discrimination as such. While many southern Socialists formally supported economic equality for blacks, most also eschewed "social equality," a code word for integration. In the twenties, Socialist party leaders had allied themselves with the officialdom of the AFL and took little initiative to organize industrial workers. By the early thirties, the shell of the Memphis Socialist party that remained consisted of a few elderly Jewish men and a few white middle-class supporters holding regular meetings at the Arbeiter Ring Hall at Jefferson and Orleans Streets, a building run by the Workmen's Circle, a Jewish fraternal group. Devoid of contact with blacks and differentiating themselves from their "bitterest enemy—communism," the Socialists seemed inert, but in the early thirties they began to show life and agitate for an end to free market capitalism.[32]

They obtained a sympathetic hearing from Edward Meeman, the Republican and Unitarian editor of the Memphis *Press-Scimitar*. Although no radical, and staunchly anticommunist, Meeman provided the most influential voice of opposition to the Crump machine, a voice the machine never succeeded in silencing. Meeman was one of an estimated twenty-five hundred who turned out to hear Socialist presidential candidate Norman Thomas speak in Memphis in September 1932. Thomas received surprisingly favorable treatment by both of the city's newspapers and obtained about 2,000 votes in the state; a Socialist mayoral candidate polled 358 votes; and a Socialist gubernatorial candidate received 168 votes in Memphis. Of participating Memphis voters, 853 had chosen Socialist or Communist party candidates, an indication of a more significant potential base for radicalism in the city than one might have supposed.[33]

This potential, however, fell victim to the prevailing anticommunist rhetoric fostered by city leaders and the newspapers. After the election, Socialists helped organize a local movement called the Unemployed Citizens League to find work and food for the jobless, with support from William Amberson, a Socialist physics professor at the University of Tennessee Medical School, George McClean, a sociology and education professor at Southwestern College, Protestant minister Alfred Loaring-Clarke, and a few other reformers. Red-baiting within the organization, sensationalized in the media, caused this relatively apolitical group to quickly fall apart. H. W. Pyle, first elected to lead the Unemployed League and then discharged for his incompetence and divisiveness, struck back by calling McClean, Amberson, and another board member "communists," while the professors, for their part, also called Pyle a "red." Although the president of Southwestern denied that McClean was a "communist," the college terminated the professor. Split over the supposed "communist issue," the League disappeared and the Socialists lapsed into inactivity.[34]

The real Communists, of course, had already been obliterated. Yet the fear of communism, whether grounded in any semblance of reality or not, would be raised over and over again by the news media, the police, and city officials whenever threats of organized activity, particularly labor or interracial activity, appeared. The appeal to this fear had varying degrees of success, and at times even those who used it may not have believed their own rhetoric. Nonetheless, red-baiting remained one of the favorite devices of those who opposed movements for change. The fear of communism, like the fear of "social equality" (integration), provided one more reason why Memphians were not supposed to think for themselves about the increasingly pressing difficulties caused by the Great Depression.

RACIAL REPRESSION AND THE ECONOMIC CRISIS

Just as the disastrous economic conditions of the early thirties led to increased repression, they also heightened the tensions inherent in the South's repressive racial order. The economic hardships shared by blacks and whites in the early thirties did not necessarily translate into labor solidarity, and the early New Deal economic recovery programs seemed to only exacerbate occupational and wage discrimination against blacks. Faced with massive unemployment, whites generally viewed blacks as a threat rather than as potential allies. A flood of some forty thousand into the Memphis labor market brought the percentage of the black population in Memphis to about 40 percent, its highest point since 1900. Crowded urban conditions highlighted disproportionately high black mortality rates, while crime and unemployment rates in the African-American community doubled or tripled those of whites. Black migrants had little choice but to accept jobs at seven cents an hour at local sawmills, and although poor whites also migrated to Memphis, many white city dwellers singled out impoverished blacks as the source of worsening urban conditions. White workers more specifically identified them as competitors for jobs.[35]

Thus began the "Negro Removal" campaign of the thirties. Under the pressure of widespread unemployment, whites urged employers to turn over some of the employment usually reserved for blacks—operating elevators, digging ditches, repairing railroad track, waiting tables—to them. Loewe's Theater in Memphis responded by firing black ushers and replacing them with whites at the same low wages they had paid the blacks.[36]

"Negro Removal" campaigns reached their ugly height in the mid-South between 1931 and 1934, when white vigilantes, paid twenty-five dollars for maiming and one hundred dollars for killing a victim, killed ten black railroad workers in Mississippi, Tennessee, and Louisiana. Members of the white railroad unions, who numbered some four thousand in 1934, demanded that the Illinois Central and other railroads running through Memphis employ whites only, encouraging and perhaps funding the killings. Although police in Memphis and Mississippi arrested five of the conspirators, only two of them received even brief jail sentences.[37] A less deadly but no less effective campaign continued for the rest of the decade. By 1940, thousands of African-American stokers, break and switch operators, and flaggers had been replaced by whites, and those blacks who remained worked mainly as laborers in the yards or as porters, jobs whites still rejected. The eventual switch from steam to diesel engines, which turned dirty jobs into clean ones that required fewer workers, only led to more black unemployment. "The Negro's work ends where the machine begins," wrote Charles Hamilton Houston, one of their attorneys (and later a leading legal architect of the NAACP's fight for desegregation).[38]

The plight of the black railroad employees demonstrated throughout the thirties the depths to which many whites would sink to obtain jobs, as well as the failure of state and federal authorities to protect black rights. The Association of Colored Railway Trainmen, founded in Memphis in 1918 by blacks excluded from the white railroad unions, repeatedly appealed for federal intervention in support of their civil liberties and job rights, to no avail. Perry Howard, who worked on the case with Houston, pursued damages and a restoration of seniority rights for the workers all the way to 1945, without results.[39] Railroad jobs, a civil rights attorney observed, "are just too soft and the pay too good [for whites] to permit these jobs to be held by Negroes."[40] Association leader George Washington finally concluded that the government would only protect white rights, leaving blacks to be "reduced to peonage and Slavery, besides murder and abuse as in the past."[41]

The existing labor movement in Memphis during the early thirties failed to find a strategy that could unite workers instead of dividing them into competitors for a limited number of jobs. Nor did the New Deal provide remedies for a racially divided labor market, one that continued to pit white and black workers against each other. The "trickle down" version of the early New Deal, as embodied in the National Recovery Act of 1933, failed to make much-needed structural economic changes; as a result, it in some ways reinforced existing inequalities. NRA wage codes—established by boards dominated by the very industries being regulated—put a federal stamp of approval on wage differentials that continued to disadvantage blacks. In public works projects, government authorities, contractors, building trades unionists, and others colluded to assure that jobs went first to whites. In 1933, construction gangs involved in early Works Project Administration (WPA) jobs were 90 percent black, and blacks otherwise ended up in the least desirable, worst-paid public works jobs, such as garbage collection. Memphis whites even forced removal of a black Civilian Conservation Corps camp to a location outside of Memphis. The federal government attached few strings to its projects that would force employers or building trades unions to open higher-paying employment to blacks.[42]

William McDowell later wrote to Works Project administrator Harry Hopkins that "as a member of the Negro race I do not feel that my people are given a fair deal with the New Deal in Memphis," pointing out that "the majority of us are required to work as common laborers no matter what we are qualified to do." In his own case, he had completed two years of college at Howard University in Washington, "and yet I am forced to work as a common laborer." Another WPA worker, Cora McKinney, wrote to President Roosevelt that "I cant see why [it] is the W.P.A. official will let the white people work, wont let we poor Colored People work. . . . We Colored People down hear is not treated right on the W.P.A." These and other letters from workers in the WPA files testified to the continuing force of racism in labor markets.[43] In Mississippi, 98 percent of the Civilian Conservation Corps jobs went to whites, in a state over half black.[44]

Neither local federal administrators nor the craft unions, and certainly not employers, challenged white supremacy in determining wage rates or in allocation of jobs. Hence New Deal recovery programs, despite valiant efforts of southern liberals like National Youth Administration director Aubrey Williams to end government-funded discrimination, in some ways only entrenched the old order of white supremacy.[45] Federal policies on race seemed unlikely to change. To get elected, Roosevelt had maintained strong links to southern Democrats, who controlled over half the committee chairs in the Congress and could block any New Deal legislation they pleased; Crump's increasingly powerful position in the Democratic party also forced the president to take particular care not to offend him. The lack of significant structural economic reform or federal political intervention in Memphis further enabled the Crump regime throughout the thirties to pursue business as usual, to continue tightening its hold on the electorate, and to serve as a broker for the city's economic interests.[46]

Against this background, during the depression decade, Crump's regime increasingly resembled a ruthless police state rather than the popular image of Crump as a paternalistic, benign despot. Violence at the hands of the state remained a part of the everyday reality for African-Americans throughout the segregation era, but it seemed to worsen during the turbulent thirties. As more blacks migrated to the city from the countryside, whites became increasingly apprehensive. Newspaper images of blacks as criminals or clowns cultivated a deadly climate, as they carried front-page stories from as far away as Virginia when they concerned alleged black male crimes against white women, along with daily cartoons in the *Commercial Appeal* featuring a folksy but ignorant character named "Hambone" speaking in "Negro dialect." In this atmosphere, the police and courts proved that whites could literally get away with murder when it came to African-Americans. In one case, far from the eyes of the public, a black woman testified that police had beaten a nineteen-year-old black youth until his neck snapped "like a chicken neck," for the "crime" of hanging out near a white house of prostitution. It took a great deal of nerve to even swear out such an affidavit, for those who protested this system of southern justice did so at great risk. In a more public case, whites packed the courtroom to witness the sentencing to death of a young black man on a murder charge; when a black minister and others tried to observe the trial, the police drove them out into the street.[47]

Blacks witnessed or experienced this police state atmosphere almost every day. Virtually every outside observer commented on the ever-present reality of police brutality against Memphis blacks. Civil liberties investigator Laurent Frantz recounted numerous incidents he discovered during his brief stay in Memphis in which police shot and sometimes killed blacks based on mere suspicion of even minor crimes. Accounts of seemingly mindless and random acts of violence by the police appeared regularly in the *Press-Scimitar*, whose editor, Edward Meeman, continually decried police brutality. In a May 1937 incident, police broke into the home of a black gas station attendant, taking him and a fellow worker to jail and beating them both until they passed out in an attempt to force them to confess to a crime they knew nothing about. Their employer later testified that they had been working for him when the crime occurred.[48] The police brutalized suspects at the jail as standard practice, beating one young black man for ten days straight until he "confessed" to a crime. The police on more than one occasion used a torture chair, on which during one interrogation they placed a suspect face down with his head hanging through the rungs while one officer put his heel on the back of the victim's neck and another beat the man with a rubber hose.[49]

The rampant police brutality in Memphis provided a graphic example of how the segregation system's utter disregard for black rights created an atmosphere of repression that undermined civil liberties for everyone. The police exercise of almost absolute power against blacks and radicals easily extended to industrial union organizers and even to middle-class whites. In a long letter to the U.S. Justice Department in May 1939, E. L. Lung, a white man who came to Memphis to sell off property left to his wife, told of an incident in which police officers invaded his home and beat senseless two drunken men who had come to buy goods at his yard sale. When Lung called the police department to protest this brutality, the same officers returned, burst in his door with their guns drawn, arrested him, and dragged him down the front steps. The city convicted Lung on charges of resisting arrest and disturbing the peace. Following the assault by "these two bandit policemen," he had a heart attack and left Memphis without disposing of his wife's property. Lung recalled that in his eighteen months in Memphis the police had murdered three blacks that he knew of; he described Memphis as "one of the rotten spots of our great land." [50]

While Lung's experience certainly did not represent the experience of most white homeowners, among the strongest supporters of Crump's rule, it did indicate the pervasiveness of the disregard for civil liberties in Memphis. It appeared as if nowhere in the established order could the average working person, white or black, find help against arbitrary violence by police or company thugs. As police officers became accustomed to exercising absolute power, local and federal civil authorities either gave tacit approval or looked the other way. Rarely did the federal government even make symbolic protests. When FBI chief J. Edgar Hoover addressed the opening of the Memphis Police Department's 1937 crime school, which was headed by a former FBI agent, he apparently said nothing about the repeated police violations of civil liberties in Memphis. Neither did the U.S. attorney in Memphis, who was practically a Crump appointee. Local citizens wrote to the federal government a number of times for help, as in the case of James Hatley, who wrote to the president about the murder of his brother by drunken Memphis police; "look as if negros is nothin but Dogs," he told Roosevelt. When the Justice Department ultimately received such complaints, it gave a standard reply: such matters belonged in the province of the local police department and the federal government could do nothing to help. [51]

The police, like the people they served in the Memphis social and class hierarchy, had a particularly visceral dislike for black trade union activists, as illustrated by the arrest and beating of railroad porter Williams Glover in January 1938. According to an affidavit Glover swore out against the police, they arrested him on the fantastic charge, made by his white supervisor at the Illinois Central Railroad, W. H. Bucher, that Glover had openly propositioned a white doctor's nurse during a company physical and had made remarks about having an eighteen-year-old white girlfriend. These charges against Glover, a porter with sixteen years' seniority, a Baptist church elder, father of four children, and a respectable member of the black middle class, seemed far-fetched at best. But Glover had run into trouble with the railroad before, when it fired him from his job as a brake operator for chairing a union grievance committee. His leading role in the Memphis Brotherhood of Sleeping Car Porters set him up again for attack. Police Chief Will Lee told Glover that Bucher had told him to "get that black son of a bitch and do what you want with him." Incensed by the charge that the porter had propositioned a white woman, Lee and another officer arrested Glover, beat him with a blackjack, and kept him in jail incommunicado and bleeding from numerous head wounds, all the while threatening him with death. Glover's fellow porters organized a mass meeting of fourteen hundred people at Centenary Church to protest his arrest, and Lee finally released him on the condition that he leave town. Aided by a dozen or more union members, Glover gathered his family and left his home and job behind, never to return.[52]

By crying rape, a charge repeatedly used in the South to frame black men for crimes they did not commit, the Illinois Central Railroad rid itself of a black unionist who had been organizing porters since the twenties. And in this and other cases the police demonstrated how few rights they felt obliged to respect when it came to blacks, unionists, and for that matter, the average white. Such violence against people trying to exercise civil liberties and civil rights was by no means confined to Memphis but was more or less characteristic of the South.[53] The repression of black civil liberties generally, and of labor and civil rights activists in particular, reflected the long unchallenged dominance of an oligarchy that felt it had the perfect right to protect its interests with violence if necessary against any threats to the existing racial or economic order.

*   *   *

During the thirties, the racial division of the working class seemed to be growing stronger rather than weaker. The collapse of the cotton economy, the decline in urban employment, and the invasions by whites into work previously reserved for blacks on the railroads and in service occupations loosened the tenuous hold of African-Americans on employment even further than in earlier decades.[54] "Negro removal," police violence, and soaring unemployment made the thirties a disastrous decade for blacks. But in the early part of the depression decade, no real challenge to existing power relations emerged for white industrial workers either. In catering to the economic and racial imperatives of the South's upper classes, both the early New Deal and the craft unions left the southern caste system untouched or actually strengthened it. The basic conditions that kept southern labor unorganized and underpaid remained in place. At the same time, one-man rule grew stronger, providing one of the starkest examples of a repressive social order found all across the Deep South. Organizers, however, would increasingly challenge this order, as the failure of the National Recovery Act and renewed labor activism all over the country pushed events in a new direction.

I I

Labor's Struggle
for the Right to Organize

The ruling classes of the South, whose vested interests are in the status quo, are not going to sit idly by and permit the work of labor organizers to engulf them in the real revolutionary possibility in the South—that of solidarity between white and black workers. It can be taken for granted that the ruling classes will employ the race issue and all other issues for all they are worth.
—Ralph Bunche

Oh, the river's up and the cotton's down
Mr. Ed Crump, he runs this town!
—sung by black stevedores

CHAPTER THREE

The Rise and Repression
of Industrial Unionism

I have no intention of recognizing any union. I am firing when I please and hiring when I please. I have always done it and I will continue to do so as long as I operate the business. And as for your being fired, you were not fired, you just quit. The minute you joined the union you were automatically fired.
—Memphis Furniture president to his workers

Imported CIO agitators, Communists and highly paid professional organizers are not wanted in Memphis. . . . Their tools are violence, threats, sit-down strikes, destruction . . . we will oppose CIO violence, threats, un-American policies from the start to finish. Let them go elsewhere, if anyone wants them. We don't and won't tolerate them.
—Mayor Watkins Overton

In the New Deal era, an upsurge in union organizing and strikes occurred across the United States. Although the New Deal's National Recovery Act had codified discriminatory wage differentials and bolstered the role of big business in the economy, it also set the stage for labor upsurge. The act's section 7(a) put the federal government in the role of mediator instead of its customary role as strikebreaker in labor disputes. Seeking to establish a basis for industry-labor cooperation within the act's framework, 7(a) stated that "employees shall have the right to organize and bargain collectively . . . free from the interference, restraints, or coercion of employers." Although backed by no powers of legal enforcement, 7(a) encouraged workers to join unions and led to rapid union expansion among workers in mining, clothing, textile, auto, longshore, trucking, and other industries.[1]

However, the New Deal dream of voluntary industry compliance with the law conflicted with the reality of class interests at war. In the South, most employers would ignore 7(a) and, later, the more substantial guarantees for the right to organize enacted in the 1935 Wagner Act. Most industrial workers in the South as well as the nation lacked basic rights to organize, to speak out, and to bargain collectively, and rights granted on paper translated into organization only as the result of great struggle. Unionism for many became a kind of freedom movement to gain both economic rights and the right to organize, veteran Tennessee union organizer Ed McCrea later observed. Like the black civil rights movement of later years, in the thirties the union movement provided a wedge to open up the South to new influences and a hammer to break down the repressive social system inherited from slavery and enforced by segregation. In the circumstances of the thirties, unionism often took on the aura of a more general struggle for democratic rights.[2]

In the mid-South, the struggle for the right to organize unions also set off an interesting new interplay of black, white, female, and poor working-class constituencies. These workers sometimes organized through AFL unions, sometimes through CIO unions, and sometimes with no union support at all. One of the most startling of the new movements took place in eastern Arkansas, across the river from Memphis, where Socialist party members organized sharecroppers, tenants, and day laborers into a kind of all-inclusive industrial unionism in the fields. The Southern Tenant Farmers' Union (STFU), drawing on agrarian radical traditions of populism and socialism, arose in response to massive evictions of rural workers precipitated by the New Deal's Agricultural Adjustment Act of 1933. This measure paid millions of dollars to plantation owners not to grow crops, on the theory that creating scarcity would increase agricultural prices. With such resources, planters preferred to hire their workers seasonally, rather than let workers live on the land and share the crops at the end of the year. Although the law mandated that they share federal subsidies with sharecroppers, many simply forced them to leave. Hundreds of thousands of sharecroppers found themselves forced to work on plantations in labor gangs or to move into the cities to obtain wages. Inspired in part by the rise of unionism across the country, many of them organized, demanding an end to evictions, a fair distribution of Agricultural Adjustment Act payments, higher wages, and in the long run, the creation of agricultural cooperatives.[3]

Neither 7(a) in 1933 nor the Wagner Act in 1935 covered agricultural workers, and the potential solutions to the sharecroppers' problems had to be fundamentally different from those for factory workers. Yet the patterns of struggle that emerged in the Arkansas cotton fields had great significance for southern industrial unionism. From the outset, union leaders recognized that allowing themselves to be divided by race would be fatal. In 1919, in Elaine, Arkansas, whites had killed and imprisoned scores of black sharecroppers when they attempted to organize. To protect the union against such attacks, the STFU created a strong interracial leadership based on the "United Mine Workers' formula"—whites at the top, blacks in secondary positions. Whites remained a minority of the members in a labor force dominated by blacks, and union locals, corresponding to the composition of the work force on a given plantation, were often all black or all white. Nonetheless, the union held frequent interracial mass meetings, in which blacks and whites sang, prayed, and voted together. White union leaders used respectful titles such as "Mr." and "Mrs." for blacks, and black orators, singers, organizers, and officers infused the union with a powerful expressive culture and proved to be some of its strongest supporters. An elderly black survivor of the Elaine massacre summed up the union's philosophy at its founding meeting in 1934, stating that "we colored can't organize without you . . . and you white folks can't organize without us. . . . The same chain that holds my people holds your people too. . . . It won't do no good for us to divide because that's where the trouble has been all the time."[4]

Interracial unionism in the Arkansas cotton fields provided a model of success during the harvest season of 1935, when some five thousand laborers held a "sit-down" strike that forced the planters to grant a 50 percent wage increase. After this victory, union membership soared. During a planting season strike in the spring of 1936, however, planters evicted many families, forcing them to live in tents or in the woods. Vigilantes walked into black churches during union meetings and beat up everyone in sight, waylaid organizers on the back roads, and rounded up hundreds of people to work in the fields at the point of a gun. The union's leading speakers and attorneys endured mob attacks and near-lynchings, and one mob leader warned, "There's going to be another Elaine Massacre, only the next time we'll kill whites as well as niggers." Appeals for help to the national AFL and to the fledgling CIO did no good: neither wanted to take on the expense of organizing field workers, who had little dues to pay back into the unions. Neither did appeals to the federal government, which feared to intervene in the districts of senior members of Congress from the Delta. During the strike, a number of black unionists were killed, and many others, black and white, fled into the night for Chicago or Memphis.[5]

Memphis became the main refuge from the Arkansas labor wars, with numerous unionists reaching the city only after wild escapes from vigilantes on the Arkansas side of the river. John Allen, a sixty-seven-year-old black organizer, reached Memphis after walking forty-five miles of back country at night and sleeping under bridges in the day, only to be subsequently murdered in Mississippi. Unionists may have had some hope that supporters in the city, where the union had located its main office, could help save the strike. But support for agricultural workers proved to be weak in Memphis, dominated as it was by commercial agricultural interests. The chamber of commerce asked relief officials to channel the city's unemployed into the cotton harvest as strikebreakers, and WPA officials cut workers off from federal payrolls to force them to do just that. Memphis police arrested picketers at the Hanrahan Bridge for urging day laborers not to cross the river to work as scabs, arrested escaped sharecroppers, and conducted a number of raids on the STFU office and the homes of unionists. The Memphis *Commercial Appeal*, dubbed "the voice of the the Arkansas planters" by H. L. Mitchell, ran a continuing diatribe against the strike, and only the *Press-Scimitar* gave it any favorable coverage. John Handcox, the poet laureate of the STFU, summed up the situation during the Memphis "Cotton Carnival," held in May 1936: "Thousands of flags was hung in the street / But they left thousands of sharecroppers . . . with nothing to eat . . . / When Cotton is King of any nation, / It means wealth to the planter—to the laborer starvation." Like many others, Handcox was forced out of the Delta region by vigilantes, wandered about, and later settled in San Diego.[6]

Few Memphians proved willing to protest the blatant suppression of civil liberties in the Arkansas Delta. With the exception of Herman I. Goldberger and Newell N. Fowler, attorneys as well as reporters feared to go to the centers of repression in Crittenden County and Marion, and did nothing to intervene. University of Tennessee Medical School professor William Amberson got fired for his support of the STFU. Outside organizers could expect worse. David Benson of the Workers' Alliance, a Communist-led union for WPA workers, came to Memphis to help the STFU but ended up in an Arkansas jail and barely escaped a lynching. Only federal intervention could have saved farm laborers from the ravages of planter repression, but despite a number of investigations the federal government did little to enforce labor's civil rights in Arkansas, the home of U.S. Senate Majority Leader Joseph Robinson. After 1936 the union never succeeded in establishing a strong bargaining relationship with employers, and the union leadership splintered. The union eventually merged with the CIO and then the AFL, but its days as a militant voice for rural workers came to an end. Continued mechanization and enclosure of the land by agribusiness in succeeding years made the elimination of the sharecropper irreversible.[7]

The struggle mounted by the sharecropper's union, like many lost battles in American labor history, provided important lessons for organizers, as is documented by a rich literature on the revolt in the cotton fields. First, the movement demonstrated that blacks and whites, even in Ku Klux Klan country, could join together when it became clear to them that their survival depended upon it. Blacks had almost always been willing to do this, but at this time a number of poor whites also recognized the necessity of organizing with blacks. According to union president J. R. Butler, "People knew that it just had to happen. They all knew that they were in the same boat and that they all had to pull together." Secondly, the determination of black sharecroppers and tenants to support the union demonstrated the falseness of the belief, common among whites, that blacks were docile, contented laborers who would not organize. On the contrary, blacks provided the most reliable supporters of unionization. Observers noted that rural African Americans had a longer and more coherent tradition of collective organization and were less self-centered and class-divided than the whites. African-American churches provided meeting places when others closed their doors, and black religion provided a rich culture of songs and inspirational rhetoric that helped to hold the movement together. African-American women also played a powerful role in the union, which enrolled all members of a family whenever one member joined. Women's voices in union affairs strengthened the sharecropper movement enormously.[8]

The STFU's "industrial unionism in the fields" pointed to the significant role that African Americans might play in the union movement and offered obvious lessons for industrial-style organizing in the city. But in the city, as in the countryside, the degree to which black workers could get white support remained critical to success or failure. That support remained problematic in Memphis.

LABOR REBELLIONS: AFL UNIONS

The midthirties rise of industrial unionism, in which all employees in a given industry organized into one union instead of into competing units based on craft, is typically associated with the CIO. But the movement was much larger than that. Grass-roots rebellions such as the sharecroppers' energized a variety of working-class constituencies, and craft versus industrial distinctions did not always have much relevance in organizing situations. Militant unionism in Memphis became associated with demands for organization among a variety of workers, black and white, and with AFL as well as CIO unions. This new worker assertiveness led to the doubling of southern AFL membership by the spring of 1934, and in Memphis, the Trades and Labor Council claimed a total of sixteen thousand workers, up from twelve thousand in 1928. AFL growth emboldened Memphis Typographical Union leader Robert Tillman and a few other craft unionists to call for wholesale organization of Memphis workers to "throw off the yoke of slavery."[9]

If the early New Deal stimulated organization, however, its trickle-down approach to the economy had also been problematic for workers, with the government bailing out big banks at the expense of small ones, giving subsidies to large landholders at the expense of tenants, and relaxing the antitrust laws against large corporations at the expense of consumers.[10] New Deal funds created jobs but did not change or even modify the structures of economic power. As one Memphis unionist complained, "Every member of the NRA committee here is a member of the Chamber of Commerce, all big moneyed men an antagonistic to union labor of any kind. How in the name of high heaven can a laboring man expect a chance with a conglomeration such as this?" Furthermore, when wages went up, particularly in industries where craft unions had some influence over NRA code making, many southern business leaders went into total opposition to the NRA. Led by Tennessee Association of Manufacturers president John Edgerton, at a Chattanooga meeting in 1934 they formed the Southern States Industrial Council, which became one of the most virulently anti-union and anti–New Deal groups in the South. Opposition to unionism in the media and among employers remained bitter. Although most Memphis business leaders supported federal spending to put new life into the economy, hardly any supported the right of industrial laborers to organize or strike.[11]

Moreover, despite membership growth, the response of the existing AFL unions to opportunities presented during the NRA period proved to be weak. On the one hand, they failed to challenge racial wage differentials or open up significantly to blacks. "The little black union hall in the back [in the servants' quarters behind the AFL building] was symbolic for how the white union members treated the blacks," George Holloway recalled. "The whites didn't want the blacks in the union, and they weren't going to have them." Further, most AFL leaders, compromised by their comfortable relationship to the Crump regime, remained unwilling to launch a general organizing drive among the Memphis lower classes. Robert Tillman, the AFL's main advocate of industrial unionism, later explained that many AFL members "just didn't believe in organizing the unorganized."[12]

Most craft unionists continued to concern themselves mainly with controlling labor markets by excluding the unskilled and the nonwhite and clung to their economic and political advantages. Yet this labor conservatism, many unionists discovered, did not pay off very well in the thirties. Following the initial spurt of union growth after the passage of 7(a), labor organizing efforts crumbled almost everywhere in the United States. When the Supreme Court undermined the National Industrial Recovery Act in the *Schechter* decision of May 1935, it capped another period of setback for the union movement in which membership declined, wages dropped, and hours of work lengthened.[13] In Memphis, the AFL's *Labor Review* complained, the abolition of government wage and hour codes set off a new round of wage reductions, extensions of the work day, and firings of union activists. One Memphis grocery warehouse responded to the NRA's demise by dropping the wages of its white workers from the code minimum of forty-two cents an hour to thirty-seven cents and replacing striking protesters with blacks making twenty-five cents an hour.[14]

Although many Memphis AFL members wanted to maintain a respectable place for unions in the city's establishment, the readiness of business owners to take advantage of labor weaknesses forced the craft unions in the second half of the thirties to take a more aggressive stance. When Trades and Labor Council president Jake Cohen resigned following the 1934 election in order to devote his time to political office, a feisty Irish bricklayer named R. S. McCann, formerly a labor supervisor and contractor and then a business agent for a bricklayers' local in Helena, Arkansas, took his place. McCann came from one of the few Memphis craft unions with a significant number of blacks in its membership. A relative newcomer to Memphis, and, at the age of forty-four, relatively youthful, he had less invested in the Crump machine than did most labor leaders. McCann and other AFL leaders in the spring of 1935 called for organizing the unorganized and "social justice for all," leading to AFL support of strikes and organizing efforts among white production workers, grocery store clerks, fire fighters, city teachers, and construction workers on New Deal Works Project Administration jobs. The AFL's detente with the Crump machine momentarily collapsed as the AFL began a significant effort to organize the unorganized.[15]

Congressional adoption of the Wagner Labor Relations Act in July 1935 proved to be the key to the AFL's changed attitude. The Wagner Act empowered the National Labor Relations Board (NLRB) to review labor disputes and enjoin or fine employers who engaged in "unfair labor practices." These practices included such standard union-busting techniques as the establishment of company-controlled unions, interference with freedom of speech and assembly, firing or otherwise discriminating against union members, and refusing to bargain in good faith. Workers could petition the NLRB for a government-supervised election to determine by majority vote whether a union would be established, thereby interposing the federal government between workers, employers, and local governments. These provisions meant that in Memphis unionists no longer had to rely entirely on the goodwill of the Crump regime, but could obtain federal support through mediators and the courts for their right to organize.[16]

Following passage of the Wagner Act, the Memphis Labor Council passed a resolution authored by Robert Tillman, whose typographical union strongly favored industrial organization,[17] calling on all unions to "extend a helping hand to oppressed workers" and to "strike back" at employers for abolishing wage increases and lengthening the working day after the NRA's collapse.[18] Almost before the ink on the resolution had dried, Memphis workers put it to the test. The first major response to the Wagner Act emerged among white female production workers—machine tenders, labelers, and packers—at the Plough pharmaceutical company in August. Some one hundred women formed a local of the AFL's Cosmetic Workers' Union to protest wage cuts, a lengthening of the work week from forty to fifty hours, and the introduction of piece rates, which left some workers with a weekly take-home pay of less than five dollars. Abe Plough, an unreconstructed member of the "rugged individualist" school of capitalism, fired the members of the fledgling union. At the same time, he proclaimed 1935 to be the company's most profitable year and announced a million-dollar expansion of the plant. When ninety-nine outraged cosmetics workers walked out of his main plant, he claimed they had "quit their jobs" and called for scab labor to take their places. General Motors, Remington Rand, Ford Motor, and other corporations used labor spies and established huge weapons arsenals as part of the "Mohawk Valley formula" for destroying industrial unionism; Plough too hoped to break the union through blatant intimidation. Though this flagrantly violated the Wagner Act, he and others hoped the U.S. Supreme Court would overturn it, just as it had the National Recovery Act.[19]

The conflict at Plough became a major focus for employer-worker conflict in Memphis. When Plough tried to reopen his plant with scabs, several thousand union supporters, including husky white bricklayers from R. S. McCann's union, blocked anyone from entering. McCann became involved in two fistfights with supervisors, and picketers from other AFL locals continually obstructed the entrance to the plant. Surprisingly, city police chief Will Lee refused to escort scabs through the throngs of union supporters. According to Robert Tillman, Plough's attacks on the living standards of white factory women had set public opinion and even the Crump machine against him. The militancy of the strike supporters reached its high point in a nationally publicized incident, when union women ripped the clothing from two strikebreakers. Helen Murray, president of the local, told the press, "We will tear their clothes off again" if they continued to scab. Union and community support for the female strikers remained so solid that the company abandoned its efforts to bring in scabs and accepted negotiations under the auspices of the federal Conciliation Service. Plough's unbending attitude toward the union prolonged bargaining, but the union finally obtained a 25 percent wage increase and a work week of forty-four hours, reinstatement of workers fired by Plough, the establishment of seniority rights, and time-and-a-half pay for overtime work.[20]

The aftermath of this victory for low-wage industrial workers, however, indicated the weakness of AFL unions in dealing with union-haters such as Plough. Wages still remained below those established under the NRA codes, and Plough followed his agreements with the union by hiring efficiency experts to speed up production. He also fired older women in the shop because, according to one federal conciliator, "their callused [*sic*] old hands won't fly as they once did." Furthermore, a mediator reported, after the strike Plough set up "a system of espionage" aimed at eliminating "all trace of organization," and eventually succeeded in breaking the morale of the unionists. Plough, according to the mediator, also threatened that "McCann would be rubbed out and expressed the greatest aversion to him." The AFL made little response to these attacks. It had also failed to respond during the strike when Plough tried to replace white strikers with blacks; although strikers persuaded them to leave, neither the cosmetics union nor the AFL organized blacks working in the two Plough plants. Such weaknesses by the AFL would be seen repeatedly in industrial organizing situations.[21]

Although evidence of a new militancy existed among Memphis unionists, inspired in part by the sit-down strikes of workers in Akron in early 1936, so did increasing anti-unionism among employers and the city government. According to one union leader, the city would do anything to bring in "big Industries and Chain stores from the North," but did little to help raise local wage rates and even used nonunion printers. When McCann pressed on in support of the AFL's Retail Clerks' Local 962, which struck seventy-seven Memphis grocery stores in January, business leaders and the city administration became openly hostile. Employers considered the clerks' demands for a closed shop, an agreement that all employees would have to be hired through the union, outrageous. The bitter strike dragged on for months until the AFL's southern representative, George Googe, interceded, leading workers at Kroger's to settle on the basis of an open shop. On the heels of this settlement, some five hundred workers struck nine different bakery shops, again demanding that all workers be hired through the union. Firings led to talk of a general strike among food store workers, and only federal mediation finally brought about a compromise agreement. Tensions escalated further when Police and Fire Commissioner Clifford Davis fired fifteen local fire fighters who organized a union and the Crump machine blacklisted them from any further city employment. Three hundred business leaders held a special meeting to endorse the firings and blacklistings and supported Mayor Overton's denunciations of McCann as an "agitator" and "trouble maker" who "is not working for the welfare of Memphis," a charge publicized by banner headlines in the press. Overton published an open letter that implied opposition to the organization of all public workers, and when schoolteachers formed a chapter of the American Federation of Teachers, the board of education ordered them to renounce in writing any affiliation with labor unions or lose their jobs. The city also fired truck drivers in PWA jobs for demanding a union pay scale, blacklisted them from other city work, and ordered contractors to fire anyone paying dues to the Teamsters. Under city pressure, public employee unionism collapsed.[22]

The city's hostility to public employee organizing also encouraged private employers to hold the line against unionists. Memphis Furniture, a locally based company with close to five hundred workers, more than half of them black, carried on a virulently anti-union campaign after increasing work to between fifty and sixty hours per week and cutting wages after the NRA's demise. In response, the United Brotherhood of Carpenters and Joiners (AFL) took the unusual step of asking blacks to join, in hopes of reviving a dormant local in the plant. When Alonzo Dabney and other black workers came to an April 1936 union meeting at the Carpenters' Hall, however, company supervisors had placed the meeting under surveillance and the next day fired or threatened to fire all those who attended. One woman and her husband both lost their jobs, even though the woman had worked for the company for fourteen years; she was making the grand total of $15.00 to $16.50 per week when fired. Other companies blacklisted fourteen laid-off workers from Memphis Furniture. Although the NLRB in July 1937 ordered the company to reinstate the fired workers with back pay and to cease interfering with the union, the damage had already been done. Subsequent AFL and CIO efforts to organize the plant during the thirties failed.[23]

Despite the upsurge in worker activity in late 1935 and early 1936, the unions made little progress in the face of a more or less solid front of opposition from employers and the Crump machine. Although the machine had traditionally tolerated the AFL unions and had refused to side with Abe Plough's callousness toward white female production workers, Crump and his representatives nonetheless made it clear that unions would exist only on the machine's terms. These terms ruled out industrial unionism, interracialism, and the organization of public workers. As the result of the city's hostility to McCann's aggressive organizing, a federal mediator commented in April, "It has been impossible to get any of the manufacturers here to agree to anything."[24] McCann became a hero among Tennessee labor supporters, who elected him president of the Tennessee Federation of Labor in 1935 and gave him a standing ovation and reelected him in 1936 for standing up to the Crump machine. But his labor supporters could not protect McCann from the power of Crump. In late 1936, men from the machine roughed him up, and not long after that the Trades and Labor Council replaced McCann with Lev Loring, a plumber with close ties to Crump. Several years later a 280-pound steamfitter beat McCann into unconsciousness outside the Labor Temple, causing a skull fracture, internal injuries, and broken teeth. McCann said the incident resulted from conflicting union jurisdictions over a labor project. A newspaper writer, however, told a federal investigator looking into charges of corruption in Memphis unions that McCann's beating stemmed from having gotten on the "wrong side of the fence" from Crump. Although McCann had pleaded with Secretary of Labor Frances Perkins to enforce the Wagner Act against the city, the Roosevelt administration had done little to discipline the Crump machine. McCann quickly went into obscurity and died at an early age from cancer.[25]

Although AFL unions would be involved in a number of tense conflicts with employers in subsequent years, the new AFL leader Loring ceased support for organizing public workers and tread lightly when it came to industrial unionism. His reassertion of conservatism reflected a state and national trend in the AFL. Delegates to the 1936 Tennessee Federation of Labor meeting, many of them members of the rapidly expanding United Mine Workers of America (UMWA), had attacked the AFL's policy of organizing along craft lines and called for unrestricted chartering of industrially organized locals. But by the 1937 convention, the United Mine Workers and other industrially organized unions had withdrawn from the

Tennessee Federation of Labor in favor of the CIO. The remaining unionists gave a standing ovation to an organizer's red-baiting speech against
labor radicals, resolved that any delegates with a "CIO inclination" should
be removed from the state federation, and replaced McCann as state president with Nashville plumber Gerald Foley. Subsequent denunciations of
the CIO as communistic and "inimical and repugnant to the ideals and
principles upon which our craft unions were formed" became standard
fare in the state AFL and in the Memphis AFL's *Labor Review*. Pressures
from the Crump machine, combined with the conservatism of local craft
unionists, many of them strongly connected to the American Legion, the
Baptist Church, and to local business leaders, had a predictable effect.
After McCann's brief foray into militant trade union activism, the city's
craft unions moved quickly back within the limits of respectability set by
the local power elite.[26]

LABOR REBELLIONS: CIO UNIONS

By removing the unruly R. S. McCann and replacing him with the more
compliant Lev Loring and by taking a harder line against union organizing,
Memphis leaders momentarily quieted AFL threats to the city's vaunted
labor peace. But it would take more than this to stop the tide of industrial
unionism that swept the country after the Wagner Act. At a national level
the law had the effect of encouraging a break with the old guard of the
labor movement, which at the 1935 AFL convention had refused to grant
industrial charters authorizing the organization of all workers in a given industry into one union. The AFL's continued policy of dividing up workers
along lines of skill, occupation, and race fragmented labor solidarity and
undermined the possibilities for organization of mass-production industries. United Mine Workers' leader John L. Lewis called for the adoption of
all-encompassing forms of organization whenever a workplace fell within
the jurisdiction of more than one craft, but instead the AFL reaffirmed
the protection of "jurisdictional rights of all trade unions organized along
craft lines." Lewis gathered disgruntled union leaders into the Committee
for Industrial Organizing, and by August 1936 the AFL had suspended the
committee's ten unions.[27]

If Memphis leaders could not tolerate the AFL's extension beyond its
traditional jurisdictions, they viewed the emerging CIO with even greater
alarm, equating it with communism, racial equality, and the potential destruction of the city's efforts to attract industrial investments from the
North. In their view, the worst feature of the CIO was its effectiveness. En-

couraged by the overwhelming reelection of Roosevelt in November 1936, CIO unions met remarkable initial success. In the early months of 1937, auto workers occupied General Motors plants in Michigan and soon forced it and Chrysler to recognize the United Auto Workers' as the sole bargaining agent in all their plants. U.S. Steel signed a contract in March with the CIO's United Steelworkers' union, while strikes and organizing drives swept through electrical, rubber, packinghouse, and other industries. By late 1938 the CIO (renamed the Congress of Industrial Organizations) had nearly four million members and became a permanent federation with thirty-two member unions, temporarily eclipsing the AFL as the largest labor federation in the United States. Along with this rapid expansion, the U.S. Supreme Court's validation of the Wagner Act in April 1937 offered potential protections to outside organizers; both factors made the CIO a real threat to unorganized southern industry.[28]

However, the first CIO organizing in Memphis did not threaten major mass-production facilities and received a muted response from city authorities. Without strikes or fanfare, white-collar workers at the Memphis *Press-Scimitar* and *Commercial Appeal* in late 1936 established one of the first new unions organized under the Wagner Act. For years newspaper management had used reporters' and editors' pride in their work and their white-collar "professional" status as a substitute for paying them a living wage. Despite their clean hands, these workers on average earned a mere fifteen dollars a week, while typesetters and other mechanical workers organized by the International Typographical Union earned two to three times more. The illusory nature of white-collar privileges struck home in September when Frank Ahlgren, the *Commercial Appeal*'s editor, fired seven senior staff members as an economy move. Following this incident, the drama critic Harry Martin overcame the fear among the workers and organized the first chapter of the American Newspaper Guild at both papers. Within a year, the local chapter won a written contract guaranteeing a forty-hour week at a minimum salary of twenty-five dollars and up to forty dollars for workers with three or more years of experience. A "guild shop" agreement allowed management to hire whomever it wanted, but required that they join the union within thirty days.[29]

Though the guild first belonged to the AFL, in 1937 Heywood Broun and other left-wing activists led the international union into the CIO. Memphis delegates to the guild convention voted against CIO affiliation. Thus, through no action of its own, in 1937 the Memphis news guild chapter became the first official CIO local to sign a contract in the city—and according to some accounts, in the South. Ironically, white-collar newspaper employees shared more in common with the middle class of craft-conscious white workers in the AFL than with poor white and black industrial workers, and the Memphis guild remained a member of the Memphis AFL's Trades and Labor Council for three years after joining the CIO. Blacks had no opportunity to write for the white commercial media, and, according to guild charter member Paul Coppock, most guild members remained conservative and strongly anticommunist. Yet because of their writing and administrative skills, Memphis American Newspaper Guild chapter leaders would play a role disproportionate to their numbers in the local CIO and in leading attacks in subsequent years on integrationists and radicals within their international and in the Memphis CIO.[30]

Although some later claimed the guild chapter provided "the cornerstone of the CIO in Memphis," the real potential membership base for CIO unionism obviously resided among the uneducated, black, and poor white workers in the city's labor-intensive and low-wage industrial plants. The first successful CIO effort to organize these workers occurred among white women in the spring of 1937. Numerous northern garment companies, like many New England textile companies before them, fled northern unions by moving South, establishing small shops staffed mostly by young white women desperate for work, most of them holding their first industrial job. These small businesses paid rock-bottom wages, provided no job security, produced cheap goods for local markets, and often collapsed during periods of economic decline. A number of these sweatshops migrated to Memphis to escape unionization after passage of the Wagner Act, and the International Ladies Garment Workers' Union (ILGWU) sent in organizers to stop them from undercutting its northern locals.[31]

White women in Memphis dress shops initially feared unionization, and many unionists considered them impossible to organize. Yet the ILGWU discovered that much like the "disorderly women" in some of the South's textile towns, once the dress shop workers took the step of joining a union they conducted extremely militant strikes.[32] Public opinion also proved very hostile to companies trying to chisel their profits out of the low-wage labor of white women. The ILGWU remained on friendly terms with the AFL (it later left the CIO to return to the AFL fold), and received support from Lev Loring and friendly treatment in the press, which did not even identify the ILGWU as a CIO union. This relatively favorable terrain led to a surprisingly quick initial victory at the Tri-State Dress Company when 150 white women struck for three days in March against low wages and long hours of work, demanding union recognition and a contract. As in the Plough strike, fistfights erupted between strikers and scabs, and some one thousand union supporters surrounded the plant to stop strikebreakers from working. This mass demonstration forced Mayor Overton to condemn wage cuts the company had instituted after the NRA's demise, which had resulted in wages as low as seven dollars for a fifty-four-hour work week. Failing to gain support from the city, the Tri-State management gave in to demands that all workers belong to the union and granted a forty-hour week and a twelve-dollar minimum weekly wage.[33]

Working-class women, it appeared, quickly stepped off the pedestal assigned to them by white men when they had the opportunity to get organized. This victory for female workers inspired the ILGWU to set up a Memphis office for organizing the tri-state region. It also fired the imagination of Ida Sledge, a graduate from Wellesley College and a member of a prominent Memphis family who quit her job at a Memphis welfare agency to join the ILGWU staff. Low wages, she told the press, remained the root cause of southern poverty and only unionization could rectify that. Her conversion to the ILGWU provided it with important middle-class support when women workers on 22 March struck the Kuhn Dress Company after the management rejected as "un-American" their demand for a union shop. Three days later, women at the Nona-Lee Dress Company also struck, demanding higher wages, shorter hours, a contract, and a union shop. The city government, fearing the spread of strikes and union shop demands, backed away from its earlier role of supporting negotiated settlements, while the dress companies refused to even discuss a union shop.[34]

With Kuhn already shut down, the union shop battle came to a head at Nona-Lee, described by union organizer Merle Zappone as "one of the worst little prisons I ever saw." When a third of the nearly one hundred women workers walked out on 25 March, a female supervisor named Dewey Parker led some forty nonstrikers in an assault against them. With long fingernails cultivated, according to the press, for just such situations, Zappone counterattacked, tearing Parker's clothes to shreds. Other union women joined the fray, and the city arrested eleven of the strikers, called "CIO Amazons" by the newspapers, which carried provocative pictures of the strikers attacking male as well as female opponents. The city took no action against the strikebreakers led by Parker, but the union had so intimidated strikebreakers that some forty of them refused to leave the shop, working and sleeping in the factory in a "reverse sit down." The city then began working to help break the strike. A local court granted the company a sweeping injunction forbidding the union from picketing, displaying signs or placards, or even from urging other workers to strike, while city police ushered company officials taking food and blankets to strikebreakers through crowds of angry strike supporters.[35]

The strikes at Kuhn and Nona-Lee lasted a month and nearly led to a shooting match when Nona-Lee hired black women as strikebreakers. As in the Plough strike, white workers reacted with special fear and hostility to the threat of their jobs being turned over to blacks. When two female strikers angrily confronted the company vice-president in front of the plant demanding that he stop using black scabs, he pulled a pistol. The police arrested all three of them. Only the mobilization of community support for the strikers by Rev. Alfred Loaring-Clark, chair of the newly formed Social Justice Committee of the Memphis Ministerial Association, finally forced a settlement. Both Nona-Lee and Kuhn signed union shop agreements, and on 19 April approximately one hundred union members went back to work.[36]

The tenacity of ILGWU organizers and white women in the dress shops achieved an unusual, if short-lived, victory for industrial unionism in Memphis. Industrial unions would struggle for years over the demand for a union shop, anathema to employers and the city government alike because it offered one of the quickest routes to making Memphis a union town. The female strikers not only won on this issue, but galvanized support from the community and the AFL unions in a way that few others could. Images of the youthful and attractive Ida Sledge advocating workers' rights and even the media image of "CIO Amazons" did not appear so threatening as had striking city employees or grocery workers whom the public directly depended upon. The support of Reverend Loaring-Clark helped to make a moral issue of the poverty suffered by industrial workers, and the determination of the women themselves captured the imagination of many white middle-class city dwellers. When young female workers who had been living together in a group house during the long strike expressed jubilation over the victory and told a reporter that "all labor should be organized," they struck a deep chord of idealism that motivated many during the thirties to sympathize with unorganized workers. Though white women made up a handful of the industrial work force in Memphis, their victories in the dress shops helped to inspire what the *Commercial Appeal* called an "epidemic" of "strikitis" among a variety of workers that continued throughout much of 1937.[37] Participants in this "strikitis," however, also included black workers, who would receive much less public support.

LABOR REBELLIONS: BLACK WORKERS

The restlessness that followed the passage of the Wagner Act infected blacks as much as any other group of workers, but in many cases they could find no union that would represent them. Prior to the formation of the CIO, the national AFL steadfastly opposed any special effort to organize black workers, repeatedly rejecting pleas by Brotherhood of Sleeping Car Porters president A. Phillip Randolph for a campaign to organize African Americans and insisting that the "autonomy" of AFL member unions made action against segregation and racial exclusion in the federation impossible.[38] The AFL could claim its policies merely reflected the racist sentiments of white workers in the ranks, and yet white workers in CIO unions often had the same racist attitudes. But unlike the situation in the skilled crafts, African Americans composed a significant portion of the unorganized industrial work force, and the CIO could not ignore them. Indeed, black support proved critical to CIO organizing in most basic industries; United Mine Workers' efforts to reorganize the Alabama coalfields, for example, remained heavily dependent on black miners, who composed 60 percent of the membership of the locals organized there in 1934.[39]

The AFL's backward racial policies, then, primarily reflected its lack of interest in the unorganized mass of industrial workers, who could hardly be organized without bringing blacks and whites into the same union structures. This reality held true in Memphis, where blacks composed 80 percent of the unskilled factory work force. These workers desperately needed organization, as Robert Tillman discovered when he began volunteer organizing at Fisher Body and then Chickasaw Wood Products. Fear of unionism, he concluded, was at that time still "bread and meat" with many poor whites; in contrast, blacks, as in the Arkansas cotton fields, proved to be "the most loyal supporters of the union movement you could find." Although no racial liberal, Tillman believed that industrial unionism absolutely required the organization of black workers, who he found "fifty times more faithful" than white workers. His observations would be borne out over and over again in Memphis, yet the response of AFL unions to black workers remained inadequate at best.[40]

If the AFL's attitude of neglect encouraged white unionists to ignore the plight of African Americans, by the spring of 1937 ignoring black workers became increasingly difficult. In the steel industry in Birmingham, as well as in a variety of other industries throughout the South, they had already begun to play a critical role in the post–Wagner Act unionization efforts, and black worker dissatisfaction began to effect the Memphis labor scene as well. On 9 March 1937, one day after one thousand white workers had turned out in support of the white female strikers at the Tri-State Dress Company, some two hundred blacks struck at the E. L. Bruce Lumber Company in Memphis. As the South's largest hardwood flooring plant and with subsidiaries in Mississippi, Nashville, and other parts of the South, E. L. Bruce offered the largest potential base for the organization of wood-workers. Most of these workers were black, however, and the AFL had done nothing to cultivate them. Asked by the press, "Where is the boss of this strike?" one of the workers replied, "We haven't a boss"; asked, "What's the name of your union?" he replied, "We haven't got a union. We don't know how to organize one." The black workers had demanded a five-cent-an-hour wage increase and walked out when the company conceded only half of this demand. When the workers went to the Labor Council for advice, Lev Loring told them to go back to work, saying, "Wildcat strikes hurt the labor movement and the city as a whole." Loring claimed the Labor Council would organize any group "into a legitimate union," but took no steps to set up a union among the black workers. The E. L. Bruce payroll numbered nearly five hundred, and some of the whites in the plant apparently belonged to one of the AFL craft unions, but this local did nothing for the black production workers. In contrast to the experience of the white female garment workers, the blacks could get no union support for their demands and went back on the job the next day. The AFL had lost a major organizing opportunity.[41]

Ten days later, some one hundred black women walked out of the Memphis Pecan and Walnut Company after the owner refused to raise wages. Working under dreadful conditions, these women made the miserable wage of six cents per pound of nuts they shelled, a maximum of four dollars in a six-day week. Their request for an increase to ten cents a pound would have increased their wage to a little more than seven dollars a week, still a miserable wage even by Memphis standards. In response, the owner of the shop threatened to turn their work over to the destitute under the supervision of local charities. In a marginal industry and with no union support, the pecan workers, like the E. L. Bruce workers, had no choice but to give up their strike.[42]

In industry after industry, black workers confronted similar difficulties. Concentrated in the lowest-paying jobs, often in marginal industries, and usually with no union backing, they had little leverage with employers. Even those nominally represented by AFL federal unions had little bargaining power. Federal union status affiliated them directly with the AFL national executive board instead of with an international union and gave them no leverage over the local Labor Council or even their own union representatives. As a result, white AFL business agents did little to respond to black needs. At the Southern Cotton Oil company in Memphis, for example, the white organizer of the AFL's federal union made more of an effort to avert a strike by black workers than he did to support their demands. Unable to bring their case before the Trades and Labor Council and with their federal union ignored by a company that refused to sign any written agreement, the cotton oil workers received no relief. In a few cases where blacks belonged to an international union, they fared better. When black and white workers at Chickasaw Wood Products walked out together under the auspices of the Coopers' International Union on 11 March, they gained a five-cent-an-hour wage increase for the plant's four hundred workers. But such alliances between blacks and whites remained fragile, especially in the face of a determined anti-union employer. A ten-day strike of Memphis Furniture workers in March, for example, gained little, despite apparent cooperation between white and black.[43]

The insecure or nonexistent status of African Americans within the established union structures provided continuing opportunities for employer manipulation of racial divisions. At a local mop and handle company in August 1937, the management provoked a walkout of unionized white workers by training nonunion blacks to take their place. As in so many other instances involving AFL unions, the white workers did not try to recruit blacks, who initially composed 150 of the 250 workers in the shop. In other cases, companies used the racial division of the work force to stop unionization before it had gained a foothold, as at Kroger's Bakery where the management fired thirty-three of thirty-four black truck drivers and replaced them with whites, successfully stalling an organizing drive. As long as unions left blacks outside their doors, employers could continue to manipulate white-black, union-nonunion divisions to the disadvantage of all workers.[44]

Although the AFL's record of relating to blacks remained dubious, black workers seemed to feel that organizing within the segregated confines of the AFL proved a better alternative than no union at all. And AFL unions, under the pressure of independent black activity and CIO organizing, began to pay more attention to them in late 1937. Even committed segregationists increasingly recognized that AFL unions lost ground to the CIO after the Wagner Act in part because of craft unionism's racial exclusion, according to black journalist George Schuyler. In his August travels in the South, he found that black workers, with little if any aid from the black middle class or white unionists, had undertaken independent organizing activities that forced employers and unions alike to heed their demands. In Memphis, AFL leader Loring told Schuyler that "in the last six months there have been more Negro workers susceptible to labor organization than ever before" and that the AFL would soon bring in an international organizer to help unionize them. Local 52 of the International Hod Carriers' and Building Laborers' Union, headed by a black man named Edwin Smith, claimed a membership of two hundred with the relatively high wage of sixty-two cents an hour. Smith told him that due to black protests AFL leaders had quit using the epithet *nigger* when in their presence. According to Schuyler, some three hundred blacks belonged to the International Longshoremen's Association; a scattering of blacks belonged to bricklayers', cement finishers', and plasterers' unions; and one black local of thirty members and one white local of four hundred members belonged to the carpenters' union. A few black painters, steamfitters, and structural iron workers also belonged to craft unions, and a black stokers' and oilers' union headed by a black president and a predominantly black switch operators' union existed in the railroad shops. In the coopers' union, blacks constituted 175 of the 250 members, as well as 250 members of a federal labor union of 500 at the American Finishing Company. In all, Schuyler thought that African Americans comprised 3,000 or more of some 16,000 organized Memphis workers, which led him to conclude that "Memphis Negro workers are slowly awakening" to unionization and receiving some of its benefits.[45]

Schuyler's figures did not indicate that blacks had drastically changed their position within the AFL, but he nonetheless believed the AFL leadership was "tossing the burden of Negrophobia overboard" and that the discriminatory racial practices of the Memphis craft unions would "almost disappear when the CIO begins to supply the competition which elsewhere has been like a breath of fresh air to the labor movement." Like many other observers, his prediction of the liberalizing effects of unionization on race relations in the South proved far too optimistic. Only where blacks dominated in both membership and leadership, as in the dockworkers' union, could blacks exercise any significant power within the AFL. The handful of organized black carpenters, bricklayers, cement finishers, and plasterers who belonged to segregated AFL locals received adequate representation before employers only insofar as such an effort also benefited white unionists, and most craft unions still excluded them from apprenticeship training. The Trades and Labor Council recognized black unionists by including them in the annual Labor Day parade in 1937, one of the largest in AFL history to that point. But African Americans still remained separated from power and influence within the AFL by a shroud of racism and narrow self-interest on the part of most white unionists. Blacks in Memphis remained on the bare margins of organized labor.[46]

INDUSTRIAL UNION DEFEAT

The pall of racism and repression that hung over Memphis not only undermined organizing among white female and black workers but frequently stymied organization among white male workers as well. Ben McCullough, a white worker on the assembly line of the Memphis Ford Motor Company's Riverside plant, discovered this for himself. In August 1937, he responded to a leaflet from the United Auto Workers' union (UAW) by voicing sympathy for the CIO union among his fellow workers. Several days later, a group of men grabbed him as he came through the factory gates, took him to Riverside Park, and blackjacked and kicked him. Two days later unidentified men from the plant knocked him down in the street, kicking him in the kidneys and beating his head against the pavement. In the meantime, the Ford management organized a company union that held a demonstration denouncing the CIO as a Communist organization and vowing "to fight any outside attempt to interfere with our jobs."[47]

No one in Memphis expressed surprise that the police took no action and the city courts issued no indictments against McCullough's assailants, even though he swore out complaints against them. City leaders feared the obvious potential for rapid union expansion at Ford and other major industries, for in the first six months of 1937 some two thousand workers had joined Memphis unions, most of them in the AFL but a few in the CIO as well. These new union recruits included bus drivers, auto mechanics, elevator operators, and furniture sellers, as well as garment workers and a diverse scattering of other factory workers. Considering this trend, Mayor Overton wrote to Crump only days after McCullough's beating, "I am afraid Firestone won't expand much here if CIO gets busy. We will have to form a definite policy of some kind. Have you any suggestion?" Crump's "policy" is not recorded in any correspondence, but CIO organizers never had any doubts about what it was. As subsequent events made clear, city leaders would do almost anything to stop CIO organization of mass-production industries.[48]

On 7 September UAW organizer Norman Smith came to Memphis, openly announcing the location of his headquarters and his intention to organize Ford's fifteen hundred workers. A week later Mayor Overton issued a lengthy condemnation of the CIO as a violent and "un-American" organization linked to communists and declared that organizers trying to stir up "strife and conflict" would not be tolerated. Chamber of Commerce president W. H. Jasspoon, deeply involved in efforts to "sell" outside investors on locating in Memphis, warmly endorsed Overton's statement, calling it a "constructive step" toward ensuring labor peace. Police and Fire Commissioner Clifford Davis followed with a full-scale investigation of outside organizers and declared, "We have started today and will free Memphis of these unwanted people." He specifically singled out Norman Smith, saying the city "will take care of that situation very soon." [49]

The day after Davis's promise, a gang of thugs attacked the labor organizer with battery cables and coke bottles, beating him mercilessly. Smith had earlier been surrounded in his car by attackers, and thugs had beaten up his assistant, a Ford worker named Charles Phillips. But Smith refused to be intimidated and agreed to meet with a group of workers at a restaurant at Hollywood and Jackson in north Memphis. The meeting turned out to be a setup. Robert Tillman later discovered that the police not only knew who beat Smith and Phillips but that a city official participated in planning the attacks, instructing thugs to beat Smith but not to kill him. Tillman noted that the incident followed the typical pattern employed by Henry Ford's anti-union enforcer Harry Bennett, who sent agents, often ex-convicts whose whereabouts were difficult to trace, to contact local police and to recruit local thugs to do his dirty work. To no one's surprise, the Memphis police never arrested anyone for the murderous attack on Norman Smith, and instead arrested Smith. Only through the intervention of Tillman did the police take him to John Gaston Hospital to have him treated for multiple gashes and a possible fractured arm. [50]

The Smith beating evoked national protest, with the American Civil Liberties Union declaring that "vigilante violence has apparently had police participation in Memphis." But neither the ACLU's offer of a one-thousand-dollar reward for information about the identity of Smith's attackers nor the demand of the *Chattanooga Times* for federal intervention made any difference to local officials. The mayor once again denounced the CIO for supposedly trying to close down Memphis factories and "stir up violence." Ford thugs and city detectives frightened auto workers away from talking to Smith by following him constantly, but the detectives were nowhere to be found on 5 October, when six or seven assailants dragged Smith from his car and beat him nearly to death with a machinist's hammer and pistols. The attackers inflicted seventeen head cuts and fractured Smith's skull while one man held a gun on Smith's UAW bodyguard Harry Elder. Scores of appeals for federal intervention from UAW locals across the country produced an investigation of the second incident, but no indictments. The police had eyewitnesses to both beatings of Smith, and Mayor Overton admitted to federal officials that he had the license plate numbers of Smith's attackers, but refused to divulge them. In public he continued to insist that all CIO organizers get out of Memphis, which he claimed had already been satisfactorily organized by the AFL. Governor Gordon Browning, who would himself be run out of Memphis in 1938, called the Smith incident a "fist fight" and refused to intervene; Police and Fire Commissioner Davis called the beating "the outcome of an inter-labor dispute." When four women from the ILGWU attempted to visit Smith in the hospital, a car full of men warned them to get out of town; when the women went to the police station for protection, the police made them leave. Chief Will Lee told the press the women were merely seeking publicity and law-abiding citizens had nothing to fear in Memphis.[51]

No appeals to the Constitution or the Wagner Act moved authorities to protect civil liberties in Memphis, and the UAW removed Smith, who apparently planned to go right on with his work. The atmosphere of intimidation only worsened. When four workers came to town from out of state to apply for work at the Ford plant in early November, a group of men wearing Ford badges surrounded them at a local restaurant. When the new arrivals refused to disclose their feelings about the CIO, the leader of the group told them, "Get out or we'll lynch you." Escorted by two police officers and some one hundred men, most of them Ford workers and some of them supervisors, the four hapless suspected organizers crossed into Arkansas. According to a *Press-Scimitar* reporter at the scene, some of the local Ford workers had been laid off and others feared that they would lose their jobs if the CIO succeeded in its organizing drive. The management of the Memphis plant and the Memphis denied knowing anything about the incident.[52]

The climate of fear inculcated by city leaders and employers effectively thwarted any efforts to rally public opinion in support of civil liberties. When Alabama civil liberties organizer Joseph Gelders and a group called the National Committee for People's Rights sent Laurent Frantz, son of a well-known University of Tennessee professor, to set up a defense group in Memphis in late November, the police promptly arrested him. Without a warrant, police searched his hotel room and seized all his papers, and Chief Will Lee then held a press conference identifying Frantz as a communist, a charge Frantz denied. Gelders, himself soon to be brutally beaten and left for dead on an Alabama roadside by thugs hired by the Tennessee Coal and Iron company, observed that the political leaders of the city looked on anything that smacked of liberalism as "foreign." Furniture worker organizer Leroy Clark discovered this attitude in the early fifties, when police threatened him because his car had "foreign" New York tags and because his skin was black. In such a town, the terms *communist, foreigner, agitator,* and *nigger lover* served as interchangeable epithets hurled at anyone who stood up for industrial unions or black civil rights.[53]

Opposition to the CIO unified the city administration and the business community and revealed how little regard existed among the city's leaders for the right of others to exercise their constitutional liberties. Chamber of Commerce president Jasspoon met privately with Mayor Overton after Smith's first beating and stayed in close touch with police and city officials during the campaign against the UAW. His role became evident when he ran into Rev. Alfred Loaring-Clark and another liberal religious figure outside the mayor's office. The men had come to urge Overton to tone down his anti-CIO rhetoric, but within hours of talking to Jasspoon they received personal visits by chamber representatives warning them to stay out of the CIO issue. Other chamber representatives visited numerous church members in subsequent weeks, telling them to stay out of the conflict with the CIO "if they know what's good for them." Jasspoon and other chamber members also sat on a grand jury in preparation for possible prosecutions of outside labor "agitators."[54]

In the wake of the Norman Smith case, such local pressures frightened away what little middle-class support for industrial unionism existed. Black scholar Ralph Bunche, in a field study of the South compiled in 1939, noted the apparent "total absence of a liberal group in Memphis," while Joseph Gelders stated that those few liberals who did exist looked "outside rather than to themselves for strength and leadership." Gelders believed a locally based civil liberties committee would do more to slow down the attacks of the city's leaders "upon everything liberal" than outside intervention. Laurent Frantz similarly hoped that a movement for the right of all citizens to exercise their constitutional rights could become a rallying point for the city's disorganized progressives. But no such group emerged. The Attorney Herman I. Goldberger, one of the few true liberals and labor supporters in Memphis, mysteriously died in an Arkansas car accident, leaving only Newell N. Fowler, a Republican antagonist of the Crump machine, for unions to depend upon for legal support. By December the city had begun foreclosing on Fowler for back taxes to punish him for work done on the Norman Smith case, and he ultimately left to take a job out west. By December, a member of the Southern Tenant Farmers' Union observed, "only undercover men" could work in Memphis.[55]

The ILGWU, the only really successful CIO industrial union, also went down to defeat. Contrary to the hopes of the ILGWU, its early victories in Memphis did not open the way for mass organizing. When the union tried to extend the gains made in Memphis to the surrounding area, it ran into a stone wall of anti-union opposition and violence. In June the union had sent Ida Sledge into Tupelo, Mississippi, at the request of local garment worker Jimmy Cox. Located in the congressional district of John Rankin, one of the most violent anti-union and antiblack politicians of the Deep South, Tupelo maintained three garment factories with some nine hundred workers. When Sledge came to town, mobs twice visited her at her hotel and forced her to leave on threat of death. Another vigilante group kidnapped and beat Jimmy Cox, who left Tupelo to protect his life as soon as he got out of the hospital. A citizens' committee of business leaders went to the three garment factories and "persuaded" the workers to form company unions, predicting bloodshed if the workers did not disown the ILGWU.[56]

With the Mississippi organizing effort crushed in the summer, the ILGWU attempted to organize white women in the dress and fur sections of the major Memphis department stores and recruited three hundred alterations workers at Goldsmith's and elsewhere. Store owners responded with a combination of voluntary wage increases and firings, bringing organizing to a standstill. Meanwhile, the "Roosevelt recession" in the fall of 1937 hit the textile and garment industries, causing Kuhn and Nona-Lee to fold up shop, as they had threatened to do if they were unionized. Desperate to hold on to its unionized base in the North, the ILGWU pulled Ida Sledge and other organizers out of Memphis to work on keeping the stronger northern companies organized. Victimized by local repression, an unstable national economy, and the fly-by-night nature of the garment industry, the ILGWU effort to organize the mid-South collapsed.[57]

* * *

By the end of 1937, a number of opportunities and problems associated with industrial unionism had come to light. Organizing opportunities clearly existed. The visible exploitation of white female workers in numerous small shops stirred broad support for the right to unionize, and according to Laurent Frantz, many Memphians condemned, at least in private, the Crump machine's blatant violation of the Bill of Rights in the Smith case. A small degree of community sympathy for labor rights appeared in early 1937, a high point for President Roosevelt and the labor coalition that had helped to keep him in power. In such a climate even supposedly timid white women and blacks could turn into militant strikers and solid union supporters. On the other hand, the economic recession triggered by Roosevelt's late-1937 pullback from massive federal spending destroyed in one swoop much of the leverage workers and organizers had struggled hard to gain, throwing many out of work and turning fearful Ford workers against unionization. The brutalization of labor activists also made it clear that the chances of success remained small when the power of the state joined forces with employers in concerted efforts to break union organizing. In both Mississippi and Memphis employers and law enforcement officers demonstrated the techniques used over and over again to destroy union organizing in the South. With the ILGWU and the UAW gone and the STFU drastically weakened, only Robert Tillman and the local News Guild actively represented a CIO presence in Memphis at the beginning of 1938.[58]

The incidents surrounding the UAW campaign came at a time when the industrial growth promoted by business leaders and Mayor Overton had begun to succeed. Their increasingly open collusion in protecting industry from unions seemed to Laurent Frantz to be part of an ominous movement in a fascistlike direction. National political trends had moved away from New Deal reformism and toward a defensive reaction against labor unions and liberalism. The "Roosevelt recession" fractured the president's New Deal congressional coalition, while Roosevelt's efforts to replace some of the most reactionary southern Democrats with liberals in the 1938 congressional elections for the most part failed. Republicans and conservative southern Democrats in Congress established the House Un-American Activities Committee, headed by Martin Dies of Texas, for the purpose of red-baiting labor, civil rights, and leftist movements, and purged the NLRB of its more liberal members. These national political developments further worsened the prospects for any kind of change in Memphis. Fearful that southern Democrats would sabotage his programs in Congress, Roosevelt became even more reluctant to speak out against civil liberties violations in Memphis. For among southern Democrats, none was stronger than Crump.[59]

Memphis compress workers moving a bale of cotton, November 1939. (Photo by
Marion Post Wolcott, Farm Security Administration, courtesy of the Library of
Congress)

Picking cotton, Phillips County, Arkansas, September 1938. Conditions had
changed little since the Elaine race riot in the same county in 1919. (Photo by
Russell Lee, Farm Security Administration, courtesy of the Library of Congress)

Jobs were scarce during the depression, as African Americans lined up outside the segregated state employment service in Memphis, June 1938. (Photo by Dorothea Lange, Farm Security Administration, courtesy of the Library of Congress)

An ironic billboard promotes investment in Memphis, February 1937. Wages in unionized areas of the North were far higher and African Americans did not share in the "American Way." (Photo by Edwin Locke, Farm Security Administration, courtesy of the Library of Congress)

Even Beale Street, the mecca of entertainment in the black South, fell on hard times during the 1930s. (Photo by Marion Post Wolcott, Farm Security Administration, courtesy of the Library of Congress)

Poor blacks and whites line up with poll tax receipts in hand to vote for the candidate of Crump's choice, 4 August 1938. (Courtesy of the Mississippi Valley Collection, Memphis State University)

Picket Line Hair Pulling Class for Men

Of all the nation's strikes, probably none got down to hair pulling with greater zest than the one which produced these scenes in Memphis. After Tri-State Dress Manufacturing Co. workers in a C. I. O. union walked out, women tussled with luckless men on the picket line.

Women at Memphis dress factories set off the public confrontations in 1937 over the right to organize, as "Amazons" (according to the media) led the way in fighting company supervisors and scabs. (Courtesy of the Mississippi Valley Collection, Memphis State University)

Red Davis (*back row, right*) with deck crew aboard the motor vessel
Herbert Hoover in Memphis, 1939. (Courtesy of W. E. Davis)

The NMU's Inland Boatmen's hall was one of the few places where black and
white could meet together. Here white river workers pose with blacks from other
industries being organized into the CIO, circa 1940. (Courtesy of Mary Lou Koger)

White tire builders at the Firestone Tire and Rubber Company first opposed but eventually provided a militant core of support for the CIO. (Courtesy of the Memphis Room, Memphis/Shelby County Public Library and Information Center)

CHAPTER FOUR

Black and White Unite

In every port . . . instructions went out to the men . . . to carry on as though they had done nothing but strike all their lives. The strike lasted for three weeks, and the company and the top A.F. of L. officials made desperate attempts to destroy the unity between I.L.A. and the Inland Boatmen, but they failed. We went into the strike united, and we came out united.
                                        —Felix Siren

Following the much-publicized beating of Norman Smith, CIO efforts came to a near standstill in Memphis. Action shifted for a time to AFL unions, which by 1938 had regained some of the strength lost in the early depression years. According to that year's *City Directory*, seventy-six AFL and railroad unions existed. This growth partly reflected the popularity of AFL leader Lev Loring with the Crump machine (the mayor even wanted Loring appointed commissioner of labor for the city). It also reflected the boost given to craft unions by New Deal jobs and construction programs, increased organizing efforts, and growing militance among workers. Militance within the AFL framework peaked in the spring of 1938, when Teamster union members undertook a twenty-three-day strike against Yellow Cab company. In one incident, white workers overturned cabs and smashed in windows, leading to more than a score of arrests. Brewery Workers' union members around the same time conducted an eighty-four-day strike at Seven Up bottling, which won a closed shop and reinstatement of all fired strikers. The city apparently accepted such labor militance within the framework of the Crump-Loring detente. White AFL unionists, even militant ones, by no means threatened white supremacy or machine rule, and as long as they stayed out of public employee organizing, they escaped the sort of merciless repression visited on CIO organizers.[1]

Especially in contrast to the AFL, the CIO appeared to be weak indeed. Workers interested in CIO unions still met in the dark, in people's homes, in garages, storefront churches, or wherever they felt the police would not intrude. Black worker Clarence Coe's first organizing experience led to a beating and the loss of his job, and so it was with many others. But late in the decade industrial unionism emerged from its shadowy underground existence. During the spring of 1939, an unusual coalition of black workers in the AFL's International Longshoremen's Association (ILA) and white workers in the CIO's Inland Boatmen's Union (IBU), an affiliate of the National Maritime Union (NMU), joined together in a strike on the inland waterways. The solidarity of black and white workers during the strike produced one of the first union victories over racial division in Memphis, established a CIO beach head, and helped to change the course of union history in Crump's town.[2]

Waterfront workers had a long history of racial conflict and employer obstinacy to overcome. Ever since the Memphis race riot of 1866, in which whites from Fort Pickering had gone on a rampage through the African-American community, labor relations on the Mississippi had revolved around the color line. The replacement of Irish workers by freed slaves after the war had been one of the causes of the riot. Afterwards, blacks increasingly dominated dock work, and though they obtained some cooperation from other black laborers during an 1877 strike, black-white labor solidarity completely collapsed. Later on, unions vanished on the Memphis waterfront altogether as commerce declined on the waterways, with railroads and highways carrying an increasing share of goods out of the region.[3] In contrast to Memphis, the ILA had succeeded in some ports in getting blacks and whites to share jobs and organize on a cooperative basis, although usually in separate locals. In New Orleans, this arrangement led to a number of startling examples of interracial cooperation, producing some of the highest wages for dockworkers in the country. But even in that city the unions broke down under the weight of state repression and white racism in the early twentieth century. Race had always been one of the keys to union success or failure in the southern port cities.[4]

In the thirties, when strikes and organizing drives revived trade unions among maritime and longshore workers on the East and West coasts of the United States, organizers began to hope for a resurgence of riverfront unionism in the South. The possibility for such organization in Memphis resulted in part from a renewed growth of traffic on the river. In 1924 Congress had established the Inland Waterways Corporation (IWC), an agency of the War Department, which by 1937 had substantially revived commerce on the waterfront. The IWC owned and managed the Federal Barge Line, and the Memphis terminal had become one of its largest operations. New Deal construction of port facilities and grain elevators on the river, when linked with railroads and the interstate highway system, made Memphis the hub of commerce for the mid-South. As the only port safe from flooding for some five hundred miles, harbor facilities in Memphis were valued at $9 million in 1939, and over $112 million worth of goods passed through them each year. Not surprisingly, Memphis traders prized the nonunion labor that assured cheap shipment of goods up and down the river.[5]

Unrestrained by unions, employers on the inland waterways blatantly disregarded the rights of their employees. They also rigidly segmented the labor force along racial lines also obviously played a role. On the docks, in places such as Memphis, Baton Rouge, and Helena, Arkansas, black stevedores did all of the hot, heavy work, wheeling nearly five-hundred-pound cotton bales and other goods onto the boats for less than thirty cents an hour—at about a third of the wages paid in northern ports. Employers contended that these wages were high compared with the wages typically paid to blacks for chopping cotton or working in a sawmill. But in fact work came so irregularly that most black dockworkers had to supplement their incomes with field work or other seasonal employment; even those dockworkers employed steadily throughout the year averaged only $652 in 1938, placing them well below the minimum standard of living. While blacks worked as freight handlers, sweepers, and general laborers, employers hired whites in the higher-paying jobs as clerks, inspectors, machine operators, mechanics, carpenters, warehousers, and supervisors. Some of these white men joined AFL unions, but they usually had little sympathy with the blacks whom many of them supervised.[6]

On the rivers, long hours, low wages, and bad conditions afflicted white riverboat workers almost as much as the black dockworkers. Except for captains and pilots, white riverboat workers (nearly all male) made slightly better wages than black dockworkers, as much as eighty dollars per month. Yet they did so only because of the huge number of hours they put in: deckhands commonly worked eighty-four-hour weeks in staggered shifts, sometimes putting in eighteen to twenty hours a day. With these long hours, wages could average out to as little as eight cents an hour. As quasi-federal employees, these workers were not covered by federal minimum wage standards enacted in 1938. Riverboat workers had other complaints, including the fact that they often slept with eight deckhands in a fifteen-by-twelve-foot room, typically had only two showers for sixteen men on a boat, and were served green meat and weevily bread. Most deckhands did not consider themselves to be craftworkers, so they began to join up with the CIO's Inland Boatmen's Union.[7]

Workers on the riverboats, as on the docks, however, remained divided along color lines. Three departments of deck employees, engine room workers, and stewards existed on most boats. Whites worked in the first two departments as deckhands, engine room workers, and as captains, mates, and pilots. Blacks worked in what were thought of as more menial jobs in the stewards' department as waiters, laundry workers, and sometimes as cooks. Blacks had once worked as deckhands but by 1939 black deckhands had been eliminated. By that time, on a typical boat on the lower Mississippi, blacks in the stewards' department comprised only 4 or 5 of 30 crew members. Blacks constituted at most 30 of the 180 employees on the Federal Barge Line's six boats operating between New Orleans and St. Louis. This minority of riverboat workers received the lowest wages and worst treatment, with waiters averaging $55.00 and launderers averaging $62.50 per month. A few black women worked in laundry and cook positions below deck; they not only made terrible wages but suffered from the sexual advances of white supervisors.[8]

Employer hiring policies played the major role in enforcing racial divisions on the waterfront. Nevertheless, as unions developed during the middle and late thirties they also played a role. Neither the ILA nor the IBU ever threatened to upset the system of occupational assignments by race. For the unions, racial employment patterns at least settled the question of who got which jobs, reducing fratricidal disputes over job distribution. Racial discrimination excluded blacks from the highest-paying jobs, but on the docks blacks outnumbered whites in every southern port and therefore provided most of the leadership for the ILA. In the IBU, on the other hand, whites overwhelmingly dominated employment and the affairs of the union. Only in the ports below Memphis did the IBU succeed in organizing interracial locals among shoreside workers, and on the boats only a handful of black stewards joined the union. One official noted that unionization had always succeeded most quickly on boats where employers excluded blacks from deck jobs. IBU organizers did not attempt to change such racist hiring policies for fear of turning whites against the union.[9]

Despite the existing racial divisions, the riverboat workers, most of them white, and the dockworkers, most of them black, had common economic grievances and often worked for the same employer. All of the workers lacked any form of job security, compensation for injuries, or pensions for old age. Besides the hard labor, poor pay, and bad working conditions, riverboat workers and dockworkers hated the dictatorial, company boss systems on both the docks and the boats. Even family ties did not mitigate the arbitrary behavior of employers, according to Red Davis, who quit his first river job when his uncle would not let him off the boat long enough to go on a date. Black dockworkers received far worse treatment than white riverboat workers. Company supervisor John Lynch at the Federal Barge Line terminal in Memphis regularly exercised his personal power over the dockworkers at the point of a gun. In a petition to the NLRB in July 1937, fifty-three of them detailed how white supervisors subjected them to threats and beatings and forced them to give bribes of whiskey or money in order to keep their jobs. Lynch, like the other supervisors, was frequently drunk, prominently displayed guns, and even killed one unarmed worker in 1937. The workers charged that "if any man should happen to speak of these conditions," he "would be discharged, beat up, run off the job or subjected to all three."[10]

Conditions for both shoreside and river workers worsened when, under the direction of IWC president and army general T. Q. Ashburn, local supervisors in port cities sought to increase company profits during a one-million-dollar expansion of Federal Barge Line facilities in 1937. Management's autocratic behavior, preemptory firings, brutality, and general bad behavior increasingly became a focal point of discontent. Like many industrial workers in the CIO era, river and dockworkers sought an end to oppressive management behavior as one of the major goals of unionization. Throughout the 1939 strike unionists focused their anger on the Federal Barge Line superintendents, calling them names such as Hitler, Mussolini, and a "one eared rat," and called for the removal of the worst supervisors as well as Ashburn.[11]

Owners of private companies often treated the workers even worse than the Federal Barge Line officials. Riverboat and dock owners Russell Warner and Frank Tamble, whose operations had dominated the river traffic around Memphis since the twenties, personified employers' grim opposition to unions. Both men gained their early reputations as liquor runners during Prohibition, and Tamble had gained notoriety in 1933 for killing a man during a drunken gunfight in a Memphis hotel he owned. According to Red Davis, Warner's and Tamble's reputation for violence included the murder of black workers and a brag that "nobody can organize this place, we'll kill them." According to an FBI agent, during the 1939 strike Russell Warner told him that nonunion crews on his boats "were armed with shotguns and rifles and that this practice was nothing new to any private concern operating on the Mississippi River." Warner added that "he had given specific instructions to all members of his organization . . . that if anyone attempted to attack, disable, or in any way hinder the work of his company they should blow them to hell." The son of a river man who floated lumber down the Tennessee River in the 1850s, Warner retained a strong attachment to frontier ways and violent anti-unionism.[12]

Blacks began to change these oppressive conditions with the aid of organizers in the St. Louis office of the ILA, who realized that as long as Memphis remained unorganized it would continue to drag down wages on other parts of the river. Frank Hargraves, president of a white dockworkers' local in St. Louis that had successfully combined with a black local to raise wages for both groups of workers, set off the organizing drive. Before Memphis police could locate him and arrest him for his "communist" agitation, he had signed up a majority of the Memphis dockworkers. When the workers went on to elect black leader Thomas Watkins to bargain for the union in 1937, Federal Barge Line superintendents P. H. Patton and G. E. Taylor chased Watkins and other unionists off the job with a pistol. The Barge Line's refusal to recognize or bargain with the union prompted over one hundred dockworkers to strike the company in July. Only the intervention of a federal mediator forced the Barge Line representatives to agree to a ninety-day truce. Local officials, stating that "we have had no labor trouble for 10 years and the Memphis negroes were satisfied until outside agitators began to stir up trouble," took this to be the end of the dispute.[13] To their surprise, on 25 October the workers struck again, this time in greater numbers and demanding a sixty-cent hourly wage (a demand they later lowered to forty cents), a forty-eight-hour week, and time-and-a-half pay for overtime. In November the strike spread to the American Barge Line, the Mississippi Valley Barge Line, Jones and Loughlin Steel, and the Union Barge Line, bringing commercial enterprise on the waterfront to a halt.[14]

During the 1937 strike, black dockworkers demonstrated their ability to shut down traffic on the Mississippi and gained significant bargaining power. However, the Federal Barge Line refused to meet directly with blacks, insisting instead that all negotiations go through AFL leader Lev Loring, who until this point had little to do with the ILA organizing. Police made numerous arrests of picketers, including one mass arrest of twenty-eight strikers, but behind the scenes Mayor Overton and a city commissioner, fearing the dispute would harm the city's economy, pressured the Federal Barge Line to reach an agreement. Following fifteen days of meetings supervised by federal mediators, company officials finally guaranteed the workers an eight-hour day and forty-eight-hour week, reduced the weight they required workers to carry, and increased the number of "pushers" for each job. But they refused to recognize the union and left the question of wage increases to be settled by future arbitration. Although the Memphis press played down the events "because of the strike being a colored man's strike," according to a mediator, the settlement nonetheless represented a partial victory. The dockworkers returned to work on 16 December after some six weeks on the picket line, forty arrests, and four injuries.[15]

The strikes against the Federal Barge Line in July and October, though gaining only minimal benefits, led to a union revival on the Memphis waterfront, one that paralleled a similar development in other southern ports. As the result of a series of strikes in 1935, 1936, and 1937, black workers established ILA locals in Cairo and East St. Louis, Illinois, and New Orleans, and fledgling locals in the less secure ports of Vicksburg, Baton Rouge, and Helena, Arkansas. Existing within the segregated confines of the AFL, ILA locals developed surprisingly strong black leaders. Harry Bridges attempted to bring some of these locals into his International Longshoreman's and Warehouseman's Union, as did the newly established IBU. These leftist CIO unions, officially opposed to racial discrimination, seemed to provide new vehicles for the reorganization of southern black dockworkers. But as long as the AFL allowed them relative autonomy, most blacks remained quite willing to stay within the ILA, where they had an established leadership, one the biracial policies of the CIO might have threatened. Nonetheless, black dockworkers in the ILA were more than willing to work with whites in the CIO, who built a series of IBU locals by working in tandem with the ILA revival. Both the ILA and the IBU locals consolidated their ranks during a twelve-day strike against the Federal Barge Line in 1938, during which national officials agreed to bargain under binding arbitration of the Department of Labor. Local company bosses still refused to recognize union representatives or increase wages, but by early 1939 a core of organizers and union leaders clearly existed on both the docks and the riverboats.[16]

BLACK MILITANCE AND UNION RACISM

Thomas Watkins quickly emerged as the undisputed leader of black dockworkers in Memphis, playing a key role in organizing strikes and work slowdowns on the docks. Nearly six feet tall and weighing almost two hundred pounds, Watkins was a hard worker with a powerful demeanor. He gained attention as a work gang leader by the way he could maintain strict control over the use of his crews by employers. He became the business agent for AFL federal local 1549, composed of deckhands, pump tenders, coal workers, chute tenders, stokers, and guards working for the

West Kentucky Coal Company. He also became president of ILA locals of freight handlers (1490) and warehousers and freight loaders (1595) at the Wheeling Steel Company. The only AFL riverfront local Watkins did not lead was the ILA Local 1539, composed of white checkers, clerks, mechanics, guards, and a few laborers, but even this local maintained a peaceful coexistence with him. No other unionist, white or black, rivaled Watkins's power as a leader on the docks.[17]

The most unusual thing about Watkins was his refusal to back down when in confrontation with white authorities. He had battled racism all of his life. At a young age a white Texas plantation owner had forced him to leave school to work the land. He later had a terrible experience in a juvenile home after his family fell apart. In the military, his resistance to white authority led to eighteen months at hard labor in Fort Leavenworth Penitentiary. His personality had been shaped early by such confrontations with whites. Subsequently, he traveled widely as a member of the army of the unemployed, suffering numerous arrests for vagrancy and train riding. His travels and his work in a variety of occupations, from plumber to steelworker, made him far more knowledgeable than most Memphis workers and less willing to be intimidated. By the time he began a family with Arlene Wynne and settled into dock work in Memphis in 1934, he was worldly and tough. The police soon had him under surveillance, listing him as a "labor trouble maker" and (inaccurately) "CIO organizer." His extraordinary ability to unify the dockworkers made him a special target for company supervisors and the police, who one night beat him up on President's Island. After this, fellow dockworkers regularly served as his bodyguards as he went from the docks to his home or to the union office, an apartment several doors from his residence on West De Soto Street.[18]

Watkins's hard-driving unionism helped to build the ILA locals from the ground up, but his audacity as a leader also placed him directly in conflict with southern racial mores. Watkins displayed a militancy almost unheard of in Memphis. In the course of his altercations with officials of the Federal Barge Line, Watkins wrote to the secretary of war (who had supervisory authority over the IWC) demanding the dismissal of local officials and President Ashburn of the IWC. Employers soon identified Watkins, rather than bad work conditions and low wages, as the source of all trouble on the docks. Predictably, during an FBI investigation in 1939 riverboat owner Russell Warner told the FBI that "the entire labor disorder presently in force in Memphis could be laid to Tom Watkins, as he is a radical individual and apparently has aroused the colored longshoremen to rebel against any contract not suitable to Watkins." Others accused him of "procommunist tendencies." [19]

Watkins's assertiveness would led to repeated conflicts not only with employers but with white representatives of the AFL. During the months leading to the 1939 river strike, tensions between Watkins and AFL president Lev Loring increased in direct proportion to Watkins's attempts to exercise his power as a union leader. AFL leaders especially targeted him as a troublemaker when he put that power to use on behalf of blacks outside his longshore local. For two years Watkins had been working with a group of black building trades workers, along with Lucien Searcy and Nebraska Jones of the Urban League. In March 1939, Watkins and the other men organized them into the Independent Craftsmen's Association for the purpose of obtaining jobs for blacks on federal construction projects. Black surveyors' assistants, painters, electricians, and plumbers had failed, after five years of trying, to gain entrance to AFL locals. When the national AFL rejected their request for a "federal" charter, they protested, only to be branded by the Memphis Trades and Labor Council as "Communistic," while the Urban League was threatened with having all of its funds from the Community Chest cut off. An "Americanism" committee set up by the local AFL brought in Searcy for "questioning" and shortly forced Jones to leave town. "Communism" in this case apparently meant anything white AFL leaders didn't like, and they particularly didn't like blacks demanding equal rights. The black union group disbanded, and Watkins gained a reputation in the AFL for being a radical. [20]

Meanwhile, Loring began to build a case against Watkins because of his audacious conduct on the docks. He first denounced a strike Watkins called for union recognition and a contract for Local 1549 as "unauthorized," and, according to an affidavit filed by Watkins with the FBI, told Watkins that "he, Loring, was head of the labor movement in Memphis and if Watkinz [*sic*] thought differently he had only to start something." Loring's threats to "tear up" the ILA local, according to Watkins, forced him to abandon the strike. Watkins had earlier piqued Loring's anger by leading the successful strikes in 1937 before some ILA locals had even been recognized by the local AFL. According to Watkins, authorization for his actions came from the ILA national office; according to Loring, all decisions of the local ILA had to be cleared through him. When Watkins on his own initiative once again called a 1 March 1939 strike of Wheeling Steel Company warehousers after negotiations over earlier promised wage increases stalled, Loring countermanded the strike, apologized to Wheeling officials for it, and told the local to accept the Wheeling company's previous offer or expect trouble with the police. Watkins refused to accept Loring's intervention into the affairs of ILA locals and complained about the settlement to the NLRB. The police promptly arrested him. Watkins later told the FBI that during the police lineup Chief Will Lee remarked, "There's a negro who has been making trouble for quite awhile. The best thing to do is either put a weight around his neck and drop him in the river or else put him in jail and throw the key away." The police held Watkins seventy-two hours and then released him without charges. His attorney, Ben Kohn, himself a victim of Crump terror, only secured Watkins's release by threatening to take the matter to the federal government. When Watkins got out of jail, he once again went over Loring's head, asking ILA international president Joseph Ryan to disapprove Loring's contract. In the end, a federal mediator convinced the local to accept Loring's proposal on a temporary basis, but reported to his superior that tremendous friction existed between the black workers and Loring. "The whole situation was dangerous," the mediator concluded.[21]

The settlement at Wheeling—which included a small wage increase, a forty-hour work week, overtime pay, and three holidays—represented progress for the workers. But in the aftermath of the struggle to control the negotiations, conflicts between Loring and Watkins came to a head. Watkins admitted that he deliberately called strikes without seeking Loring's approval because he did not trust him to fully support black demands. "I well knew the policy of the Central Trade and Labor Council and avoided contacts with it as much as possible," Watkins told the FBI, "because I knew the Council was not sympathetic toward the organization and advancement of Negro workers." Watkins's attempt to get ILA president Joseph Ryan to overturn the settlement Loring imposed at Wheeling failed, but Watkins made a further effort to get outside help against Loring. He wrote to William Green, national president of the AFL, charging that his ILA local had to pay a twenty-five-cent per capita tax to the local Trades and Labor Council, which Watkins called "the highest rate charged by any Council in the United States." Watkins intimated that the money was being misused by the Memphis council, and in response the AFL sent representative Paul Aymon from Atlanta to investigate the council's books.[22]

The mortification of being investigated for financial irregularities due to the accusations of an uneducated black worker proved to be the last straw for Loring. On 13 April, he and fellow plumber Pat Hackett, who had arrest powers as the city's plumbing inspector, cornered Watkins on Illinois Street near Marine Hospital. According to a witness at the scene,

Loring pulled off his coat and ran at Watkins, demanding to know if he had written the letter to the AFL in Atlanta, and Watkins tartly replied, "Yes, I wrote the letter and I'm going to write another." Hackett promptly made his arrest while some twenty white workers called by Loring from a nearby construction site surrounded Watkins. The city held the longshore leader in jail for two days with no charges and then accused him of assault with intent to murder, resisting arrest, disturbing the peace, and threatening breach of peace. In court, Loring testified that he had only approached Watkins to ask him a question, but the black leader "was abusive in his answer and told me he didn't like the way the council was run." Loring also claimed Watkins pulled a hammer and tried to attack him. Two witnesses at the scene, however, stated that Watkins didn't try to strike anyone, and three witnesses testified that Watkins did not resist arrest. According to Watkins, Loring told him during the altercation that "if you think you're going to make trouble around here for me, nigger, I'm going to dig your grave and do it within 24 hours." Despite this testimony, the city fined Watkins eighty dollars for resisting arrest and disturbing the peace. The judge turned him over to the state on the assault charge.[23]

Two days after the arrest, the Executive Board of the Trades and Labor Council expelled Watkins's ILA local, stating it could not be returned to Labor Council membership until it removed Watkins. Calling him a "disturbing element in the Memphis labor movement," the council charged Watkins with having "broken solemn agreements between the union and its employers" by calling unauthorized strikes. It further indicted him for writing to AFL president Green. During the council meeting Loring read from some of the letters Watkins had written and ridiculed his untutored style and charged that Watkins's organizing efforts "resulted in loss of prestige to the Memphis labor movement." The *Memphis Labor Review* highlighted the case of Watkins with banner headlines, accusing him of "violent agitation" and relating the "outrage" of AFL members at his letter to Green. The entire city establishment, of which Loring was a part, by this time viewed Watkins as a subversive presence, one they would soon remove permanently.[24]

THE GREAT RIVERFRONT STRIKE OF 1939

In the midst of these conflicts between Watkins and Loring, negotiations between the Federal Barge Line and waterfront unions completely broke down. Previous work stoppages conducted against the Federal Barge Line by the ILA and IBU had won short-term agreements from the largest company on the lower Mississippi but had not resolved the grievances of the workers nor provided any form of security for their unions. The Federal Barge Line had not accepted unions as legitimate bargaining agents and denied workers rights to seniority, job security, and guarantees of minimal hours of work. Constant layoffs due to intermittent demands for labor continued to place workers at the mercy of those who rehired them and allowed supervisors and company officials numerous opportunities to discriminate against union members. Both riverboat workers and dockworkers felt they needed a hiring hall that would allow the union to parcel out available jobs according to seniority and allow new workers to come into rotation as more jobs appeared. Federal Barge Line and private employers alike vehemently opposed the closed shop "rotary" hiring hall for the same reasons as other employers: it in effect accepted the union as a permanent institution with considerable control over the allocation of jobs. Although the Federal Barge Line had accepted preferential hiring of union members and a closed shop in Cairo, East St. Louis, and Peoria in its 1938 agreements, in 1939 it refused to allow this system to spread further south.[25]

Three weeks of bargaining for a new agreement had failed to produce a contract. On 24 April, the Federal Barge Line offered no major wage concessions and called for a ban on the union's proposal of a closed shop or preferential hiring agreement. If the company position stood, the unions would have no basis for developing or even maintaining their strength on the waterfront. Coupled with a threat by IWC president Ashburn to impose an "embargo" on shipping, i.e., to lock the workers out and stop shipping goods, many workers considered the company's "offer" a declaration of war. During negotiations, ILA and IBU locals from St. Louis to New Orleans had formed a leadership group for the unions called the General Council of Riverworkers. On 26 April the council called a strike against the Federal Barge Line, demanding higher wages, union hiring halls, and the removal of Ashburn and local officials from this "reactionary agency of the progressive New Deal." The IBU members, variously estimated at between 250 and 1,000 employees, walked out first, but some 2,500 to 3,000 AFL dockworkers joined them within a day. The joint action of the IBU and the ILA locals shut down the Federal Barge Line and the smaller Mississippi Valley Barge Line, halted much of the river traffic between St. Louis and New Orleans, and threw the shipping economy and employers alike into an uproar. Taking place around the same time as a strike of NMU maritime workers in ports on the East Coast and in the Gulf of Mexico, the strike paralyzed a significant portion of the internal commerce of the Mississippi Valley.[26]

The General Council of Riverworkers, headquartered in St. Louis, represented an uncommon alliance. Composed of black and white workers and of AFL and CIO unions, the council sought to resist the racial divisions that had repeatedly broken strikes and unions on the river. In Memphis, Watkins of the ILA and Frank Bruno of the IBU served as co-members of the Port Council, and in New Orleans IBU leaders Robert Himmaugh, white, and Ernest Scott, black, similarly served as co-members. IBU members dominated the Port Councils in Helena, Vicksburg, Baton Rouge, Mobile, Louisville, Cincinnati, and Pittsburgh, while ILA members composed the Port Council in Cairo and occupied four of the five positions on the General Council's executive board. By organizing jointly, blacks and whites in the two unions hoped to avoid some of the tragic failures of the past.[27]

However, by taking joint action with a CIO union, ILA locals incurred the wrath of southern AFL representative George Googe and Memphis AFL leader Loring, who placed their opposition to the CIO above the concerns of black longshore workers. Loring apparently believed the accusations of Federal Barge Line officials and the police that Watkins was "acting under the guidance of some white men" in the CIO with the objective of taking the ILA locals out of the AFL, and declared the ILA strike an unauthorized "sympathy strike" with "CIO boatmen who are trying to destroy AF of L unions." Self-interest made it apparent that the dockworkers would have more bargaining power if they struck in concert with the riverboat workers, and in fact R. A. Walton, ILA vice-president in Chicago, had telegraphed Watkins to take the Memphis ILA locals out on strike. Based on this telegram, Watkins's Local 1490, composed of black freight haulers, voted to strike on 27 April. Loring, however, publicly denounced the black workers' strike as illegal and made the strange claim that an order from Googe for the strikers to go back to work took precedence over orders from the ILA international office. But when Loring held a meeting to try to convince black dockworkers to return to work, they refused to even vote on the question unless Loring allowed Watkins to be present. Infuriated, Loring told them, according to Watkins, that "since you all are out, there will be no getting back, so start hunting for other jobs." If he could not overturn the decision of the black workers, however, Loring did succeed in getting whites in Local 1539 to continue working. The refusal of Watkins and the black dockworkers to bend to Googe and Loring would have momentous consequences, beginning a period of all-out war between the white AFL, the police, and business leaders on one side and Watkins, black dockworkers, and white riverboat workers on the other.[28]

The only real source of strength for the black dockworkers and the white riverboat workers lay in their alliance and in hopes that federal intervention might secure a modicum of civil liberties protections during the strike. The importance of the civil liberties question became clear as police and company officials began a concerted campaign to intimidate union picketers all up and down the river. In Memphis, Police Chief Will Lee advised IBU organizer Frank Bruno and IBU port agent Pat Matthews that he would not allow pickets to operate on the riverfront without permits and that he would not allow such permits to be given out. According to Bruno, Lee told him the "best thing for them to do was to return to their boats and stop calling these continual strikes." While Lee and Police and Fire Commissioner Clifford Davis banned mass picketing at Federal Barge Line terminals, they allowed police to escort black scabs to work for the Federal Barge Line, which advertised for "able bodied men" to work at forty-three cents an hour, a little above the previous wage. According to Southern Tenant Farmers' Union secretary Evelyn Smith, the riverfront "was packed with police and squad cars who would not allow the strikers to even congregate in small groups." Superintendent Patton declared that boats would be unloaded with nonunion labor even if it led to violence, a contingency for which Commissioner Davis had promised him protection. Encouraged by support from both the AFL and the police, Patton addressed a message to striking black workers appealing to their loyalty to the company and urging them to go back to work under the same conditions as existed before the strike; an emissary from Googe likewise urged them to return to work. Instead, Watkins's local reaffirmed its support for the strike by a vote of 134 to 0, and Watkins publicly called for Patton's dismissal.[29]

The refusal of a black-led union local to give in to company and police intimidation set a precedent in Memphis that many whites wished to erase and soon led to what appeared to be a dangerous provocation. Tensions escalated citywide on 5 May when someone cut loose five joined and loaded barges owned by the Warner and Tamble Transportation Company, letting them drift dangerously down the Mississippi. The unsupervised barges passed within shouting distance of an excursion steamer loaded with hundreds of prominent white society women of the Junior League and drifted twenty-five miles downstream before a Tamble tugboat brought them to bear. According to a guard aboard the barge, a party of white men with handkerchiefs covering their faces cut the barges loose. Union workers remained under strict orders from strike leaders not to harm Federal Barge Line property during the strike, and many felt that someone had manufactured the incident to turn public opinion against the strikers. This suspicion grew when police later claimed an anonymous caller had told them that

Watkins had perpetrated the crime; and the guard, apparently terrified of his employer, Tamble, then claimed he could not tell whether the men who cut the barge loose were black or white. Under pressure from his employers and from strikers, he told an increasingly confused and contradictory story, until the FBI concluded that he was trying to cover something up.[30]

In an attempt to undercut intimidation against strikers, union supporters began a campaign for federal intervention. The IBU's Pat Matthews contacted Senator Robert La Follette, Jr.'s, civil liberties committee in Congress, and numerous people sent telegrams to the Justice Department complaining of the police refusal to allow picketing. The campaign produced some results. For the first time, the Justice Department actively intervened against civil liberties violations in Memphis. U.S. Attorney General Frank Murphy sent FBI agents to Memphis and other port cities to investigate, and according to news accounts, gave U.S. attorneys instructions "to prosecute any person violating the civil liberties statutes." At the same time, Evelyn Smith, claiming that the police "are doing everything they can get away with to terrorize the workers," set about organizing a local civil liberties committee that included a Unitarian minister, the wife of a corporation lawyer, and the wife of John Rust, the inventor of the new mechanical cotton picker. In response to these pressures, Chief Will Lee allowed groups of three to picket in front of the Cotton Exchange Building, where the Federal Barge Line had its offices and where pickets had been arrested earlier. The intervention of outside forces had similar effects in Vicksburg, where a local sheriff released five workers he had held without bail.[31]

Civil liberties protests failed to squelch what workers called police "scab herding" at the Memphis terminal, however, where AFL president Loring began supplying the Federal Barge Line with unemployed union laborers to take the place of strikers. Federal Barge Line officials also recruited a scab crew for the Steamer *Vicksburg,* with the Memphis police picking up vagrants and offering them the alternative of going to jail or working on the boat, without ever telling them of the strike in progress. The hapless crew of black and white laborers worked the boat from Memphis to Cairo, where they learned of the strike and quit. Strikers in Cairo then helped them successfully demand that the Federal Barge Line pay them for the trip even though they had refused to finish their tour of work. The incident with the *Vicksburg* ended peacefully, although Federal Barge Line officials claimed five hundred striking workers had riotously boarded the boat and thrown its captain overboard (FBI officials never substantiated the charge).[32]

Throughout the strike, such rumors of violence and actual violence swept the riverfront. Federal Barge Line officials played up rumors that CIO members had guns and dynamite ready to use to keep scab crews off the river, while CIO workers passed the word that Warner and Tamble's company had armed their boats with machine guns in order to transport scabs up and down the river. In one incident, a nonunion barge worker attempted to quit his job on a steamer while in port at Memphis in order to join the strike. According to an affidavit sworn out by the worker, "When I attempted to leave the vessel, I was struck across the stomach by a uniformed watchman employed by the Federal Barge Line, who threatened to beat me to death if I made any attempt to bring any or all of the crew of the *Memphis* ashore with me." The worker also complained that the police aided Federal Barge Line officials in frightening other workers from walking off the boat. Although unions had won limited rights to picket in Memphis, they had almost no control over what happened on the docks or on the boats, and throughout the strike Federal Barge Line officials used Memphis as a disembarkation point for nonunion crews coming up from New Orleans, something they could never get away with further north in Cairo or St. Louis.[33]

South of Memphis, in towns such as Baton Rouge, Mobile, and New Orleans, Federal Barge Line authorities responded with even greater hostility to the strike than in Memphis. In Mobile, worker affidavits alleged that company supervisors gave pistols to nonunion employees and told them "to kill any damn CIO," and one anti-union deckhand used brass knuckles to knock a CIO picket unconscious, forcing unionists to flee from the docks. FBI officials reported that in New Orleans a professional strikebreaker known to have shot a truck driver during a Teamsters strike there in 1938 led a gang of men to attack Robert Himmaugh and Ernest Scott, as well as other union members. In Vicksburg, according to Felix Siren, company officials attempted to provoke a riot and police ran a union organizer out of town.[34]

Workers sometimes responded to such intimidation by fighting back. In New Orleans, they hauled the officers and crew off the nonunion *Natchez* and held them overnight in the union hall, while in Cairo CIO workers refused to allow ships coming into port to tie up and beat up a nonunion ship's captain. The newspapers played up such incidents, which barge line owners called "gangsterism." Company reports that workers carried machine guns and dynamite seem to have been complete fabrications, however.[35] While union workers on occasion used force to stop the use of scabs, their main defense was to seize on all reports of company violence in an attempt to involve the federal government in settling the strike. Memphis CIO organizers in the past had tried this without much luck. In this case too the FBI proved useless to anyone wishing to prevent an act of violence, for as one agent explained, their purpose was to investigate and take the facts to the local U.S. attorney, not to stop an act in progress. But perhaps because the turmoil on the river was so extensive, FBI and Justice Department officials urged local police to restrain themselves and provided no encouragement to the Federal Barge Line officials either. In effect, implied threats of federal prosecution against both the workers and the companies had the effect of making each group more cautious during the strike.[36] Company officials also failed to get enough support from local authorities to crush the strike. Especially in Cairo, where city officials and even the governor of Illinois refused to side with management, Federal Barge Line officials could work up little public antagonism to the strikers. Exasperated by local authorities "wholly in sympathy with the strikers," they again asked federal Justice Department officials to protect scabs, and again the officials insisted that their job was to stop violations of federal law, not to help defeat the union. The *Chicago Tribune* and others condemned the failure of government to support "loyal men" who wanted to work, but employers simply could not get the government intervention they needed to break the strike.[37]

In the midst of the virtual civil war up and down the Mississippi River, the unity of the strikers remained unbroken for some three weeks. During this time whites and blacks coordinated picketing, held joint meetings, and warmed their hands by the same fires. Efforts by the Federal Barge Line to make separate settlements with the black AFL workers repeatedly failed to break up this common front. According to the *Pilot*, the newspaper of the NMU, IWC director Ashburn offered to mediate the strike with the ILA locals if they would settle without the IBU, but the dockworkers refused to make such a settlement. A worker writing to the union newspaper declared that the strike proved that the long-standing belief that ILA and NMU unions could not work together had been destroyed.[38] In fact, the ability of the black union members in Memphis to resist efforts of the AFL's Loring to turn them into strikebreakers proved critical to the entire ILA-IBU effort. Since white ILA workers already had refused to join the strike, had Watkins's local gone back to work, it would have turned Memphis into a stronghold of anti-unionism and perhaps have opened the way to strikebreaking at other points on the river. "Without the support of the black dockworkers we never would have won," white striker Red Davis later recalled.[39]

The solidarity of Watkins and his fellow black workers with the white riverboat workers and their refusal to buckle to AFL demands presented both the Federal Barge Line officials and AFL leader Loring with a difficult problem of saving face. At the local level, they continued to fight against the dockworker locals, even after the IWC finally decided to settle the strike. At the direction of the IWC, officials of the Federal Barge Line agreed to bargain, but mysteriously failed to issue instructions to local officials to comply with a settlement. As a result, Memphis officials refused to sign any agreement with ILA locals and continued to rely on scab bricklayers and hod carriers brought in by the AFL's Building Trades Council. Loring, meanwhile, tried to establish a new longshore union in which Watkins would have no role. Federal Barge Line officials in Memphis recognized Loring's tactic and put the scabs to work instead of taking back the strikers. In protest to the conditions in Memphis, union members up and down the river continued their strike for several days beyond strike settlement, until Barge Line officials realized they had no choice but to compel the acceptance of the Memphis local if they wanted to settle the strike elsewhere. The company discharged the AFL's scab laborers, and on 22 May the last of the strikers in Memphis went back to work.[40]

Hence, the first CIO strike victory in Memphis forced the Federal Barge Line to grant the ILA and the IBU recognition as the sole collective bargaining agents in their respective workplaces. The company further agreed to return strikers to their jobs without discrimination as work became available and to preferential hiring of union laborers. The unions did not win wage increases, which were to be settled in subsequent bargaining. Still, union officials called the strike a "clear cut victory." The IBU was the first CIO union in Memphis to strike and win, while the ILA was the first black-led AFL union in Memphis to exercise independent leadership against white leadership in the Trades and Labor Council. By maintaining labor unity, the dockworkers of the AFL and riverboat workers of the CIO won a victory that would prove important to the future success of industrial union organizing in Memphis. "We have won every round because of our unity," Siren proclaimed. "We will continue to do so."[41]

AFTERMATH

However, obtaining a viable contract and acceptable relations with supervisors after the bitter three-week strike proved to be almost more difficult for riverboat workers and dockworkers than winning the strike itself, and in the aftermath of the strike local authorities moved to extinguish the independent black leadership of the ILA. During the summer and fall of 1939, local officials of the Federal Barge Line and numerous smaller private companies sabotaged much of the strike settlement by refusing to implement the new contract. And with federal authorities and the newspapers less in evidence since the strike had ended, Thomas Watkins and his black local of the ILA became the first and most serious casualties of anti-union forces after the strike. By the time the Memphis ILA members returned to work on 22 May, Lev Loring, Barge Line superintendent Patton, and officers of the Memphis police had already held a meeting in which they plotted to remove or kill Watkins. Said Watkins, Loring "told me himself that he was going to dig my grave and see me in it." Pierce Thomas, a black union committee member, informed Watkins that a Memphis police officer had told him, "I have nothing against you, but that negro Tom Watkins is either going to get run out of town or get killed." [42]

On 26 May, the police carried out this threat. The arrest of Watkins and his wife in the middle of the night, the nearly successful attempt of the police and Russell Warner to kill him, his dramatic escape into the Mississippi River, and the almost ludicrous stories they concocted to cover up the assassination effort (recounted in the Introduction) hardly caused a ripple of official concern in Memphis. After making his investigation of the case, which mainly consisted of talking to local police, the U.S. attorney in Memphis excused their actions and told U.S. Attorney General Frank Murphy that with the removal of Watkins "complete harmony" had returned to Memphis. The police for their part remained so unconcerned about the Justice Department "investigation" that they did not even bother to press charges against Watkins to cover up their attack on him. Watkins's escape from death in Memphis, aided by black women and union members, and his exile to St. Louis proved once again the frailty of civil liberties protections for blacks in Memphis. [43]

The larger purposes and ramifications of the attempt to decapitate the Memphis local's black leadership became clear immediately following Watkins's plunge into the Mississippi. Before Watkins's disappearance even became public knowledge, Federal Barge Line general superintendent of the Mississippi terminals G. E. Taylor, describing Watkins as a "CIO leader," had flashed to all boats that Watkins had been shot or drowned. The significance of the message was not lost on either unionists or company officials. In New Orleans, renowned anti-union superintendent L. E. Barry warned IBU leader Ernest Scott that he and other blacks could receive the same treatment as that "smart nigger" Watkins, and reassured Scott that the New Orleans police, as in Memphis, "would do anything" the company wanted them to. Barry refused to let Scott onto the dock to supervise the new contract and organized a company union to enforce the "seniority" of strikebreakers. Instead of allowing all laborers equal opportunity to receive available work, Barry placed scabs at the top of his hiring list, making it unlikely that unionists would ever get regular employment. Company superintendents in Mobile similarly penalized union workers for the strike, and in Memphis Superintendent Patton set up a company union among boat captains and mates and told them they would all be fired if they joined the CIO. The company did fire William R. Henderson, a cook on the steamer the *Hoover,* which Red Davis and other Memphians worked on, for being on the NMU's negotiating committee.[44] Similar threats and harassment against unionists during the summer blossomed on the lower Mississippi, as they did also in a separate strike battle in the Gulf ports of Texas.[45]

In short, despite the strike victory of 1939, the struggle over union rights had not ended, either in Memphis or in any other southern port. The removal of Watkins was a body blow aimed at black unionists. And even though the Federal Barge Line had signed an agreement with the unions, wages still had to be negotiated and the hiring hall and other union rights remained to be implemented. According to the *IBU News,* by the end of June local officials had broken every agreement written into the contract gained by the strike. Top officials of the Federal Barge Line in Washington showed no intention of doing anything about these violations. They treated with derision petitions and complaints from workers about local noncompliance with the contract and reprisals against union workers. One administrator ridiculed the charges against superintendent Barry as "petty complaints" by black workers "who are too sensitive to be 'cussed' or called 'niggers' since they are unionized." In response to the complaint about the brass knuckles beating of Herman Wonzy during the strike in Mobile, an IWC official shrugged the attack off as a "typical negro row which they try to blame on the Federal Barge Line." As if to prove that racial insensitivity ran all the way to the top of the company, IWC president Ashburn called the complaints of blacks "petty."[46]

Once again, only intervention by higher-ups in the federal government brought the companies to heel. The Commerce Department maintained ultimate authority over the IWC, and when it employed Monsignor Francis J. Haas of Catholic University to investigate conditions on the river, he substantiated virtually every charge made by the unions. As a result of the Haas investigation, Assistant Secretary of Commerce J. Monroe Johnson demanded that Ashburn force local officials of the Federal Barge Line

to implement the 1939 contract "without reservation" and to cease their attacks against unionists. But not until November did labor relations on the
riverfront take a turn for the better, when the Commerce Department fired
Ashburn after discovering that he had been operating a government yacht
at twenty thousand dollars a year for his own pleasure and had received
grants of five thousand and ten thousand dollars from the government for
"personal" expenses—at a time, noted Johnson, when "river hands were
up in arms over low pay and poor food."[47] Chester Thompson took over
as president of the IWC, phased out the worst of the anti-labor superintendents, and began negotiating seriously with the unions over wage increases.
In 1940, he began an ambitious modernization and expansion program
that would reduce the number of jobs done by hand and make it easier to
pay higher wages to those who remained.[48]

In Memphis, the ILA's black Local 1490 signed a one-year contract that
recognized the union, established a grievance procedure, an hourly rate of
forty-seven cents for laborers (still low compared to northern rates), an
eight-hour day, time-and-a-half pay for overtime or work on Sundays or
holidays, acceptance of seniority rights, and a preferential hiring system by
which the union would supply all new laborers to the company. In effect,
this granted all of the major demands made in the 1939 strike. In return,
the union agreed not to strike during the duration of the contract. White
members of ILA Local 1539 signed a separate contract, winning similar
provisions even though they had refused to take part in the strike.[49]

The terms of these contracts, signed by Federal Barge Line officials
throughout the system, represented an enormous advance for southern
dockworkers and established a new standard by which workers would
judge every transportation company on the inland waterways. Although
Warner and Tamble's operations and a number of others remained nonunion, most workers on the Federal Barge Line, the largest on the river,
belonged to unions. Further wage increases brought the highest-paid dockworkers in Memphis up to sixty cents an hour by 1941. Unionized riverboat
workers, who became direct members in the National Maritime Union
when it dissolved the IBU as a separate division, also achieved full union
rights and substantial wage increases, but they still worked eighty-four
hours per week and saw their families only one day a month. Government
regulation during the war years eased some of these conditions, however,
when the National War Labor Board recommended that riverboat workers
be granted six days of leave for every thirty days of work and increased the
wages of the lowest paid workers on the boats, thus easing the differential
between white and black workers. These settlements did not mean the end

of conflict or union activism on the inland waterways; the southern wage differential remained, and the struggle for pensions, health care, and other "fringe" benefits had yet to be launched. Nonetheless, the strike and the government's conciliation with the unions finally improved wages and stabilized conditions dramatically.[50]

These developments aided the creation of strong unions in Memphis, where the NMU local became one of the most important and continuing sources of support for CIO unionism in the city. Veterans of the strike continued to preach to workers that the "only salvation is in organization," and NMU leaders such as Frank Bruno, Robert Himmaugh, and Sam Despaux as well as younger rank-and-file activists such as Red Davis and William R. Henderson all gained much of their authority and experience as unionists during the 1939 strike. For Davis, like many others, the strike proved to be a personal turning point, leading him to a lifelong preoccupation with the labor movement and radicalism. He and other husky young veterans of the strike, toughened by long hours of work on the boats, subsequently sparked many CIO picket lines and organizing drives, and the NMU hall on West Illinois Street became the hub of the CIO movement prior to World War II. Along with a few black churches, the hall offered the only shelter for interracial gatherings and one of the very few institutional signs of the CIO's existence. Despite the persistence of racially exclusive employment patterns on the riverboats, the NMU officially opposed all forms of discrimination, and rank-and-file whites frequently took an active role in supporting the strikes and organizing drives of blacks in Memphis. The NMU became a base for white support of black organizing, and its Communist leadership, including Himmaugh, Bruno, Despaux, and later Davis and Lawrence McGurty, likewise made it a base for radical activism within the Memphis CIO.[51]

The aftermath of the strike for ILA members turned out quite differently. Despite the tremendous demonstration of labor solidarity during the strike, with Watkins removed the ILA local in Memphis once again came under the authority of the AFL leader Loring. Moreover, the ILA international union, steeped in corruption under the rule of Joseph Ryan, did little to break down job segregation or build up local black leadership in the South. In subsequent years conflicts between black workers and management would be resolved within a framework established by white union leaders and in an international where rank-and-file democracy remained at low tide and corruption flourished.[52] Furthermore, dock work shifted away from Memphis toward the modernized port facilities in nearby St. Louis and Helena, Arkansas, reducing the leverage black dockworkers could use against local employers. Hemmed in by AFL control and lacking the added strength of a united movement with the white workers of the CIO, black workers on the docks had decreasing opportunity after the thirties to exercise independence from employers or white labor leaders.[53]

Blacks who worked for private companies still remained unorganized and subject to the deadly rule of racists such as Warner and Tamble, whose company remained nonunion. The case of black longshore worker Robert Cotton, reported by CIO troubleshooter Lucy Randolph Mason, provided a case in point. Cotton attempted to sue Warner and Tamble for back wages over a work dispute. According to Cotton's sister, his employers asked him to come to work on 12 September 1940 for a "conference," and she never heard from him again. But according to some of Cotton's fellow workers, they "saw a floating body dressed in clothing similar to the clothes worn by Cotton" while working on a steamer on the Mississippi, but their captain would not lower a boat to investigate. Further reports indicated that the marshall of West Memphis, Arkansas, had met with Warner and Tamble on the Arkansas side of the river, where it was suspected that the men weighted Cotton's body and threw him in. Matthew Williams, the black vice-president of the ILA local at West Kentucky Coal Company, a local organized and led by Watkins, had also "disappeared" as the result of his union work, according to Mason. Williams had been fired by the company for union activities and had persistently fought his case through federal labor agencies, which ordered the company to cease their anti-union efforts. Following his victory before the labor board, police picked up Williams at his home and took him to the police station, where the desk sergeant told him, "You are a troublemaker and the best thing for you to do is to catch a cotton picking truck to Arkansas and not be caught on the streets of Memphis again." Williams, in hiding, made his account available to Mason, but ceased his agitation for reinstatement at Kentucky Coal.[54]

* * *

The loss of Watkins and other black ILA leaders proved to be a mortal blow to unionism on the Memphis docks. One can only guess what kind of impact Watkins might have made in Memphis had he been allowed to pursue his natural role as a leader of workers. Surely he would have become an authoritative figure in the labor movement had AFL leaders, employers, and the police tolerated him. Indeed, when he finally moved to the shipyards of Portland, Oregon, he helped organize city employees and remained an active adviser to black unionists. He remained "subversive" enough to the FBI, which continued to track his activities until 1973, and he remained a powerful and impressive figure well into his twilight years. According to one of his best friends, Watkins was still "like a lion" in his eighties. Without him, black dockworkers in Memphis never again experienced such compelling and independent leadership.[55]

In the forties, white workers on the riverboats and black dockworkers conducted largely separate struggles, and the brief high point of interracial unity on the riverfront faded from view. But although the ILA locals ceased to be a significant influence, the NMU and its cadre of organizers remained, soon to be joined by a new group of black workers who would form the early basis for successful CIO unionism in Memphis. The first step toward unity of black and white working-class interests had been taken.

CHAPTER FIVE

Race, Radicalism, and the CIO

When I started organizing the CIO I was called a Communist anyhow, and one thing I noticed was that the Communists were the most dedicated union supporters. In 1939 I wasn't a Communist, just a militant young guy caught up in the class struggle. . . . But I became acquainted with the Communists and I found myself defending them because they were the best organizers. I got caught up in the struggle, and at that time the big issue was black and white unity. I could see from experience there was no way to achieve organization without unity between black and white.
—W. E. "Red" Davis

The CIO has brought more hope for progress to Negroes than any other social institution in the South—and that, sadly, includes the church. . . . Of first significance to Negroes is the acknowledgment of themselves as persons entitled to democratic respect.
—Lucy Randolph Mason

During the thirties, a new breed of homegrown radicals emerged in the South. Communists, Socialists, and religious followers of the social gospel across the region became active in agitating for unemployment relief, unionization, and in opposition to racial repression and segregation. These radicals, and even many liberals, came to identify the working class as the central force in changing social conditions in the region. At the same time, the success of Hitler fascism clarified the need for a broad alliance of centrists and leftists against the threat of right-wing forces. Fascism's progress during this period demonstrated how quickly master race doctrines of white supremacy led to the destruction of human rights and democratic government, a lesson not difficult to grasp in Mississippi, eastern Arkansas, or Memphis. Antifascism and antiracism became increasingly popular themes as the objectives of leftists, labor organizers, civil rights advocates, and New Dealers began to merge. During the "popular front" era of the middle and late thirties, leftists and Communists attained the height of their influence within the New Deal coalition. The influences of this period proved crucial to the success of the CIO.[1]

As Hosea Hudson's narrative and the writings of Robin Kelley have documented in Birmingham, it was the Communist party's unprecedented activity in support of black self-determination and labor rights that established much of the groundwork for an ongoing civil rights and labor alliance in the South. Communist party activists organized councils of the unemployed, demonstrations for relief, and unions. The party's International Labor Defense launched the Scottsboro Boys campaign, the most massive defense against southern lynch laws ever seen. Party propaganda directly challenged white supremacy, even declaring support for the dreaded "social equality" by stating that "whom a worker shall marry is up to the man and woman involved and no one else." From Gastonia, North Carolina, to Harlan County, Kentucky, Communist labor organizers had also risked their lives in bloody organizing battles that AFL unions refused to touch. Although state and vigilante repression crushed many of their efforts during the first half of the decade, Communist party activities nonetheless helped awaken the nation to the plight of workers and African Americans in the South.[2]

The Socialist party had a very weak base in the South and often looked reformist at best in contrast to the Communists. Nonetheless, some of the Socialist party's southern radicals such as Howard Kester, H. L. Mitchell, John Handcox, Myles Horton, and others played important organizing roles and often condemned capitalism and racism as militantly as any Communist. At the same time, Communists all over the world turned from earlier go-it-alone tactics to building left-center coalitions. In the South they began to organize with their former "class enemies" in the Socialist party at the All-Southern Conference for Civil and Trade Union Rights in May 1935. An assortment of southern radicals cooperated at Highlander Folk School, which aimed to establish common ground among working people and promoted the idea that organized workers could solve their own problems. The nonhierarchical labor school, founded by Myles Horton and Don West in 1932 outside of Chattanooga, became a major educational center for southern labor organizers. Although closely linked to the Socialist party, Highlander provided a space for the free exchange of ideas on the left. Similarly, for a time radicals of various persuasions cooperated in organizing the Southern Tenant Farmers' Union.[3]

The Southern Conference for Human Welfare, established in Birmingham in 1938, provided perhaps the most important regional expression of the popular front. The Southern Conference brought together labor leaders, leftists, Eleanor Roosevelt, and, for a short time, a number of lead-

ing politicians and media figures. These people sought to transform southern economic, social, and political life by unseating reactionary elected
officials, supporting union organizing and industrialization, and improving race relations. The CIO and the Southern Conference developed cooperation and mutual support that would last until the cold war years.
The more leftist Southern Negro Youth Congress, a Communist-led civil
rights group located in Birmingham, also began to make important regional efforts. As these and other groups with broadly related interests and
objectives emerged, industrial unions and the left in the South seemed to
have a promising future. Although the Socialist party went into decline
after opposing Roosevelt's reelection in 1936, the Communist party grew in
influence and strengthened its alliances with the Democratic party and the
CIO. Although still red-baited everywhere in the region (including within
the Southern Conference), the Communist party partially emerged from its
underground status in the late thirties, calling not for revolution but for a
"people's front" to open up the South to democracy. Its goals then roughly
coincided with that of the Southern Conference, civil rights groups, and,
most important, the CIO.[4]

Although all the radical, liberal, and grass-roots movements of the
period provided an important basis for change, the growth of the CIO,
nationally and in the South, provided the essential moving force in the
popular front politics of the era. All those who wanted change realized that
without the organization of the industrial working class, economically and
as voters, major social reforms could not move ahead, particularly in the
South. At the same time, the CIO needed the New Deal and popular front
to flourish. Successful industrial organizing, history had shown repeatedly,
required sympathy from the middle class and the government. Equally important, industrial unionism needed the support of black workers, who
by the thirties made up a critical percentage of the industrial working
class in numerous industries. In the South, unions simply could not succeed in mining, steel, and in a variety of agriculturally related industries
without African-American participation. The development of black civil
rights organizations, like the development of unions, played an important
role in the development of the popular front. In short, none of the popular
forces for change in this period could survive alone, a fact that lent particular urgency and power to the appeal for a broad-based, interracial, and
interclass popular alliance.[5]

In this context, it became possible and even necessary for the CIO
to take a strong stand against union-sponsored racism. It took increas-

ing pains to appeal directly to black workers and to civil rights groups for support. At its official founding convention in 1938, the CIO unanimously resolved "uncompromising opposition to any form of discrimination, whether political or economic, based on race, color, creed or nationality." Denouncing race prejudice as an employer weapon to "create false contests between Negro and white workers," the CIO in contrast to the AFL made it incumbent on member unions to organize whites and blacks into the same locals on a nondiscriminatory basis. CIO leaders rarely spoke about racism as such, but they understood the necessity to fight it on a practical level, endorsing antilynching legislation and calling for abolition of the poll tax. John L. Lewis and others realized that past failures to incorporate blacks into industrial unions in the meat-packing, steel, and coal-mining industries, to name but a few examples, had allowed employers to manipulate racial conflict and destroy strikes and organizing drives time after time. In an effort to avoid such strategic mistakes, a number of CIO unions hired black organizers and incorporated Communists and left-led civil rights groups such as the Southern Negro Youth Congress, the National Negro Congress, as well as the NAACP, into their organizing. Communist-led packinghouse, maritime, and other unions helped to establish a strong reputation of CIO egalitarianism, while the support of blacks and mainstream civil rights organizations such as the NAACP proved critical to CIO successes in the Steel Workers' Organizing Committee campaign, in the battles to organize Ford Motor, and elsewhere.[6]

The left-center coalition within the CIO, joined as it was to egalitarian racial principles and a broad movement for progressive government, produced a distinctly different and more promising vehicle for southern industrial unionism than that offered by the AFL. Communists, black workers, and civil rights groups within and outside the CIO often made the difference between success and failure in union organizing and helped to generate a new vision of labor solidarity in the South. By the end of the decade, for the first time in a long time, a number of southern whites willingly defied the racial taboos of the Jim Crow system. The popular front emphasis on the struggle for democratic rights also put pressure on the national Democratic coalition to part ways with southern Democrats such as Crump, who tried to crush the very reform forces the New Deal had encouraged. And while some in the Democratic party moved to the right, many southern workers moved to the left. The interracial organizing that occurred during the 1939 riverfront strike perhaps would not have succeeded in the early thirties, when the city had crushed all manifestations of interracialism and radicalism. But new possibilities existed by the end of the decade. Radicalism in Memphis emerged later than in other large cities, but it finally did emerge, and mainly from the ranks of the working class.

THE GROWTH OF A WORKING-CLASS LEFT

Red Davis, nicknamed for the color of his hair, not his politics, personified a new type of working-class radical in the South. With six children in his family and his father recently dead, he left the tenth grade in 1938 to make a living on the Mississippi River. He worked fourteen to sixteen hours a day, seven days a week, shoveling coal on his uncle's riverboat, making just enough money to get by and send a few dollars to his widowed mother.[7] He aspired to be a riverboat pilot, but when the CIO's National Maritime Union (NMU) began organizing the riverboat workers his interests turned to the union movement. In 1939 he joined the union and began his life-long career as a rank-and-file organizer of southern workers. The strike of inland boat workers and black dockworkers in the spring of that year proved to be a turning point in his life, bringing him into closer contact with black workers and convincing Davis of the necessity for black and white labor unity. As Davis walked the picket lines and huddled around fires with blacks, sharing in the common hardships of a bitter strike, he developed enormous respect for the leadership of people like Thomas Watkins and an appreciation for the ability of black rank and filers to survive in the most difficult situations.[8]

That a poor white from a Mississippi River town deep in the Delta cotton country should not only join interracial union activity but become a lifelong radical indicates the important changes taking place in a period when radical and union activity blossomed simultaneously. In the aftermath of the river strike, a core of working-class leaders developed who would set the tone and direction of the Memphis CIO in its formative years. As the result of the strike Davis met Communist riverboat organizers such as Bob Himmaugh (whose daughter he later married) from New Orleans, Sam Despaux from Louisville, and Frank Bruno and Pat Matthews, local men from the Fort Pickering neighborhood. In later years Davis also became acquainted with Blackie Myers and other top Communist leaders of the NMU. Davis did not himself join the Communist party until after World War II. Raised as a southern Baptist, he did not approve of the sexual freedom espoused (and practiced) by some of the Communists he met. However, he did begin to read everything he could get his hands on, including Aristotle, Plato, Tom Paine—and Karl Marx. Based on his associations with Communist union stalwarts, his reading, and his experience,

Davis began to form a new view of the world in which, as he later explained it, "class struggle" provided the moving force in history. Tied to this understanding of class struggle came a deepening awareness of the role of racism in holding back working-class movements.[9]

The NMU's position against racial discrimination contributed to Davis's increasing awareness. The union, like many in the CIO, included an antidiscrimination clause in its constitution. Unlike most CIO unions, the NMU elected a black leader, Ferdinand Smith, as vice-president. Under his leadership, the union undertook a concerted campaign to break down discrimination against blacks on ocean-going vessels, on at least one occasion expelled a member accused of stirring up racial prejudice, and instituted the rotary hiring hall partly as a means of providing black workers equal access to available jobs. On the inland waterways, the NMU opposed the poll tax, lynch law, and other aspects of segregation, even while racial segregation on the job remained the rule on the Mississippi River.[10]

Davis's experiences in the Memphis CIO following the 1939 strike gave him additional perspective on the race question. During various stints organizing rubber workers, steelworkers, and woodworkers in 1939 and 1940, Davis developed an abiding respect for the leadership abilities of black workers. "During this time a process of thinking was developing among black workers, producing a strong black working-class leadership," he later observed. "Industrialization was changing the whole situation, producing a new type of black leader in the industrial centers, men such as Hosea Hudson in Birmingham." Davis came to know blacks as some of the most solid union members and as some of the most dedicated party members as well. Other influences in the CIO also expanded Davis's view of the world. In 1939 he and workers from the Memphis J. R. Watkins plant, which he helped to organize, gained contact with movements from around the South while attending Highlander Folk School. The experience helped dispel feelings of regional isolation and inhibitions against taking a leadership role. "Highlander played a key role in helping working-class leadership to develop," Davis later recounted, "teaching workers how to make leaflets, organize and chair union meetings, and speak in public." As the result of his experiences at Highlander and his contact with black and white union militants, Davis was on fire with enthusiasm for the CIO. At age eighteen, Davis felt like he was "organizing twenty-four hours a day."[11]

These new experiences forced Davis through some profound and wrenching changes. He explained: "I was an average, white southern kid. . . . I lived as a small kid with black neighbors. We played together and fought together. As I grew older and moved into a white neighborhood, I picked up the prejudice that white kids pick up. Going to school, of course, it was all white schools and black schools; they were segregated. I didn't learn better until I got into the CIO." The changes in Davis's attitude when he became a union activist opened up serious differences with white neighbors and family members. Davis recalled that unionists met frequently in black churches, the only places besides the NMU hall that would allow interracial gatherings. It seemed logical to Davis to ask his own Baptist pastor to let him hold a union meeting in church, but the minister would not allow blacks to meet there. Although he'd been baptized, Davis recalled, "I told him I wasn't a member any longer, and I haven't been to church since then." Due to the hostile attitude of most of the white church leaders toward the labor movement, Davis, his brother Morton, and his sister Mildred all ended their Baptist affiliation, and all three of them eventually became Communists while others in his family remained Baptists. To some extent, this split the family along religious and political lines, "a product of the times," according to Davis.[12]

By the end of the thirties, a milieu existed within the southern CIO that allowed white workers to function within a more radical political world than would have seemed possible earlier. The progressive changes in government enacted by the New Deal made it possible to hope for a better future, while at the same time the CIO and grass-roots movements also made it possible to think about race in a new way. Davis was not the only one affected by the changes taking place. Frank Bruno was one of the first Communists Davis met. From the poor white section of Fort Pickering, Bruno served as NMU port agent and ran the NMU's dilapidated union hall on Illinois Street, providing the CIO with a modest but visible presence. Muscular white riverboat workers, used to long hours and heavy physical labor, also could be called on at a moment's notice when they were in port as shock troops for picket lines and leafleting. Such rank and filers built not only the NMU but other CIO unions, including unions of black workers. Communist NMU members such as "lying Bob" Himmaugh and Sam Despaux traveled up and down the river bringing contact with the outside world and materials from NMU educational director Leo Huberman. Leftist organizers brought bags of books, pamphlets, and newspapers on board the boats, conducted political discussions about labor history and the need for labor solidarity, and even reviewed Marxist classics with workers. Particularly after World War II, when the NMU established undisputed control over hiring procedures and work practices on unionized river lines, employers could do little to interfere with such practices by "red" unionists.[13]

Still, only a few river workers adopted socialist beliefs or became strong supporters of black civil rights. According to Larry McGurty, who later married Davis's sister Mildred and worked on the river himself, the politics of most river workers did not extend beyond the struggle for union rights. Even Bruno, a member of the Communist party, lacked an understanding of the fundamentals of Marxist theory, McGurty believed. Davis later concluded that the ideological level of the Communist party prior to World War II "was very low," particularly in terms of race relations. Not surprisingly, left-wing activists found themselves frustrated by the vested interests white riverboat workers had in job segregation by race. NMU activists such as Davis and his brother Morton were well versed in trade unionism and class struggle philosophy. But although both of them developed strong commitments to racial equality and often engaged in shoreside organizing with blacks, they could not get whites to oppose segregation on the riverboats; indeed, bringing this up with white workers during the depression did not even seem like a possibility.[14] Although NMU members provided much of the backbone for the early CIO movement, the NMU itself did not provide a vehicle for organizing blacks.

However, at the same time that NMU activists built an almost entirely white organization, leftist members of the United Cannery, Agricultural, Packing, and Allied Workers of America (UCAPAWA) built a mostly black union membership in the cotton warehouses and compressing and seed oil plants in Memphis. UCAPAWA would play a key role as one of the early left CIO unions in Memphis, establishing a base among black workers and developing a core of organizers who would help spread the CIO to other industries. It started its Memphis office with donations made by a fundraising committee in Philadelphia (just the sort of "foreign interference" the Crump machine railed against) that contributed fifty dollars a month to the mid-South district. The small Communist party organization in Memphis and a district organization in the state provided additional help by bringing in outside "free-lance" organizers, such as Ed McCrea of Nashville. Despite their limited resources, UCAPAWA organizers dared to do what others had failed to do: organize blacks in the sweatshops of some of the city's most plantation-minded manufacturers and begin interracial organizing.[15]

An interesting combination of people provided the keys to unlocking the Crump antiunion stronghold in the cotton industry. Among them was Harry Koger, UCAPAWA's first local organizer, who came to Memphis from Illinois, where he had taught school, gone to business college, and spent twelve years as a YMCA secretary. His earlier career included fighting in World War I, working as a sailor on the Great Lakes, selling life insurance, running a tin-mining business in Mexico, and working on a daily newspaper in Texas. There he became involved in a local strike of UCAPAWA shrimp workers, most of them black. He saw one man killed during the strike and then joined in organizing black sharecroppers and tenants in East Texas. Koger came to Memphis as a UCAPAWA organizer and worked closely with the charismatic leftist minister Claude Williams and his People's Institute of Applied Religion. Koger, like Williams, believed the principles of Christianity supported class struggle, equal rights, and socialism. Deeply committed to the struggles of black and poor white workers, at age forty-seven Koger became UCAPAWA's first paid representative in Memphis at between fifty and seventy-five dollars a month.[16] Koger became part of a network of organizers, some of whom belonged to the Communist party and others of whom did not. These people had the common aim of empowering the working class, and their base centered in the Fort Pickering neighborhood. Industries in this mostly white working-class area produced jobs for both black and white. Koger lived in this neighborhood, in a house next door to the Inland Boatmen's hall at the foot of Illinois Street, about a block away from the former residence of Tom Watkins. According to Red Davis, "It was a poor working-class neighborhood, and they were all strong union people. There was a strong bond of solidarity between the longshoremen and the NMU. So this was really the base of the organization effort in Memphis; it was the only safe haven." The few bars, churches, and stores in the area supplemented the Boatmen's hall and the houses of workers as gathering places and sources of community information. In the black neighborhood near Hernandez and Beale streets, a few minutes' drive from Fort Pickering, dockworkers met regularly in a black church, while the whites tended to congregate at Coon Hill Tavern near the water. Black dockworkers, cotton warehouse and compresses workers, young white women in the J. R. Watkins plant, and white riverboat workers all conducted organizing drives in and around Fort Pickering. Community, neighborhood, and family ties helped to produce both a vibrant CIO movement and a small branch of the Communist party. Said Red Davis, "The strong bond between black and white workers was the basis for CIO organization and unionization at the first stage. CIO organizing started in Fort Pickering and spread from there."[17]

However, although the Communist party in Tennessee in this period grew to an organization of three to four hundred members, according to Ed McCrea, the Memphis party unit developed later than most and remained a small underground organization. McCrea, state party organizer in the late thirties, recalled that in Memphis for security reasons "only one or two people would know who was actually in the party, outside of the little groups they would be in; they wouldn't know who else was in the party." Despite its small size the Communist party in Memphis played a pioneering role in developing working-class leaders and mobilizing union campaigns. The early Memphis CIO, McCrea commented, wasn't produced by "the kind of spontaneous leadership you could sometimes get when people just got mad and took action, and then somebody develops as a leader . . . it was not spontaneous combustion, with all these natural leaders spewing forth, you know." In McCrea's opinion, the most class-conscious activists of the NMU and UCAPAWA, who extended their organizing into a variety of industries, laid the groundwork for CIO success in Memphis. Even their strongest opponents admitted that leftists played an important early role in the Memphis CIO. Indeed, the fate of both the NMU and UCAPAWA remained symbiotically tied to the development of a working-class left within the CIO.[18]

The significance of leftist activity among workers was not in numbers but in its role in developing a nucleus of black and white labor activists. As Robin Kelley found in Birmingham, the party in particular served as an educational vehicle for workers, especially African Americans who had been denied adequate formal schooling. Literate party activists taught non-literate workers, some of them white as well as black, to read and write; educational sessions in party meetings familiarized workers with organizing techniques and union strategies; and party activists taught labor history and sometimes African-American history. Black UCAPAWA leader Henderson Davis, as one example of this schooling in the left, had almost no education and learned most of what he knew about unions as well as how to read and write in the local Communist party. He eventually became chair of the Memphis Communist party. John Mack Dyson, later UCAPAWA local president and the key to UCAPAWA success, similarly "learned the ropes" of trade unionism in the party. Dyson, according to Davis, provided one example of a "natural leader," his great sense of humor and gentle manner repeatedly disarming hostile whites and winning over nervous blacks to the CIO. "There are people that have the confidence of their fellow workers, and these are the people you have to seek out," said Davis. "Mack Dyson took the chance of getting fired and had the ability to talk to his fellow workers, and they believed in him." The party offered such individuals literature and an alternative news media revealing what was going on in the world but was not printed in the local press, comradeship and support from both white and black workers, discussion of the class struggle and local union organizing, and literacy skills that should have been gained in primary school. With the party's aid, Dyson became a skilled union leader. Although at first he could barely write a leaflet, over the years Dyson became an effective public speaker, union leader, and contract negotiator. "Once you find the natural leader in a shop, the rest will follow and you'll have the place organized," Davis reflected. When party members could find no such leader as Dyson in a given shop, Communists "colonized" it by sending in an outside organizer, as they did when they established a CIO local at Wabash Screen Door company in 1940. By such methods, Communist party members in Memphis helped to establish an early core of CIO leaders.[19]

Not surprisingly, in this early period working-class activists found the immediate goals and tasks of the Communist party to be almost indistinguishable from those of the CIO, and it remained very difficult for many to know the difference between trade union and Communist activity. Workers joined the Communist party not so much out of ideological conviction but because it offered them an active organizational vehicle at a time when few others existed. According to McCrea, "People were so ready to join the CIO that they would really flock into whatever seemed to be effective at the time." A lot of party members, Davis also recalled, joined to advance specific struggles, but "never understood or studied the broader issues." In part because of such realities, anticommunists later held that the Communists had no legitimate roots in the working class, that it manipulated unsuspecting poor and working-class people in order to "infiltrate" or "subvert" the unions. Similarly, in this view, the Communist party only "used" African Americans to further its ulterior purposes.[20]

These assertions ignore the fact that people joined the Communist party of their own free will, used it to the extent that it served their purposes, and left when they felt it necessary. Those who joined, unless they were police agents, did so because the party had something to offer. In a period when AFL unions remained essentially conservative and the CIO unions remained weak, the party attracted workers because it provided the most class-conscious organization around. Moreover, the disciplined activity and growth of the Communist party built the labor movement, serving the very purpose desired by rank-and-file workers. According to McCrea, a number of important CIO leaders in Tennessee, including Matt Lynch, who helped lead the Tennessee CIO and later the AFL-CIO, gained their early experience through contact with, if not membership in, the Communist party during this period. McCrea himself came to Tennessee via New York, where he joined the Communist party, and before that from rural Maryland, where the banks foreclosed on his boyhood home during the depression. Although he did not come from an industrial labor background, he, like many others, identified his self-interest and that of the country with the working-class movement and with the Communist party. He felt that party activities and education helped many people develop skills and class consciousness that greatly benefited them as individuals and the southern CIO.[21]

The lack of written material, the faulty nature of human memory, and the efforts of the authorities to label nearly everyone working for the CIO as a Communist often makes it difficult to assess with certainty the role that Communists played in the southern CIO. Party members in most situations refused to deny or admit membership, a tactic used to avoid purges from AFL unions in the twenties and early thirties. These tactics remained necessary if people wanted to keep their jobs. In any case, many of the most active organizers during the popular front era paid little attention to whether a person actually was or was not a member of the Communist party; people worked together around goals that they could all agree upon and did not debate the finer ideological questions. On a practical level, whether Communists played a role in a given situation or not, employers and the police could be counted on to claim that they did, using the label of communism to fragment worker's movements and alienate middle-class support. "Everyone who didn't agree with the status quo back then was called a 'red,'" McCrea recalled. After the 1938 formation of the Dies Committee on Un-American Activities in the House of Representatives (later known as HUAC), Congressional investigators, FBI agents, employers, the news media, and AFL unionists alike red-baited CIO organizing drives indiscriminately. Since opponents of the CIO rarely troubled themselves with political distinctions between the various rank-and-file labor militants, it made little sense for the workers to trouble themselves on that score either.[22]

The charge of "common-ism," as southern anticommunists often called it, had a special relation to the question of race. According to Morton Davis, an early organizer for various CIO unions, "communism equaled nigger lover to most people in the South." Southern journalist Wilbur Cash related a similar equation that applied throughout the South: "labor unions + strikes = communists + atheism + social equality with the Negro." FBI agents following Harry Koger around made this equation clear: his statements to black workers claiming they were as good as whites, the agents wrote to their superiors, provided proof positive that he was a Communist. Merely organizing on an interracial basis usually proved sufficient to qualify someone as a "commonist" in the minds of authorities.

According to Myles Horton of Highlander, red-baiting proved more effective in intimidating liberals than in scaring off workers; UAW leader Walter Reuther, who once called red-baiting "the bosses game," also thought the real target of red-baiting was the middle class. Since authorities used the charge over and over again against unionists, any dedicated organizer had to become to some extent oblivious to the charge.[23] In any case, trying to identify southern leftists by party affiliation proved misleading at best. HUAC spent millions pinning labels on individuals, but many working-class activists formed political views by participation in labor struggles rather than by debating questions of doctrine. "It was hard to tell who was a Communist and who was not," party organizer McCrea later recalled, "because everybody was so damned mad about the conditions." The Left in the depression-era South embraced a wide range of people with anticapitalist and antiracist sentiments, only some of whom joined an organized left party.[24]

The equation of unionism with social equality and communism certainly scared off some white workers, but it often had the opposite of its intended effect on black workers. According to Memphis CIO activist Dan Powell, blacks recognized red-baiting and race-baiting as two sides of the same coin, and such attacks on the CIO only strengthened their interest in the organization. At a 1940 national convention of UCAPAWA, black leader Owen Whitfield explained this reaction. He described an incident in which a plainclothes police officer came around to a UCAPAWA meeting in Missouri asking whether anyone had been there speaking about overthrowing the government. Whitfield related how a white police officer told black unionists, " 'If they come around, let me know, because there is a bunch of damn reds around here fooling you niggers.' " According to Whitfield, "Everybody sat quietly, and we had a boy everybody called 'Big Boy.' He said 'Listen, you white folks, what is them things you are talking about? We don't know anything about the Russians and reds you are talking about, but we do know the southern whites. We want to make this plain. We learned one thing—we learned to love the things you white folks hate.' " According to Whitfield, blacks had stopped paying attention to red-baiting because it seemed that "everybody who wants a home or a loaf of bread is a red or backed by reds."[25]

Observers had particular difficulty in politically classifying black workers, who drew on religious traditions, folklore, and common sense for their analysis, while often participating in left-wing unions that seemed to have dangerous radical goals. An NAACP observer traveling through Tennessee in September 1937 wrote to Thurgood Marshall about a meeting of hundreds of blacks gathered on Beale Street as if he were observing a scene from the Russian Revolution. Colorful banners with slogans such as "to the disinherited belongs the future," mass singing, and an emphasis on inter-racial organizing marked the occasion as a significant departure from what most whites thought of as the traditions of the South. These black workers, already members of a Socialist-led union, the Southern Tenant Farmers' Union (STFU), were joining a Communist-led union, UCAPAWA, as part of a labor federation, the CIO, denounced in Memphis as subversive of all that was holy. STFU leader H. L. Mitchell later recalled the spirit of the times. "We thought, and our people thought that the CIO was going to sweep the whole country . . . they were going to bring about a complete change in the lives of everybody and make things better." Whether these workers in the main knew "communism from rheumatism," as the say-ing went, or cared about the doctrinal debates between the Socialist and Communist parties, they surely understood that they were embarking on a radical undertaking.[26]

The popular front effort to bring together doctrinal leftists and unionists of all stripes had its share of failures, however. The merger of the STFU and UCAPAWA, for example, lasted only briefly. Conflicts over high CIO dues rates, the STFU's lack of autonomy within UCAPAWA, agricultural versus urban industrial organizing, black demands for greater leadership in the STFU, and jurisdictional, ideological, and leadership disputes all soured the relationship between the two unions. And although farm worker orga-nizers, from the Imperial Valley of California to the Black Belt of Alabama and the Delta of Arkansas, all suffered tremendous repression, this pres-sure sometimes splintered their ranks rather than drew them together. In March 1939, the STFU disaffiliated from UCAPAWA and the CIO, never to return. Both unions found the problems and expenses in organizing the southern rural sector overwhelming, and neither of them recaptured the rural base the STFU had at its high point of success. The STFU in-creasingly shifted its work to the West Coast, while UCAPAWA shifted its work to urban areas. As the Socialist party went into decline, especially in the South, the Communist party was on the upswing and increasingly dominated the staff positions in UCAPAWA.[27]

UCAPAWA, even without the presence of the STFU, represented the CIO's best efforts to organize racially and ethnically oppressed workers. Chicano and poor white cannery and farm workers in California and Texas, Indian and white cannery workers in Alaska, Polish and other ethnic white workers in soup canneries in Chicago and New Jersey, black and poor white tobacco and peanut workers in the Carolinas and Virginia, and black cotton compressing and seed oil processing workers in the Deep South all belonged to UCAPAWA. This diverse lot had much in common: they worked in some of the lowest-paying industries in the United States and belonged to left out, despised ethnic groups, and many of them, in some industries at least, were women. Unlike most CIO unions, UCAPAWA's newspaper, its conventions, and the composition of its leadership increasingly reflected the presence of these "minorities," who made up the majority of the union's membership. Radicals played a key role in the union from its inception, and UCAPAWA at its founding and subsequent conventions passed numerous resolutions against racial discrimination, lynching, and the poll tax and emphasized the importance of organizing the South. Praised by John L. Lewis as a representative of the "forgotten man," the union during the forties developed a strong educational and shop steward program and organizational base among some of the most disinherited workers in the United States.[28]

Nowhere did the importance of this experiment in multiracial unionism become more evident than in the South. By the end of the decade UCAPAWA locals aided voting rights drives and the community struggles of African-American and Chicano workers and produced especially strong black leadership in the Carolinas and in Memphis. Cottonseed oil and compress companies employed few women in Memphis, but in the Carolinas UCAPAWA produced strong female as well as black leaders. UCAPAWA locals would be among the fastest-growing in the southern CIO, and in Memphis UCAPAWA produced the only CIO local headed by a black president. However, in the late thirties organizing progress came slowly, requiring the union to first establish a core of local leaders versed in trade union procedure and organizing strategies. Employers and others in authority would not bargain directly with African Americans, making the union's commitment to a strong shop steward system and black leadership at the top of the union especially difficult to pursue. Wages paid to workers in the cottonseed oil and products industry and in cotton storage and compress companies also remained far below the wages paid to many other manufacturing workers. In all respects, UCAPAWA workers in Memphis and across the South had further to go and faced more obstacles than workers in most other industries.[29]

At a September 1939 meeting in Memphis, the union brought together a handful of leaders from Oklahoma, Arkansas, Texas, and West Tennessee, and in December it established the Southern Cotton States Council, which claimed one hundred locals in six states. The union elected Harry Koger as president of the council and chief organizer in the region, and he opened a Memphis office in July 1940. In some of the rural areas of District Four the union began a program to establish buying clubs and cooperatives, halt evictions, improve federal agricultural policies, and improve wages for rural workers and organized around community issues such as better schools and black voting rights.[30] In Memphis, the focus was on union organizing. UCAPAWA's two-week leadership training school in August 1940, held at the Inland Boatmen's hall, involved some sixty members under the direction of Claude Williams and Koger. At this school, Williams preached a broad conception of the union movement as an instrument for social change. Besides addressing the mechanics of collective bargaining procedure, the school concentrated heavily on labor history, politics, and the fusion of class struggle and religion that characterized Williams's ministry in the South. Myles Horton of Highlander, UCAPAWA International president Donald Henderson, and the religious radical Jack McMichael, president of the American Youth Congress, all spoke at the school, providing a mix of trade unionism and social radicalism. Rural workers, whose powerful religious culture and songs raised the meetings to a high emotional pitch, intermingled with urban factory workers in discussions of how to organize both sectors. While these meetings affirmed Williams's belief in the radical potential of the workers' movement, the *Commercial Appeal* saw only Williams's "red connections" and described the black workers as gullible and ignorant.[31]

The Memphis school stressed the problems of rural workers, but its most visible result was to produce a core of black leaders for the sudden expansion of the industrial union movement in Memphis. In the two months following the school, in September and October 1940, the union won three NLRB elections and organized a number of locals among cotton workers and in a variety of other low-wage industries. As the result of the NLRB elections, UCAPAWA established its first solid base in Memphis. At the grain company of L. P. Cook and Sons the union established a model contract for its future organizing, providing a five-cent-an-hour pay raise and including preferential hiring for union members, a seniority system, and three years' leave of absence in case of military service. UCAPAWA also established locals at a Pillsbury Flour plant, Indiana Flour company, Dixie Pickery, and DeSoto Oil company. Membership ranged from a unit as small as five workers at Indiana Flour to some forty workers at Dixie Pickery. UCAPAWA also established a local of the Steelworkers' union at Wheeling Steel, whose president, Sylvester Skipper, had helped organize the earliest UCAPAWA locals at Bosworth bag company and at Federal Compress.[32]

Although these locals remained extremely small, according to the union newspaper total UCAPAWA membership across the mid-South soon reached over one thousand in sixteen different plants. In Memphis, and probably throughout the region, blacks provided almost all of the elected leaders. These included outside organizer William DeBerry, first president of Local 19, covering the oil mills and cotton warehouses, and Roosevelt Brown, president of Local 4, covering flour mills, parts of Federal Compress, and the Cook grain company. Mary Huffman, vice-chair of the Dixie Pickery local, became UCAPAWA's first elected female officer, and other black women served as treasurers and financial officers for Locals 19 and 4. Black officers also led the workers at DeSoto oil mill, Cook, Humphrey's Oil, and Riverside Compress. While blacks in UCAPAWA served as officers and handled the finances, however, only one served on union negotiating committees; most employers would not bargain directly with black workers, while whites typically had better education and better access to the courts. Although a few whites continued to play critical roles, the fact that blacks constituted the main leadership of the union made it unusual in the southern CIO, where white officers often dominated even when African Americans made up most of the work force.[33]

UCAPAWA growth among low-wage black factory workers in cotton-processing industries had a domino effect, spurring the formation of unions among blacks within other low-wage industries. A handful of white Communist party organizers played a key role in this development. Based on Koger's success with UCAPAWA, the International Woodworkers of America (IWA), a union with a left-wing leadership based in the Pacific Northwest, hired him as a full-time organizer. He remained president of the Southern States Cotton Council and continued to work as a volunteer organizer for UCAPAWA, while the NMU's Bob Himmaugh went on full-time staff for UCAPAWA, engineering most of the successful election campaigns in the fall. Himmaugh's landlord kicked him out of his Ft. Pickering apartment, but such harassment did nothing to stop the increasingly successful organizing by NMU, UCAPAWA, and IWA activists. Morton Davis of the NMU, for a time a Communist party member, later helped organize in Memphis, Mississippi, and Helena, Arkansas. By no means all early organizers belonged to the Communist party, however. William R. Henderson of the NMU, decidedly anticommunist, played a key role for the CIO in Memphis and Helena. Despite ideological differences, by working collectively organizers built these and other CIO unions without the jurisdictional disputes that had plagued the old craft unions of the AFL (these would later plague the CIO as well), and established the basis for the CIO's woodworkers', steelworkers', and furniture workers' unions in Memphis.[34]

At the December 1940 UCAPAWA convention in Chicago, union officials showcased Locals 4 and 19 in Memphis as examples of the union's rapid expansion in the Deep South as well as in the rest of the country. As the result of this kind of growth, UCAPAWA had shifted decisively toward organizing industrial and urban locals. This shift undercut farm worker organization, but urban workers provided a more solid dues base and cost much less to organize, for the city work force was not so spread out as in the countryside. Urban UCAPAWA locals, in other cities as well as Memphis, also provided a ready base for CIO expansion into other industries. Seeing the potential for success at last among workers in agriculturally related industries, UCAPAWA at its 1940 convention centralized its financial structure in order to provide more funds for campaigns in the urban industrial centers. To strengthen its base in Memphis, the union likewise eventually consolidated food Local 4 and cotton Local 19 into one UCAPAWA Local 19, headed by John Mack Dyson. Communist organizers and black workers continued to build the UCAPAWA local into a sturdy organization that, along with the NMU, became a stronghold for labor's left within the Memphis CIO.[35]

Surprisingly, the Crump machine paid relatively little attention to leftist organizing among black workers in cotton processing and other small-scale industries. "The comparative lack of interference with the organization of these smaller plants," the CIO's civil liberties investigator Lucy Randolph Mason explained, resulted from an agreement the AFL made with the Crump machine "to lay off of organizing any large plants." In return, Crump allowed craft unions a free hand in the smaller shops and ignored the CIO in these shops as well. But while the AFL organized only a handful of white skilled workers and overseers, or more often did nothing, UCAPAWA and the IWA aggressively organized among the blacks who predominated in the woodworking, furniture, chemical, fertilizer, food, and cotton-processing industries. To be sure, Memphis remained "a hot and dangerous spot for CIO unions," Mason observed. CIO organizers scheduled meetings in one place but held them in another, usually under the cover of night, to avoid spies and police. The dilapidated Inland Boatmen's hall, packed with crowds of black workers in their overalls, still provided the only place other than black funeral homes and churches that allowed them to meet. But despite the violent anti-CIO climate in Memphis, leftists avoided the frontal attacks the Crump machine had visited on Norman

Smith in 1937. Quietly, the CIO began to build a solid base of organization among poor blacks and a not insignificant element of poor whites.[36]

In the North, CIO organizers in the major auto and steel plants had organized massive industrial memberships virtually overnight based on a few dramatic incidents that turned the tide of popular opinion against employers. Many of these actions, especially in auto plants, resulted from years of previous shop organizing, often by Communists and other radicals. Yet some saw the northern CIO model as one in which organizers approached industrial workers like fruit ripe for the picking, going after the largest industries first. This seems to have been Norman Smith's approach at the Ford plant in Memphis, for example. Such a strategy rarely worked in the South. Smith's organizing among predominantly white industrial workers at Ford had been easily smashed. Workers at Ford made some of the highest industrial wages in Memphis, and blacks played a marginal role in the shop. Except for a courageous few, whites at Ford either remained passive or turned against the UAW efforts, making it relatively easy for vigilantes and the police to run Smith out of town.[37]

At the end of the decade, a different model of organizing developed in Memphis. The 1939 river strike had opened the door to industrial organizing by activating a significant core of black and white workers; these efforts produced a CIO union hall and obtained a degree of federal protection. The process of activating workers went another step with the establishment of UCAPAWA. Led by a core group of leftist organizers, the CIO made rapid headway among black cotton-processing workers and woodworkers. Black urban workers, like the black agricultural workers of STFU, had a cohesive culture and sense of collective aspiration that made them far more receptive to unions than most whites. Communists more than others understood and sympathized with the oppression of the black working class and saw the organization of blacks and whites into common unions as the key to changing the segregationist South. It is therefore not surprising that unobtrusive organizing by leftists and blacks provided the earliest core of CIO support in Memphis. In later years, some in the Memphis CIO would claim that Communists "infiltrated" the unions. The truth was, they built the unions from the ground up.

THE BLACK FREEDOM MOVEMENT AND THE CIO

Memphis organizers would find over and over again that the strongest CIO support resided not among white workers in mass-production industries such as Ford and Firestone, but among the poorest echelons of the black working class. This became clear even to outside observers such as Lucy Randolph Mason. In the fall of 1940, she reported to Eleanor Roosevelt on the great change occurring in Memphis. "I have not seen anywhere more spontaneous activity on the part of workers, with the large number of Negroes especially interested and desperately needing organization," she wrote. As these black workers established the early base for the Memphis CIO, they also began to break the bonds of Jim Crow.[38]

Union organizing meetings at times revealed a fervor among southern African Americans comparable to that seen during the black freedom movement of the fifties and sixties. The quest for black freedom in both eras drew on a strong base within the black church, on African-American music and culture, and on a long tradition of resistance to oppression that went back to the days of slavery. This tradition and culture, long used in daily life as well as life-and-death struggles, now became a potent force in the struggle for unionization. Mason noticed that while whites usually organized the CIO meetings, blacks dominated their spirit and content. In a book about her experiences in the South, she later recalled:

> Those meetings were deeply religious. A colored member would pray and lead in singing and dismiss the gathering with a blessing. In one group there was an elderly Negro who 'lined out' the Lord's prayer verse by verse while others repeated the words after him. They were praying for more of the Kingdom of God on earth. Sometimes they would ask the white organizer to lead in prayer, and the white man always responded. Sometimes I was the one who prayed and I was always so moved by the spirit of the Negroes that it was hard to steady my voice. I think I never heard people pray more sincerely than did those humble union folk.

Workers in these meetings used variations on the Lord's Prayer as an invocation for unionism, conveying "a wit and aptness of expression" that fascinated Mason.[39]

Black speakers at union meetings often articulated their sense of determination and unity in religious terms, but these meetings demonstrated more than the well-known piety of the African-American community. Religious revivalism shored up the determination needed to get organized in spite of the threat of layoffs or police and company violence. Black workers shook the union hall with songs and speeches celebrating not just their faith in God but their newfound power of organization. As Mason reported it, one speaker enunciated the mixture of religion and unionism quite clearly. "We must have self-confidence in God. Self-confidence is self-help," he stated. "We must put our arms around each other and lift each other up. Let us cling together and rise together. Living is God's gift to us. We got to use it right. This union is part of our living and we got to stick by it." On other occasions blacks spoke in more secular terms, but with the same emphasis on solidarity and collective action. One man declared that "the company stooge who tells the boss who is a member of this union is taking pork chops off your wife's and children's plates. He is stealing their food. We got to stick together to help us and our families." [40]

Black workers recognized in the CIO a mechanism for getting organized at the workplace that could not only improve their economic conditions but defend their dignity in a society dominated by the demeaning system of segregation. Once organized, the sense of determination and even defiance inspired among the workers in their union meetings transferred to the workplace and began to change the nature of relations between white bosses and black workers. Employers who might normally treat blacks with contempt, or at best with paternalism, suddenly had to respond to them as workers with the power to hinder or shut down production, and this sometimes forced employers to change their attitudes and their practices. Mason wrote of an elderly and dignified black man who reported "at length on the wonders of the CIO," stating, "This CIO is a great thing—it makes wonderful things happen. After he heard about our union, our boss called some of us in his office—that never happened before. He made us sit down in the big chairs in his office, and he asked us what we wanted, and what would satisfy us. We told him we would have to talk to the committee before we could say what we wanted. He had never asked what we wanted till we had a union." The union steward in the same shop added, "The bosses asked us what we wanted so they could keep us from organizing, but they were too late, we had already organized." [41]

Black workers, with a union behind them, could sometimes drop the obsequious behavior demanded of them by whites, in defiance of southern racial conventions. Mason noted the words of a black union president, who related a conversation with his boss: He "asked me what was this he heard about our going to organize a union. He said he knew I would tell him the truth about it. And I said 'We *have* organized.' He looked surprised and asked what we want. I told him we would let him know what we want after we had thought about it and made our plans." In an unusual gesture, the boss then "asked me which way was I going and did I want to get taken home, and I said 'no,' I was not going home yet." Another black union officer related that his boss came by his workplace and said, " 'Are you feeling good?' and I said 'yes.' Then he said 'How did you like that three cents an hour raise I gave you last week?' I said, 'The committee will talk to you about that.'" Such curt assertiveness by blacks, without organization, would have been likely cause for firing or worse. With organization, taking a clearly defined position relative to employers became reasonable behavior, part of a bargaining relationship.[42]

Black articulation and organization within the CIO awakened Mason and many others to the extraordinary power of black unionism and the radical change it might potentially bring to social and class relations across the South. Assertiveness and spirit among black workers provided an essential element needed for building the CIO, and even white racial conservatives within the union movement had to accept it. Robert Tillman, raised in the old school of white paternalism, nonetheless recognized that blacks "were a hundred times more faithful" to unionism than whites. Communists and leftists thought the struggle for black union rights would ultimately serve to challenge the entire segregation system. Ed McCrea, who lived in Nashville but came to Memphis to work in various CIO campaigns, found black workers especially receptive to appeals that went beyond the question of improved wages and working conditions. In a speech to black cotton compress workers at the the NMU hall in 1939, he recalled, "All I talked about was what it meant to get organized, the only way workers could ever get a decent living or any kind of freedom." According to McCrea, "You didn't have any trouble explaining this to blacks, with the kinds of oppression and conditions they had. It was a question of freedom." As if to emphasize that point, police broke up the meeting and reportedly beat up a number of workers; McCrea barely escaped unharmed. Still, the fact that a white person would speak in favor of black freedom, according to McCrea, visibly strengthened the commitment of blacks to the CIO.[43]

The power and inspiration of the intensely religious culture of the African-American community, evoked regularly at union meetings, could be overwhelming and gave rise to a number of musical expressions that in many ways defined the spirit of the union movement in the South. In 1936, black STFU organizer John Handcox had transformed the black gospel tune "Roll the Chariot On" into "Roll the Union On," a song that became an anthem for southern unionism, much as had white Appalachian Florence Reece's "Which Side Are You On?" Similarly, at the Memphis school in August 1940 black sharecropper Hattie Walls transformed the traditional hymn "Gospel Train" into a union song. She replaced the song's religious lyrics with "it's that union train a coming," and as she lined out

traditional verses such as "there is no second class on this train, no difference in the fare, get on board, get on board," other workers substituted
"CIO, CIO" for the last phrase. These workers, Claude Williams thought,
transformed spirituals that "seemed to be saying [something] about heaven
and God" into songs "saying something about earth and man"—a practice
that fell into the historical tradition in which slaves had used spirituals
to speak of freedom, but in words that the master class would not suspect. Only now, during the CIO era, the words were more direct. Pete
Seeger, Woody Guthrie, and the Almanac Singers popularized the Memphis school's "Union Train" in front of CIO audiences all over the country.
The insertion of union lyrics into religious songs gave a powerful double
meaning to the proceedings in the labor school and other union meetings,
one which equated industrial unionism with the historic black freedom
struggle.[44]

The decisive role of black workers in organizing drives suggested that an
alliance of industrial unionism and black civil rights could be a powerful
vehicle for change. It also increasingly forced white workers to reconsider
their relationship to blacks. Industrial unionism in places such as Memphis
could not succeed without incorporating blacks into the mainstream of the
labor movement, and at least some white workers came to understand this
reality. "It was a question of self-interest on the part of whites," Red Davis
recalled. "I saw that and other white workers saw it too." Davis realized,
for example, that white riverboat workers would have never succeeded in
organizing the riverfront without gaining the cooperation and support of
black workers on the docks. For the first time, whites in many industries
could not ignore the fact that they needed the support of black workers. It
also became increasingly clear that industrial workers had more power and
were less likely to become divided when organized into common unions,
rather than into the segregated units of the old craft unions. By the late
thirties, a new stage in the development of the southern labor movement
seemed to have been set.[45]

The importance of black support for the CIO became apparent not only
in Memphis but in other southern industrial centers where blacks made up
a sizeable portion of the working class. In a 1939 survey of worker attitudes
in Birmingham, Horace Cayton and George Mitchell confirmed the patterns evident in Memphis: African Americans provided the most reliable
support for industrial unionism. Referring to the difficulty in getting industrial workers organized, one white unionist told the authors that "if we
could get the co-operation of the white people like we can that of the Negro
we would have the whole thing whipped." Another Birmingham white

unionists observed that blacks "had shown unsuspected power in talking about union affairs" and formed the backbone of CIO locals in mining and steel industries. In the face of these realities, Cayton and Mitchell found that in Birmingham white workers had begun to moderate some of their racial attitudes in order to achieve some level of cooperation with blacks. When confronted with the need for interracial organization, many white workers accepted it with surprisingly little hesitation. Once organized into racially mixed unions, existing hostilities—based on past racial exclusion by white unions and strikebreaking by blacks—declined. Once organized, for example, white and black miners began riding together into the mines instead of riding separately, as was the previous practice. "White men relieved of the fear of Negro competition, and aware that the absence of the threat depends upon reasonable treatment of the Negroes in their unions, have a double reason for a more kindly attitude toward Negroes," Cayton and Mitchell observed.[46]

However, if success depended on the CIO's ability to bring whites and blacks together, white supremacist beliefs and the physical limitations imposed by the segregation system clearly limited the extent and nature of this cooperation. Interracial union situations forced whites to at least partially change their conduct, but it did not require that they totally reverse their attitudes. Cayton and Mitchell found that in Birmingham many white workers supported the "mixed unions" of the CIO because they felt they allowed them to exercise more control over blacks than if blacks established separate unions. Furthermore, they expected blacks to act with deference and formality toward whites. Whites typically addressed blacks by their first names, while blacks had to be careful to call a white "brother," or better still, "mister," and on strike duty it remained unacceptable for a black to stop a white scab from crossing the picket line. Such temerity by a black "who behaves above himself," as whites expressed it, could lead quickly to violence. Black deference and white paternalism remained essential elements of the CIO scene in Birmingham. Red Davis similarly observed that whites in Memphis during the late thirties became more willing to organize a union with blacks, but few changed their deep-seated feelings of racial superiority. Among whites, he believed, it was primarily those who joined the Communist party who experienced a deep change in attitude. For white workers generally, changes in racial attitudes were "a self-interested attitude change, a white worker realizing that he couldn't have strength in the union without the black workers in the same union. But that was as far as it would go." In other words, as one southern historian noted, race relations in most CIO unions remained decidedly paternalistic.[47]

Cayton and Mitchell observed other developments in Birmingham that had strong parallels in Memphis. In unions where blacks remained a minority, they received few opportunities to conduct themselves without bowing to the pattern of racial deference required by Jim Crow. One black worker summed up the situation to Cayton and Mitchell, explaining that "where Negroes are in a majority they are given advantages in expressing their ideas; in those where they are in a minority, 'they are Jim-crowed mightily.'" Only in unions where blacks predominated overwhelmingly did they control their own affairs. In these situations, blacks kept union records, carried on correspondence, served on shop committees, represented the interests of the workers before employers, and held high union offices, carrying out their responsibilities in a forceful manner. In contrast to Birmingham, Memphis industry remained smaller and much less organized at the end of the decade, but similar racial dynamics applied. Blacks overwhelmingly dominated the small CIO base that existed in the woodworking, cotton-processing, and related industries, and in these industries Communist organizers and black leaders could afford to take a relatively forthright position in favor of black rights. On the other hand, in Firestone and other shops where white workers constituted a clear majority, blacks could expect few gestures of solidarity from white workers.[48]

Across the South blacks had little choice but to adhere outwardly to southern racial etiquette and accept a secondary status within most unions, with the hope of improving their conditions later. Red Davis observed that "their first objective was to get organized; after that, they wanted to start working on the discrimination." Cayton and Mitchell likewise observed that "apparently the Negro has both immediate and long term objectives; the immediate ones [are] usually a rise in pay, and the remedying of minor shop grievances. Remotely he [*sic*] hopes for the softening of the now rigid line between white work and Negro work, promotion by ability and not by color." The CIO as a vehicle for black freedom had decided limitations. Yet under the horrendous conditions imposed by segregation, according to George Holloway, blacks regarded any step in the direction of freedom as clearly "the first step" in the right direction. Hence, few southern blacks debated the tactics of racial pragmatism in the initial stages of CIO organization. The biggest problem for black workers, in Memphis and other southern centers, remained that of gaining union rights in the bitterly antiunion shops of both local and national companies.[49]

THE DECLINE OF THE POPULAR FRONT

Neither unionists nor Communists in Memphis had a prayer of influencing American foreign policy. Yet, just as the popular front era developed in part out of struggles going on overseas, events overseas also led to its decline. For many in the national CIO, the turning point came in September 1939, when the Communist party switched from a strong internationalist antifascist position to condemning the conflicts in Europe as "inter-imperialist rivalries." Party leaders supported without qualification the German-Soviet "nonaggression" pact, which in fact allowed aggression by both countries against neighboring states and took to calling those who disagreed "social fascists." The party's isolationism actually placed it closer to the position taken by John L. Lewis and most Americans prior to the bombing of Pearl Harbor, and its lack of real power within the CIO hierarchy hardly placed it in a position to challenge those at the top of the federation. Nonetheless, its sudden pacifism put it in an antagonistic position to President Roosevelt and to some of his most influential supporters in the CIO, who increasingly feared the Communist presence would ruin the CIO's coalition with the Democrats, and hence its effectiveness on the domestic political front.[50]

The events happening in Europe seemed far removed from local concerns in Memphis, but what happened in the CIO conventions had a vital bearing on the future of local industrial unions. Delegates to the 1940 CIO national convention, Communists included, took the first step toward dividing the CIO along ideological lines, voting to condemn "foreign ideologies" of all sorts and equating fascism with communism. In this vote and a vote over national leadership in the convention of the UAW, the party's leaders sacrificed principles and power in order to maintain CIO unity, but these sacrifices did not stop the anticommunist drift within the labor movement. When John L. Lewis stepped down as head of the CIO and Philip Murray took his place in 1940, only the need to keep the CIO intact against the competing forces of the AFL kept CIO leaders from purging the Communists altogether. The party reverted to supporting Roosevelt's position of war preparation as a result of the German invasion of the Soviet Union in June 1941, but these switches in policy left "a legacy of antagonism toward them that persisted in the CIO," according to the historian Robert Zieger. Questions of ideology and power began to divide the CIO more intensely than in its first few years, destroying much of the fragile unity existing at the local level.[51]

As the united front within the CIO disintegrated, anticommunist purges or bans against Communist office holding provided liberals and conservatives with an opportunity to increase their power at the expense of the left. In Tennessee, the state CIO Industrial Union Council in late 1940 took the path of the national CIO by lumping Communists, fascists, Industrial Workers of the World, and Ku Klux Klan members together and banned them all from serving as officers or representatives to the state CIO council. Although Communists helped to build the CIO while fascists and Klan members tried to tear it down, the CIO had circumscribed them both as enemies of the labor movement. These developments provided a catalyst for conservative members of the Memphis American Newspaper Guild chapter to seize power in their national union. The conservative journalists in Memphis had twice rejected joining the guild, partly due to its leftist leadership; once in the guild, Memphis leaders Harry Martin, William A. "Red" Copeland, and Malcom Adams put together an anticommunist faction that split the 1938 national guild convention. When the guild held its next annual convention in Memphis in July 1940, Martin, representing himself as the candidate of the "solid South," led the removal of guild officials considered by some to be Communists, even holding a "trial" of the former vice-president of the guild on charges of "communism." Ironically, Boss Crump withdrew the city's previous invitation to the guild to hold its convention in Memphis, claiming that the organization, as a member of the CIO, was Communist. Despite Crump's disinvitation, the guild proceeded with its July convention, and, according to Memphis journalist Paul Coppock, removed "every reddish official" from the guild national leadership. At the end of the convention, Martin emerged as national president of the guild, with Memphis copy editor William A. Copeland serving on the executive committee.[52]

The purge within the guild and the CIO's shift to the right enhanced the reputation of Memphis news guild leaders in the national CIO and put them in a position to take over formal leadership of the emerging Memphis CIO. Guild leaders, representing an all-white and white-collar membership, could barely relate to the CIO's new organizing base. Copeland at the 1940 convention praised the segregationist Trades and Labor Council as "one of the best American Federation of Labor unions in the country"; William R. Henderson, an NMU member allied with Copeland, told guild delegates a racist joke about "one of the worst old darkies in the country" who was always stealing chickens, giving them a chance to laugh about the supposed ignorance of southern blacks. Despite obvious signs that leftist whites and black workers in the new Memphis CIO would have little in common with such leaders, CIO director of organization William S. Haywood would soon appoint both Copeland and Henderson as full-time CIO organizers in Memphis. Ironically, the FBI investigated Copeland when he got this position to see if he was a "communist." Only the wartime truce against Communists prevented him from purging leftists from the Memphis CIO.[53]

*   *   *

CIO politics in the forties would become wrapped up in left-right divisions, which in the South revolved in large measure around the question of how far and how fast to move on the racial question. Although blacks and a number of leftists made up the organizing and membership base of the early CIO, conservative, white anticommunists would be put in charge of it. Conservatism at the top hardly stopped leftist organizing. In fact, for some time to come a de facto popular front involving left, right, and center forces would continue among organizers in the Memphis CIO. But no consensus existed on the role of blacks or Communists in the unions, nor was there a unified vision of the future. Leftists continued to seek the transformation of all aspects of the southern way of life, including an end to segregation, while rightists sought better wages, working conditions, and the continuance of segregation. Statements made by some white CIO leaders in the South that industrial unionism in no way threatened segregation did not represent a passing or unusual belief.[54]

Looking back to this period, Ed McCrea concluded that "the biggest problem in the South, the biggest impediment to actually organizing the workers, was the ideological struggles and the split in the labor movement." According to McCrea, "There was only a period of time for the first two or three years in the CIO that there was any kind of unity at all. Soon after the initial successes, after the basic industries like rubber, steel and so forth were organized . . . the struggle started for the control of the international unions." This struggle would ultimately have momentous consequences for blacks and civil rights advocates within the CIO.[55]

CHAPTER SIX

Black Scares and Red Scares

Harry Bridges, the alien CIO leader, practically wrecked San Francisco and other Pacific Coast towns. Neither he, John L. Lewis nor Earl Browder will wreck Memphis. . . . Labor has always been dealt with fairly, but the type that proposes to deal with our industrial situation like it has in Akron and Detroit (sit-down strikes) will not be tolerated in Memphis.

—E. H. Crump

They will not be allowed to conduct themselves in Memphis as if they lived in Chicago, Pittsburgh or Philadelphia. We have never had it before and we will never have it. For after all this is a white man's country.

—Joe Boyle,
Memphis Police Commissioner

If the Federal Government doesn't do something about the reign of terror in Memphis, they might as well haul down the American flag over the city hall and replace it with the Nazi Swastika. Hitler would never have to invade Memphis; all he would have to do would be to issue it a charter of affiliation.

—Henry McCallister,
Workers' Defense League, September 1940

As Europe plunged into World War II, new possibilities for industrial unionism and civil rights advances emerged in the United States. Federal military spending increased the demand for labor, providing a favorable climate for hundreds of strikes for union recognition and higher wages that finally defeated the efforts of numerous industrial giants to keep the unions out. Industrial expansion and CIO growth raised expectations among African Americans, as evidenced by the massive black support for A. Phillip Randolph's threatened march on Washington in early 1941 for jobs and equal rights.[1] But growing union and civil rights mobilization in the prewar era also stimulated a frenzy of anti-unionism and anticommunism. Union opponents everywhere condemned strikes in armaments-related industries as the work of "fifth columnists," equating fascism with communism and communism with labor and civil rights activism. In 1941 the *Atlanta Constitution* called strikers "American Mussolinis" who would "deliver this country . . . into the hands of Nazidom," and it claimed that union leaders had "hidden, ulterior motives" on behalf of foreign powers. Tennessee and other southern states considered new sabotage and sedition acts, and laws curtailing unions passed the legislatures of sixteen states in the South and Southwest; similar measures appeared in Congress. Lucy Randolph Mason characterized the campaign for these laws as a "skillful admixture of patriotic sentiments and invitation to institute labor baiting and witch hunts." [2]

The national government, thought to be a friend of labor and a supporter of civil liberties, fanned the flames of suspicion as it sought to deport West Coast union leader Harry Bridges as a communist, prosecuted Trotskyites, and sent in troops to stop CIO strikes in defense industries. Federal witch-hunting made its way into the bucolic Memphis environs by way of Texas member of Congress Martin Dies of HUAC, who circulated a "red list" of southern CIO activists such as Owen Whitfield of UCAPAWA. The Military Intelligence Division of the army also investigated union activists "alleged to possess Communist tendencies," including Thomas Watkins, William R. Henderson, and Frank Bruno from Memphis, and established a list of people subject to military detention, including Robert Himmaugh and other labor organizers. The FBI for its part placed a mail cover on Harry Koger, and probably others, recording the names and addresses of all his correspondents. [3]

Such federal actions only encouraged the growing paranoia among the South's elite and much of its middle class concerning interracial unionism and demands for black civil rights. In the South anti-unionism coincided with what Harry Koger called a "growing wave of race hatred, which is being fanned by some of our more conservative preachers." In Texas race-baiting and anti-unionism led to a revival of the Ku Klux Klan, and in the Carolinas, Klan activists helped terrorize CIO textile organizers. In Georgia, Lucy Randolph Mason wrote, the Klan, politicians, and the news media used popular fear of U.S. involvement in the war to cultivate "a hysterical campaign of super-patriotism." In Alabama, authorities launched a "little red scare" against all leftists and civil rights workers. [4] In Memphis and other parts of the South, rumors spread that black domestic workers had formed "Eleanor Roosevelt Clubs," to register blacks, who in fact had already been voting in NLRB-sponsored union elections. Efforts to repeal the poll tax in Tennessee and other states also threatened to change the status quo via the ballot box. [5] Many whites reacted viciously to threats of black voting: when a group of black west Tennesseans tried to register in Brownsville during the summer of 1940, whites beat, stabbed, and drowned El Williams and ran NAACP supporters out of the area.[6]

The shift to the right, a preview of the red scare that would take place after World War II, had a palpable effect in Memphis. Whereas the repressive Crump regime had looked increasingly out of step with national politics during the popular front, in 1940 Crump and other southern Democrats could identify their opposition to unions and civil rights with a rising national tide of anticommunism and patriotism. The Memphis media, Lucy Randolph Mason reported in September 1940, practically ceased any favorable coverage of issues important to the CIO, while a new paper appeared that devoted "a large portion of its columns to the fifth column activities of the CIO and the need for eradicating this cancer from Memphis and the U.S." The police, in cooperation with the FBI and federal military officials, responded to the new climate with the arrest of UCAPAWA's Robert Himmaugh and his wife on suspicion of being German agents and the arrest of Roy Pierson and other CIO unionists at Wabash Screen Door as "fifth columnists."[7]

Appeals to the rhetoric of national security and anticommunism made it easier for the Crump machine to crack down on an increasingly restless African-American community as well as on the CIO. In reality, the existing organizational base for black civil rights remained extremely weak. The NAACP and Urban League, as researcher Ralph Bunche discovered, still reflected the interests of small business people and preachers. These people, as in many southern cities, were in no position to mount an effective challenge to the existing regime; many of them were tied to the Crump machine's spoils system and had no interest in doing so. Even so, black Republican leader George Lee saw a big change coming. He predicted that the rise of industrial unions would promote the "growth of class consciousness among the Southern white masses" and thereby "remove the necessity of demanding rights on the basis of race and color and . . . place our struggle on the plane of class interest."[8] Many city leaders feared just such an alliance, while the white middle class feared the growing black urban population, which in 1940 reached its highest point since 1900. As African Americans continued to flood into the city from rural areas, reaching more than 40 percent of the city's total population, black radio personality Nat D. Williams dubbed Memphis "the Harlem of the South"—an image not reassuring to most whites.[9]

The southern upper classes, Ralph Bunche predicted, would do everything in their power to prevent class alliances between blacks and whites. In the case of Memphis that power, concentrated in the hands of the Crump machine, was considerable. Crump illustrated the strength of his one-man rule in the 1940 election, when he forced Mayor Watkins Overton, who belatedly declared he would no longer give the "Nazi salute" to Crump, from office. Crump ran for mayor himself. He had his lone opponent, a local clerk who felt someone should stand up to Crump, fired from his job and run out of the city. Crump recalled member of Congress Walter Chandler from Washington, and after being sworn in as mayor, turned the job over to Chandler on the same day. Crump then had Clifford Davis, who Crump apparently felt had become too popular in Memphis, appointed to Chandler's old job until the next election. These electoral shenanigans proved that Crump could do virtually anything he wanted in Memphis and still get rubber-stamp approval by the voters.[10]

Crump's consolidation of political power produced increasingly repressive treatment of the black community. Following the state's 1939 repeal of Prohibition, the machine attempted to shore up Crump's image with the white middle class by shakedowns and closings of black businesses, legal and illegal. Whites took over some of these businesses, and black ward heelers and saloonkeepers on Beale Street, once an important source of kickbacks and poll tax money, became expendable. For instance, when Luther Miller and John Henry Webb, two black men, set up a restaurant and beer hall, the police arrested them, wrecked one of their homes, and drove them out of Memphis. Their lucrative trade, by prearrangement with the police, went to a white owner of numerous cafes, reportedly the biggest bootlegger in town and a ward boss for the Crump machine. As profits and poll taxes on Beale Street and in black wards came under almost complete control by the Crump machine, its arrogance toward the African-American community and its leaders grew.[11]

Just as Crump relied on the police and the "brown screws" in the machine to control the black community, he relied on the police and the AFL to the control the working-class movement. The AFL, not only in Memphis but across the country, provided a pliable instrument. In its efforts to compete with the CIO, the AFL red-baited it before the Dies Committee and even went so far as to support employer-backed amendments to weaken the Wagner Act, which it thought favored industrial unions. At the AFL's Southern Labor Conference in March 1940, President William Green appealed to business leaders to support the AFL's belief in "union-management cooperation," its avoidance of sit-down strikes, its support for "the institution of private property," and its lack of interference with southern "local autonomy"—i.e., segregation. Such appeals to employers, stressing the AFL's "southern" character and its cooperation in keeping "communism" out of the workplace, made by AFL southern director George Googe and local leaders such as Lev Loring, became a staple of AFL organizing. On occasion the AFL even collaborated with the Klan to defeat the CIO. Memphis political leaders appreciated this attitude and clearly viewed the AFL as a conservative bulwark against the CIO. Particularly as the CIO began to make headway among blacks, the AFL with its long history of white supremacy became a desirable alternative for many employers as well.[12]

The reason for this confidence in the AFL remained clearly evident in the furniture industry, one of the few places where an AFL union attempted to organize both black and white industrial workers. At Memphis Furniture, where blacks constituted the great majority of production workers, they remained frozen out of all but laboring positions. White male machinists, with a few black male helpers, and white female upholsterers, with a few black female helpers, controlled all the higher-paying skilled jobs. The AFL proposed to do nothing to change this, but even so some whites opposed the AFL Upholsterers' Union out of fear that "unionization of the common laborers would give the vote control to negroes." The company, however, once faced with potential threats from CIO organizers, quickly saw the necessity of accepting the AFL. In early 1941 the upholsterers' local succeeded in organizing all but forty of the seven hundred workers; arguing that "60% of the employees were Negroes, who were susceptible to CIO propaganda," it asked for a closed shop to keep the CIO out. Instead, management won the right to fire any worker or group of workers that failed to "maintain harmony."[13]

The agreement, praised by Lev Loring and company attorney Phil Canale, served as a kind of white covenant to keep the biracial CIO out. The U.S. Bedding company gave similar protections to the AFL in a "preferential shop" agreement, while at Gates Lumber Company employers even granted the AFL a union shop. The AFL won these protections with little activity, in industries that normally fought to the death against even a hint of the union shop. Employers could safely assume that AFL unions would be under more or less unquestioned white control. Furthermore, white-run AFL unions in black-dominated workplaces were notorious for ignoring the needs of most of the unskilled laborers. In the mass-production industries, Lucy Randolph Mason believed, the AFL's main purpose was to block the entrance of the CIO, not to improve conditions for the majority of the workers. Her analysis of the role of the AFL would be clearly borne out at the Firestone plant, where a CIO union mounted one of the most daring assaults against the Crump citadel in the prewar period.[14]

FIRESTONE: NORTHERN MANAGEMENT, SOUTHERN SEGREGATION

For a number of reasons, in the fall of 1940 the Firestone plant became the most important single target for CIO organizers in Memphis. To establish its legality in the city and its legitimacy among the workers, the CIO needed to organize a major industrial plant with a biracial work force. UCAPAWA had proven the possibility of organizing blacks in local industries; white as well as black workers had proven their willingness to organize and to strike in numerous instances since the passage of the Wagner Act; and biracial unionism seemed increasingly possible, even within some AFL unions. But it would take more than the organization of workers in small and weakly capitalized local shops to make Memphis a union town. CIO supporters hoped that, as had happened in the North, if they could win over the workers in one big industrial plant, those in smaller industries might begin to organize. They also thought a northern-based industry might be easier to deal with than locally owned enterprises. The Firestone Tire and Rubber Company, employing nearly three thousand workers in Memphis by 1940, about two-thirds of them white, obviously fit the bill.

The CIO as an international federation had its own reasons to make Firestone a high priority. The campaign to organize the American rubber industry constituted a major battlefront for the CIO. Since the late nineteenth century, various unions, including the Knights of Labor, the Industrial Workers of the World, and AFL affiliates, had attempted to organize the rubber industry, without success. The sit-down strikes of tens of thousands of workers at the four major rubber companies, including Firestone, headquartered in Akron, Ohio, in 1936 and 1937 broke open the rubber industry and at the same time started the CIO on the road to national success. By 1938, the CIO union had organized all of the rubber plants in Akron except Goodyear. But in the South, the Goodyear management crushed union organizing at its plant in Gadsden, Alabama, by firing union activists, installing an espionage system, and hiring thugs to beat up CIO leaders; city officials aided them with a law outlawing black-white meetings. Hoping to take advantage of such a climate, Goodyear, Firestone, and other companies transferred work to the nonunion South during the 1937 recession, setting up runaway plants that could undermine the unions in Akron. United Rubber Workers organizers hoped they would not have to relive the terrible Gadsden experiences in Memphis, however, for Firestone had been among the first of the Akron industries to accept the CIO in its plants. In any case, by 1940 the Memphis plant had become the largest nonunion rubber factory in the country and a key player in the "decentral-ization" strategy. Northern unionists had little choice but to take it on if they wanted to maintain a strong base in the industry. But keeping the Fire-stone plant nonunion also remained key to the Crump machine's efforts to keep the CIO out of Memphis. Hence, the fate of workers in this plant and the fortunes of the local CIO became indissolubly linked.[15]

Despite its image of relative moderation in Akron, Firestone proved to be nearly as hostile to unionism in Memphis as Goodyear had been in Gadsden—and as willing as any southern company to exploit racial divi-sions. Forrest Dickenson, who later helped organize the factory, recalled that the Firestone management "liked to sponsor big events and so forth for the workers, but you talk about being liberal with respect to work, no soap. Firestone was never liberal in labor relations, in Akron or anywhere else." Nor was it liberal in race relations. Its "A, B, C" classifications of separate wages for black and white, with blacks getting the lowest wage, along with its rigid segregation of work and plant facilities, proved as impervious to change as that of any southern company, and as divisive. The company hired workers for jobs according to their race, confining blacks to depart-ments in which they did the dirtiest, hottest, heaviest labor at the lowest wages. Only whites could work as mechanics, machinists, tire builders, or in other higher-paying positions in the plant, while blacks hauled, lifted, and cut the rubber or did skilled work, classified as "helpers" to whites, all at minimum wages. No matter their work, blacks got the worst wages. In the forties, for example, when the company changed work on the Banbury machines (hot churns that mixed pigment and rubber) from white to black, it also lowered the wage scale. Though the Banbury job remained one of the most difficult in the plant, the black workers running the machines continued to receive some of the lowest wages in the factory.[16]

The segregation system within the factory reinforced racist attitudes among white workers, intimidated blacks, and established barriers to friendly interaction between the two groups. Blacks could be fired for drinking out of a "white" fountain, using a "white" bathroom, going through the "white" turnstile, or using the "white" parking lot, which was paved, instead of the "black" lot, which was not. According to Matthew Davis, few white workers would fraternize with blacks or even talk to them on the shop floor. Hillie Pride, another black Firestone worker, remem-bered how the racial system placed white production workers in a position similar to that of a supervisor. "The whites had all the supervision over you. You had to do what the white people told you. . . . You'd work next to a white man doing the same job, but you didn't make what he made, oh no." [17] White workers believed they gained something by subordinating blacks, and in many ways they did. But as the organizer Dickenson pointed out, segregation also ensured powerlessness and low wages for black and white alike. Hence, while Memphis Firestone workers ultimately made a top wage of $.70 cents an hour before World War II, in Akron unionized workers made $1.40 an hour—even though, according to organizers, they produced less than the workers in Memphis.[18]

The rural background of the overwhelming majority of Firestone workers made it especially difficult to overcome racial divisions and to unionize. Because of the heavy nature of work in tire production, Firestone looked for the strongest, largest workers it could find, black or white. The farm laborers from the rural areas and small towns of Tennessee, Arkansas, Mississippi, and Missouri who fit this need seemed unlikely to join unions. Matthew Davis, hired off the street because of his strength (he weighed 220 pounds), came originally from rural Mississippi. He had completed a high school education but knew nothing about unions. Similarly, George Clark, a white from rural southeastern Missouri who went to work at Firestone in 1938 as soon as he finished high school, had no knowledge of unions. According to Clark, "Back in the early days of the CIO, people didn't know the first thing about unions. The skilled men knew no more than anybody else. There were no leaders in the plant." Hiring large numbers of blacks would not necessarily aid unionization either, Clark thought, since "no one knew what the response of blacks toward unions would be in the early days." Both Clark, who later became president of the union at Firestone, and Davis became CIO stalwarts, but only after hard experiences in the work force.[19]

The composition of the Firestone labor force, according to Clark, raised difficult racial barriers. For one thing, because of the workers' unfamiliarity with unions, "it was easy for the foremen to pass around the idea that the CIO was a black man's union." But even those who knew about unions had no inclination to support biracial organization. Richard Routon, a white worker from the small town of Paris, Tennessee, unlike Davis and Clark, knew family members belonging to AFL craft and railroad unions. This provided him with more union contact than most rural workers, but it still offered him no model for industrial organization. These unions had been built on racial and craft exclusion, a fact encouraging Routon's initial negative attitude toward what company supervisors referred to as "the Communist nigger-loving CIO." Like many of the whites applying for work at Firestone in the late thirties, Routon was newly married, jobless, racially prejudiced, and hungry for work. He got his job by standing in line with four hundred others in the dark hours of the morning. It is not surprising that, once hired, he initially would have nothing to do with the biracial unionism of the CIO, even though he too also later became president of the CIO Rubber Workers local. For Routon and thousands of others like him, it was simply unheard of to meet with blacks on any basis other than that of superior and subordinate.[20]

Lack of union knowledge, white racial prejudice, and job hunger often made recent migrants to the city a tractable labor force, and the Firestone management took full advantage of this fact. Although northerners from Akron, such as Cliff Reynolds and Raymond Firestone, set the labor policies, they hired local people as supervisors and superintendents, and these people instituted a dictatorial reign of coercion in the factory. Like the workers, supervisors had little or no experience with unions or other organizations advocating worker's rights and brooked no opposition. They drove the workers to their limits, carrying out company policies that did not allow employees to leave their machines until lunch time, when they got a mere fifteen minutes to eat. During three eight-hour rotations, workers changed shifts without ever turning off the machines. They had no paid vacations or paid holidays, and they were not allowed to talk on the job. Supervisors fired people for the slightest infraction of the rules, and workers could not even go to the bathroom unless a supervisor agreed to take over their position on the line. Some supervisors, such as Joe Woodall, a former prizefighter who had lost all the fingers on one of his hands, used their newfound power to act out their own personality disorders, harassing and intimidating workers and sometimes becoming sadistic.[21]

Workers, especially blacks, found conditions under this regime to be nearly unbearable. Black workers regularly pushed skids weighing as much as 5 tons and handled rubber blocks weighing up to 250 pounds. Matthew Davis recalled working on the "wash line," hanging rubber up to dry with water dripping all over him in the midst of winter, cold air blasting him from the doors opened to the receiving dock; with so much noise, he could not hear the supervisor speak. Due to such conditions, men like Davis ended up with arthritis and impaired hearing. Those who worked with lampblack spent years trying to get the tire pigment out of their pores, and many developed cancer. According to black worker Edward Harrel, "Even with light-skinned blacks you couldn't tell who or what they were after they got that lampblack all over them." Hillie Pride recalled, "We didn't have no union, no help, no nothing. You had to do what they said or you were out the door. . . . You were just like mules and hogs." According to Davis, "A lot of people worked only a couple days and then left; the work was so bad, they couldn't stand it." Of those who stayed, neither white nor black workers felt the management paid any attention to their needs as human beings. "We were chained to the machine, with no rights to speak of," Routon recalled.[22]

Although the racial conditions in the plant militated against unionization, the hardships of work caused many Firestone workers to consider the advantages of joining a union. Although workers appreciated having stable jobs and initially considered themselves privileged to receive higher wages than existed in most industries, after several years of exhausting labor many began to wonder about their future. H. B. Griffin, a young white worker hired at Firestone in 1937 who later held a series of elected offices for the CIO union (including president of the local), recalled, "I knew I couldn't work like this forever. No breaks, fifteen-minute lunches, efficiency experts always watching." As he and others like him began to think about unionization, the CIO's United Rubber Workers began putting out feelers in the plant during the summer of 1940. Although many whites reacted negatively to the CIO's interracial policies, the organization had a far better record of organizing industrial workers than did the AFL unions. "The main thing that finally sold me on the CIO," Griffin recalled, "was when the company put a sign on the bulletin board saying anyone with five years' seniority would get a one week paid vacation. They did this as part of their campaign to keep the CIO out. I thought, if they would do this just to keep the CIO out, what would we get if we had a union?"[23]

Noel Bedgood, nicknamed "Chink" because of his slanting eyes, became one of the early local supporters of the CIO at Firestone after his personal experiences there convinced him of the necessity to fight back against management. Bedgood quit school in 1928, held a number of jobs until Firestone hired him in 1937. He worked his way up from unskilled labor to seventy-five cents an hour as a machine operator. Once he learned this job well, however, the company made him operate three machines at once. When he protested this overwork and also pointed out that workers doing his job in Akron made twice the pay, the company demoted him to a sixty-cent-an-hour job. Worse, he was forced to teach his old job to a new employee who began bossing him around, making Bedgood do some of the tasks the new hire should have done himself. When he finally had an altercation with the man, who he considered a "company stooge," Firestone fired him. This treatment at the hands of the supposedly paternalistic Firestone management turned Bedgood toward the labor movement. He had no job to lose. While looking for work, Bedgood met an attorney named Charlie Wylie, who put him in touch with United Rubber Workers' organizer George Bass. The three of them began organizing Firestone in August 1940.[24]

THE BATTLE FOR ORGANIZATION

George Bass in some ways seemed like the perfect person to organize the Memphis Firestone plant. A native of Winchester, Tennessee, he moved to Akron in the twenties as did thousands of southerners leaving the depressed rural areas looking for work in the industrial North. His seventeen-year stay in Akron culminated in the dramatic sit-down strikes and street confrontations of the thirties under the banner of the CIO. In 1940, he volunteered to take a one-year leave of absence from Local 5 (he later became its president) to go South to unionize the southern rubber companies. He came to Memphis at age thirty-seven, a self-assured union veteran and not easily intimidated by company thugs or police. If he had a flaw, it was his weight of over two hundred pounds. Out of shape and unarmed, he provided a juicy target for anti-union thugs.[25]

Within two weeks of his arrival, Bass had signed up some eight hundred of the over two thousand Firestone employees eligible to join the union, apparently unbeknownst to Firestone's labor superintendent Cliff Reynolds. How he did this in an anti-union town like Memphis tells much about the role of race in the union struggle. Blacks constituted the great majority of those initially signing union cards, and for good reason. George Holloway, schooled in the ways of trade unionism by his Pullman porter father and a student for two years at the famous Tuskegee Institute, became a leader of the organizing drive. His influence quickly moved the black workers toward the CIO, but he could only take this stand because Bass made it clear that the CIO opposed the conditions of discrimination that relegated them to the worst jobs in the plant. "George Bass came in and began to talk about some of these things, that we should have these opportunities too," Holloway recalled, and that made all the difference to the black workers. Opponents of the union used this fact throughout the ensuing months to turn the white workers against what they called the "nigger unionism" of the CIO. According to Holloway, "Whites were afraid they'd lose privilege and seniority. If they opened departments to us, they were afraid they would get bumped" from their positions. Some later criticized Bass for taking an openly egalitarian position on race, but without the initial base among the blacks, there probably would have been no organizing drive at all.[26]

Bass went public with the organizing campaign on 23 August, informing the acting police chief, Carroll Seabrook, of his activities and of a union meeting planned for two days later. This call on the police inaugurated a nightmarish series of violent attacks on Bass. That night Bass held a meeting at the Claridge Hotel with four white union supporters at Firestone—Claude Parker, Jack Forsythe, a Mr. Howard, and a man identified as Mr. Holcumb. The meeting had barely started when four anti-union Firestone employees, led by the former prizefighter Joe Woodall and another man named Ben Baldwin (both of whom had already made threatening phone calls to Bass), banged on the door and tried to get into the room. In an attempt to protect the identity of the men inside, Bass stepped into the hallway and blocked the men from coming in. Woodall, spotting Parker in Bass's room, told him he was fired and if he returned to the plant to work he would "beat hell" out of him. In the hallway, the men told Bass, "We intend to see that you are run out of town and you will wind up in the river." Bass tried to reason with the men, who had been drinking, arguing, "We live in the United States and we have laws to govern such things. If you have anything against me or my organization, take it to the law." When Baldwin moved to strike the organizer, calling him "a communist S.O.B.," Bass restrained him, but a third man then went around the corner and returned with about twenty more drunken men. Bass talked some more, but the men attempted to push by him and open the door. Hearing the ruckus, the management called the police and the men dispersed. When the police arrived, they declared the incident closed.[27]

After the police left, however, the Firestone men returned, pushing Parker around and threatening to beat him up. Parker drove off and Bass walked to the police station to report the incident. When he returned to his hotel, Woodall, Baldwin, and about ten others surrounded Bass, cursing and pushing him. When Bass asked the hotel clerks to call the police, they refused. When he attempted to call them himself from the lobby, Baldwin grabbed the receiver and the two men held an impromptu wrestling match, with Baldwin attempting to twist Bass's arm behind his back. When Bass slung Baldwin up against a wall, an open knife fell to the floor from Baldwin's pocket. Alarmed, the men walked out of the hotel and Bass went to his room to call the police. The gang continued to congregate in front of the hotel, until one lone police officer finally arrived and the men left. At Bass's insistence, the officer arrested Baldwin, who was apparently too drunk to leave quickly.

Bass then began to get a taste of Memphis "justice." At the police station, the officers refused to pick up Woodall, and a local judge dismissed disturbing-the-peace charges against Baldwin for "lack of evidence." When

Bass went to Police Commissioner Joe Boyle to ask for protection, Boyle more or less told him the police would do nothing. When Bass returned to his room, the Claridge had not only canceled the CIO meeting scheduled there but demanded that Bass leave the hotel. With no place else to go, Bass stayed temporarily at the home of a black worker, another violation of Memphis racial etiquette that placed him in further jeopardy. Although the police had Bass under surveillance, they refused to give him protection; more chilling, the mayor then issued a public denunciation of Bass's activities.[28]

Saying nothing about the intimidation against Bass, Mayor Chandler condemned union organizing and ordered the police chief to prevent any disturbances that might arise out of the Firestone campaign—implying that the CIO, not the company or its thugs, was the source of the problem. "Memphis will not tolerate intimidation, or threats of bodily harm to those who wish to work, and foreign labor agitators who seek to stir up strife and trouble are not welcome here," the mayor declared. In an article titled "City Closes Doors on Labor Agitators," the *Commercial Appeal* highlighted the statement of the mayor and Police Chief Carroll Seabrook, who declared that "lives and property in Memphis must be protected," presumably against CIO labor agitators. These statements followed the same buildup the city authorities had used before the attacks on Norman Smith.[29]

Nonetheless, Bass continued to stand on his constitutional rights to free speech and the right to organize supported by the Wagner Act. He responded to the mayor by declaring, "This is the first time I ever heard a man ignorant enough to say that because I come from another county of Tennessee that I am a foreigner. He cannot run us out of Memphis." To prove it, he made sure that the union's planned meeting went ahead on Sunday. Following the cancellation by the Claridge Hotel, CIO organizers shifted the meeting to the Inland Boatmen's hall, where 135 men showed up, 75 of them black, to hear speeches by Bass, William R. Henderson of the NMU, Will Watts, an Alabama steel organizer, and Harry Koger of UCAPAWA. Unionists continued to point out that Memphis Firestone remained the largest unorganized rubber plant in the country; that the Memphis Firestone workers produced just as much or more as workers in Akron but received half the pay; and that workers in unionized plants received vacations with pay every year, had job security, and could not be fired on the whim of a supervisor. Bass urged the workers to remain peaceful and predicted that the Firestone plant would be unionized before the end of 1940. "Firestone has never refused to deal with a legal organization," he reassured the workers.[30]

These assurances could not have been very convincing, as police cars circled the block, claiming they had received a call that a "riot" was in progress and a gang of Firestone thugs stood in a sullen group across the street from the union hall. H. B. Griffin later recalled how the police scrutinized the meeting to make sure that whites and blacks abided by the laws of segregation, which they did. Either in an effort to protect themselves or as an ingrained habit, whites and blacks sat on opposite sides of the room. Bass took pains to make sure that this situation did not offend the black workers, the union's strongest supporters. "Bass apologized to the blacks," Griffin recalled, for the segregated seating. "But if we had done any different, the police would have broken it up."[31]

Although the meeting at the Inland Boatmen's hall concluded peacefully, intimidation against Bass continued. After being kicked out of the Claridge, Bass was now kicked out of the Ambassador Hotel as well. Everywhere he went, threatening phone calls followed. On Monday, 26 August, he arrived at the Forrest Park Apartments only to have the management again tell him to leave. Bass acquiesced, but as he left with Charles Wylie and Noel Bedgood, a gang of twenty men armed with two-by-four planks, hoses, and iron pipes confronted them, led by Woodall. The union men jumped in Bass's car to make a getaway, only to discover that the motor had been tampered with. The car was dead, and so possibly were Bass and his companions.

The gang grabbed the car, turned it over on its side, and began smashing all the glass out of the windows and pinning the front doors so they could not be opened. Then the mob turned the car on its back, crushing in the top. Bass heaved his huge body into the backseat and attempted to kick open one of the doors, with the mob hitting him in the ribs from both sides with two-by-fours. Other members of the gang tore off the car's license plates, screwed off the gas tank, and allowed gas to run into the gutter. One of the men struck a match, but for some reason failed to ignite the gas. Bass desperately kicked at the doors until finally one burst open. Once he emerged from the car, the mob immediately turned and ran.

Only after the mob left did a police cruiser show up. Rather than tracking down the thugs, the police wanted to tow Bass's car away, but he insisted on getting pictures taken of the wreck so that he would have evidence to present in court. When Bass and the union members went to the police station to swear out testimony, however, the police arrested Wylie and charged him with "using profanity." Wylie's exact words, according to Bass, were "it's a damn shame that a bunch of hoodlums would be allowed to run the street." The police claimed that he also cursed the "sons of bitches," which they took to mean themselves, but which Wylie claimed meant the Firestone thugs. Denied bail, Wylie stayed in jail overnight. Unlike the case of company thug Baldwin, released after his attempted assault on Bass, in the case of Wylie the judge convicted and fined the union supporter ten dollars for cursing.

After leaving the police station, Bass found that, true to his word, Woodall had also seen to it that someone "beat the hell" out of Claude Parker when he came to do his job at the Firestone plant that Monday. Although an anonymous phone call to Parker on Sunday had threatened violence if he went to work, Parker showed up at his normal time. Parker's department superintendent immediately called him into the office. He told him he could not fire him, but said his work would be watched carefully. After Parker worked his first shift, the company demanded he work another one, all the while under the scrutiny of his supervisor. Before Parker could complete the second shift, however, the management let him off an hour and a half early, while the rest of the workers continued their shifts. When Parker arrived at the parking lot, a group of ten to fifteen Firestone employees surrounded him. His ignition switch had been torn out of the car. Firestone's armed guards stood and watched as the men attacked Parker with clubs and fists, beating him to the ground. When he finally got home, Parker's sister told him an unknown party had called to inform her that Parker would get the same treatment if he returned to work on Tuesday.

Amazingly, Bass remained unruffled. On 29 August, three days after being mobbed outside the Forrest Park Apartments, Bass took Frank Bruno, eighteen-year-old Mary Lou Koger and her father, Harry, Roy Pierson, Eugene Odell, Warren Bourgeois, Walter Smith, Red Davis, and perhaps others to leaflet the Firestone plant. The leaflet pointed out that "workers under contract have *job security,* meaning that a foreman cannot fire you if he doesn't like the way you part your hair, or anything like that." It also emphasized that "United States government laws protect you in your right to join your union. . . . No employer can fire you for joining a union." To dramatize that Memphis Firestone workers made half the prevailing wage in the unionized rubber industry, the leaflet claimed that even the "spittoon cleaners" up north made as much as the highest-paid worker in the Memphis plant.[32]

The unionists finished handing out the leaflets during the afternoon shift change at the east gate of the Firestone factory on Morehead Street without incident. As they began heading for their cars, however, a group of some seventy-five Firestone employees, led by Woodall, advanced on the leafleteers with blackjacks, lead pipes, brass knuckles, sticks, knives, and at least one pistol. While some 250 workers leaving the plant stood around watching, a supervisor named Taylor shouted, "Boys, are you going to run him out of town or are you going to let him leave here?" At that, the mob broke into a run and attacked the leafleteers, isolating Bass and Bedgood from the others. The two organizers ran into the middle of the street with a crowd of men hitting them with pipes. Blood poured from wounds all over their heads as thugs pushed the other leafleteers onto the sidewalk so that they could not intervene to stop the beating. One of the bullies told Roy Pierson they were going to kill Bass and Bedgood, and then the other leafleteers would get the same. Pierson frantically ran to a nearby house to call the police for help, but the residents would not allow him to use their phone.[33]

Just when it looked as if the crowd really would beat Bass and Bedgood to death, tire builder J. R. Carroll pulled his car into the street and drove in between the labor organizers and the largest group of assailants. According to Richard Routon, a witness to the event, Carroll got out and began cursing the crowd, "calling them everything he could think of, and said, 'Now you brave sons of bitches, if you want to beat on somebody come beat on me.' They stood there and glared at him, then turned around and walked. That's what broke up the fight." This act of individual bravery by an outraged worker dispelled the mob mentality and broke up the crowd. Carroll took Bedgood and Bass to St. Joseph's Hospital to have their heads stitched. Bass had bruises all over his arms and shoulders, three deep gashes on his head, and another under his eye. Bedgood also had numerous severe cuts on his head. It required eighty-five stitches to patch up Bass and another seventeen to close the wounds of Bedgood.[34]

Throughout the attack on Bass and Bedgood, five armed Firestone guards at the gate stood by doing nothing. And although Bass had called the police chief to advise him of his leafleting of the plant, and the police had assured him he would receive protection, no police arrived. Police later claimed that because the Firestone plant was outside the city's jurisdiction and paid no taxes, they could not intervene. In reality, the city did provide fire and police protection to the Firestone plant, tax free, as part of the agreement to get the company to come to Memphis. The attack, and police complicity in it, nearly replicated the pattern of events leading to the Norman Smith beating in 1937, and a number of CIO members believed they spotted some of Ford's thugs among the attacking mob. No one ever confirmed the alleged Ford connection, but according to Red Davis a later court suit against Firestone revealed that the Firestone management had paid employees as much as one hundred dollars apiece to lead the attack, for which the company ultimately apologized. George Holloway believed the Crump machine sponsored the beatings: "There was so much money being passed around," he said, that some workers felt sure Crump was involved.[35]

As in the Norman Smith incident, the Bass beating aroused union outrage all over the country. Lucy Randolph Mason and other CIO leaders, as well as the Workers' Defense League, pressured the Justice Department to intervene against the city for violating the Wagner Act. Frank McAllister, the southern secretary for the Workers' Defense League, told justice officials that "if the Federal Government doesn't do something about the reign of terror in Memphis, they might as well haul down the American flag over the city hall there and replace it with the Nazi Swastika." Washington, however, still feared to offend Crump. The assistant U.S. attorney general urged unionists to put their trust in the same man who had whitewashed the Thomas Watkins case, local U.S. Attorney McClanahan, who "assures us that he has secured the fullest cooperation from the local authorities." When Bass called McClanahan for help, however, the attorney made the ludicrous suggestion that he contact the local police and wrote back to Washington claiming that no proof existed of any connection between the city of Memphis or the Firestone management and the attacks on Bass. If the federal government intervened, according to McClanahan, it would "place the Government and our office in the attitude of taking sides in what now appears to be a factional row" between workers. McClanahan was more concerned about the surly manners of unionist William R. Henderson, who had accused him of covering up the case of Watkins, than he was about the behavior of the police.[36]

In the aftermath of the incident outside the plant, two Firestone guards swore out an arrest warrant against J. R. Carroll, and when Carroll defied threats against returning to work, guards searched his car, produced a fishing knife from his tackle box, and had him arrested for carrying a deadly weapon. Mayor Chandler continued to refuse protection to Bass, advising him only "that there is danger of his safety as long as he remains in Memphis." Crump, for his part, issued a public warning against the CIO, linking it to sit-down strikes, Harry Bridges, and Communist party leader Earl Browder and warned that the CIO's brand of industrial unionism "will not be tolerated in Memphis." The refusal of the Memphis machine to abide by the Wagner Act remained clear for all to see. Yet the Democratic National Committee chair belittled protests, saying, "What do you want me to do about it? Go down there with a gun?" The Justice Department responded by saying it would not pursue either the Bass case or that of the missing dockworker, Robert Cotton. No one in Washington wanted to challenge the powerful Ed Crump.[37]

The Bass beating revealed the lengths to which local authorities would go to repress whites as well as blacks when they challenged the racial or class system. "They didn't think too much of the whites trying to help the Negro into organizing the CIO union," said Clarence Coe, in an ironic understatement. "That could really get you into trouble." George Hollo-way felt particularly disturbed when he realized how little he could do as a black man to help Bass, who he felt had taken an exemplary position in favor of black rights. "George Bass used to tell everyone that the CIO believed in justice for all . . . blacks should have as much right to a good job as anyone else. That's what the CIO was built on." Despite his great respect for Bass, Holloway stood by and watched while "these big huge men just came in with billy sticks and beat him like hell. I just cried." He stood at the plant gate until Bass was taken to the hospital, realizing all the while that had he tried to step in it probably would have set off a race riot, destroying any chances of unionization. "It just broke my heart to see that, and there was nothing I could do," Holloway recalled. Such were the realities of segregation in 1940.[38]

Remarkably, George Bass continued his organizing, knowing from past experience how good could sometimes come out of bad. Lacking any pro-tection from the law, he hired the muscular, young Red Davis—a football star in high school—as a full-time bodyguard. He and Davis also took a trip up to Winchester to round up some of Bass's relatives, men who had worked in the rubber factories in Akron but later returned to farm-ing in Tennessee. Company goons, cowards at heart, left Bass alone, while Davis and Mary Lou Koger handed out leaflets. Although federal authori-ties failed to intervene, the unfavorable national publicity generated in the Bass case made both the Firestone management and the Memphis authori-ties wary of mounting further attacks. Edgar Clark, himself a victim of blacklisting by Memphis employers for his opposition to Crump, reported to the Workers' Defense League near the end of September that "men are now passing out literature inside the plant without being fired." [39]

Most important, the repression against the CIO campaign seemed to have the opposite effect on the workers from that intended by the authori-ties. The beating of Bass and Bedgood by company thugs repelled many white workers. The heroics of J. R. Carroll provided one indication of a new challenge emerging against the Firestone management. Carroll made this statement to the press: "I have been an employee at Firestone for about three and a half years and I'm not a member of the union. But I can't sanction the kind of unfair beating those men got, and I'm for them from now on. . . . The men who did the beating used iron pipes, rubber hose, and blackjacks. It was the damndest thing I ever saw—all those men jumping on the handful who were passing out the leaflets." Richard Routon, initially a CIO opponent, recalled that the attack on the CIO members "was a turning point, because all of us out there . . . thought this was going to be a fair fight. . . . Instead it was a violent, vicious, ugly thing. It really turned an awful lot of us against the management." In the wake of the Bass beating, the CIO's chances of winning the Firestone plant seemed better than ever.[40]

With the failure of overt terrorism against CIO organizers, "the most disturbing new factor is the sudden appearance of an AF of L union at the plant," wrote Workers' Defense League representative Clark in late September. Apparently the city administration and the Firestone management had concluded that the workers were ripe for unionization. If so, they much preferred that the employees vote for the ineffectual rubber unit of the AFL, led by a few electricians, machine shop workers, and supervisors. AFL rubber organizers proved notoriously incompetent in Akron, Gadsden, and other locales. AFL members in the Memphis plant, said Dickenson, "were like a lost ball in high weeds" when it came to industrial unionism. Nonetheless, the city administration and the Firestone management hoped the AFL could forestall the CIO in the Firestone factory.[41]

With the entrance of the AFL into the picture, the race question surfaced as the determining issue in the Firestone campaign. Craft unionists played upon the tense racial climate of 1940 to drive whites away from the CIO. "The AFL men told us," recalled George Clark, "that this would be a white man's union if we joined the AFL." H. B. Griffin recalled the AFL's warning that "if we elected the CIO there'd be a 'nigger' building tires next to the whites." The AFL Rubber Workers local made its own position clear by establishing segregated locals, one for blacks and one for whites. Although this appealed to some whites, blacks almost unanimously rejected the AFL. When it held a joint meeting of the two units at the end of September, blacks constituted only 6 out of 300 workers attending. In contrast, at a mass meeting of the CIO's rubber union around the same time, blacks made up all but 35 of of some 350 workers in attendance. Gadsden had passed a law making interracial meetings illegal and arrested rubber workers when they violated it; in Memphis, authorities obtained the same result via the AFL. With its entrance into the situation, the workers at Firestone split clearly along racial lines, with most whites joining the AFL and almost all blacks joining the CIO.[42]

Assuming the possibility that the majority in the plant favored some sort of union, racial polarization obviously provided the best chance of defeating the CIO. The racial question had been a difficult one for the CIO to handle ever since Bass came into town. True to the CIO's position in favor of integrated unions, Bass told white workers from the very beginning that any local built by the United Rubber Workers would be "mixed," with white and "colored" in the same bargaining unit. The resulting hostility to Bass by many white workers probably encouraged the attacks against him and definitely caused many whites to turn away from the CIO. Lucy Randolph Mason related an incident in which two young whites from the Firestone plant came up to Bass and asked him, "Is it true that Niggers will be taken in this union?" According to Mason, "Bass recognized the significance of this question, but promptly said 'Yes.' The two men were obviously angry. They left in a minute or two. Bass then said their visit meant that the AF of L was stirring up the race issue in the plant. . . . 'It will probably cost us the election,' he said."[43]

The Firestone campaign highlighted the racial dilemma of the CIO in the South. Forrest Dickenson, who followed Bass as Memphis organizer for the United Rubber Workers, felt that Bass made a fundamental mistake by organizing the black workers before first building a base among the whites. The predominance of black support, Dickenson felt, gave the AFL a potent weapon to use against the CIO, making it impossible to win whites over to the union. When Dickenson came to town in 1941, he organized the whites before going to blacks for their support. Dickenson's approach, however, implied to the whites that the union would be under their control, an implication that Bass tried to avoid. "George Bass came in with the understanding that we would unite," Holloway recalled. However, Bass did also try to build an identifiable group of whites to lead the CIO efforts, and no black seems to have been included in any public leadership role. Far from being dominated by "nigger unionism," as AFL supporters claimed, the typical patterns of southern unionism in which whites dominated continued in the Firestone campaign, despite Bass's strong commitment to interracialism. And despite that fact, the AFL continued to win the whites to their side because of the continued white fear of black equality within a CIO union.[44]

The CIO seemed to be doomed on the racial question no matter what it did. As if to emphasize this point to any would-be organizers, the Crump machine initiated a major new campaign of intimidation aimed at destroying both the CIO and the handful of independent black political leaders that existed in Memphis. With eyes on both the impending November presidential election and an NLRB election scheduled for 23 December 1940, city leaders intensified efforts to stop any trend toward liberalism, interracialism, or industrial unionism.

THE MEMPHIS "REIGN OF TERROR"

In January 1941, LeMoyne College professor and NAACP supporter Collins George wrote to the national NAACP to report on one of the bleakest periods in Memphis history for the African-American community. "It seems as if Ed Crump, working through Joe Boyle, has gone stark raving mad," he wrote. "No one letter could tell of his continued campaign of intimidation of Negroes. Police enter any colored cafe at any time to paw over the patrons in search of God-knows-what. Negroes are stopped on the street, cursed, beat, kicked; they are pulled off of street cars for the dire offense of not rising to give the very last seat in the car to a white, and likewise arrested if they dare to make any audible comment about it." Far from its supposed status as a famed citadel of southern paternalism, Crump's town seemed to have become an armed camp in which blacks were not even safe to walk the streets. This condition resulted from a vigorous defense of white supremacy throughout the fall of 1940, which shattered any chance of black-white unity in the Firestone campaign and destroyed all vestiges of independent black political power in the city.[45]

Labor and civil rights organizers around the South and throughout the nation viewed the situation in Memphis with alarm. Mason warned the U.S. attorney general and Eleanor Roosevelt that the successes of CIO unions in gaining black support made it likely that, without federal intervention, "some of the leaders of these colored workers may quietly disappear, and no questions raised by the police," as in the case of longshore worker Robert Cotton. The Southern Negro Youth Congress wrote to President Roosevelt that the situation in Memphis constituted "the beginnings of an American fascist stronghold within our very borders, with its race hatreds, enmity to labor, and suppression of civil liberties." The leftist white preacher and union supporter Claude Williams sensed impending disaster, recalling how the East St. Louis race riot and the race riot in Elaine, Arkansas, both responses to labor organizing efforts, had previously destroyed interracial organizing for decades in the mid-South.[46]

These dire warnings were not far-fetched. Police Commissioner Boyle had encouraged the intimidation and violence pervading Memphis when he announced plans during the summer of 1940 to prepare for "emergency" situations by training the police in the use of gas, rifles, and even machine guns for "riot duty." Boyle announced plans to open a new firing range and to purchase five thousand dollars worth of Thompson submachine guns, gas masks, high explosives, hand grenades, and other ammunition. He rationalized the armament program as war preparedness to "meet any emergency" that might arise locally. By October the city was training thirty officers a week for the new program, and in December Boyle announced Memphis would soon have one of the "shootingest" police forces in the United States.[47]

These "war" preparations came in the midst of a crackdown on the African-American community that aimed at ridding it of all voices independent of the Crump machine. The black millionaire and Republican party activist Robert Church, Jr., who symbolized the existence of this independence, had generally been let alone by the authorities. Like the efforts of NAACP leaders to register black voters in the rural areas of West Tennessee, however, the efforts of Church and other black Republicans to support Wendel Wilkie in the 1940 presidential election led to retaliation by the white power structure, which apparently feared growing black assertiveness. As a correspondent for the *Pittsburgh Press* explained it, "For years the Crump machine has used the Negroes as a political tool," but now "the Negro vote might be developing into a Frankenstein monster and turning on its creator." Concerned that blacks might vote against Democratic party candidates, according to *Time* magazine, "Boss Crump did not want any more Negro Republicans around." But Crump and the people who ran Memphis also had the broader aim, Lucy Randolph Mason and many others believed, of setting back the CIO and all other manifestations of independence in both the black and the white communities.[48]

Prior to the election campaign the city of Memphis had already begun to move against Church by forcing him to sell off much of his land to pay back taxes that had accumulated since the depression. Church, seeing the handwriting on the wall, stayed out of town and turned Republican party campaigning over to local druggist J. B. Martin and long-time Republican "Lieutenant" George Lee. When Martin set up a mass Republican rally at Beale Street's Salem Baptist Church, city officials ordered it canceled. When Martin refused to cooperate, police staked out his drugstore and began to search the pockets, wallets, hats, and other personal effects of every customer that came through the door. The police maintained surveillance on his store for sixteen hours a day for over a month, searching even little children and forcing men to take off their shoes at the door. As justification for these humiliations, they claimed that the conservative black businessman Martin was a "dope peddler." This police "clean-up" campaign seemed aimed at intimidating black Republicans, but it continued long past the November election and increased in intensity during the weeks leading to the Firestone election at the end of December. Police raided all the black establishments on Beale Street, in one sweep arresting sixty-five "undesirables." Police intimidation forced Martin and several other black business owners to close their doors, thereby removing the few independent voices among the black bourgeoisie. Church and Martin both left Memphis completely and relocated in Chicago, opening the way for white Republicans (deemed "lily-whites" in the South) to build a completely white-run Republican party in Memphis.[49]

Following the raids on Beale Street, Police Commissioner Boyle launched an ever-widening criticism of African-American community leaders and critics of segregation and made it clear that no deviation from the norms of southern segregation would be tolerated in Memphis. Arrests of African Americans on charges of loitering and vagrancy, open threats against black ministers, journalists, and political leaders, police provocations against blacks riding the city streetcars, and other incidents continued throughout December and into the new year. For over six months, city officials cultivated an atmosphere of bigotry and repression reminiscent of the 1890s expulsion of Ida B. Wells, demonstrating how little the thinking of Memphis leaders had changed on the racial question. In a series of press conferences, Boyle attacked both blacks and whites who criticized segregation in any way and praised the "good, honest negro who does not, I am sure, approve the activities of this fanatical, unappreciative group." He also notified the community that the Memphis police had nineteen black professionals under surveillance for "fanning race hatred" and claimed "foreign-born Communist agitators" had been stirring up "a young element of the negroes" who were becoming "insolent." He warned blacks that "this is a white man's country, and always will be, and any negro who doesn't agree to this better move on." Neither Crump nor any prominent business owner repudiated him. On the contrary, Crump attacked reporters for having written "a lot of anonymous, cowardly stories sent out from here just for the money" that gave Memphis bad publicity.[50]

National and regional organizations again attempted to intervene in support of civil liberties in Memphis. The Southern Conference for Human Welfare's Howard Lee issued a public letter to President Roosevelt warning that "on behalf of the Firestone Rubber Company, E.H. Crump and the city administration of Memphis are inciting race prejudice and intimidation of Negro people" and concluded that "a race riot situation is being fanned by the authorities in Memphis." Lucy Randolph Mason came to the same conclusion and pleaded with Eleanor Roosevelt to get Washington officials to intervene against the local FBI and U.S. district attorney, who she said "are completely under Crump's domination." The national office of the NAACP likewise called for federal intervention to stop what it called the "threat of machine gun warfare" against the African-American community by Joe Boyle.[51]

As usual, protests to the federal government did little good, and police intimidation silenced the handful of blacks considered "radical" by the city administration. Following the flight of Martin, Church, and black businessman Elmer Atkinson from Memphis, the Methodist conference removed Rev. Harry Gibson, one of the ministers Boyle had accused of being a troublemaker. After Boyle called the editors of the two local black papers into his office, the owner of the *Memphis World* informed several NAACP supporters who had planned to buy the newspaper and turn it into an organ for black rights that he no longer could afford to sell it to them. Under heavy pressure to find a way to keep their positions secure, a number of black ministers and business owners groveled at the feet of the Crump machine. Black educator and minister Blair T. Hunt called Crump a "human idol," and Rev. T. O. Fuller decried black activists as "Fifth Columnists." Lee and other remaining black Republicans likewise took an increasingly accommodationist approach to the Crump machine.[52]

The machine's control of every aspect of the city's political life, combined with overt police repression, succeeded in enforcing a dismal conformity in both the African-American and white communities. When white and black ministers of the Interracial Commission asked to meet with Boyle in January 1941, he told them that he would meet only with the whites. The white ministers accepted this condition, which violated the very purpose of their organization. The meeting, predictably, produced a whitewash of the city's problems. Rev. Marshall Wingfield of the First Congregational Church announced, "We are the best right-hand adjunct the police officers have," stressing "we are all Southerners" and assuring the white public that "no such thing as race equality has ever been mentioned in our meetings." At the end of what Rev. Alfred Loaring-Clark of St. John's Episcopal Church called "a very happy conference," Mayor Chandler told the public that the ministers "expressed approval of the city's law enforcement program and assured us that their sole desire is to co-operate whenever possible." With this statement, and a headline in the *Commercial Appeal* stating "Racial Commission and City Fathers in Harmony," the white commission members appeared to place their stamp of approval on what outside critics called a police state. The ministers likewise failed to challenge Boyle's refusal to allow them to bring interracialist Will Alexander to speak in Memphis against lynching. They expressed their doubts about the city's police state methods only in private.[53]

With such a manifest failure by potential supporters of liberalization to step forward, the president of the NAACP chapter at LeMoyne College, Daniel Dean Carter, wrote to the NAACP legal counsel, Thurgood Marshall, that the masses of black people had retreated from any active opposition to the police. "The Negro mass has been terrorized to the extent that the police have had recently to deny a wide-spread rumor that Mr. Boyle had forbidden Negroes to wear high waisted pants and long coats," which could be used to conceal weapons, Carter told Marshall. An equally depressed Collins George, co-supervisor of the LeMoyne group, warned Marshall in January that he and Marguerite Bicknell, a white faculty member, expected to be arrested at any time and that according to police practice they might be held incommunicado for up to seventy-two hours without charges placed against them. "Unless one lives in Memphis," he wrote, "the complete intimidation and the accompanying brutalizing of both white and colored is unbelievable!" He added a warning that "they may, of course get after us both on a 'red' charge which is absurd or would be any where else."[54]

Memphis seemed to lack any internal democratic process to bring about social change. Hence, the CIO, the NAACP, and the Southern Conference continued to press hard for outside pressure from the Justice Department. The Justice Department did send in U.S. Attorney Amos Woodcock, but he talked only to local U.S. Attorney McClanahan and to Joe Boyle, soliciting no opinions from African Americans or critics of the Crump machine. Not surprisingly, he reported back to Washington that no basis for charges of civil liberties violations in Memphis existed. When Thurgood Marshall protested that Woodcock's report was "one-sided to say the least," a representative for U.S. Attorney General Robert Jackson insisted the Justice Department had "no jurisdiction over the behavior of the police toward Negroes or anyone else." One more attempt to gain federal intervention had come to nought.[55]

Crump reiterated that Memphis would not allow "agitators or saboteurs under the guise of teachers, lecturers, farm and industrial workers with their vicious propaganda" to roam free. The city was only defending "the right thinking, working, honest negro," Crump said, and "we are not going to let the *Press-Scimitar,* or any New York or other foreign influence interfere with us." Police Commissioner Boyle had a solution as well to the race problem, stating, "We are not going to have any race trouble here, and the best way to avoid it is to let these fresh, upstart negroes know their places. We have too many good, hardworking and honest negroes for the few bad ones to pull them down." Boyle, Crump, and the other white men who ran Memphis assumed that they knew, and had the right to determine, what the standards of "right thinking" should be for blacks. They did have that "right," as long as they had the power to enforce it. A deeply depressed Collins George wrote to Walter White in the NAACP national office in February that "the Negroes en masse remain in an apathetic dread," the local chapter of the NAACP remained dysfunctional, and no one dared to stand up for their rights. "Such is Mr. Crump's stranglehold on this town in the matter of jobs, taxes, courts, etc.," George concluded.[56]

Black novelist and scholar J. Saunders Redding described the demoralizing situation in the Memphis African-American community during a visit he made to the city before Christmas of 1940. "The Negroes were silent, sullen, cowed," he wrote. "There was no one to speak out for them, no single voice in all that city during that pre-Christmas season that uttered one word of good will. . . . The chairman of the Race Relations Group, resigned. The other members, white and colored, remained silent." Redding experienced the intimidation of the Memphis police firsthand when he asked a white police officer for directions. The officer called him a "coon" and accused him of being a dope peddler while another officer frisked him, turned his pockets inside out, examined his correspondence, broke his pack of cigarettes in half, and threatened him. Despite his immense shame and anger at his failure to resist, Redding concluded that wisdom "lay in the recognition of my impotence. A move from me, a gesture of stubbornness, a hint of refusal" could result in beating or death. Redding's experience was replicated on a large scale around Christmas, when the police stepped up their drive against "undesirables," arresting several hundred blacks on the street. In Memphis, any African American who did not know his or her "place" automatically was an "undesirable" and had no rights a white person felt bound to respect. This was the essence of living in Police Commissioner Boyle's "white man's country."[57]

At Firestone, the general atmosphere of terror and repression frightened many potential supporters away from the CIO. Just prior to the Firestone election in December, Claude Williams reported, police "circulated constantly around the homes of the workers for the purpose of intimidating the CIO members." An official of the American Legion, a doctor at Baptist Hospital, told NMU representative William R. Henderson that "he would get his neck broken if he did not get out of the CIO 'while the going was possible.'" He also told Henderson that "the American Legion was opposed to the CIO" and that the police were preparing to "to clean it out of Memphis." A member of the Interracial Commission passed on a warning to Williams that if the CIO won the Firestone election "blood would flow in the streets." If not all workers in the plant knew about these threats, they all knew about the race-baiting and red-baiting campaign of the AFL rubber union. According to Richard Routon, a majority of workers wanted a union at the Firestone plant, but many whites bought the rhetoric, labeling the CIO as a "Communist, 'nigger-loving' union." The AFL, endorsed as it was by the Crump machine, provided a safe alternative to the CIO.[58]

The city strategy of co-opting industrial unionism by channeling worker discontent into the AFL almost unraveled, however, when the Firestone company suddenly switched from an hourly to a piece rate, causing a reduction of the general wage scale. On 5 December, Firestone workers spontaneously walked out and for three days engaged in the largest strike yet held in Memphis. The AFL union, which had been counseling against strike action for nearly a year, proved unable to handle the situation. The AFL's rubber organizer vanished from town, leaving it to city officials to settle the dispute, a development which, according to a federal labor mediator brought in to cool the situation, antagonized the workers further. Crump, in his usual high-handed fashion, removed the AFL local's president, Lester Goings, because the man had served time in the penitentiary. When Memphis Trades and Labor Council president Loring, acting on behalf of the Crump machine, also criticized the AFL local president while on the picket line, the workers got so angry they nearly overturned Loring's car. After the machine smoothed over the incident by reinstating Goings, both AFL and CIO members voted to go back to work without having gained any concessions from the company.[59]

Yet, although the AFL had not presented itself in a favorable light, in a secret NLRB election held on 23 December, 1,008 Firestone workers voted for the AFL, 805 for the CIO, and 38 voted no union. Among those eligible to vote as part of the bargaining unit, white workers voted almost entirely for the AFL, while black workers appear to have unanimously supported the CIO. The company had succeeded in imposing its piece rate, and the city administration had established an AFL union in the plant it felt it could control and that the company could accept. Many white workers would later regret their support for the AFL. Routon, who became the AFL's first treasurer, later reflected that "Local 22456 of the AFL turned out to be a subterfuge fostered by the Trades and Labor Council acting at the behest of the Crump machine and the chamber of commerce. We soon found out that we'd been duped into joining an AFL union which knew nothing about industrial organization to keep out a union which understood the industrial worker's situation." George Holloway had figured this out already and quit his job at Firestone before the company had a chance to fire him for his organizing role in the plant. He went to work as a Pullman porter.[60]

*   *   *

In the NLRB election, Firestone workers had the opportunity to vote in secret and determine their own fate. Unfortunately for them, the race issue had once again won out over their class interests and foiled an opportunity to weaken the hold of the Crump machine and the business oligarchy it served. Certainly the repressive atmosphere in the nation and in Memphis played no small role in this defeat. But the multitude of divisions between white and black fostered by the segregation system and the racist beliefs deeply ingrained among white workers, more than repression, played the main role in foiling the CIO's challenge to the status quo. White workers at Firestone, by voting strictly along racial lines in favor of an inept AFL rather than risk association with the "nigger unionism" of the CIO, proved that the old divide and rule methods used to control the labor force still worked.

Unquestionably, however, civil rights consciousness continued to stir among Memphis African Americans, regardless of what the white authorities said. After Boyle's provocative order that police would patrol the street cars to prevent any "impudent" blacks from refusing to sit in the "colored" section, a number of young blacks did just that. When a twenty-six-year-old black house servant refused to go to the back of a bus on which only two other people were seated, he was arrested for "drunkenness" and violation of the state segregation laws. Anonymous protesters, "fifth columnists" according to Boyle, also set a number of trash fires, apparently in retaliation for police treatment of blacks. During the coming war, acts of individual rebellion would multiply. Hollis Price of LeMoyne College witnessed one such incident in 1942, when a plainly dressed black man refused to move from his seat on the bus to make way for a white passenger. "This is that damned democracy you all been talking about," he ruefully asserted when he got off the bus.[61]

Such deviance from the southern system would increase as the world plunged into war. Movements for civil rights and labor rights had common origins in a long history of struggles for change. Both movements required neighborhood, church, and workplace organizing. Both used picket lines and mass meetings to make demands on employers and those in power, and both sought federal intervention for beleaguered organizers in the

South. To one degree or another, both movements sought to change the way people thought about themselves and their fellow humans. And both movements had to be checked in order to maintain the southern system. What Memphis authorities feared, and what their anticommunist rhetoric covered up, was not "communism" at all, but the organization of people into movements for democracy.

III

Industrial Unionism
and the Black Freedom Movement

The organization of laborers in unions which fight for better wages and conditions of work is one of the greatest pathways toward real democracy. Inevitably the union must break down racial discrimination or fail in its objectives.
　　　　　　　　—W. E. B. Du Bois

Those same forces who are organized against the Negro people are organized against you. . . . [But] instead of saying they're against Catholics or Jews or Negroes, now they declare they're out after "Communists."
　　　　　　　　—Thurgood Marshall
　　　　to the United Packinghouse Workers' Convention

CHAPTER SEVEN

War in the Factories

Blacks were definitely part of the whole program, and that was understood. If the unions
were going to be successful, black and white couldn't be separated anymore. I'm not
saying there weren't segregated unions, because there were.
—Mary Lawrence Elkuss

The race question in Memphis right now is loaded with dynamite and . . . only experts
should be allowed to handle the fuse. . . . The worst mistake we could make right now
would be to set up an active council committee on racial discrimination.
—Pete Swim

The failure of the organizing drive at Firestone in late 1940 appeared
to signal the conclusive defeat of industrial unionism in Memphis. Instead, 1941 became a banner year for the CIO, the beginning of a dramatic
expansion that would bring the organization to a high point of thirty-two
thousand members by the end of the war. The critical turning point for the
CIO occurred in some northern industrial centers during the 1936–37 sit-
down strikes, but in Memphis that turning point arrived at the onset of
World War II. In May 1941, Lucy Randolph Mason reported from Memphis to CIO director of organization Allan Haywood that "locals with a
well paid up membership spring into being in a few weeks, largely without
solicitation on the part of organizers. The few CIO representatives on the
job are rushed off their feet responding to requests for help." In response
to this changed atmosphere, the national CIO and various international
unions placed numerous full-time staff members in the city. During the war
years, the Memphis Industrial Union Council, the CIO's city-wide organization, increasingly overshadowed the AFL's Trades and Labor Council
in size and influence. Biracial organization at this point became the key
to CIO success. It also remained, however, the focal point of continuing
struggle over the meaning of unionism as a social movement.[1]

Several factors account for the startling change in the CIO's fortunes, war production the most prominent among them. Between 1940 and 1943, the construction of scores of new industrial plants, the investment of tens of millions of dollars by private industry, and the construction of massive military facilities by the federal government produced prosperity at a level previously unknown in Memphis. During each of these years, employment in the existing manufacturing, wholesaling, and distributing enterprises, as well as in new ordnance, aircraft, and ammunition industries, expanded dramatically. Construction work on a new naval aviation base at Millington, hospitals, a quartermaster depot, and other military facilities brought thousands of new workers to the city. Craft union membership soared, but industrial employment grew even faster. In the first three years of the decade, the city gained about nineteen thousand manufacturing jobs, doubling the number of factory workers. From a depressed, secondary labor market based on industries related to cotton, lumber, food, chemicals, and a few other products, Memphis finally achieved a long-sought status as one of the major industrial centers of the South.[2]

If the war in Europe revolutionized the city's economy, it also began to change the tenor of Memphis labor relations. The chamber of commerce had avidly sought the new war industries and the federal money that went with them. In return for the great economic boom brought by the war, however, business leaders, politicians, and public opinion makers had little choice but to quiet their hostility toward the CIO. The warfare state produced prosperity and, finally, a more forceful intrusion of the federal government into labor concerns. Lucy Randolph Mason during the Firestone campaign had predicted that "it might give Crump and the city administration pause in their ruthless fight on the CIO" if federal authorities made it clear that continued anti-unionism would mean the loss of federal contracts. In early 1941, Eleanor Roosevelt made exactly this point in a speech reprinted in Memphis and Nashville papers and publicly criticized the Crump machine as her husband had never dared. City leaders collectively bit their lips, including Crump, who soon muted his verbal assaults on the right of the CIO to organize in "his" town. Although employers continued to resist unionization, without overt police and Crump machine backing they had a difficult time stemming the tide of industrial unionism brought in by the war.[3]

THE FLOWERING OF INDUSTRIAL UNIONISM

As wartime labor demand replaced the mass unemployment of the depression years during the summer of 1941, a series of strikes and organizing drives produced increasing numbers of victories instead of defeats. One of the earliest victories occurred in March, when UCAPAWA struck the J. R. Watkins plant, obtaining recognition as the sole bargaining agent for 141 workers and a contract stipulating a forty-hour week, six paid holidays, and a minimum wage of thirty-seven cents an hour. More important than these gains, the agreement required workers covered by the contract to retain their union memberships during its duration. This clause, similar to wartime "maintenance of membership" agreements soon to come, prevented Watkins from pressuring workers to leave the union and gave UCAPAWA a stable existence in the plant. In the following months, the CIO conducted a general organizing drive, led by the NMU's William R. Henderson, the IWA's Harry Koger, and UCAPAWA's William Haber aimed at replicating such contracts in other shops. CIO activists also created the Memphis Industrial Union Council, which had authorization from the national CIO to organize any workplace. This mandate more or less forced local organizers to work together and avoided the potential jurisdictional disputes that, craft union experience had often demonstrated, placed internationals in conflict with each other. The CIO thrived in this united front context.[4]

Black workers continued to provide the core of CIO support, and in industries where they constituted the majority, readily took up the strike weapon. In one conflict that lasted over eight weeks and involved some 120 workers, blacks struck Mississippi Valley hardwood company when it refused to bargain. The city police escorted scabs from Mississippi into the plant while the business community set up an employer strike fund, closing ranks behind the company. The union threatened to respond to the hardline employer stance by calling a general strike of all fifteen thousand of the city's lumber mill workers, 85 percent of them black. Lacking the power to implement this threat, workers engaged in continuous small battles for union recognition, contracts, and basic improvements in wages and conditions. A similar strike, lasting four months, occurred at Tennison Brothers steel.[5] But in contrast to 1940, city officials steered clear of the kind of violence that had given the city such a bad name. Without state intervention, even the toughest employers had difficulty stopping unionization. The IWA gained a contract at Mississippi Valley and further fruits of the CIO drive appeared in August at the Nickey Brothers hardwood flooring plant. The management there picked up the maneuver used by Firestone and other companies, supporting an AFL union to gain white loyalty. Unlike the situation at Firestone, however, blacks constituted the great majority of the work force at Nickey Brothers and they carried the NLRB election for the CIO's UCAPAWA by a vote of 208 to 91. The CIO turned the shop over to the IWA, which gained a contract providing seniority rights, paid vacations, a forty-hour week, a minimum wage of thirty-four cents an hour, a grievance procedure, and recognition of the union as the sole bargaining agent.[6]

These and other organizing victories gave the fledgling CIO a character very unlike that of the AFL. As a result of painstaking organizing, by September 1941 the CIO had gained bargaining rights in more than sixty workplaces in Memphis and surrounding environs, most of them small shops with predominantly black work forces. The IWA held a total of ten companies under contract in Memphis by August, and in its summer campaign had lost not a single election. African Americans dominated union affairs in this early stage, electing Beatrice Moore as financial secretary, making her the first black woman to ever hold office in the IWA. Black religion played a key role in the union, as preacher-worker Rev. Ernest Fields led the organizing committee and invoked "God's will" as a justification for improving the living standards of the workers. At an August picnic of one thousand black woodworkers and their families, Fields and Rev. Claude Williams preached union social gospel, with a quartet of Nickey Brothers workers providing the entertainment.[7] Blacks similarly continued to play the dominant role in UCAPAWA, the CIO's largest union. At Jackson Cotton Oil Mill and Memphis Cotton Oil, UCAPAWA workers struck for two weeks in October 1941 and won a contract providing union recognition, seniority rights, grievance procedures, five annual holidays, a one-week paid vacation, and a two-cent hourly raise for all. UCAPAWA organizing also increasingly brought poor whites into the organization. Some 350 UCAPAWA members, a third of them white women, struck Wabash Screen Door in June, obtaining union recognition and a contract despite arrests and determined employer opposition.[8]

CIO success resulted primarily from enthusiastic black support for unionization, which they did not limit to the CIO. In late May the AFL's hotel and restaurant union offered surprisingly strong support to 123 waiters, elevator operators, dining room attendants, kitchen workers, cooks, and laundry workers, who walked out at the Hotel Claridge. Their demands for a minimum pay of ten dollars per week and for a maximum sixty-hour work week for men and a forty-eight-hour week for women indicate just how badly the hotel management treated its workers. In the heady atmosphere of 1941, Lev Loring denounced "economic slavery" at the Claridge, and the Trades and Labor Council set up picket lines of white women to support the black strikers. Yet only two members of the two

white AFL locals in the hotel supported the strike. Most white unionists, including members of the AFL musician's union, crossed the strikers'
picket lines. This lack of labor solidarity among white AFL members, combined with a concerted counteroffensive by the Restaurant Association and
the local press, defeated the strike after eight weeks.[9]

Other AFL unions made efforts to reach out to African Americans, but
with dubious results. The AFL represented some 210 blacks, half of them
women, at Crescent Laundry and ultimately established a membership of
some three thousand in fourteen dry-cleaning and laundry establishments.
An AFL union also began organizing 350 workers, most of them female
and a third of them black, at American Snuff's tobacco plant. But, unconcerned by any strong threat from the CIO in these particular industries,
employers strongly resisted these AFL campaigns. Most laundry owners
refused to bargain, and one feed mill plant owner shut down completely
rather than accept AFL jurisdiction. In contrast, when CIO unions attempted to organize common laborers, most if not all of them black, the
AFL hod carriers' and common laborers' union quickly won a closed shop
agreement with the Associated General Contractors in August. This made
Memphis a closed shop town in the building industry for unskilled black
laborers as well as for white craftworkers and guaranteed the union a
bonanza of one hundred thousand dollars in joining fees. Yet the weakness
of AFL organizing among blacks remained apparent, as it continued to shut
blacks out of almost all skilled work in the building trades and engaged
in little follow-up among the laundry workers. Black AFL membership
remained concentrated in the laborers', hod carriers', brickmasons', and
dockworkers' unions.[10]

Nonetheless, blacks in some cases had good reasons to consider joining AFL unions. These had the advantage of greater acceptability to employers than the CIO, and certainly the AFL Trades and Labor Council
provided a larger base of funds and support from the Crump machine than
any CIO union could offer. AFL unions obtained closed, preferential, and
union shop agreements that employers would rarely grant to CIO unions,
covering foundry, bedding, and lumber company workers. These agreements continued to provide a convenient bulwark for employers against
the CIO. One manufacturer fired twenty-three workers belonging to a CIO
steelworkers' organizing committee, based on an AFL contract that stipu-
lated that employees must join the AFL or lose their jobs. In contrast,
employers in shops represented by the CIO proved totally unwilling to discuss the closed shop or even the union shop. Owners of Humphries Mills
articulated the common outlook of industrialists, stating they would never

grant a closed shop because "their employees are practically all negroes, the majority of them being common laborers and irresponsible."[11] However, although AFL unions had advantages over CIO unions, AFL internationals interested in organizing blacks remained a distinct minority. Most AFL unions in Memphis concentrated their efforts in majority-white plants and failed to deal effectively with interracial situations. AFL unions often represented a handful of white craftworkers out of hundreds of production workers and laborers, the vast majority of them black, as at Nickey Brothers, Anderson-Tulley lumber, Humko Oil, and other factories. Due to its segregated structure and its uniform failure to unite workers across racial lines, the AFL could provide only a disruptive presence in such situations. As a result, its appeal to a resurgent black working class in 1941 remained limited.[12]

Various incidents of violence against organizers in Tennessee and across the South demonstrated that the CIO still remained an embattled organization, but, ironically, this fact gave it an important advantage over the more prosperous and acceptable AFL: the CIO's appeal as a champion of the underdog. Highlander Folk School educator Mary Lawrence Elkuss looked back to 1941 as a great moment in the South, partly because "the CIO was a very vital crusading movement then, and it meant tremendous things to the people who came into it." The CIO's appeal rested in part on its willingness to organize even the most downtrodden and outcast workers. In a place like Memphis, this appeal necessarily implied organizing blacks as well as poor whites. Even racially conservative white organizers, such as William R. Henderson of the NMU, the first full-time Memphis organizer paid by the CIO, understood the necessity to organize blacks in the Deep South. Along with the NMU's Morton Davis and Harry Koger, during 1941 and 1942 Henderson took his life in his hands by crossing the river to organize predominantly black CIO locals in Helena, Arkansas, only to be arrested and then driven out of town by local authorities. In contrast to the AFL, the CIO remained an oppositional movement, one that represented the potential emancipation of southern workers from starvation wages and sweatshop conditions. The sense of being in a movement, and sometimes putting one's body on the line as a part of that movement, pervaded the early CIO in a way quite alien to the "business unionism" of the AFL.[13]

Trying to consolidate workers into the CIO, however, proved always to be a difficult task. Most of those joining the expanding industrial labor force in Memphis in 1941 and 1942 had no previous union experience. Many came to the city completely illiterate after years of plowing, planting, and harvesting in the countryside. Union educational programs became critical to integrating these workers into the labor movement, and numerous CIO unions began teaching crash courses emphasizing basic reading skills as well as the broadest principles of unionism, organizing techniques, and negotiating procedures. Racial conflict frequently undermined such efforts, however. The UAW, in the process of gaining a foothold at Ford Motor and Fisher Body, set up an educational conference in October 1941, staffed by Highlander member Harry Lasker. Lasker subsequently began a general education program for CIO unions, but he found it almost impossible to get people to come to meetings after work, and he questioned "just how much work I can get done in classes where the Negroes and whites are together" in segregated seating arrangements. Blacks proved reluctant at first to openly express themselves in front of whites, and their lack of education forced him to "go slow." Only when he branched out to work with Harry Koger did he discover real enthusiasm for labor education among black cotton workers, who punctuated meetings with songs and speeches. Despite his difficulties, Lasker eventually created a continuing program of education, including courses in the mechanics of union organizing that averaged sixty students per week and included workers from auto, woodworking, chemical, steel, maritime, and cotton-processing industries. Lasker's contribution would be brief, for he soon joined the armed services and was killed in the war.[14]

For the Memphis CIO, Highlander programs remained essential to creating a successful union movement. Highlander stressed the importance of workers making decisions for themselves, believing that working people could provide answers to their own questions if they sat down and discussed their problems collectively. Lasker and other Highlander educators, including Mary Lawrence Elkuss, helped Memphis locals produce their own newsletters and leaflets and set up labor history and collective bargaining workshops, often held in people's homes. They also brought some of the most active Memphis unionists to the Highlander center in Monteagle, Tennessee, exposing them to the experiences of other unionists across the South. "It wasn't easy," said Mary Lawrence Elkuss. "A lot of the education work I did was on picket lines and in strike headquarters, things like that. [But] you had that feeling that things were moving and this was going to make a big difference." By the end of 1941, workers joined unions so quickly that organizers hardly knew what to do with them. Elkuss recalled that "the problem was that the people were joining up so fast that the CIO had a hard time consolidating the gains they were making."[15]

The crusading quality of the CIO's work in 1941 was accentuated by the fact that its largest local remained predominantly black and Communist-led. UCAPAWA, with eight agreements covering twenty-five hundred members as early as October, far outdistanced the IWA and even the UAW, which had quietly organized fourteen hundred members in the Ford plant. Compared to whites at Ford and other factories, Lasker found blacks in UCAPAWA to be "great joiners" and much more ready to attend meetings and apply themselves, once they gained confidence in white organizers. In addition to UCAPAWA, the National Maritime Union, despite its small base of about one hundred union members, quickly gained strength in 1941. It had a closed shop agreement with the riverboat companies and also had a strong activist presence in the CIO. However, other forces also came to exercise increasing influence in the fledgling CIO. The Memphis American Newspaper Guild chapter maintained contracts with both major newspapers, and the steelworkers' union, led by Noel Beddow, had signed ten contracts in small shops. Following the Japanese attack on American forces at Pearl Harbor on 7 December, the CIO would increasingly broaden its membership into new industries with large numbers of racially conservative white workers and union leaders. Industrial expansion during the war finally would defeat efforts by employers, the Crump machine, and the AFL to turn it back, but would also transform the political dynamics of the industrial union movement.[16]

Six months after American entry into the war, the CIO's unionization of the Firestone plant provided the first clear signal that the CIO would win the battle for legitimacy in Memphis. The United Rubber Workers' new organizer Forrest Dickenson, who had worked as a tire builder in Akron, quickly gained white support for the CIO. Unlike the AFL organizers who had relied on support from maintenance workers (a marginal group according to Dickenson), he concentrated on building a core of CIO support among white tire builders, who could shut down the entire plant if they stopped work. His explanation of how employers used race to divert workers from their own economic interests began to convince Richard Routon and other whites to abandon the racial exclusionism of the AFL. According to Dickenson, although his grandfather had fought for the Confederacy in the Civil War, the South's defense of slavery was a "waste of life, senseless." Slavery, he explained to whites, was simply another tool of northern merchants and southern landowners "to use labor with impunity, even as employers do today." Employers used blacks as a reserve labor force to drive the wages of everyone down, and as long as blacks and whites did not join together in a union, employers would continue to do this. "It's all an economic question," Dickenson told workers, requiring labor organization to counter the power of the bosses. As to the broader dimensions of the race question, said Dickenson, "We never fooled with that damned thing. We played that down. Workers are employees to us, not black or white."[17]

George Bass, who likewise had deep roots in the South, had probably made similar appeals, but perhaps whites simply would not listen in the midst of the race-baiting and red-baiting campaign against the CIO rubber union in 1940. But after thirteen months of "white privilege" in the AFL, which failed to produce a single wage increase or to improve shop conditions, the attitude of white workers had changed. Dickenson spent a lot of time with Routon, a tire builder who had been the treasurer for the AFL union, but like many others had grown disgusted with the AFL. Routon now shifted to the CIO and took many of the tire builders with him. Routon, with typical white racial prejudices, at first opposed including blacks, but Dickenson explained to him that "you can't organize an industry in pieces" as the AFL tried to do. "You can't put workers into two unions, one white and one black. You have to be able to shut down the whole plant to be effective, and that means you have to have everyone in the same union." By the spring of 1942, that made sense to Routon. "By that time," Routon recalled, "we didn't give a damn about black or white. We didn't care if they were polka-dot. We were tired of the sweatshop conditions. We were ready to join together and do something about it."[18]

On 28 April 1942, the CIO United Rubber Workers (URW) won an NLRB-sponsored election in competition with the AFL by a vote of 911 to 521, with the AFL union only holding onto the maintenance and machine shop craftworkers. This election, which apparently included less than half of the bargaining unit in the plant, placed the most prized jewel of the city's 1930s industrialization efforts in the CIO column. Interestingly, Routon played a critical role in the election by successfully appealing to whites to overcome their racial animosities. During a walkout over a racial incident in the plant, according to Routon, "the whites were erupting about how we had to 'keep the niggers in line,' while the black people were protesting that after all, they were members of the union too, and it should represent all of them." Routon made a speech in the parking lot telling the workers they had no choice but to cooperate with each other if they wanted a union. The employees finally went back to work, and in response to his speech elected Routon as the CIO local's first president. Black laborers had also impressed the issue of mutual dependence on whites by slowing down production after the CIO lost the 1940 election, thereby cutting down the piece-rate earnings of semiskilled whites. According to George

Holloway, "The blacks put pressure on the whites by not cooperating, until they realized they needed us." The CIO union remained on rocky terrain, however. According to a labor mediator, many newly hired blacks feared to join either the AFL or the CIO, while many whites, especially those in the higher-paying jobs, still refused to join an organization "which admits negros [sic] on equal terms." Furthermore, the company refused to bargain seriously with the CIO. After winning the election, Routon and others learned, the CIO union's struggle had just begun.[19]

After Firestone fell to the CIO, however, little question remained that the industrial union movement had come to Memphis to stay. As the war ballooned the work force at Firestone, Ford, and Fisher, all of which converted to producing war goods on a mass scale, the CIO became entrenched at each one of these enterprises. Memphis industries now included tire and rubber, aircraft, meat-packing, iron, pharmaceutical, transportation, communication, and steel-fabricating, as well as the more traditional woodworking, cotton-processing, warehousing, and food and farm products companies. Organizing continued in all of these industries, and by March 1942 the CIO claimed ten thousand members. Within another year the CIO claimed fifteen thousand in fifty-four plants. These included some five thousand in the URW, four thousand in UCAPAWA (in twenty different plants), twenty-one hundred in the IWA, nineteen hundred in the steelworkers' union, and fifteen hundred in the UAW. CIO membership quickly climbed to twenty-five thousand, as employment skyrocketed to some seven thousand at both Firestone and Fisher Aircraft and a thousand or more at the plants of Anderson-Tulley lumber, E. L. Bruce flooring, Buckeye cottonseed oil, and American Finishing Company. Mass-production companies, with anywhere from five hundred to seven thousand workers under one roof, for the first time clearly dominated the economy. Memphis employed forty thousand or more wage workers, a third of them black, placing industrial-style unionism on the threshold of almost unbelievable success (see table 7.1).[20]

THE STRUGGLE FOR UNION SECURITY

Among the factors causing CIO growth, the extension of federal authority over labor relations became one of the most important. In order to obtain high levels of production, the War Labor Board (WLB) and other federal agencies guaranteed unions a role in the factories as long as the unions adhered to a no-strike pledge and played a cooperative role in helping to maximize production for the war effort. The WLB's "maintenance of mem-

Table 7.1. Number of Workers in Selected Major Industries, July 1943

Manufacturing total workers	28,113
Fisher Aircraft	6,867
Chemicals and allied	5,235
Firestone Tire and Rubber	4,209
Lumber and timber	2,326
Ordnance/ammunition	1,942
Chicago and Southern airlines	1,065
Sefton Fibre Can	817
Pidgeon-Thomas iron	500
Other manufacturing	4,842
Federal government, civilians	7,070
Transportation, communication, public utilities	3,291

Source: War Manpower Commission, Program Planning and Review Division, Reports and Analysis Unit, 1 July 1943, Memphis Files, USES, USDL, RG 183, NARA.

bership" formula, adopted in June 1942, prevented workers under union contract from withdrawing from the union during the life of the contract. Maintenance of membership clauses had already become a primary contract demand for unions in the South, where continued employer hostility so frequently eroded initial organizing victories. But the WLB did not hand its protection to unionists on a platter, and arbitration cases only came before the board after all other efforts at collective bargaining had failed. Hence, even with the increasing legal sanction of the government on their side, unionists had to struggle continually with employers and the WLB to obtain the protections supposedly guaranteed to them by their support for the war effort.[21]

The growth of industry and the extension of federal mediating powers through war contracts, combined with continual news media appeals for patriotism and unity in the war effort, constituted powerful factors validating the CIO's presence in Memphis. These factors would have meant little without worker support for the new unions, but workers joined the CIO in such large numbers that city leaders had little choice but to acknowledge the new reality. Hence, in June 1942 Mayor Walter Chandler greeted the first meeting of the Tennessee Industrial Union Council in Memphis warmly, telling state delegates, "You are genuinely welcome here." This welcome provided such a sharp contrast to Memphis in 1940 that one CIO representative commented, "I had a feeling that I must have arrived in the wrong city." But in reality, the CIO could no longer be viewed by business leaders as retarding Memphis growth, which now increasingly hinged on cooperation with the federal government and on developing a trained and literate labor force rather than on attracting industry through low wages and repression of unions. Individual employers could and did continue to fight the CIO, but the city administration could not. By 1945 Mayor Chandler proclaimed himself a progressive on labor issues and even praised industrial unions as a "bulwark of democracy."[22]

As early as 1940, when a handful of local industrialists and the Memphis Chamber of Commerce had hosted a "personnel conference," labor conciliators had anticipated that a "progressive group" of employers would begin to recognize the advantages of dealing with the CIO. The chamber of commerce began to move in that direction during the war, organizing an array of industrialists, the mayor, the AFL's Lev Loring, and even the CIO's Memphis Industrial Union Council president, Pete Swim, into the Committee for Economic Development. Phil Pidgeon, a northern transplant and owner of the city's largest iron works, chaired the group, working with a Central Committee of business leaders to prevent a return to the depression through business planning and by maintaining the purchasing power of workers. Rather than defeating organized labor, they aimed at incorporating it into a business-directed agenda for continued economic growth.[23]

However, conflicting impulses afflicted the business community. Even the "liberal" business owners in Memphis eschewed New Deal social planning and labor regulation, favoring instead "responsible" governing by business—that would recognize unions when necessary but strive to make them unnecessary. They saw the outlines of such government already developing in Washington, where "dollar-a-year" executives ran much of the war effort. However, other Memphis business leaders rejected any form of collaboration with labor and lobbied for an end to all labor reforms, especially the forty-hour work week and the union shop, labor protections many of them considered "abuses" of the Wagner Act. A number of Memphians complained about these matters to the National Defense Committee chaired by Senator Harry Truman, one lawyer calling labor protections "nauseating" and urging use of the American military to "put organized labor in its proper place." Local business leader Roane Waring went further, declaring that strikers in wartime should be shot. The war seemed to bring out savage anti-unionism among some, at the same time that others recognized that government regulation and unionism itself, within a framework of business control, could be to their advantage.[24]

Below the surface rhetoric of labor-management unity in a common cause, anti-unionism remained embedded in the practice and thinking of most local manufacturers, who for the most part continued to fiercely resist demands for union recognition, collective bargaining, and union security. Protracted battles over the most minor union gains persisted in northern-based conglomerates as well. Hence, throughout the world war, a separate war went on in the shops of Memphis. Maintaining the southern wage differential still remained the central concern for many employers. Indigenous capitalists, particularly in the furniture, woodworking, cotton, and food industries, continued to claim they were unable to pay higher wages, even though they made greater profits than ever before. National companies such as Firestone and Fisher Body, which had no problem with profit margins during the war, also resisted every effort to bring up wage standards. Memphis industrial wages in fact remained among the lowest in U.S. metropolitan areas, for exactly the reason articulated by CIO unionists: employers, usually with the tacit approval of white workers, had locked blacks into low-wage occupations and by doing so effectively dragged wages down for all workers. Even during the war, employers had blacks at the bottom of the wage and occupational heap, and they intended to keep them there.

As a result of this pervasive recalcitrant attitude among employers, CIO unions during the war spent much of their time locked in bitter struggles to bring up the low base rate of pay among blacks in unskilled and semiskilled positions. They did this not out of concern for blacks per se, but because they realized that only by doing this could they lift industrial wages generally. UCAPAWA organizers fought numerous such cases, usually winning only a few cents an hour in increases against determined employer resistance. For example, UCAPAWA brought a case before the WLB in an attempt to get the Cudahy corporation, a major national meat-packing company and producer of edible oils, to bring the minimum wage up to a mere fifty cents an hour—a rate that would still have provided an average income far below what the federal government projected as the "minimum" standard of living. The company stalled a WLB decision through procedural delays, shirked the minimal wage increases already gained by the union by reclassifying semiskilled workers into unskilled categories, and refused a union demand for a maintenance of membership clause. In the end, the WLB raised the minimum wage of forty-three cents an hour for men and thirty-seven cents an hour for women a mere three cents; it rejected UCAPAWA's demand for union security; and it did nothing to enforce equal pay for women, a principle mandated by the union's constitution. Restrained from direct action by the CIO's "no-strike" pledge, workers watched in frustration as the cost of living in Memphis increased by 27 percent within the first year and a half of the war while their wages remained stationary.[25]

The Cudahy case, the union declared, provided but one example of northern industry exploiting southern labor, while the WLB continued "symbolically tipping its hat to absentee owners who have ruthlessly exploited this Region and its people." Unionized workers experienced even greater frustration in dealing with locally owned companies. Employers in the woodworking industry remained among the worst. The IWA at Anderson-Tulley lumber company spent 352 days trying, and failing, to implement an initial contract for nine hundred black workers signed by the company in February 1943. The management in this case brought in George Kamenow, a Detroit attorney, who promised to hold meetings and never showed up, refused to talk to federal labor conciliators, and claimed to agree to wage increases that never appeared in the contract. Once Kamenow reached "agreement" on a token two-cent wage increase, the company refused to sign it, all the while telling workers in the shop that Anderson-Tulley would "never" implement either the contract or a wage increase. After the WLB stepped into the case, the management refused to implement the board's directives to increase wages. In March 1945 the WLB took the unusual step of refusing to order striking workers back to their jobs because of the company's refusal to negotiate a new contract. In the end, management destroyed the IWA in its shop, despite the fact that the union had squarely won an NLRB election there. The union had similar troubles with other employers who signed contracts but refused to carry them out or continue bargaining. Mississippi Valley Hardwood, for example, refused to negotiate a new contract in 1943, stating that it "was good enough last year, so it must be good enough this year, and that's that." [26]

CIO unions had particular difficulty in winning union security in shops where employers and AFL unions had teamed up to keep the CIO out. Locally owned Memphis Furniture—one of the oldest companies in Memphis, its owners praised by Senator McKellar as "high class, honorable men"—proved to be one of the most devious in its opposition to the CIO. The AFL's Upholsterers' International Union had gained bargaining rights in the shop and led a May 1941 strike, but in the next two years failed to produce gains for the workers. Concerned that the majority black work force was "susceptible to CIO propaganda," the company and the AFL union continued to enforce a clause allowing management to fire anyone that failed "to maintain harmony" in the shop. Yet even this covenant failed to keep out the CIO, which overwhelmingly defeated the AFL by a vote of 379–31 in September 1943. According to an FBI investigation of the plant, however, not a single white worker joined the CIO's United Furniture Workers of America, which sought a maintenance of membership clause and a union dues checkoff from workers' paychecks as crucial protections against a hostile employer and the AFL. The company responded by bringing in union-buster Kamenow, who attempted to intimidate federal labor mediators and used his whole range of anti-union tactics to stall negotiations. In the end, the all-black CIO union failed to gain the checkoff and achieved a pay raise of only four cents an hour, not a great gain for workers making a mere forty-one cents an hour. During the war, the company transformed its predominantly male work force into one that was largely female (though still mostly black). This rapid turnover undermined existing union membership and served as an excuse to keep wages among the lowest in Memphis.[27]

In these and other cases, manufacturers during the war sought to keep unions weak and to uphold an extremely low minimum wage for black labor. They had considerable success in this effort because of the continued, though declining, influence of the rural labor market. Blacks constituted more than 50 percent of the population in most of the counties surrounding Memphis, and in those areas white landholders still could use the power conferred on them by segregation to rule with an iron fist. According to a 1942 meeting of the Southern Tenant Farmers' Union held in Memphis, agricultural laborers still made as little as fifty cents for a working day that sometimes lasted from three in the morning until eleven at night. Even with the wage increases rural workers subsequently won due to the labor shortage created by the war, the wages of agricultural workers remained far below those paid to factory workers. Some five to eight thousand day laborers left Memphis every day to engage in backbreaking labor in the cotton fields, and local factory owners repeatedly claimed that industrial wage scales should be compared to the debased wages of these agricultural workers, not to the wages of factory workers in the North. In their view, Memphis factory workers should not complain about wage rates of forty to fifty cents an hour. If they did, they could always be replaced by hungry rural migrants.[28]

BARRIERS OF RACE AND GENDER

Wartime industrial employment offered agricultural workers a better alternative to the plantation system, and many of them came to the city as much to escape the arbitrary power of the riding boss and the planter as

they did to achieve higher wages. But even during wartime labor shortages, industrial jobs remained difficult to obtain in the South for those
with black skin. Delta property owners complained bitterly whenever they
lost black laborers to war industries, and some government analysts feared
that "if too many negroes are drawn into the industrial labor market . . . a
serious shortage of agricultural workers would probably obtain." In deference to the needs of the cotton economy, many of the new war industries
avoided hiring African Americans except for the most menial jobs considered unfit for whites, and black citizens in Chattanooga and elsewhere
protested at the start of the war that local industries excluded them from
hiring altogether. Even in the face of wartime labor shortages, northern as
well as southern companies frequently brought in whites from outside the
region rather than train available local blacks for semiskilled jobs. In Mississippi, for example, General Tire of Akron refused to hire blacks, as did
federal agencies in the state. Similarly, in the Mobile, Alabama, shipyards
employers, unions, and federal agencies alike did everything they could to
avoid hiring local blacks, despite unprecedented labor demand.[29]

Throughout the war, it remained unclear whether manufacturing growth
would weaken or only further entrench the racial system that undergirded
segregation and cheap wages. The U.S. Employment Service (USES) and
state employment agencies in the South consciously collaborated in excluding blacks from nonmenial factory work by setting up programs that
provided vocational training for whites, including women, while almost
entirely excluding blacks, male and female alike. In Memphis, by May
1942, vocational training programs for the war had enrolled 1,084 whites
and only 98 blacks, less than 10 percent of the total number of workers.
In 1943, black inclusion increased to a little under one-fourth of the total
in an urban labor force nearly 60 percent black. Even blacks who did get
into these programs discovered, however, that "vocational" training meant
something different for blacks than it did for whites. White men attempting to enter the industrial labor force received training for skilled work as
airplane mechanics, machine and tool operators, electricians, sheet metal
workers, riveters, and welders, while blacks trained as cement finishers, tire
changers, and in other semiskilled, low-wage occupations. Black women
received almost no training at all. The USES, via a separate division for
black employment run by southern whites, even refused to place blacks in
the semiskilled jobs for which they were trained. It was the same all over
the South, according to the federal investigator John Beecher, who gave
example after example of the "pathetic farce" of black "training" programs

devoid of content or resources. "Nearly all USES offices in this region," another investigator wrote in 1944, exhibited "open disregard" for fair employment principles.[30]

A careful study found that the pervasive pattern of USES discrimination in the South "differed from other regions only in degree,"[31] but exclusionary practices proved more difficult to break down in the South than in the North and West. Employers opened up jobs to white women or imported white workers from outside of the area to avoid hiring blacks in Memphis. Of new hires listed by June 1942, Memphis industries had hired nine thousand white women but only twelve hundred black men. So few black women made it into industrial employment that statisticians didn't even bother to provide a listing of them. At Chickasaw Ordnance, of thirty-six hundred workers only fifteen were black. As the war went on, some employers of necessity increasingly hired blacks, but the pattern of discrimination within industry never changed. While whites, female as well as male, found increasing opportunities for decent paying work in industry, blacks remained mired in common laborer and semiskilled positions at rock-bottom pay. Blacks came to Memphis from the countryside at the bottom of the economic heap, and in large measure stayed there, while whites moved up. Even housing programs reinforced this pattern: "There is not a single available house in Memphis for colored," one report noted, although housing did exist in small amounts for white war workers.[32]

President Roosevelt's Fair Employment Practices Commission (FEPC), established at the end of 1941 to prod employers with government war contracts to end employment discrimination, raised hopes for equal employment. But the conditions associated with wartime industrialization in many ways only accentuated the color line. Segregationists and anti-union employers dominated the regional WLB in Atlanta, for example, and the NAACP's Walter White complained to the president that no blacks sat on the WLB out of twelve members and twenty-four alternates. The head of the regional War Production Board, according to John Beecher, called protests against racial discrimination Axis propaganda, while the head of the U.S. Education Office responsible for employment training programs imposed segregation or complete racial exclusion at every opportunity. The FEPC itself until 1943 remained under the control of administrative authorities with little interest in efforts to end job discrimination. In Memphis, FEPC investigators maintained a list of Memphis industries discriminating against blacks, but did nothing to penalize them. Even when an FEPC investigator documented the firing of a black woman for refusing to have sex with a white supervisor, his superiors imposed no penalties. As during the New Deal, federal agencies proved of little help to blacks in ending employment discrimination in the South.[33]

Meanwhile, black exclusion from better-paying and more skilled positions remained a constant. Blacks worked as sweepers, laborers, or semi-skilled operatives and in other menial positions, while whites obtained the jobs classified as skilled work at higher rates of pay. In one clearly documented case of discrimination, Fisher Aircraft exclusively assigned five thousand or more blacks to the lowest job classifications at lower rates of pay than for comparable work in other parts of the country. When the UAW appealed to the federal Mediation and Conciliation Service to change these conditions, Memphis member of Congress Clifford Davis put in a fix with John Steelman, head of the service. Davis wrote to Mayor Chandler that "John Steelman doesn't want us to even think about the Fisher Aircraft labor matter," for he had "put this matter on the bottom of a very heavy stack of pending matters, in the hope that it might be so long delayed that the war would be over and we would have no further need to concern ourselves." The union took the case to the WLB, but not until 1945 did it finally get a ruling retroactively increasing the rates of pay for black laborers. Black complaints against the AFL building trades unions, which continued to almost totally exclude African Americans from all but laborer jobs in construction work, never did receive any action. The war had the devastating effect of further freezing blacks out of all lines of skilled craft employment. As defense contractors began going directly to the unions for employment referrals, black carpenters and other crafters had even less access to union jobs than they did in the thirties.[34]

In factories with biracial work forces, unequal wage scales and discriminatory job classifications remained visible to all. At the Buckeye cottonseed oil company, for example, employers required black millwrights with seven years of experience to handle pipe-fitting, welding, and cement-finishing jobs outside of their classification, paying them only $.44 an hour while whites doing the same work made between $.88 and $.98 an hour. At a local wood products company, black stokers made $.47 an hour, while white stokers made up to $1.00. Black bricklayers in the same plant also made $.47, while whites made up to $1.62 for the same work. At a nearby defense production plant in Jackson, a black worker complained that blacks with bachelor's and master's degrees still had to work at laborer's jobs, while whites with no education beyond high school ran machines and worked as clerks and labor supervisors. As one USES survey put it, even when some 255 black males were available for technical, administrative, and professional work, there was no "projected demand" for their labor—meaning, employers would not hire them.[35]

Similarly, the racially skewed job classification system kept blacks in the lowest-paying positions in the Firestone factory. Whereas 683 blacks, almost all male, made up about 30 percent of the 1942 work force, only 51 of these workers held skilled jobs. Another 181 held semiskilled positions and 451 held jobs classified as unskilled. And while the company almost immediately broke white women into semiskilled work when it expanded the work force, it continued to hire black men for laborer positions only. Fisher Aircraft did the same, bringing in 700 white women as riveters and operatives doing subassembly work, leaving 70 percent of the black employees (all men) in unskilled positions. The company had begun the war by laying off some 700 black men, and when it reopened the plant it refused to call the older men back. In their place, Fisher trained and hired whites. These new workers had the possibility of moving up the job ladder; remaining black employees with many years of seniority remained in laborer classifications, with the lowest pay.[36]

Although industrialists employed larger numbers of African Americans during the war than ever before, they filled the huge demand for semiskilled factory labor primarily with white women. Whereas white women in the thirties had been confined to pharmaceuticals, garment work, and a few other industries, during the war they made up half of the new entries to the factory labor force. At Firestone, white women made up one-third of the work force and 75 percent of the new hires by 1943. Because racial and sexual taboos especially forbid white women and black men from any sort of contact outside of a master-servant relationship, the entrance of white women into factory labor served as an excuse not to employ more blacks or to upgrade those already employed. Black Firestone workers recalled how tensions became acute when black men and white women worked in any close proximity; black men had to walk through the factory with their eyes down, so as not to look directly at a white woman. After the war, the plant almost erupted into a riot when a white woman accused a black man of urinating into a can when he could not get relief to go to the bathroom.[37] A similarly volatile racial and gender mix occurred in numerous other plants (see table 7.2).[38]

Industrial employment of larger numbers of white women and black men substantially increased the overall earnings of these two groups, but employers continued to tier occupations so that both groups uniformly made lower wages than white men. Average wage rates for common labor in Memphis industry in 1945, even after the wage increases granted dur-

Table 7.2. Women and Blacks in Industry

	Women				Blacks			
	1942	%	1943	%	1942	%	1943	%
Ordnance	637	47.8	1,300	43.4	93	5.0	151	7.0
Textile	—	—	1,205	51.0	—	—	1,099	46.5
Lumber	85	3.5	626	13.9	1,884	78.0	2,758	61.2
Paper	240	55.8	825	56.8	100	23.3	383	26.3
Chemicals	795	15.6	963	17.4	774	15.3	1,481	26.8
Rubber	500	18.9	1,943	33.8	700	26.5	1,660	28.8
Aircraft	—	—	577	21.0	—	—	123	5.0
Iron manufacturing	30	2.4	43	5.0	150	12.0	125	14.4
Other industries	921	20.2	1,671	31.2	2,263	9.5	2,666	50.0
Transportation, communication, and public utilities	171	5.8	723	21.6	—	—	627	18.8
Federal depots, air transports, hospitals, and naval facilities	—	—	2,158	30.3	—	—	2,123	29.8

Source: Compiled from "Labor Market Developments Report," 15 Apr. 1943 and 15 Oct. 1943, Memphis Files, USES, USDL, RG 183, NARA.

ing the war, remained low, typically ranging from $.47 to $.52 per hour. Black men continued to fill most of these positions. Semiskilled jobs paid from $.50 to $.75 per hour, and white males, joined by white women and a sprinkling of black men, filled most of these positions. Skilled jobs, at much higher rates of pay, were almost uniformly filled by white men. In the all-male construction industry, common laborers, practically all of them blacks, made $.50 an hour; semiskilled workers, black and white, made $.65 to $.85 an hour; and skilled workers, almost all of them white, made anywhere from $1.12 to $1.62 an hour—sumptuous wages by Memphis standards.[39]

Southern wages for the unskilled lagged so badly behind the rest of the United States that in 1943 the WLB took the significant step of ending wage differentials based solely on race. But this ruling did not close the economic gaps produced by occupational segregation. If wages doubled and in some cases even tripled compared to the thirties, white males in skilled positions increased their earning power much more dramatically than did black males, or white women, in semiskilled and laborer positions. At Firestone black male common laborers made $.50 an hour; white females made $.55; semiskilled laborers, white and a few black males, made $.65 an hour; and white male skilled workers made from $.96 an hour (tire builders) to $1.18 (machinists). Although everyone improved their wages compared to the thirties, skilled workers in 1943 made as much as twice the wages paid to unskilled and semiskilled workers, a much greater disparity than existed in the earlier period. This widening wage gap between skilled and unskilled industrial workers would only increase in the postwar years.[40]

While black men and white women struggled separately to improve their lot, black women remained all but ignored. Black women, government and industry analysts believed, could not be absorbed into war production and were mostly denied access to industrial jobs. Why? Black women had always worked outside their own homes in large numbers, although confined mainly to domestic tasks. Of the 20,251 black women estimated by the Memphis Negro Chamber of Commerce to be employed in 1941, nearly 12,000 worked as domestic servants and over 4,500 worked as launderers, either privately or for dry-cleaning companies. White employers of these women constantly pressured officials not to draw off their dwindling labor supply; white middle- and upper-class households especially resisted losing their domestic workers to better-paying employment. Industrial employers, influenced by this pressure as well as prevailing racist and sexist stereotypes that pictured black women as capable only of doing domestic and menial work, generally hired black women as a last resort. Hence, black women made the transition to industrial employment in the lowest-paying jobs—mainly in the lumber industry, at Memphis Furniture, in small labor-intensive shops, and in janitorial work and manual labor in a few places such as Firestone. Even these jobs paid better than domestic work or cotton picking, however.[41]

The few black women employed at Firestone did the hot, heavy, miserable work normally reserved for black men. Evelyn Bates, for example, began work in 1944 sorting tires stacked six and seven feet high outdoors in the blazing sun. She hauled tires, often filled with water and infested with bugs and snakes and weighing up to seventy pounds a piece, seven days a week. "I didn't like it," she recalled, "but I didn't have any other choice because I wanted to work . . . [and] if you quit that job you didn't get another factory job probably. Not a black woman. You might go to a little cafe, do housework or something like that, but factory jobs were hard for black women to get." Bates had to put on a big dress with a hoop skirt and many slips, making her look heavier than she was, to even get a job at Firestone; they required workers to weigh at least 150 pounds and she weighed only 100.[42]

Other jobs for black women at Firestone included stacking, hauling, and cutting bad pieces out of tires, all heavy hand labor. Alternatively, black women worked in the kind of jobs assigned to them in the domestic economy. "The idea was," said Bates, "that the white women didn't want to sweep, she didn't want to clean up no rest room, and that was a black woman's job. It's just like you got a white man's job and a black man's job. And that's the way it was with the womens too." Little if any solidarity developed between black and white women, for black women remained classified with black men as common labor, not as female labor. To get into the higher-paying category, they would have had to compete with white women for jobs in the supply room, on the assembly line, or as supervisors. "You had a white woman always over you," Irene Branch recalled. "She gonna see that you work . . . you couldn't go to the bathroom and stay no time. If you did, she'd come in there and get you." As to the hard work, "you had to take it, see," Branch recalled. "You couldn't do nothing else but had to take it or get going. Go somewhere else and get another job, you know, one place as bad as the other place. There was no use." Only after the war, when black civil rights initiatives began to break down job segregation, did the situation improve. Meanwhile, Branch related, "I just prayed and prayed and stayed on in there 'til things got better." [43]

BLACK WORKERS AND LABOR MILITANCE

The war effort seemed to promise a better deal for factory workers, but not without continuing pressure on employers from workers and the unions. In response to such pressure, employers had recognized unions and signed agreements with them, but they fought tooth and nail against the benefits workers expected to see follow from unionization. With enough resistance, employers hoped to and sometimes did kill off new CIO locals, often while cultivating support for craft unions among better-paid white workers. At the start of the war, workers tolerated this situation in hopes that the WLB would intervene on their behalf. But the federal bureaucracy moved slowly for workers, and by 1943 their patience had worn thin. Because their conditions remained so much worse than whites and angered by their difficulties in getting into higher wage categories, blacks frequently became the most volatile element of the labor movement.

At Proctor and Gamble's two Buckeye cottonseed oil and cellulose plants, employing seven hundred blacks and three hundred whites, UCAPAWA Local 19 leaders repeatedly postponed strikes for wage increases among the blacks by promising action from the federal government. But the workers became frustrated by the failure of either the WLB or the NLRB to increase their wages. As early as May 1942, UCAPAWA shop leader Edward Johnson wrote to Eleanor Roosevelt for help, pleading, "We have been working under all types of unfair conditions and we are tired of it, we have filed over thirty cases to the national labor relations board and they are stalling." John Mack Dyson appealed for help to CIO president Philip Murray, writing that "if we cant get eight cent and half starve to death we would rather for the government to take over the plant and run it." When the black workers did strike, the company, with support from the WLB and union officials, fined and suspended their leaders. Continuing to receive far lower wages than whites, they walked out again. Similarly frustrated, blacks struck other Memphis plants throughout 1943 and 1944. When striking AFL teamsters stopped bringing supplies in to Kraus cleaners, 100 black laundry workers joined the strike and in turn demanded bargaining rights for another 183 unrepresented black seamstresses. All three groups refused to go back to work until the WLB settled their cases jointly. In numerous cases, blacks proved so ready to strike that whites in some shops began to rely on their militance to push up wages for everyone. Wrote the CIO's William R. Henderson, "That has been the draw back in many of the Memphis Plants employing more negroes than white. The White men have wanted the negroes to stick their necks out."[44]

However, employers and the news media also accused white workers of "strike-itis," a new disease that afflicted everyone at the Firestone plant. Workers there, despite condemnation from the Memphis Industrial Union Council, began a series of work slowdowns and walkouts in early 1943, when the WLB failed to take action on wage adjustments. When the board retaliated for the walkouts by suspending all consideration of a wage increase, the workers walked out again. And when the company removed its piece-rate guarantee, actually lowering the wages of production workers, white female stockroom workers and male tire builders again shut down the plant. At a stormy mass meeting in April, a predominantly white group of workers heckled WLB officials and CIO leaders alike, their taunts driving URW representative Forrest Dickenson from the stage. A third of the workers voted for the federal government to take over the plant. Putting in seven-day weeks with no improvement in their wages since voting in the CIO, many workers felt sold out by the union and the government. Media cries of "treason," Selective Service threats to draft strikers, and union threats of FBI intervention finally forced them back to work.[45]

The continuing strikes at Firestone finally pressured the WLB to direct a retroactive wage increase to all the company's workers and to grant a maintenance of membership clause, requiring all current employees to remain union members for the life of the contract. While one employer on the board denounced this provision as "the destruction of private enterprise," the majority adopted the union's rationale that "complete voluntary labor organization is impossible" in a racially mixed southern plant because a certain number of whites always refused to join an interracial union. The board ruling allowed the CIO rubber union to stabilize its existence, while throughout the remainder of the war Firestone workers engaged in numerous unauthorized slowdowns and strikes to expand their power. They ultimately compelled the company to adopt an effective grievance procedure, a seniority system that protected workers' jobs during layoffs or strikes, a voluntary dues checkoff, vacation with pay, and six paid holidays—"things we never dreamed of before," Richard Routon recalled. These benefits resulted in part from war and industrial growth, but most important from militance by both whites and blacks in the workplace. Firestone workers remained so militant that in one 1945 strike it required a meeting of the entire Memphis CIO to get them back to work.[46]

While white and black frequently struck together to strengthen their bargaining power, they also struggled amongst themselves over the racial terms of unionism. Black discontent at Buckeye increasingly focused on the Jim Crow job classifications and other conditions that placed them at a disadvantage to white workers. Black painters, for example, remained classified as laborers while working alongside white painters classified as skilled workers and drawing twice the pay. When, in June 1943, federal mediators imposed a settlement that jeopardized their chances to advance to higher-paying positions, 160 blacks walked out of the Buckeye Jackson Avenue plant. The wildcat strike spread to the company's Hollywood Avenue plant, and only threats and fines imposed by the UCAPAWA's business agent finally got the strikers back to work. Yet Buckeye management continued to exclude blacks, who made up 75 percent of the work force, from higher-paying job classifications. As a result, a federal mediator reported that "the race issue is very much alive within this plant" and that black committee members would not let the job classification issue rest. In June 1944, blacks struck for one day at Buckeye's Hollywood Avenue division, and blacks at the Jackson plant later held another five-day strike. Despite the continued discontent, the conflict over job classifications remained unresolved until after the war.[47]

The Buckeye strikes made it evident that many unionized black workers would no longer accept discriminatory practices and placed business agents for the union in a ticklish position. UCAPAWA, unlike most CIO unions, included a provision against racial discrimination in its contracts, and yet strikes seemed to be the only way to implement this provision. However, the union, renamed the Food, Tobacco, and Agricultural Workers' Union (FTA) at its 1944 convention, held to a strict antistrike position during the war. In the face of this contradiction, FTA business agents took the ambivalent position of supporting black demands while imposing fines if necessary to get them back to work. William A. "Red" Copeland and Forrest Dickenson, on behalf of the national CIO, urged the blacks to put off action on job classification until after the war in return for immediate wage increases. But mediators blamed Local 19 president John Mack Dyson, who worked at the Hollywood plant, and other black "trouble makers" for continuing to agitate the issue. In reality, one labor mediator pointed out, there were no ringleaders; the Buckeye strikes constituted a "mass decision" to oppose discrimination.[48]

If black workers in other industries emulated the struggle against racial job classifications of workers in FTA's Local 19, there would have been no end to the strikes, for almost every industry maintained this discriminatory system. Most black workers did not risk walkouts over this issue during the war. However, an accumulation of grievances continued to set off labor upheaval, especially at Firestone. There tension over poor wages, speedup, long hours of work, segregated jobs, wages, and facilities, and company resistance to improving conditions produced constant turmoil. Strikes by white tire builders, white female stockroom workers, black Banbury machine operators, and relatively small groups in other departments could shut down the entire process of production for six to seven thousand workers. Recognizing this power, Firestone employees became the most testy and militant of Memphis workers. "That plant became famous for its walkouts," H. B. Griffin recalled, and was closely watched by the FBI, military intelligence, and everyone concerned with war production.[49]

The testy militance of Firestone workers made them the natural leaders of the CIO movement in Memphis. But, in the context of simmering racial conflicts, strike turmoil also potentially endangered the URW local. The danger of racial schism had been evident ever since Richard Routon had calmed down the first racial walkout there. This incident proved to be only the start of a stormy and continuing confrontation between whites and blacks over the meaning of trade unionism—with blacks wanting to use the union to batter down segregation and many whites wanting to use it to keep segregation in place. At the bottom of this conflict lay the racial wage system put in place by the company in the thirties. Firestone in Memphis employed the highest percentage of black workers of any American rubber plant, in a town that had driven black wages down to rock-bottom;

through its racially based "A, B, C" system, Firestone in Memphis established the lowest wage for rubber workers anywhere in the country. The first step toward alleviating the tension in the plant turned on the union's demand that the company raise wages for everyone, but the company continued to claim that its wages should be based on the average paid in Memphis, not in Akron or even in other parts of the South. The WLB disagreed and in 1945 raised wages for Memphis Firestone workers by 11 percent across the board; it also abolished the company's three-tiered system, which classified wages according to whether a worker was black, white, or female. Union leaders did not take the next step of calling for an end to discriminatory job classifications, however, fearing the possible backlash from challenging the prerogatives of whites, especially white males, entrenched in skilled and semiskilled employment.[50]

Amongst hard-won victories, ominous signs of racial conflict in the latter stages of the war increasingly threatened to tear the CIO apart. CIO unions all across the United States experienced discord between whites and blacks over jobs, wages, and housing. Urban crowding, long hours of work, a wage freeze, and poor conditions inside the factories produced explosive tensions, leading in June 1943 to a white-initiated race riot in Detroit that left twenty-five blacks and nine whites dead. The riot set a divisive and fearful tone within the labor movement, as hate strikes and racial conflicts escalated all over the nation. In Birmingham, white workers struck against blacks being admitted into a formerly all-white department in a local factory, and this and other job desegregation efforts nearly led to riots. In Mobile, whites shot blacks going to their jobs in the shipyards. In Pine Bluff, Arkansas, six hundred whites struck and nearly precipitated a riot over the employment of black women. Racial tension existed in Memphis for many of the same reasons, with blacks attempting to use the wartime labor demand to increase wages and find better jobs, employers trying to keep the price of labor down, and white workers trying to improve their conditions while holding onto their racial prerogatives. Racial conflict during the war, observed the historian Bruce Nelson, produced in some workplaces "a virtual civil war that served to intensify the internal divisions within the American working class at a moment when the potential for unity and concerted action seemed to be greater than ever before."[51]

RACIAL POLARIZATION AND THE CIO

By 1944, the war-induced shortage of cheap black labor had local employers of domestic workers, cotton pickers, and factory hands in an uproar. Planters in the countryside complained that blacks would not bring in the cotton, and indeed rural agricultural workers left the plantations for the cities in record numbers. In cities such as Memphis, the middle class feared "uprisings" of the "coloreds," and rumors of "Eleanor Clubs" among domestic workers abounded. Memphis manufacturers complained to the mayor that blacks "shopped around" for the highest-paying jobs and would not work on the old terms. Employers generally demanded that blacks "work or fight," regardless of wages or conditions. City police supported this demand by giving idle blacks found on the street the option of loading up on the cotton trucks or going to jail; federal officials dropped those who refused to pick cotton from relief programs; and ads by the Negro Chamber of Commerce urged blacks to take up work in cotton fields and warehouses as a patriotic duty. But many would no longer accept the pitiful wages offered for these jobs, preferring to hold out for something better. Few employers willingly accepted this new fact of life and many of them decried black "laziness." To many, such complaints seemed entirely cynical. "Yesterday the cotton planters did not need cotton workers at any price," a researcher at Fisk University reported. "Now they want them but without paying them what they are worth today. Tomorrow they are planning to release them wholesale." The problem was not black laziness, for no one worked harder than blacks in low-wage occupations; the "problem" was that blacks finally perceived the possibility of doing better.[52]

If employers had difficulty accepting the right of black workers to seek the highest-paying jobs, whites generally had even more trouble accepting the changed attitude toward segregation increasingly evident among African Americans. Opposition to Jim Crow, usually covert, became increasingly overt, as individual challenges repeatedly occurred in the streets and especially on buses. Black naval recruit Willie Hall and his white sailor friends, as one example, told a bus driver, "Hell no, we ain't going to the back of the bus" and sat down in the "white" section. When police arrested a black teacher for refusing to give up her seat to a white, her minister and two thousand members of her church protested to the mayor. Working-class preachers such as Rev. Roy Love, a former laborer at DeSoto Hardwood flooring company, increasingly made their churches available for union and civil rights meetings. In 1944, the African Methodist Episcopal minister and civil rights activist D. V. Kyle came to Memphis and began working with Local 19 and a revived NAACP, whose membership increased tenfold during the war, from four hundred to four thousand members.[53]

The new racial militance had everything to do with the war. Blacks provided 50 percent of the city's early draft registrants, 10 percent more than their percentage of the general population, and fund-raising drives for the war made Memphis the "Negro War Bond Capital of the U.S." With blacks supporting the war against fascism abroad, new demands arose for a war against Jim Crow, which some viewed as a form of fascism at home. Yet domestic racism remained as rampant as ever. The owner of White Rose Laundry, where 150 blacks worked, blithely ignored a petition campaign to take down racist advertisements, police violence escalated in the streets, and the city's censorship board continued to cut parts of films that showed blacks in nonmenial roles "not ordinarily performed by members of the colored race in real life." Added to such daily insults, stories appeared regularly of black soldiers beaten and lynched in southern military camps, while German prisoners of war in Louisiana and Mississippi seemed to receive better treatment than local blacks. Under such circumstances, many doubted the antifascist rhetoric of the war. In one poll taken among Memphis blacks in 1942, 75 percent of the respondents thought they would be treated better than they currently were if Japan conquered the United States (although only 55 percent said this when interviewed by a white). Even before the United States entered the war, a black Memphian had protested to Roosevelt that "a German can come to U.S. and have more to say then We do" and went on to write: "The other day We told our Sons that they soon would have to go. to War. And they reply Why. I said for Your Country. they Said that Was not they Country. And it brought to me a thought. We Work hard For Our Children And raise them up and I think that we Should have Some thing to Say After All." The writer concluded by demanding equal pay with whites, blacks on juries, black police in black neighborhoods, and an end to rape frame-ups.[54]

Black workers bore the brunt of racism and grew increasingly angered by the contradictions of the war against fascism. They knew that the daily practices of discrimination in the plants where they worked violated the spirit if not the letter of federal policy, which at least rhetorically prohibited employment discrimination. They also knew of the beatings, lynchings, and other assaults on human dignity occurring in the South. George Holloway experienced the contradictions of the war for "democracy" when white officials forced him and other Pullman porters to eat in the kitchen during a stopover in Little Rock, while German prisoners of war dined in a luxurious hotel restaurant for whites only. Clarence Coe and others at Firestone heard about this incident and of numerous white attacks on black soldiers stationed in the South. In protest, Coe signed up hundreds of NAACP members at the plant. He became so disgusted by stories of Jim Crow in the military that he decided, "I wanted no damn part of this" and used his asthma to avoid the draft. But his unremitting work in the factory was not much better than being in the army. "I had to work seven days a week . . . and there was one whole year that I didn't see the sunset," he recalled. But blacks got no respect for their contributions from white supervisors, who could make up any lie to dismiss black workers. "Whatever a white person said, that was it," Coe remembered bitterly.[55]

During the final two years of the war, race relations reached their boiling point in Memphis. In 1943, a major confrontation began when the National Urban League appointed a militant young African American, a former Teamster organizer, as its executive secretary in Memphis. Benjamin Bell, like Nebraska Jones in 1939, decided that the demand for black labor rights was the key to changing Memphis. He began speaking and writing boldly against discrimination in local employment, protesting the exclusion of blacks from skilled work and industrial jobs, and helping to organize black laundry workers. When he refused to sit in segregated seats on a city bus, a white bus driver beat him and threatened him with a pistol. Just as they had replaced Jones, the Urban League, under pressure from the Crump machine, replaced Bell with someone more compliant, a minister named James McDaniel. But Bell then became involved with a chapter of the Brotherhood of Sleeping Car Porters, which invited the union's black president, A. Philip Randolph, to speak at Rev. Roy Love's Mt. Nebo Baptist Church. The invitation set off a six-month free speech battle and became mixed up with growing racial turmoil in Memphis factories.[56]

The Crump machine came down hard on every black leader it could find to stop the Randolph meeting. The county sheriff ordered twenty black leaders to the county jail, where, according to Randolph, county attorney Will Gerber "told them that the white people of Memphis were arming themselves with clubs and guns and were going to break up the meeting." Although Randolph had been speaking at union meetings all over the South without interference, Love and the others felt compelled to cancel his Memphis meeting. Randolph was not so easily denied, however, showing up at a private meeting sponsored by the Southern Tenant Farmers' Union (now part of the AFL) in November 1943. At the meeting and in his subsequent travels around the United States, Randolph denounced the Crump machine's violation of civil liberties and black rights, setting off Crump diatribes against "imported negroes" stirring up race trouble. According to Crump, "about 99 per cent of the negroes in Memphis appreciate what has been done for them," but "about 1 per cent of the negroes will never be satisfied . . . unless there is complete equality." He concluded that Memphis would run its own affairs "and no outsiders will ever run them for us."[57]

Crump had not changed, but others had. Southern AFL leader George Googe supported the Randolph meeting, as did Robert Tillman and other AFL leaders, with only Lev Loring finally blocking local AFL support. And when police attempted to stop Rev. George Long from holding the rally in his Beale Street Baptist church, Long announced, "I take orders only from Christ. . . . I did not ask Mr. Crump if I could come to this town, and I am not going to ask him if I may stay. . . . The issue raised by Mr. Crump is the issue around the world—Freedom." Long declared that "Christ, not Crump, is my Boss," and if blacks could fight and die for freedom overseas they could do it in Memphis as well. Finally, on 31 March 1944, an interracial gathering of eleven hundred, most of them union members, met at Long's church to hear Randolph denounce Jim Crow and call for the establishment of nonsegregated AFL locals and for black and white unity within the labor movement. He drew clear parallels to the police state atmosphere in Memphis and fascism abroad, saying Crump had "out-Hitlered Hitler." For perhaps the first time in the twentieth century, a public meeting had been successfully held in Memphis articulating what many had long believed but feared to say.[58]

Following this victory against fascism at home, however, a wave of repression began that touched even the most highly respected black leaders. The fire department's condemnation of Reverend Long's church as a fire hazard was a minor harassment compared to brutal police treatment of numerous blacks on the streets. Thugs also came back into the Memphis picture, attacking Reverend Long and black Republican leader George Lee with knives and clubs and trying to attack Bell in an alley with an iron bar. The same two men cornered Rev. L. O. Taylor of Olivet Baptist Church and Rev. Roy Love with lead pipes, and thugs also beat two prominent black physicians. Detectives warned even the conservative "brown screw" in the Crump machine, high school principal Blair T. Hunt, that he too was in for a beating, and anonymous callers warned Nat D. Williams, editor of the *Memphis World*, not to publicize the incidents. Many believed these assailants had previously done undercover work for the Memphis police department. It seemed clear enough, said black AFL organizer Cornelius Maiden, that the attackers intended "to terrorize the negroes." The beatings of leading figures like Lee, who "is sort of a God to all Negroes," according to Maiden, demonstrated to blacks that "if he can be attacked any one can." Maiden reported that "the Negroes think the next phase will be some sort of attempt at a race riot so a lot of Negroes will be killed," and that even conservative blacks such as Hunt had taken to carrying guns.[59]

Increasing racial polarization in the factories paralleled the violence exploding in the streets of Memphis, and the possibility that the racial crisis would destroy the young industrial unions haunted the CIO. Conditions at the Firestone plant became especially tense. Blacks remained quite aware that the company's management had, with the cooperation of the USES (which referred not a single black among the 200 trainees it provided Firestone in early 1944), kept higher-paying jobs closed to them, primarily by hiring white women instead of blacks for many of the semiskilled positions. Hence they reacted strongly in January 1944 when the company made plans to remove 168 black operators of Banbury machines, used to mix chemicals and raw rubber. Six months earlier these semiskilled positions had been held entirely by whites. The management replaced them on an experimental basis with blacks in order to alleviate labor shortages, but now claimed blacks could not handle the job. A strike by the blacks forced them to back down. White union leaders, realizing that further changes in job classifications would throw the plant into chaos, covertly supported the blacks—according to the FBI, "personally advising the employees to stop work while at the same time officially urging them not to stop work."[60]

Worried URW leaders viewed racial divisiveness as the potential Achilles' heel of the union. It had been used by management and the AFL repeatedly to the detriment of the CIO. One company official had aborted an early CIO attempt to upgrade the wages of whites in the curing room, for example, by simply threatening to make it "a nigger job." Such tactics of divide and rule remained especially effective when white machine operators and maintenance workers still supported the AFL and continued to agitate against any advances for African Americans. Some of them even demanded that the union make blacks go into the union hall by the back entrance or have separate doors for whites and blacks, a request denied by union leaders. Incidents of racial violence against blacks by plant personnel also threatened disruption. In June 1944, two thousand blacks walked out, protesting the treatment of a worker by a company guard, and struck again a week later when five plant guards beat up a black man who they claimed came to work drunk. Police responded by arresting the man from his hospital bed for carrying a pocketknife. Only dramatic efforts by the CIO's Forrest Dickenson, who drove to Birmingham to speak to a labor conciliator at one o'clock in the morning, averted chaos in the shop. Based on the labor conciliator's recommendations, the company held a special meeting of plant guards, union officials, and union committees and outlined a program of "fair and equal treatment for negro employees" before the assembled group. As a result of the company's promise of better treatment, the blacks went back to work.[61]

An even more inflammatory racial incident occurred in March 1945. For black Firestone workers, this incident symbolized the degrading practices enforced by both the company and the city government. Clarence Coe explained: "The buses would come and turn around right there in front of the gate. And the whites would load first. And if there were any vacancies on the back seat, you could pay your fee up front, then go around to the back door. They weren't going to let you in the front," for fear that blacks would touch up against whites. This practice got the better of one black woman. After a long day of hot, exhausting work in the plant, she refused to wait for the whites to load up and boldly attempted to take a seat on the bus. A white plant guard, a native Mississippian, grabbed her by the arm and took her to the guard shack. When she cursed him out, the guard slugged her in the mouth, knocking out several of her teeth. The police, predictably, arrested the woman and did nothing to the guard. When blacks going to work on the second shift learned of the incident, they walked out. Hoping to quiet the situation, the company fired the woman and transferred the guard. Then six thousand whites walked out, protesting the guard's transfer, and the blacks refused to go back. Between them they closed the entire plant for three days.[62]

As if attempting to exacerbate the conflict within the factory, police began harassing black workers in the parking lots, pulling their cars apart in supposed searches for contraband and roughing them up. In one incident, sheriff's deputies arrested blacks on the street and slapped around men who admitted to membership in what they called "that damn CIO nigger union." When the union tried to hold a meeting outside the plant to calm the situation, a police car drove up with its sirens wailing. Two officers jumped out with shotguns. One of them shoved his gun into the stomach of white union official H. B. Griffin, and when local president Richard Routon tried to calm the officer, the other officer arrested him. They drove off with him in the car, one of the men cursing and threatening to beat him all the way to the police station. After the union bailed him out, Routon recalled, he returned to the plant to find black workers "all over the place," waiting to see if he would be returned safely. Only several days later, when URW international president Sherman Dalrymple threatened to revoke the union cards of all those who remained on strike, did workers return to the plant.[63]

These incidents came at a time of stiffening employer resistance during CIO contract renewals, and CIO director William A. Copeland suspected that the AFL and the Crump machine together were collaborating "to incite so many walkouts that even good CIO members will become disgusted . . . and be suckers for any suggested changeover." Routon based similar suspicions on direct experience. During the strike over the bus incident, an emissary from the police took Routon downtown to Crump's real estate office. According to Routon, "Crump sat there with his gold phone, with Joe Boyle sitting by him, chain-smoking. Crump turned and looked at me and said, 'We ain't gonna have any Chicago, Detroit, or New York in Memphis, Tennessee. We ain't gonna have any nigger-loving communist union in Memphis, Tennessee.'" Routon responded, "Mr. Crump, it is not a nigger-loving communist union, and we've got thirty thousand CIO members in Memphis today. You say we aren't gonna have 'em, but we already have 'em." According to Routon, Crump then went into a tirade about the CIO, and the union leader got up and left. Crump obviously realized that the industrial sector he had promoted so heavily was becoming a battleground over the assigned role of blacks in southern society. The New Deal and then the war had also run the Democratic party into a period of racial liberalism that jeopardized the entire structure of race and labor relations in the South. Crump and other southern leaders took direct action to stop this trend at the 1944 Democratic party convention, where they defeated Henry Wallace's renomination for vice-president in favor of the more conservative Harry Truman. In the postwar years, Crump and other southern "Dixiecrats" would take increasingly extreme measures to roll back the tide of civil rights demands.[64]

For CIO unionists inextricably bound up in the changes occurring in the southern economy, no such simple answer to black demands for more equal treatment existed. Blacks had proven themselves to be the first to join and the last to abandon industrial unions and the most ready to risk what little they had in strikes. They had also gained a somewhat stronger, though still precarious, position in industrial employment as a result of the war. Although the percentage of whites in the CIO had increased substantially compared to their percentage in the prewar CIO, industrial unionism could not continue to grow without black support. Once blacks had gained bargaining rights and initial improvements in their conditions, however, they raised their expectations. For the CIO to attract their continued support, more action for fair employment practices would be required. The national CIO recognized this reality, establishing the Committee to Abolish Racial Discrimination in 1942. President Roosevelt's 1943 Executive Order 9346 explicitly included unions as groups forbidden to discriminate in war industries, and by 1944 the CIO had established a semipermanent national antidiscrimination committee. The national CIO then called on local unions to set up their own committees to implement equal rights practices and urged internationals to put antidiscrimination clauses in their contracts.[65]

However, many if not most whites remained resistant to any change in the segregation system within the factories or union halls. Copeland and Memphis Industrial Union Council president Pete Swim, both members of the all-white American Newspaper Guild local, strongly opposed taking any public action against discrimination. Swim, in a letter to CIO secretary-treasurer James Carey in May 1944, bluntly informed the CIO, "Our council has not set up an active committee on racial discrimination and will not do so in the near future if the advice of council officers is heeded." Swim contended that the CIO must maintain a "completely economical" approach to the race problem, raising blacks out of poverty through collective bargaining, but maintaining a "hands-off" policy on what he called "the social angle." Setting up an active antidiscrimination program, he felt, "would be cutting our own throats." Although no one would have argued with Swim about the need for continued economic gains and organizational expansion, he said nothing about how to overcome the racial antagonisms of white workers or the obvious inequalities being protested by black workers. These problems could not be solved by the "hands-off" policy or administration by "experts" that he suggested.[66]

As in other regions, white CIO members in Memphis desperately needed educational programs to prepare them for the more racially egalitarian period to come.[67] Rather than extending Highlander-style education into the area of race relations, however, racially conservative whites concluded that racial matters should be hushed up. Their influence over CIO decision-making had grown during the war. In 1943, Tennessee CIO director Paul Christopher and the national CIO's director of organization, Allan S. Haywood, had chosen Copeland as full-time regional director for the CIO in the tristate area, partly on the basis that he would keep control over the left-wing unions and could not be tagged by union opponents as a Communist or an integrationist. Copeland, a copy editor at the local newspapers, personified patriotic anticommunism and white racial conservatism, regarding any white person who supported black equality with deep suspicion. He attacked Highlander's Mary Lawrence Elkuss as a Communist, in part because she insisted upon using formal titles when addressing blacks, whom Copeland habitually addressed by their first names or, worse, referred to black men as "boys." Copeland generally opposed strikes and racial mixing, reflecting his roots in a white-collar strata of the working class quite alien to the mass of white and black production workers. Guild leaders Harry Martin and Pete Swim served as successive Memphis Industrial Union Council presidents, while Copeland served on practically all of the government labor boards and conducted many of the contract and wage negotiations for CIO locals. As Copeland and his colleagues made themselves indispensable during the war expansion, they became increasingly vocal against civil rights and pushed the CIO in a conservative direction that blocked any real solution to its racial problems.[68]

CIO national leaders considered Copeland, as well as other white racial conservatives who staffed many of the CIO operations in the South, "safe" leaders for the region. But their refusal to implement the CIO's antidiscrimination policies potentially undermined CIO support among blacks, who, along with white radicals, had assumed the union movement would help to tear down segregation. Black workers in the Communist-led FTA, not only in Memphis but in Winston-Salem and other locales, had made strong gains during the war, indicating the possibility for union expansion into industries with large numbers of black workers, based on an equal rights policy.[69] Copeland increasingly attacked such policies. During an October 1944 meeting of the Memphis CIO staff, he complained that Local 19's hiring of a black office secretary forced white visitors to meet a black woman in order to make contact with the union and suggested she be moved into a back office. He considered the office situation symptomatic of the local's insistence on projecting blacks and whites as equals and complained that the union's white organizer, Joe Hellinger, had also employed an African American to represent the local before a government board and was working a black organizer into negotiations with Memphis companies. Black Local 19 president John Mack Dyson's prominence in the CIO's Political Action Committee and the mixing of black and white workers at union parties also drew his attack.[70]

Schisms over the racial question in the Memphis CIO were not resolved and became increasingly tangled in left-right divisions. Joe Hellinger, Local 19's white business representative, had been run out of nearby Brownsville for his efforts to organize blacks and made no apologies for supporting the national CIO's pledge to combat racial discrimination. Copeland, on the other hand, wanted blacks to play a distinctly subordinate and muted role in the CIO and continued to complain about Local 19's racial practices to Tennessee CIO director Paul Christopher. His complaint that the union's leaders had no interest in organizing whites but would go to any lengths to get black support went to the highest levels of the CIO, causing Director of Organization Allan S. Haywood to confront the union's international president, Donald Henderson, who, according to Christopher, "flatly denied that it was UCAPAWA policy to favor or cater to Negroes." Such assurances had no effect on Copeland; he viewed the commitments of leftist organizers to black civil rights as primarily ideological and believed that their egalitarian policies would scare away white workers. Through his own ideological prism, he could not help but view leftist organizers and their equal rights tendencies as a hindrance in the South.[71]

Copeland's views had a good deal of support in the southern CIO, and his antagonisms toward leftist unions in 1944 prefigured postwar schisms over racial politics. These schisms became especially evident where CIO staff members participated in organizations with a somewhat broader agenda than trade unionism. At a meeting of the Southern Conference for Human Welfare in Nashville in 1942, according to John Beecher, Noel Beddow of the steelworkers' union delivered "a passionate and incoherent harangue to the general effect that there was far too much attention given the Negro question when the conference should be concerning itself with the underprivileged of both races in the South." Although liberals, not Communists, had raised the issue of racial discrimination, racial conservatives accused them of "playing ball with the Communists," suggesting the discrimination debate was really over political doctrine. In a sense this was true, for while Beddow and other CIO staff members disclaimed any intent by the CIO to disturb segregation, many others in the Southern Conference hoped to overturn it altogether. In a less politically charged incident in the spring of 1945, when Paul Christopher proposed that the southern CIO hold an integrated session at Highlander Folk School, he got an almost hysterical response from regional staff members—all of them white. "Watch your step on this question, do not go an inch further than is absolutely safe," warned one regional director. In response, the school at first decided not to bring any blacks to the session and at the last minute chose Memphis organizer Henry White to attend as an "outstanding" black. His skin was so light that some whites did not even realize the school had been "integrated."[72]

*   *   *

Such controversies revealed the unsettled and unequal nature of race relations within the southern CIO. Even where blacks made up a large portion of the membership, whites typically dominated union affairs; segregated seating arrangements in union meetings remained the norm; and only rarely did unions enlist blacks as organizers or union representatives. Most hurtful to black workers, discriminatory job classification systems and wage differentials remained unchallenged by the unions. Blacks themselves increasingly challenged these conditions inside the unions and factories, but they got little overt support from most white unionists. This situation flowed naturally from CIO strategy in Memphis, where CIO organizers had sought to keep questions of equal rights in the background, emphasizing instead the goal of gaining collective bargaining rights.

However, by January 1945, unions had won tremendous gains, with the Memphis CIO claiming a membership of 32,500 workers in 117 different plants. In September, the Memphis Industrial Union Council adopted a "postwar policy statement" that set as its goal "the organization of every unorganized plant in Memphis."[73] With a war against fascism nearly won and the complete triumph of the union movement expected, blacks demanded more equal treatment. The strategy of Memphis CIO leaders of placing racial questions on the back burner did not fit the new situation, where racial change was so evidently on the front burner. At this point, divisions over principle and tactics on black civil rights began to emerge as central issues in the industrial union movement, with differences increasingly split along political lines.

Clarence Coe remembered one incident that revealed the coming struggle over desegregation. A black member of the armed forces named Mayo William, he recalled, returned from the war after sixty months in England, Italy, and Japan. One morning Mayo came from the locker room to his job at the Firestone plant and forgot that he could not drink out of the "black" fountain until a white man had finished drinking out of the "white" fountain, both of them connected by a single water supply. The incident nearly caused a riot in the plant, and when Coe defended the black man's action as an understandable lapse of memory, management called him into the front office. "That man has been out of the country for five years, and he still has a little more freedom," Coe told the supervisors. "It's going to take him some time to adjust."[74] But the question was whether Mayo William wanted to adjust. In the postwar era, the CIO in the South would have to decide whether, and how far, to move forward on the crucial question of race.

CHAPTER EIGHT

The CIO at the Crossroads

[The post-war era] was the high point of the CIO in the South. Everybody felt good; there was victory over fascism. We had a coalition with the Soviet Union over Nazism. The feeling was that things were unlimited and we could build the unions and have peace. The United Nations was being set up, and we thought that war could be eliminated. Everyone was enthusiastic, and we were all caught up in it. Then all of a sudden they pulled the plug on everything and started the cold war.
—Red Davis

The biggest impediment to organizing the workers was the ideological struggles and the split in the labor movement; there was no unity in the labor movement.
—Ed McCrea

For those who who had suffered through the dismal thirties, the possibilities for change in the South seemed enormous at the end of World War II. During the war the number of southern industrial workers had jumped from 1.6 million to 2.4 million. Government war labor boards had forced many employers to accept higher wages, maintenance of membership provisions, and other union rights and benefits for their workers. Labor union membership nationally was higher than it had ever been, with 10 million AFL and 4.5 million CIO members. Union members sat on government wage boards as near equals with employers, and, boosted by its influential role in the 1944 elections, the CIO remained a significant player in the Democratic party. Although the unions had a more precarious position in the South, nonetheless union membership there had climbed to 400,000 for the CIO and to 1.8 million for the AFL; in Memphis, the two federations appeared about equally matched at about 30,000 each at the high point of the war.[1] Under these conditions, according to Lucy Randolph Mason, politicians and the news media had come to treat unionists with a degree of respect in the South. "Six years ago it was practically impossible for a CIO representative to appear on a college campus, before a civic association, or ministerial forum," but no longer, she wrote.[2]

Although the AFL had the much larger membership of the two federations nationally, based on construction, service, and transportation sector growth during the war, CIO activists felt confident of industrial unionism's postwar future even in the South. The war had profoundly altered the southern economy, and with it, the prospects for social change. Massive migration had urbanized and proletarianized millions of southerners, including hundreds of thousands of African Americans and women. Although many of these recent entrants into the factories lost their positions when GIs returned home, most of them remained in the urban economy, ripe for unionization, after the war. Urbanization, the expansion of industrial jobs for blacks, and the growth of black income during the war offered potential sources of postwar union strength, at the same time providing a strengthened base for black civil rights activity. Likewise, the larger number of women in the work force seemed to offer a potential base of new union members. These developments seemed far more favorable to the CIO than the AFL.[3]

If the war had changed the economic situation, it also seemed to suggest a change in the way many people thought about unions and about race. The antifascist and prodemocratic ideology of the "people's war," as some called it, had raised expectations for an end to Jim Crow among African Americans and exposed white southerners to new ideas and influences as well. Returning GIs, white and black, expected a better standard of living than before the war and generally had less tolerance for the poll tax and other undemocratic measures. As one example of this, in Athens, Tennessee, returning war veterans overturned one of the Crump regime's "satellite" governments after a six-hour gun battle between the veterans and leaders of the local courthouse ring. Armed GIs nearly lynched the sheriff and his deputies for beating a white veteran and shooting a black voter in the back and ultimately won control of the city government, as did GIs in a number of other southern prodemocracy revolts during the 1946 elections. GI militancy seemed to herald a change in direction in the white South. In Memphis, the appearance of the small but integrated American Veterans Committee also suggested a new tone in race relations.[4]

Many liberals and labor supporters hoped that a broad coalition headed by the CIO could avert a repeat of the conservative reaction that followed World War I and create a kind of second "popular front," potentially much more powerful than the first.[5] Its elements already appeared at hand. The

Southern Conference for Human Welfare by 1946 had numerous state committees, published a South-wide newspaper, and gained over one thousand members a month; it sought a majority coalition of labor, liberals, and African Americans that "could transform the South from the most reactionary influence in national politics to the most progressive."[6] The CIO donated much of the funding that made the conference's growth possible and called it the "natural and appropriate spearhead of the liberal forces in the South."[7] The success of Highlander Folk School, which taught labor history, collective bargaining, and how to write leaflets and newsletters, speak in public, and engage in political action, also suggested the development of a much more sophisticated southern working-class leadership. By the end of 1946 Highlander had hosted over seven thousand unionists in residence and twelve thousand in field extension courses. Highlander graduated most of the leading CIO activists in Tennessee, creating a core of union leaders with a greater understanding of unionism and range of skills than had existed before the war. The UAW called Highlander the "bulwark" of the southern labor movement.[8]

At the war's end, labor and civil rights advocates increasingly focused their attention on ending racial segregation. But they recognized that the CIO, which in the words of southern liberal Will Alexander offered "the most promising force for correcting . . . our racial patterns," remained the key to change. CIO leaders provided major backing for the Southern Conference's 1944 petition to kill the poll tax; they also played a major role in its 1946 meeting in New Orleans, which frankly declared opposition to all forms of discrimination.[9] Highlander too relied on union backing as it launched a six-year program to increase racial understanding and to integrate all of its programs. The UAW, the FTA, the International Union of Mine, Mill, and Smelter Workers, and other unions held explicitly interracial programs after the war; and, following the struggle over the "integration" of the CIO southern staff institute during the summer of 1945, Tennessee CIO staff training schools became interracial as a matter of policy. Biracial labor organizing more than ever seemed to provide a basis for union progress, democratization, and liberalization.[10]

National CIO leaders recognized the opportunities in the South and the importance of the race question. In 1946, Philip Murray announced a program, dubbed "Operation Dixie" and funded with several million dollars from the CIO and its affiliates, to organize the South. Significantly, he characterized the southern campaign to unionists as a "civil rights crusade" as well as a drive for union rights. As an attempt to fully extend unionism to the South, Murray called it "the most important drive of its kind ever undertaken by any labor organization in the history of this country." Organizing the South would be critical to the future of the CIO, and organizing blacks would be critical to that effort. Director of Organization Allan Haywood pointed out in a talk at Highlander that Operation Dixie could not compete with the numerically stronger AFL without black support. "We cannot continue the record of progress we have made up to now unless we are united," said Haywood. "We must stamp out all forms of discrimination. Only with a united movement, based on equal rights, can we win our fight for economic security for all. Haywood, like the national CIO, for some time had increasingly stressed that successful unionism required a strengthened fight against racism, including the inclusion of antidiscrimination clauses in contracts and extension of the Fair Employment Practices Commission.[11] The CIO shift toward a more explicit emphasis on civil rights not only aimed at gaining black support for the CIO over the AFL but accorded with the CIO's vision of social change. If the CIO had disappointingly little to say about the status of women in the Operation Dixie plan, in contrast to the still-conservative vision of the AFL, its calls for political action, coalition building, support for pioneering social legislation, and an end to racial discrimination seemed to place it at the forefront of progressive social change.[12]

However, union and civil rights supporters quickly learned of the potentially disastrous possibilities in the postwar South. As African Americans, particularly veterans, increasingly verged on open rebellion against Jim Crow, the issue of race became more volatile than at any time since the Civil War. A negative example of the possibilities after the war appeared in the small town of Columbia, Tennessee, where white police led a race riot against the black community, while militant black war veterans took up weapons to resist. Whites later killed two African-American veterans in their jail cells in February 1946. In July, a mob lynched two black workers and their wives in Walton, Georgia; in early 1947, thirty men dragged Willie Earle, accused of murdering a white, from a Greenville, Mississippi, jail and lynched him. The lynching of some forty African Americans in the war's aftermath—many of them veterans—demonstrated the explosive racism of the postwar years. Murray had linked antiracism to antifascism in the closing years of the war, and now the CIO joined civil rights organizers in actively opposing white mob violence.[13] The upsurge in racial violence continued, however, with employers, politicians, and the news media using racism and anticommunism interchangeably to overcome union organizing and demands for social change in the South.[14]

In the face of such opposition, the CIO's postwar southern strategy relied on continued support from black workers and on the hope that black and white workers in places such as Memphis could transcend the old boundaries that divided them. Although the war experience had offered examples of heightened racial confrontation, it had also demonstrated increased interracial cooperation.[15] The CIO's successes in getting whites and blacks to join together in unions during the war, in the opinion of many southern progressives, had been a long stride toward ending the racial division afflicting the South for generations. Highlander's Mary Lawrence Elkuss felt "the CIO accomplished wonders" in Memphis by organizing blacks and whites together. "Yes, they would often segregate themselves when they came to the meeting hall, blacks on one side and whites on the other," she recalled, "but at least they were in the same meeting hall." To this extent, she believed, "the CIO pioneered in bringing people together." Lucy Randolph Mason also commented that in Memphis, with such a large percentage of blacks in the industrial work force, "it was easier than usual to get both white and Negroes into the unions right from the beginning, because the white workers realized that without the colored they could not represent the majority needed to build a union."[16]

The simple act of bringing blacks and whites into a union could sometimes change racial attitudes quite dramatically. During the war, Richard Routon of the United Rubber Workers had moved from a position of overt racial prejudice and support for the AFL to supporting the CIO's biracial policy as the only effective way to organize. Following his election as Local 186 union president, Routon consciously attempted to overcome his own prejudices and those of the other whites. "I started experiencing a change in my attitude toward black people," Routon recalled, "though the emotional feelings were still there at times, and I had to suppress them." Routon credited other unionists and Highlander with breaking down his racial feelings. "Southerners who attended Highlander," he observed, "had a complete change of character for the better. They came to hold a more liberal and tolerant viewpoint and a positive attitude." Highlander had a particularly strong effect after the war when it recruited increasing numbers of blacks, who ate and slept in the same facilities with whites. Unionists such as Routon and fellow rubber worker H. B. Griffin had started out with strong prejudices, but increasingly abandoned them in part as a result of experiences at Highlander.[17]

Other experiences influenced whites as well. Routon's local established a tradition of electing four blacks out of eleven executive board members, and in 1944 it also began setting aside one out of four delegate positions for an African American. Routon, Griffin, and a white millwright who had opposed electing blacks soon found themselves riding a train with black committee member Mose Lewis as delegates to the union convention in Washington. Lewis had to sit in a segregated car until they got past Virginia. The union whites became increasingly angry at the indignities Lewis experienced, and when a Washington restaurant owner told them to "get that nigger out of here" Griffin exclaimed, "What the hell, this is the capital of the U.S. Are you telling us we can't sit down to eat together? To hell with it, then." The men got up and walked out. They had similar problems trying to get hotel accommodations, and shared beds in a sleazy Washington hotel rather than split up and stay at fancier, segregated facilities. By the end of the trip, according to Routon, even the white millwright had become sympathetic toward Lewis.[18]

Taking the first step of biracial organization did not abolish racism, but could and did lead to important changes in the thinking of many whites. By the end of the war, in a burst of optimism, Mason even claimed that white southern workers had gone beyond union-building strategies to support equal rights for black workers.[19] In reality, however, few white workers had reached this point. Joining together with blacks on a class basis was only one step toward breaking down white prejudices, and other steps did not necessarily follow. Though many white workers came to realize the necessity for the CIO's interracial policy, it remained far more difficult for them to abandon deep-seated racial attitudes.[20] When Mary Lawrence Elkuss helped set up the Memphis Industrial Union Council armed forces canteen during the war, for example, she was unable to break down Jim Crow conventions among whites or blacks. "When it came to social things like the canteen dinner," she recalled, "it was impossible in that day and age to have a mixed situation. . . . It was so accepted there that you didn't break the color line that I don't think a black service man ever came to the white canteen." She also recounted how some whites "just turned around and left" when they discovered blacks at Highlander after the war. Although Local 19 observed integrated staff and social activities, segregated seating and social arrangements continued to prevail in most CIO locals and in the Memphis CIO hall.[21]

Within most unions, the basic difficulty remained that of getting local whites to recognize that a problem existed. The CIO's early strategy of appealing to immediate economic interests and avoiding discussions of race failed to raise white consciousness or to address the issue of how blacks would be treated inside the CIO once unionization succeeded. By the middle forties, many black workers had experienced unionization, increased wages, and improved conditions. Now they expected the CIO to begin to deliver on its larger promises of support for equal rights, promises that most whites opposed. Although still pragmatic, blacks became increasingly impatient, as whites continued to almost invariably fill positions as presidents, organizers, and business agents. Except for Local 19 and perhaps a few other locals, this typically occurred even in predominantly black unions. According to Red Davis, "It was a question of self-interest on the part of whites" to have biracial organization, but "the weak point was, once you got organized, who got elected to office." [22]

Racial compromises acceptable to most black workers in the early years became more problematic as the CIO grew. Unions raised wage rates, but barely narrowed the differences between whites in skilled employment and blacks in unskilled and semiskilled positions. The War Labor Board had taken steps to increase black wages relative to whites, but its influence ended with the war. While whites in the highest-paying positions could make an increasingly good living, those in the bottom wage levels continued to merely exist. [23] Furthermore, as United Furniture Workers of America director of organization Ernest Marsh observed as late as May 1945, "Manufacturers in Memphis absolutely will not settle agreements with a colored representative." These and other humiliating segregation practices by management only reinforced the distance between blacks and white workers, who did not want to let go of their privileged positions in the factories. And although Local 19's black president, John Mack Dyson, had already begun duties as a negotiator, few other unions would fight for the right of blacks to directly represent themselves. Hence, while a multitude of injustices faced black workers, they continued to have great difficulty in winning union office and in placing demands before the CIO and employers. [24]

Aside from the entrenched nature of the racial system at the local level, other factors obstructed change. Whether white workers in a place such as Memphis would have the courage to practice or even to openly express racial tolerance hinged to a large degree on the directions taken by the larger society, the news media, and by national union leaders and politicians. The political decisions made by federal agencies, especially the NLRB, as well as the president and Congress, would have tremendous impact on the success of industrial unions in the postwar years. So would the increasingly provocative question of "communism." Race riots and red scares after World War I had combined to help crush the labor movement; since that time the southern establishment had resisted threats to the social order by crying "communist." The accusation lost its bite during the wartime alliance of the Soviet Union and the United States—as one UAW member at its 1945 summer session commented, "We used to fall for this redbaiting stuff, but we know now what it's used for."[25] But patriotism could easily be reattached to anticommunism in the war's aftermath, and as questions of equal rights came increasingly to the fore segregationists renewed their charges that civil rights equaled communism. In the postwar era, the southern industrial union movement entered its most critical organizing period. The success or failure of Operation Dixie would provide a measure of how much change could take place, and how fast, in the South.

POSTWAR PROBLEMS AND POTENTIALS

The postwar economy presented both obstacles and opportunities in the struggle for industrial union organizing. On one hand, increased competition for jobs could not help but intensify social tensions and racial conflicts. Some forty thousand Memphians had served in the armed forces, and most of them came back looking for work. Following government closure of the city's war production plants, the USES reported in February 1946 that it had ten times more applications for work than available jobs. Factories laid off thousands of blacks and women, on the "last hired, first fired" principle that ruled employment. And although the period from 1940 to 1950 saw industrial jobs as a percentage of total employment in Memphis increase from a meager 7 percent to about 20 percent, the elimination of war industries pushed the number of manufacturing jobs down below the peak level of the war years. Expected improvements in living standards for the working class under these conditions did not materialize. Veterans, one government report noted, had "living standards, aptitudes, and ambitions which unfit them for straight laboring occupations," and yet few of them had the technical skills needed to take jobs in the growing number of clerical and technical occupations (see table 8.1). These jobs in any case did not pay as well as some expected, nor did most Memphis manufacturing jobs, in a period of contraction, sustain the expectation of higher wages.[26]

Not surprisingly, under postwar conditions the African-American community suffered acute economic dislocation. Thousands of black GIs returned to a crowded housing market and declining demand for unskilled labor. Black women who had taken common labor jobs in the war lost most of those positions to veterans, forcing them into lower-paying domestic and service work. White craft unions further tightened the barriers to black workers, as they typically did during periods of increased unemployment, while government agencies provided only a few, mostly ineffective, job training programs to increase the skills of black veterans.[27] Aside from

Table 8.1. Shelby County Employment, 1943–52

	Manufacturing	Nonmanufacturing
July 1943	28,113	—
May 1945	45,800	124,500
Sept. 1945	36,700	126,100
July 1946	37,600	134,500
Jan. 1947	38,500	133,300
July 1947	36,400	133,100
Jan. 1948	39,600	—
1952	42,150	130,550

Source: "Basic Employment Data for Shelby County, Tennessee," July 1947 and Feb. 1948, in Tennessee Department of Employment Security, Research and Statistics Division, *The Labor Market* (Nashville: 1948); *A Survey of Industrial Facilities in Memphis, Tennessee* (Nashville: 1953).

these economic pressures, police repression and white racial hostility became alarmingly evident. During a series of publicized incidents in 1945 and 1946, white police brutally attacked African Americans on the streets, two of them raping a black woman in one incident. In another case an all-white jury sentenced a black sixteen-year-old to die in the electric chair, even though it appeared doubtful he committed the crime. And although the African-American community raised increasing protests, the war had tempered the outlook of Crump and older white leaders of the city very little. At age seventy-one, Crump's opposition to all forms of liberalization became increasingly pronounced. The attitude of white craft unionists was often no better. George Weaks, of the Brotherhood of Railway and Steamship Clerks, spoke for many of his fellow white unionists in 1947 when he declared that "we here in the South want to keep the Negro just where he Belongs He has a place and so has the White Man. and the Negro cannot take the White Man's Place."[28]

However, despite a decline in the number of manufacturing jobs and growing racial polarization, the Memphis CIO believed it had a potentially fertile field ahead of it. Although its membership declined due to the closing of war industries, the CIO in early 1946 represented somewhere between fifteen and twenty thousand workers (see table 8.2). In the industrial arena, it far surpassed the AFL's influence, servicing contracts in 195 plants, compared to 21 industrial plants under contract with the AFL. And although AFL unions monopolized the construction, transportation, and skilled craft sectors, as AFL head Lev Loring began his tenth term in office it seemed unlikely that craft unionists would reach out to indus-

Table 8.2. Estimated Major CIO Union Memberships, January 1946

Union	Membership	Plants	Potential gains
United Rubber Workers	4,484	2,350	
Food, Tobacco, and Agricultural Workers	3,245	262,200	20 plants
United Auto Workers	2,785	3,300	
United Steelworkers	1,054	161,500	15 plants
International Woodworkers	800	113,000	14 plants
Gas and Chemical Workers	340	71,400	12 plants
United Furniture Workers	300	71,500	17 plants
United Packinghouse Workers	166	3,400	7 plants
American Newspaper Guild	147	235	
National Maritime Union	100	—	
Other	421	181,040	

Source: W. A. Copeland to Paul Christopher, 30 Jan. 1946, Reel 28, TOC, OD microfilm.

trial workers. Furthermore, the CIO's William A. "Red" Copeland pointed out, another twenty thousand potential union members existed in some 340 unorganized plants. Although the CIO had already organized most of the manufacturing companies employing one hundred or more workers, a multitude of smaller enterprises remained unorganized, including airlines, dairies, feed and grain mills, meat-packing companies, laundries, bottling companies, chemical and steel-fabricating plants, woodworking and furniture-related plants, restaurants and hotels, gas stations, car dealerships, and railroad yards. If the CIO organized these workers and reached out to white-collar workers (thirty-five hundred worked at Sears Roebuck, another twenty-five hundred in department stores), possibilities for expansion still seemed immense.[29]

Black workers remained at the core of the potential new base of CIO members. Most unorganized companies had sizeable numbers of African Americans, most of them underpaid and, as Copeland had suggested in 1943, "waiting for someone to turn to." Although job competition intensified after the war, all evidence showed that blacks remained highly receptive to organizing. They lived and worked within relatively small and easily reached industrial zones, and because they remained in the lowest-paying jobs had the most to gain from unionization. Common laborers typically made only the federal minimum wage of $.40 an hour, and most of them had no paid holidays, vacations, or extra pay for overtime. In contrast, unskilled workers in unionized enterprises often made $.50 to $.60

an hour when first hired. Union wages for unskilled industrial laborers remained pathetic in comparison to skilled building workers, who made from $1.25 up to $1.94 an hour. But even in the lowest-paying union jobs common laborers had gained time and a half for overtime, at least a few paid holidays, and grievance procedures. Unionization clearly offered the quickest route to improvements for common laborers throughout Memphis industries.[30]

Female workers also offered potential hope for the CIO. Although many white female factory workers became homemakers at the end of the war, black women and many white women as well either held onto their jobs or found new ones. "Women who were drawn into the labor market for the first time during the war, were definitely not willing to withdraw," observed an analyst for one state agency.[31] In contrast to the thirties, when women made up a very small fraction of the industrial work force, in 1949 they made up 20 percent and 43 percent of the nonmanufacturing work force; they continued to represent one-third or more of the whole labor force in Shelby County even when leaving the more than ten thousand domestic workers out of the calculations. White women played an especially important role in white-collar service, government, and trade employment, as did black and white women in blue-collar employment in apparel, tobacco, paper, furniture, and electrical industries. Nearly seven hundred women still worked in the Firestone plant, and some five hundred later worked at a new General Electric light bulb plant established in 1949.[32] Gross and systematic discrimination affected practically all of these workers, who almost always made lower wages than men; the wage gap grew worse instead of better after the war.[33] If the CIO could appeal to and incorporate female talents and leadership into the union movement, it could tap into a major new source of potential members (see table 8.3).

Particularly for women and blacks at the lowest end of the wage scale, postwar economic conditions cried out for a vigorous union movement. But all workers rapidly began to lose what they had gained during the war. Hours of overtime shrank and inflation soared due to the lifting of government wage and price controls, and by June 1946, compared to 1939, the cost of food in Memphis had gone up by some 70 percent, the price of housing by nearly 40 percent, and the price of clothing nearly 50 percent. Yet while the real wages of workers eroded, statistics showed corporate profits all across the country at all-time record levels. Local business owners, as everywhere in the country, nonetheless resisted demands for wage increases.[34] Despite peace agreements made in Memphis and other cities by labor and management at the end of the war, no peace could exist

Table 8.3. Female Postwar Employment, Selected Industries, May 1949

Industry	Number	Total employed	Female employed	Percentage female
Manufacturing				
Apparel	7	861	643	75
Chemicals	13	2,222	359	16
Electrical	4	1,139	666	59
Fabricated metals	7	568	57	10
Food	19	3,415	511	15
Furniture	4	1,385	487	35
Lumber	12	3,863	258	7
Machinery	4	3,009	124	4
Paper	5	1,358	511	38
Rubber	1	4,443	648	15
Textiles	2	1,011	261	26
Tobacco	1	373	165	44
Manufacturing total	94	26,278	4,982	20
Nonmanufacturing				
Government	5	4,720	1,342	28
Service, nondomestic	16	3,595	2,282	63
Trade	66	11,084	5,690	51
Transportation, utilities	11	3,890	895	23
Nonmanufacturing total	117	24,832	10,783	43
Total	211	51,110	15,765	31

Source: Annual Report, Memphis Labor Market, prepared June 1949, Box 353, USES, USDL, RG 183, NARA.

under these conditions. The largest strike wave in American history shook the nation in late 1945 and much of 1946, a year in which President Truman not only removed controls on prices and profits but called out the armed forces to break strikes. The alliance between the CIO and the Democrats in the federal government crumbled, with President Truman appearing to be as much an enemy to the unions as any Republican. Many called for a labor-based third party, as all pretense at peace between workers, owners, and the federal government collapsed.[35]

ORGANIZATION AND FRAGMENTATION

In the context of these developments, the CIO's inauguration of the Operation Dixie organizing drive in May 1946 became a critical test of the union movement's ability to maintain and extend its power. But certain problems with CIO national strategy emerged immediately. The Operation Dixie campaign sought to replicate experiences in the North in which workers in a few mass-production industries organized virtually overnight. The CIO hoped to create a "transforming moment" similar to the 1937 sit-down strikes in the North, in which it would sweep through unorganized industries across the South. But even in the CIO's strong points such as East Tennessee, where twenty plants employed one thousand or more workers (only five such plants existed in West Tennessee), this turned out to be an unrealistic expectation. In isolated mountain and rural communities, company towns, anti-union police, and religious fundamentalists made it extremely difficult to organize. The concentration of Operation Dixie leaders on southern textiles as the key industry focused the CIO on some of the most hostile companies in the South and on workers who were far less likely to organize than other workers, particularly blacks, in a variety of other industries. Indeed, most of those who could do so moved out of the textile industry during the war, and those who remained had little intention of jeopardizing their jobs in union campaigns. On the other hand, to unionize blacks in most furniture, woodworking, cotton-processing, tobacco, and other industries required slow organizing of small shops one by one. This would not produce the quick results and large numbers needed to encourage northern unions to pay for the campaign, and the CIO had little taste for it.[36]

Yet organizing among black workers in small shops during Operation Dixie's first year produced some important results. Given the wartime experience and the continued existence of the Wagner Act, immediately after the war even some of the most hostile employers still accepted labor's right to organize.[37] In Memphis, newly appointed black organizer Henry White, president of the local union of baggage handlers, or red caps, quickly began winning elections. Under the direction of Copeland, a Southern Organizing Committee (SOC) staff of four organizers claimed no large successes, but over the course of the summer workers in wood, furniture, food and tobacco, steel, chemicals, textiles, and paper elected unions in numerous small shops with a preponderance of blacks. In at least three cases CIO unions took shops out of the hands of AFL organizations of long standing.[38] By June, CIO membership had gone back up to thirty thousand, and by February 1947, Copeland could brag that the Memphis CIO had won 157 elections in the last four years and lost only 12, a startling record.[39]

Throughout the summer and fall of 1946, Operation Dixie across the South seemed to be at least partially achieving its aim of organizing the unorganized. The CIO claimed ten to twenty new southern locals per week;

in its first year and a half, it claimed eight hundred new locals with four hundred thousand members—a doubling of CIO southern membership. Tennessee, rapidly becoming the South's most industrialized state, led the way with somewhere between seventy and eighty-five thousand new CIO members signed up by February 1947. At the end of 1946, the CIO claimed to have lost only 54 of 288 NLRB elections in the South.[40] Black support and leftist leadership proved the key to success in many of the places where the CIO excelled, as in food-processing, woodworking, and packinghouse industries. And significantly, despite the CIO's lack of direct attention to women in its public statements, women made up some 50 percent of the new CIO union members during the Operation Dixie drive. FTA, which excelled at organizing both women and ethnic minorities, led the way by winning 111 elections among tobacco and cotton workers in the upper and lower South. FTA gained fifteen thousand new workers in Operation Dixie's first two years, bringing in more new members at that point than any union except the International Woodworkers of America. In Memphis, FTA Local 19 sparked many of the CIO's election victories and wage increases in small shops.[41]

In response to the CIO, the AFL launched its own southern drive. Apparently fearful that the CIO would raid the AFL's base among southern blacks, who made up 450,000 of the AFL's 650,000 total black membership, the AFL employed seventeen black organizers and made special appeals to blacks not to be fooled by the "communistic" CIO's pretensions to support black rights. The AFL claimed it had more black organizers and leaders in its segregated unions than the CIO did in its integrated organizations—which may have been true. While the AFL tried to convince blacks that it was not discriminatory, it openly appealed to employers to accept the AFL over a supposedly radical CIO—which, the AFL's George Meany claimed, "has openly followed the Communist line and is following it today." Even with these conservative appeals, the AFL ran into considerable opposition in unorganized parts of the South. It variously claimed some 250,000 to 500,000 new members as the result of its southern drive.[42]

Despite its appeals to blacks, in nearby Laurel, Mississippi, the AFL lost a major campaign by a vote of 812 for the CIO to 637 for the AFL at the Masonite woodworking plant. There, as in many places, the AFL lost due to black support of the CIO, and in Memphis AFL unions likewise had little success in predominantly black shops. AFL unions did better and were more aggressive where they had a homogeneous white or black work force. AFL Teamsters, for example, in early 1946 led a bitter strike against Greyhound Bus company in Memphis that lasted for over three months, proof of the tenacity of white craft unionists. In contrast, employers could easily replace unskilled workers, white or black, leading CIO unions to take a more cautious approach. Indeed, Red Copeland boasted that the Memphis Industrial Union Council had not sponsored a strike since 1942, which leftists pointed to as one cause of the continuing low wages in many CIO-organized factories. Despite its potential advantages, however, the AFL in Memphis did little to organize the unorganized, most of whom were black. Instead it concentrated its efforts on civic campaigns and on attacking the CIO as "communist," and in fact seemed to pay little attention to expanding its ranks. In any case, by the fall of 1947 the national AFL dropped its southern organizing drive.[43]

The AFL's ineffective efforts did not necessarily signal the doom of southern labor organizing, however. The CIO's biracial Operation Dixie, with its initial successes among black workers in southern-based industries, seemed to hold out much greater hope for change in the South.[44] But its limits also became quickly apparent, according to the historian Barbara Griffiths. The SOC did not have adequate staff or resources to cover the entire South, or even to do a good job on a local basis, and no equivalent of the WLB existed to ease the way with employers. In Memphis, although the CIO lost a few elections due to determined employer opposition, its main problem was lack of staff and resources to meet the demands placed on it by the many workers who sought organization. Copeland's staff of four organizers often worked eighteen-hour days. Each of the small shops they organized required many rounds of leafleting, meetings, and considerable paperwork, as well as time spent cultivating personal contacts. This small staff, along with the representatives of the international unions in Memphis, remained entirely inadequate to the task of organizing twenty thousand potential new industrial workers. Earl Crowder of the United Steelworkers, for example, serviced twenty-one different plants with some eighteen hundred members and tried to organize three thousand potential new ones. In contrast, when the AFL's International Association of Machinists decided to compete for these same workers it put six organizers into Memphis. Crowder's impossible task helped put him in the hospital, and Copeland too ended up with ulcers and heart trouble as the result of trying to carry an impossible load of organizing, negotiating new contracts, and editing the Tennessee edition of the *CIO News*.[45]

The CIO adopted a centralized command structure during the Operation Dixie campaign that not only placed too much strain on too few people but led to inappropriate decisions. While the AFL responded to CIO victories in Memphis by bringing in ten more organizers during the summer months, the Southern Organizing Committee in Atlanta, headed by Van Bittner, began to take organizers out of Memphis to use them in other parts of the South. The SOC, apparently hoping to exert more control over NLRB decisions, additionally required that all petitions for elections from Memphis be sent to the Atlanta office of the NLRB. This policy slowed down petitions for elections, which normally went directly to a subregional office of the NLRB in Memphis. And whereas CIO unions previously had been free to operate on their own initiative, under Operation Dixie the SOC "annexed," according to Copeland, the entire Memphis CIO operation. Not only Copeland's staff, hired at the national level by CIO director of organization Allan Haywood, but the representatives of various international unions in Memphis came under SOC discipline. Since Copeland had been designated a subregional director by the CIO and head of Operation Dixie in Memphis, this meant that every organizer fell under his authority.[46] This arrangement led to no end of political trouble in Memphis, where Copeland had always been unpopular among left-wing unionists.

Bittner exacerbated such political tensions by his policy of excluding trade union leftists, among them some of the best organizers in the South, from Operation Dixie's staff. In their stead he hired militant anticommunists such as Pete Swim of the Memphis American Newspaper Guild chapter, who became public relations director for Operation Dixie, and George Baldanzi of the textile union, who ran much of the southern campaign. The SOC even excluded Highlander from the campaign, rejecting its offer to conduct educational programs. Highlander's Myles Horton years later pointed out that the SOC's hiring policies saddled it with a number of organizers who lacked the nerve and know-how needed for southern organizing. Some of the SOC's organizers would not even associate with blacks, were racist in private conversations, and often did not know how to effectively relate to white workers either. According to Barbara Griffiths, many of the SOC's cautious white organizers "simply could not bring themselves to go beyond perfunctory efforts to organize blacks" and projected "an unconscious aura of white supremacy." In their quest to present an uncontroversial image to the white South, the SOC turned aside job applications from blacks and seems to have hired far fewer black organizers than the AFL. The campaign was also almost completely male dominated. When two highly qualified women, one black and one white, applied to work for the SOC, Paul Christopher referred the black woman to the CIO's antidiscrimination department and offered the white woman work as a secretary. By ignoring opportunities to put women and blacks into organizing roles, the CIO lessened its chances of reaching its potentially most responsive constituencies. Such backwardness, according to Horton, stemmed from an ineffective top-down approach, which reduced organizing to a question of how many people had signed union cards.[47]

Operation Dixie's virtual banning of blacks, women, and suspected Communists, as well as an air of suspicion directed at white racial liberals outside the CIO, crippled the whole movement for change in the South. Bittner began this divisive trend in April 1946, even before Operation Dixie had formally begun, when he attacked allies on the left with a widely publicized statement that "no crowd, whether Communists, Socialists, or anyone else will be permitted to 'mix-up' in the campaign." Bittner specifically attacked the Southern Conference for "interference" with the CIO because one of its black field staff had criticized CIO locals for imitating AFL segregationist practices. CIO leaders in Richmond picked up the charge almost word for word a few days later, and Philip Murray himself reiterated the theme during the May 1946 United Steelworkers' convention, denouncing "outsiders," leftists or otherwise, who "meddled" in CIO affairs.[48] These statements signaled the beginning of the end of CIO support for the Southern Conference, already under increasing siege by segregationists— Mississippi senator Bilbo, for example, attacked it as an "un-American, negro social equality, communistic, mongrel outfit." CIO national office donations to the Southern Conference ended, and in early 1947 the CIO removed it from its list of organizations approved for funding. The cutoff of funds and subsequent withdrawal of most CIO representatives from the conference helped precipitate the decline of an important CIO ally.[49]

The rejection of allies on the left and the conservative tone adopted by SOC leaders did nothing to improve CIO organizing among white textile workers, however. Union opponents by the autumn of 1946 had effectively defeated the critical CIO campaign in textiles, which SOC leaders considered the key to organizing the South. On the other hand, left-wing unions such as the FTA and the International Union of Mine, Mill, and Smelter Workers continued to make some of their greatest advances, despite their official exclusion from the SOC. Organizers from such unions, and even some centrists in the southern CIO, felt that their emphasis on racial equality and aggressive organizing among women and ethnic minorities in fact placed them more in accord with the CIO national program than did the policies followed by conservative unions. Nonetheless, national CIO leaders did little to support them. On the contrary, suspicion against the left at the highest levels of the CIO buttressed the conservative policies of the Operation Dixie campaign.[50]

At the local level, the Memphis CIO played out all of the weaknesses apparent in Operation Dixie. Although no signs appeared that workers had turned against the CIO, its organizational campaign increasingly bogged down as SOC resources proved inadequate to the task of reaching people in the shops. Already, organizers had begun to complain about the one-man control over SOC activities in Memphis. "An organizer can get along in Memphis only if he cooperates with Mr. Copeland," furniture union organizer Walter Carson complained. Henry White, the Memphis SOC's only black organizer, resigned in midsummer, perhaps because the SOC paid him almost one hundred dollars a month less than its three other Memphis organizers—all of them white and with far less experience.[51] Another SOC staff member resigned around the same time, with no explanation, and Copeland also lost Richard Routon, one of his most experienced SOC staff members, to the CIO's Political Action Committee. Copeland's organizing committee received yet another blow in October, when his assistant, Lawrence McGurty, precipitously resigned rather than make a pledge not to engage in activities considered left-wing by Copeland and the SOC in Atlanta. By the fall, a drop-off in NLRB elections contrasted to the gains made by the unions during the spring and summer.[52]

Even during the summer's organizing victories, however, the fracturing of the CIO campaign along political lines had become apparent. The marginalized position of CIO leftists surfaced publicly during the 1946 congressional elections, when Crump and his protege Senator Kenneth McKellar denounced the CIO's Political Action Committee as "communistic." Richard Routon, the new Memphis Political Action Committee director, responded by disowning the CIO Left, emphasizing that the Tennessee Industrial Union Council constitution banned Communists from attending as delegates or serving as officers and that the Memphis CIO banned Communists as delegates or even as visitors to meetings. In fact, the CIO Left and Right continued to work together, despite official statements to the contrary. FTA poll watchers, working in cooperation with the Political Action Committee, made the first open challenge to the Crump machine's control over the voting booths during the August 1946 primaries. But the quiet collaboration between the CIO Left and Right, which had produced victories in organizing drives, did not stop CIO-backed candidates from going down to defeat. Many union voters, disgusted with the failure of Truman and the Democrats to uphold the interests of workers and consumers, failed even to go to the polls. The Tennessee CIO Political Action Committee's candidate, Carmack, received fewer votes in the primary against McKellar than he had four years earlier in a campaign against Tennessee's other senator, Tom Stewart.[53]

Following the primaries, pressures increased on the CIO to oust its left-wingers, and internal conflicts escalated. During October, the FTA's Karl Korstad, John Mack Dyson, and Larry Larsen, as well as Red Davis of the NMU, set up a meeting at Lemoyne College to organize a chapter of the National Negro Congress, a Communist-led national organization supporting black labor and civil rights. A Memphis newspaper reporter informed Copeland that he planned to turn the story into an expose of the Memphis CIO that claimed Communists had controlled it from 1940 to 1942, had lost control to the Memphis Industrial Union Council after that, and now were trying to regain the upper hand by recruiting black workers. These were Copeland's views exactly, but he did not want such a story in the press. The newspaper planned to run the story the same day that over one thousand FTA workers shut down the Buckeye company over a contract dispute and on the eve of an important NLRB election at a furniture plant where the AFL had charged "communism" against the CIO furniture union. Copeland succeeded in getting the reporter to at least hold up the story until after the furniture election. He then called together Local 19 leaders to remind them that all left-wing activities in the CIO were to be suspended during Operation Dixie and made them agree that all future leaflets and nonunion activities would be first cleared with him and the SOC staff. At this point, McGurty, whom Copeland considered "the most popular and trusted" of his staff, resigned rather than pledge that he would take all orders from Copeland and cease his relationships with the FTA.[54]

The McGurty incident revealed how far political restrictions and a centralized command structure had come to dominate Operation Dixie, which in Memphis revolved around the decisions of one man. It also revealed the clashing racial politics of left and right trade unionists. Copeland had been grooming McGurty for a major leadership role, unaware of his recent marriage to Red Davis's sister and his growing attraction to the Left. McGurty to some extent admired the hard-driving Copeland, a dedicated, capable administrator who never took vacations. In 1946, McGurty knew little about Marxism, but the Left's activity on the racial front, as well as McGurty's personal links to the Davis family, drew him away from Copeland's influence. McGurty had been the first white in a small Memphis packinghouse to join an all-black CIO union, and he believed that his job as a CIO member was to convince whites to join with blacks and to throw aside Jim Crow. Hence his attraction to the National Negro Congress, whose meeting he attended, and to FTA's Local 19, the only union where he found strong interracial friendships. He later recounted how at one of its picnics "to my utter amazement [I] found the entire union membership,

Negro and white, drinking beer, shooting craps, and having a great time together." Copeland, in contrast, thought interracialism and black union leadership should be played down and tolerated blacks only so long as they followed southern racial conventions, including segregated seating arrangements. When McGurty argued that such practices contradicted the antidiscrimination program of the national CIO, Copeland told McGurty that he, not the national CIO, made policy in Memphis. This argument over race, McGurty recalled, cast him as a Communist sympathizer in the eyes of Copeland. "The fact that I had agreed with Communists on that one question [of racial equality] had branded me."[55]

The Buckeye strike, occurring at the same time as the confrontation between McGurty and Copeland, further revealed the conflict between Left and Right on racial questions. In a company with a work force that had become about 40 percent white, interracialism became the key to Local 19 success during the strike. One black and one white worker co-chaired the Welfare Committee, which gave out union benefits to strikers; one black and one white, leaders of the Buckeye company's two plants, acted as cocaptains of the picket lines; and throughout the strike, picket lines remained integrated. CIO unions in other plants had often placed black pickets at the back of struck plants, whites at the front. Members of Local 19 referred to everyone at union meetings by titles, thus avoiding the disrespectful white practice of referring to blacks by their first names only. In the CIO, in contrast, Henry White used the title *Mr.* when addressing Copeland, who called White by his first name.[56] More important, according to the FTA business agent Karl Korstad, Local 19 had built up a strong working unity between leaders and workers, with little distinction between black and white. The shop steward system provided the key to Local 19's strength. The union emphasized shop stewards taking on and settling grievances at the first stage of a dispute—in the factory, during break times, with final disposition of issues made between the steward and the supervisor in front of the workers. By following such procedures, the union built confidence among the workers in settling their own disputes; it also made it possible for a core of black leaders such as John Mack Dyson, William Lynn, Tom Roach, Allison Stokes, George Isabell, Leroy Boyd, Earl Fisher, and others to gain respect from both white and black in the shops. Hence, George Isabell at Buckeye handled grievances for white as well as black workers, and John Mack Dyson became the CIO's first black negotiator in Memphis. The FTA's ability to organize electoral activity in the African-American community also resulted from the respected role of people such as Dyson. The union continued to hold many educational functions, even bringing the historian Herbert Aptheker to Memphis to speak to the local about African-American history. Local 19's grass-roots, interracial unionism, according to Korstad, contradicted the practices and outlook of many white CIO leaders, however. Copeland, for example, spoke of "industrial democracy" and expected cooperation from companies if unions behaved in a "reasonable" manner—which in Memphis meant that unions would adhere to segregation and "represent" the workers rather than have the workers lead the union.[57]

Based on its core of support among the workers, especially blacks but whites as well, Local 19 up until mid-1947 proved to be one of the most durable and dynamic of Memphis CIO unions. Media stories about "Communist infiltration," printed in the middle of the Buckeye strike, had no apparent effect on the outcome: all of the workers gained fifteen cents an hour, an unprecedented wage increase in the southern cotton-processing industry. Such across-the-board increases, over time, reduced the distance between the wages of the unskilled and the skilled, while the percentage wage increases gained by most CIO unions increased the wage gap between skilled and unskilled. FTA also led successful strikes of blacks at the Buckeye plants in Corinth, Mississippi, and Montgomery, Alabama. By November 1946 FTA had brought its membership in Mississippi Delta cottonseed oil, grain, and other food-processing plants up to 7,594, more than double its membership in 1944, and reported twenty-seven plants under FTA contract in Memphis. Local 19 president John Mack Dyson (also a vice-president of the national union) at this point made the same salary as Korstad, the business agent, making them equally organizers and bargaining agents for the union. By November the union began setting up organizing committees in each Delta local as part of Operation Dixie, and its organizational expansion in the Delta soon allowed the union to begin negotiating regional contracts for all the Buckeye plants.[58]

FTA's achievements won it strong support from blacks, particularly in unskilled occupations. FTA organizers thought the union should have won strong support from the leaders of Operation Dixie as well, regardless of some of its members' political beliefs or affiliations.[59] However, the right to hold one's own political beliefs counted for less and less. In 1946, the Southern States Industrial Council, "Christian America" (funded by right-wing Texas oil company executives), the Ku Klux Klan, local police, politicians, and the news media set off an incendiary storm of anticommunism and anti-unionism throughout the South. Vigilantes kidnapped, beat, and even killed CIO members, while states made picketing illegal and required unions to pay exorbitant fees for a "license" to organize, and privately funded groups saturated radio and the mails with anti-union literature. The Southern Conference dubbed the combination of anti-union laws and extralegal terror during 1946 as a renewed form of "southern fascism." But the problem wasn't only southern. It was not only the House Un-American Activities Committee, which got its strongest support from southern Democrats, but General Electric, the National Association of Manufacturers, chambers of commerce, and other groups at the national level that red-baited New Deal liberalism and CIO unionism—and with as much vigor as any segregationist. Conservative Republicans such as Richard Nixon in California reaped the benefits of the growing fear campaign during the 1946 elections, which decisively set back the Democrats and liberalism in Congress. While the reaction appeared in its most brutal form in the South, the red scare was national.[60]

Industrial unionists in Memphis did not suffer the direct violence being visited on organizers in the Deep South, for the Memphis CIO at this point in its history was too large to be defeated by overt repression. However, they experienced the same growing propaganda barrage against unionism and "communism" apparent everywhere in the nation. The media campaign gradually destroyed their credibility with the public and pushed the CIO to the right internally. The Memphis *Commercial Appeal,* as well as the AFL's *Memphis Labor Review,* echoed the anticommunist sentiments of the House Un-American Activities Committee and other such groups, inundating readers with a barrage of headlines and articles on communism the "anti-Christ" and warning that the "reds" controlled various CIO unions. FBI director J. Edgar Hoover was so impressed that he wrote a special letter to Memphis readers saying, "The Memphis *Commercial Appeal* is rendering a real public service in bringing to its readers the mission of Communism in America." Already, the FBI had begun opening letters addressed to CIO leftists in Memphis and kept them and many others under surveillance for many years to come. They even considered putting people like Red Davis on their "security index," presumably to be rounded up in case of "national emergency."[61]

The barrage of hostility took its toll on southern organizing. By the end of 1946, the Operation Dixie campaign had fallen into disarray. CIO international unions, dismayed by the lack of results in textile plants and their own tightening budgets, increasingly failed to pay their per capita tax for the campaign. At its national convention in November 1946, the CIO drastically cut the Operation Dixie budget, knocking the props out from under the campaign in Memphis and everywhere else. As a result of budget cuts, the SOC in Tennessee immediately lost half its staff. In Memphis, Copeland relied primarily on volunteers and organizers paid by various internationals for continued Operation Dixie efforts. Tennessee director Paul Christopher likewise attempted to replace paid staff with a campaign to involve every CIO member as a volunteer organizer. Moreover, in the early months of 1947, organizing in the state became much more difficult. In Greeneville, for example, state officials red-baited FTA organizer Mary Lou Koger, while the chamber of commerce paid for ads urging local townspeople and farmers to ally with business owners against the "outsiders" of the CIO. Operation Dixie increasingly lost such contests in eastern Tennessee. The growing red scare and the increasingly obvious failures of Operation Dixie put tremendous pressure on the CIO organizing that continued.[62]

The CIO had weathered storms of red-baiting in the past, but under the pressures of the cold war and organizing failures a great temptation existed to turn inward. As CIO members indulged in this temptation, a climate of anticommunist paranoia set in amongst the SOC staff; one textile organizer, for example, later insisted to Myles Horton that the Communists, who had no role in textile campaigns, were the cause of the CIO's failure in that industry. In this atmosphere, Highlander's policy of allowing all unions to use its facilities came under attack. The CIO's Willard Townsend told Henry White, according to Copeland, that "Highlander was pretty well tinted with pinkoism." By the end of 1946 Copeland himself had begun building a case against the school for allowing leftist trade unionists and civil rights groups to hold classes and organizing meetings there. By early 1947 he would no longer recommend Highlander for CIO financial support, and at his behest the Tennessee CIO set up an "investigating committee" to scrutinize the school's politics. Throughout the South, Copeland and other CIO leaders spoke of people who "played ball" with the "communist element" and spread rumors about the politics of individuals they hardly knew. Brownie Lee Jones, director of the Southern School for Workers in Virginia, threatened to sue Copeland for defamation of character if he did not stop spreading rumors that she was a "red," but Copeland responded that "if she was not guilty" she should get up in a CIO convention and "denounce the Commies." Copeland at some point also began meeting regularly with the FBI to inform them of left-wing CIO activities across the region.[63]

In effect, Operation Dixie had placed the most fervent anticommunists and racial conservatives in control of the southern CIO, and when the organizing campaign failed they began to use the CIO Left as a scapegoat. Although Communists continued to work in the southern CIO for the next two years, by 1947 the shaky left-center unity that had prevailed since the thirties had fragmented. This development occurred in the context of a widespread shift to the right in the nation's ruling circles, in a period when people made their careers out of demagogic appeals to fear—fear of renewed depression, fear of change in the world order, and fear of racial integration. In 1947 the Truman Doctrine shifted American foreign policy toward economic and military support for repressive right-wing regimes while the president began a loyalty program that placed the private beliefs of millions of Americans under government investigation. In the new cold war atmosphere, the passage of the Taft-Hartley Act set the stage for the final dissolution of the left-center alliance in the CIO and the demobilization of the southern organizing drive.

THE TAFT-HARTLEY ACT AND THE END OF CIO UNITY

Despite growing difficulties in the CIO, in early 1947 it continued to win elections in numerous small Memphis shops.[64] But passage of the Taft-Hartley Act by Congress in June finally reversed this trend and prepared the way for further CIO fragmentation and defeat. Dubbed the "slave labor" act by unions, the law eviscerated the organizing protections gained in the thirties. Following a year in which everyone from Memphis Chamber of Commerce president Edmund Orgill, the Ku Klux Klan, and the media to Van Bittner had denounced "reds" in the unions, the Taft-Hartley Act established a political litmus test that divided the trade unions along ideological lines. Every union official had to swear they did not belong to the Communist party. Noncomplying unions could no longer gain a place on NLRB ballots in union representation elections. Secondary strikes, boycotts, and other union pressure tactics likewise became illegal. The NLRB could be used by employers to decertify unions, which had to file complicated reports with the secretary of labor on their internal structures and finances as well as prove their leaders had no Communist party affiliation. The law prohibited closed shops, union expenditures in elections, strikes by federal employees, and made individual labor leaders liable for breaches of union contracts. It also provided for an eighty-day "cooling off" period during which the government could prohibit strikes in various industries and allowed federal troops to replace union members during strikes in violation of the act. It even removed the federal Mediation and Conciliation Service from the jurisdiction of the Labor Department, deemed too sympathetic to unions. Perhaps most damaging in the South, section 14(b) made it permissible for states to outlaw union shops. Southern state legislatures followed with "right to work laws" that undermined this crucial means by which unions maintained their membership against anti-union employers. Tennessee passed its law in February, even before passage of the Taft-Hartley Act.[65]

Taft-Hartley's disastrous provisions received instant support from business owners and industrialists in Memphis and across the state. Employers flooded Tennessee Democratic senator McKellar's office with pleas to pass Taft-Hartley to stop "communists" and the "union dictatorship" over business. The head of U.S. Bedding company in Memphis felt the law was "too mild" and the Memphis Chamber of Commerce wanted more drastic action as well, including the outlawing of industry-wide bargaining, strikes for union recognition, and wildcat strikes. On the other hand, Memphis business owners protested proposed legislation to raise the minimum wage to a paltry sixty cents an hour and to limit the work week to forty hours. In supporting restrictions on unions and opposing them for employers, business owners thought they were fighting for their freedom. But workers, who wrote Democrat McKellar by the dozens protesting his support of Taft-Hartley, saw these measures as undermining freedom. "I had 2 sons in over-seas service for this to be a free country in the last war," one Memphis worker wrote, "and you turn around & place shackles on our necks by lining up with Republicans . . . at the command of National Assn. Mftrs. as though you owed labor no obligation." Labor protest did no good: McKellar voted for Taft-Hartley and to overturn President Truman's veto of the bill.[66]

Aggressive anti-union laws in 1947 for the first time pushed the AFL, the CIO, and the railroad unions into a united campaign to protect union rights. This unity reached its high point in Memphis during the August Labor Day parade. Fifteen to eighteen thousand members of all three groups paraded through the streets, with twenty thousand spectators in attendance; it took workers lined up six abreast over an hour to march past a reviewing stand. Black workers marched with whites and carried banners and placards urging "support for FEPC," "everyone to vote," "equal justice to all," and "equal job opportunities." Following the parade United Steelworkers' secretary-treasurer David McDonald declared that "labor finds itself faced with a Congress under the influence of the mightiest combination of wealth and power in history" and with "just one purpose—turn back the clock; beat labor, break the unions." The march began a series of long-term efforts by the AFL, the CIO, and the railroad unions to close ranks in support of progressive candidates for office and for joint lobbying in the state legislature.[67]

The unions hardly had time to mobilize politically, however, as employers used the new laws to reopen contracts and challenge maintenance of membership clauses and other union security provisions. In response to Taft-Hartley, the CIO's SOC first adopted a policy of noncooperation: it not only refused to file petitions with the NLRB but withdrew the petitions already before the NLRB. Deprived of NLRB protections and kept off the ballot in NLRB-sponsored elections, fledgling CIO unions often had no choice but to go on strike in order to win recognition. The SOC endorsed gaining recognition "the hard way," but did not have the resources to finance recognition strikes, thus placing greater burdens on individual unions. In Memphis, lack of NLRB coverage forced the CIO's chemical union into a twenty-seven-day strike for recognition at Willard Battery. The absence of government mediation likewise forced a number of locals to resort to strikes to obtain better wages, including three conducted by Local 19 against cottonseed oil mills in the fall of 1947.[68] The CIO, however, had little success in gaining recognition or representation without the NLRB; only two CIO efforts to organize new shops outside of the NLRB framework succeeded in Memphis. And the shops it had already organized, including the J. R. Watkins plant, faced decertification efforts by employers and AFL unions.[69]

Following passage of the Taft-Hartley Act, organizing drives faltered as numerous CIO unions failed to get on NLRB ballots, and competing AFL unions became a more potent force. The SOC saw five months of textile organizing in East Tennessee destroyed in August because it could not get on the NLRB ballot; at the Vultee Steel plant in Nashville, the NLRB's refusal to certify the steelworkers' union, which had previously defeated an AFL union by a two to one vote, forced an unwanted strike that jeopardized the local's continued existence. Meat-packing companies especially took advantage of the precarious condition of southern locals of the CIO's United Packinghouse Workers' union, refusing to apply wage increases won at the national level and precipitating a number of local strikes. As nearly ten thousand disputes arising from the new law clogged the NLRB national dockets, local unions that would have previously gained certification within months remained uncertified for a year or more, thus losing the confidence and enthusiasm of workers, who in many cases turned to the AFL. When the CIO finally decided to comply with Taft-Hartley, the law's requirements tied them up in endless legal bureaucracy; even NLRB regional director Paul Styles had to enter law school, and he suggested to Paul Christopher that he and other CIO leaders do the same in order to cope with the new law. Under these conditions, Operation Dixie practically ground to a halt. By April 1948 the campaign gained about five locals per week as compared to twenty per week gained previously. Indicative of the unfavorable trends, by June 1948 wages had gone up on average only 14 percent in comparison to price increases of 30 percent since the war's end.[70]

Taft-Hartley not only stymied CIO organizing but accentuated its internal divisions. The national CIO left each union to decide for itself whether to sign the act, setting off internal strife and raids between complying and noncomplying unions. Within the UAW and the NMU, union leaders began purging officials who would not sign the noncommunist affidavits or who were deemed to be Communists. The Operation Dixie staff began openly raiding noncomplying left-wing unions. Under these conditions, previous alliances within the CIO dissolved.[71] The dire effects of the Taft-Hartley Act on CIO unity could be seen in the United Furniture Workers of America (UFWA), which had significant Communist and leftist leadership at the national level and had been among those CIO unions with high hopes for Operation Dixie. A multitude of workers in furniture and related shops, among the lowest paid in the country, remained to be organized in the South, and blacks played a major role in the industry. Accordingly, the union consigned nearly half of its organizers to recruiting southerners. Soon Local 282 in Memphis had reached a new high point of strength, with contracts in thirteen shops, and furniture locals seemed to show promise in other parts of the South as well.[72] But with passage of the Taft-Hartley Act, the union's hopes of southern expansion went up in smoke. Top leaders refused to sign the act's anticommunist provisions, leading to prolonged internal conflict; top union officers finally signed the Taft-Hartley oath in 1949, but by then the damage to the union had already been done.[73] Other CIO unions, seeking to make up their own losses, began raiding the union's membership, a development one UFWA veteran called a "disgrace" to the labor movement. Internally divided and under attack by employers and other unionists, the furniture union went into drastic decline, an example of industrial unionism's weakening position all across the South.[74]

*   *   *

In Memphis, the pressure of the Taft-Hartley Act, the red scare, and resistance to growing civil rights demands heightened white-black schisms as well as political tensions within the CIO. Increasingly, white workers resisted joining with blacks in the CIO's biracial structure, while CIO unions hesitated to take strong action to attract black support. At Southern Air Lines, Henry White succeeded in organizing all of the black laborers, but whites voted to join a separate UAW unit. Worried that the blacks might pull out of the CIO and join a competing AFL union, CIO organizer J. D.

Harris met with the whites to ask them to open their ranks to blacks. Instead, the UAW members voted eighteen to three to exclude them.[75] A similar situation developed at a new bottling plant of the Coca-Cola Company, where the AFL's Teamsters sought to take the plant away from the CIO's brewery workers' union. The union had organized 90 percent of the black drivers, dockworkers, and helpers on the trucks, but it put almost all of them on "work permits," which allowed them no rights in the union. Most of the whites refused to participate. This dis-unity put the union in a highly vulnerable position when it became clear at the end of July that the CIO would have to strike the plant in order to gain recognition. "You may run into plenty of trouble in Memphis with only Negroes on the picket line if the whites try to go through," Paul Christopher warned Harris. While Harris tried to avoid a strike, blacks, who received as little as $19.30 for forty-eight-hour weeks and $27.50 for seventy-six-hour weeks, demanded action. Seeking to take advantage of discontent with the CIO, Coca-Cola brought in black ministers, doctors, and other professionals to convince black workers to forget the CIO and join a company union. The CIO had no satisfactory response, and the situation dragged on without resolution.[76] Also indicative of growing black alienation with a number of CIO unions, in December 1947 the International Woodworkers of America (IWA) lost the E. L. Bruce Lumber Company, with a predominantly black work force, to the AFL's Carpenters' and Joiners' union by a vote of 1,135 to 774. At the J. R. Watkins plant, where blacks played a much smaller role, the CIO barely defeated a decertification effort by a vote of 49 to 33. Among both blacks and whites, the CIO's momentum of 1946 and early 1947 had dissipated.[77]

If black support for some CIO unions declined, however, in other cases blacks continued to feel they had a tremendous stake in joining the CIO. Leroy Boyd, a shop steward at Local 19's Federal Compress plant, recalled how much the union meant to him. He and several hundred other blacks worked at Federal Compress for a mere forty or fifty cents an hour and received no help at all from the AFL. White supervisors, he recalled, "were people right off of the plantations in Mississippi. They believed in working you just like the people worked you down there on the plantations . . . that was the sentiment of the company from top to bottom." Reminiscent of how white overseers treated black dockworkers in the thirties, one supervisor pulled a gun on a worker, and others fired anyone who crossed them. "You had to *act* like he was your boss," said Boyd. "If you disagreed with him, you couldn't tell him he was lying, even if he was lying . . . they were rushing you, and cursing at you." With great difficulty, FTA organized this shop in 1946. In 1947, black FTA member Earl Fisher took up the first grievance, and the local held a series of unofficial work stoppages to force a response from the company. One of these got Fisher fired. Boyd recalled that he and co-workers carried on a continuing battle at Federal Compress throughout the postwar years and for decades after that. "We were fighting them, and they were fighting us."[78]

Without an effective union, such protracted struggles for change on the shop floor would be impossible, and in most cases CIO unions, despite the increasing limitations of some of them, continued to provide a far better vehicle for blacks than did the AFL. And within the CIO, the leftist unions, despite their own liabilities, still remained the most reliable supporters of black rights. The Communist party had lost significant labor support during the war by demanding that workers continue a no-strike pledge indefinitely, and in 1944 Earl Browder took the popular front idea to its extreme by temporarily dissolving the party altogether. Party leaders had frequently alienated people by their bellicose attacks against those with whom they disagreed, and it was relatively easy for CIO leaders to isolate Communists in the postwar years. But in 1946 and 1947 the Communist party had also experienced a revival in the South, based on an increasingly aggressive effort to organize among blacks. In North Carolina, black tobacco workers swelled party membership to 150 or more members, and in Memphis the party reached its high point of influence, with perhaps a score of members, many of them in shops. Postwar campaigns against "white chauvinism" and increasing emphasis on civil rights, while alienating some whites, strengthened the party among blacks. And many whites, on the riverboats at least, also accepted the Communist party, according to Red Davis. For a time, at least, "it was popular to be a Communist. There was no stigma attached." Indeed, Davis sold the *Daily Worker* openly in the CIO hall and gave out Marxist literature on the riverboats, where the NMU had some four hundred members. According to Davis, in 1946–47 "you could be an open Communist in Memphis"—a far cry from the thirties.[79]

Many blacks in leftist unions, Leroy Boyd among them, considered white radicals as among their strongest allies and ignored the growing red-baiting campaign against them. "During that time, of course, a lot of our people were branded Communists," he recalled. Blacks "didn't pay any attention, because they knew how white men felt about another white man speaking up for the Negro. He was just branded as a Communist." Boyd spoke as if the fact that some of these white civil rights supporters *were* Communists was irrelevant; and to him, it was. Many blacks like Boyd remained intensely loyal to Local 19 at the very time that a number of whites began to fall away. They also recognized leftists, both white and black, as a group that could undertake enough initiatives to make a real difference in the racial politics of the CIO. Communist party members included Red and Carmen Davis, Bea and Ed McCrea, John Mack Dyson, Earl Fisher, Henderson Davis, Lawrence and Mildred McGurty, and others in cotton-processing, chemical, and furniture industries; a handful of white and black teachers and professionals belonged as well.[80]

Although small, the Communist party influenced many workers in strikes, union meetings, and organizing drives. During its high point in the postwar years it also organized groups for civil rights, such as the National Negro Congress and the Civil Rights Congress. According to one probably inflated report by an Urban League field secretary, as late as 1951 550 to 600 Memphians subscribed to the *Daily Worker*—some 500 of them black. The Communist party stood ideologically against racism, but more important, its members put their beliefs into action. White party members could be relied upon to join picket lines and organizing drives with blacks, in sharp contrast to many other white unionists, who were willing to join biracial unions but did little else to demonstrate solidarity with black workers. Indeed, many white union officials, including Copeland, "just had no association with blacks," according to Red Davis. "They'd never go to lunch with them, and they just had a condescending attitude towards them. . . . They would openly oppose any step toward integration; they'd make no bones about it." CIO success over the long haul required a larger understanding of the race question. Communist party members in the CIO promoted genuine concern and commitment on racial questions and built alliances between blacks and whites. White workers, Davis observed, changed their racial beliefs at a deep level "only when they joined the left or through left influence." If for no other reason, Communists remained an important component of the CIO as a movement.[81]

Yet Communists, by their own accounts, made major mistakes in the postwar years. Ed McCrea, for example, believed that not signing the Taft-Hartley Act set the left unions up for destruction. Most workers, in his experience, could not understand why the unions should sacrifice their place on NLRB ballots over a political issue. McCrea quit the party in order to sign the anticommunist affidavit, based on the belief that "you can't take a position that you can't justify with the workers. After all, you're their leadership, they elected you to fight for their benefits." Other Local 19 leaders who belonged to the party did the same. McCrea also felt the party hierarchy pushed Communist trade unionists to take positions on foreign policy questions, such as opposition to the Marshall Plan, that were "way in advance of the thinking of the rank and file" and thereby exposed them to attack by the Right. Karl Korstad similarly believed that the FTA's out-front support for Henry Wallace had unnecessarily exposed the union to CIO attacks, while McCrea also felt that Communist party over-exuberance in campaigns against "white chauvinism," although attracting the support of blacks, also alienated white workers at a time when their support for unions was desperately needed. At the same time, McCrea believed, the party failed to produce a realistic program that would move whites away from the reaction of the period. Communist party national leaders thought they were "out to win the war for socialism," and, according to McCrea, often sacrificed the labor movement to do it. He felt that party leaders pushed almost recklessly to the left at a time of great danger, when their directives to organizers in the field could and did have disastrous effects.[82]

However, the main obstacle to continued unity within the labor movement remained the general drive toward reaction in the country, not the faulty vision of party leaders or the mistakes of trade union leftists. No matter how dedicated they might be, neither the handful of Communist and leftist activists in the southern CIO nor the CIO itself could stop the upsurge of the larger forces of the cold war era, nor could they halt the segregationist reaction against growing black civil rights demands. No matter what positions leftists might have taken, it would not have saved them from the onslaught to come. However, the heightened political divisions within the southern unions initiated by Operation Dixie leaders in many ways encouraged rather than resisted the growing climate of reaction. Ironically, this would have more long-lasting effects on the fate of southern unionism than did Operation Dixie's organizing successes. CIO organizing continued, but by the end of 1947 a brief window of opportunity in the postwar South was about to be firmly closed shut, as the unions themselves joined in purging some of their best organizers. In the Memphis CIO, this would have quite negative consequences for union growth and stability. "The leftists were the only ones who could mobilize white supporters to support a black picket and strikes of black workers," Red Davis recalled. "When they broke up the left coalition, then they began to lose the strikes."[83]

Crowded conditions threw black and white together in new and uncomfortable ways during the war. Greyhound bus station, September 1943. (Photo by Esther Bubley, Farm Security Administration, courtesy of the Library of Congress)

An unprecedented strike wave after the war had the potential to involve black and white together, even during the strike of AFL Teamsters at Greyhound Bus company, February 1946. (Courtesy of the Mississippi Valley Collection, Memphis State University)

Women played a growing role in the economy and the unions during and after the war, as this May 1947 photo of telephone strikers in Memphis indicates. (Courtesy of the Mississippi Valley Collection, Memphis State University)

George Holloway (*center*) became the first African American on the bargaining committee of the new UAW Local 988 at Memphis International Harvester, May 1948. (Courtesy of the Mississippi Valley Collection, Memphis State University)

During the 1948 strike against the Nickey Brothers lumber company African Americans received critical support from whites in left-wing NMU and FTA locals. Pictured here are Red Davis (*back row, third from left*), Larry Larsen (*back row, fifth from left*), Ed McCrea (*back row, third from right*), Lawrence McGurty (*front row, third from right*), and George Bentley of the IWA (*left of McGurty*). (Courtesy of W. E. Davis)

FTA Local 19 leaders, 1948, include Lee Lashly, future president (*first row, third from left*), George Isabell (*first row, last on right*), Larry Larsen, regional director (*second row, first on left*), Ed McCrea, business agent (*second row, third from left*), and John Mack Dyson, president (*third row, second from left*). (Courtesy of Ed McCrea)

Paul Robeson (*second from right*) came to Memphis in October 1948 to support Progressive party presidential candidate Henry Wallace. Also present are Ken Clark, state organizer (*far left*), and Louis Burnham, national organizer (*next to Clark*). (Photo courtesy of Clara Vincent)

By 1967 Firestone workers had won the right to sit wherever they liked, but when the *Commercial Appeal* printed this photo they cropped the black workers out of the picture. (Courtesy of the Mississippi Valley Collection, Memphis State University)

Dr. Martin Luther King, Jr., (left) and George Holloway of the UAW symbolize the meeting of civil rights and labor concerns. The political leader George Lee is in the background. (Courtesy of George and Hattie Holloway)

A mass march following the death of Martin Luther King, Jr., in 1968 brought AFSCME national president Jerry Wurf and Rev. Ralph Abernathy, King's successor as president of the Southern Christian Leadership Conference, together with local civil rights and labor leaders. Pictured are Rev. James Lyke (*far left*), Jesse Epps, (*third from left*), followed by Rev. Ralph Jackson, AFSCME president Jerry Wurf, Rev. Ralph Abernathy, Miriam Decosta Willis, and Rev. Ezekial Bell. (Courtesy of the Mississippi Valley Collection, Memphis State University)

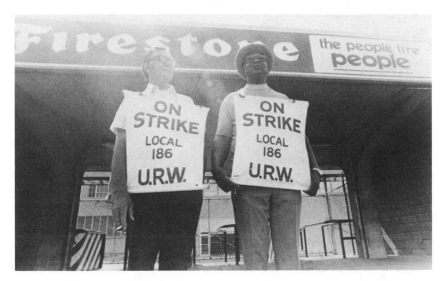

Workers became famous for their militance at the Firestone plant. This strike took place in 1976. (Courtesy of the Mississippi Valley Collection, Memphis State University)

CHAPTER NINE

The Cold War against Labor and Civil Rights

All members of the Memphis CIO should again be reminded of and warned against permitting these traitorous agents of a foreign government to infiltrate into the ranks of the Memphis CIO local unions . . . for the express and avowed purpose of dividing, weakening—and ultimately destroying—the Memphis CIO movement.
—Memphis Industrial Union Council

Since the majority of the CIO membership is Negro people they appear to be very concerned with the civil rights program . . . but only find their supiors [sic] interested in getting rid of the reds.
—Gene Day

A lot of our people were branded Communists. Any time a white man spoke up for the rights of the Negro, he was called a Communist.
—Leroy Boyd

However much the media, Congress and the president, and local politicians and employers focused on "communism" in the cold war years, the polarization building up throughout the South remained explicitly racial. And behind the accelerating racial confrontation lay decades, even centuries, of efforts by ruling elites to maintain their privileges and power. Unionization and growing working-class access to the vote, to education, and to higher income threatened these privileges and power in the postwar period, as did demands for black civil rights. As in the past, opponents of change sought to obscure and undermine potential alliances between working-class whites and blacks with racial demagoguery. Mississippi senator Theodore Bilbo in 1946 had attacked the Southern Conference for Human Welfare as that "un-American, negro social equality, communistic, mongrel outfit"; Crump, once renowned as a paternalist, increasingly veered toward such vitriolic rhetoric as well. In his twilight years, Crump, like other segregationists, mounted a last defense of Jim Crow, wrapped in the patriotic flag of anticommunism. In 1948, he endorsed South Carolina senator Strom Thurmond's "State's Rights," or "Dixie-crat," party, a breakaway movement that signaled the end of the "Solid South's" support for the Democratic party, which had endorsed African-American civil rights in its platform. Crump even banned the American Heritage Foundation's "Freedom Train," a traveling exhibit of original copies of the Declaration of Independence and other historic documents that toured the country in late 1947. Crump claimed that the founda-tion's requirement of integrated viewings of the train's documents would cause whites and blacks to jostle each other and lead to race riots; Mayor James Pleasants claimed Freedom Train supporters wanted to "poison the minds of the people." Although the train went to Atlanta, Little Rock, New Orleans, and Richmond on an unsegregated basis, it did not stop in Memphis.[1]

The South's accelerating racial polarization became clearly manifest in Memphis factories. In April 1948, 450 unskilled black workers struck the Nickey Brothers lumber company, one of the oldest plants in Memphis. The strike started when the International Woodworkers of America (IWA) sought a seventy-five-cent-an-hour minimum wage, a vacation plan, and a provision for checkoff of union dues. It quickly revealed the racial schisms within the work force. White workers in the plant's upper-level wage cate-gories, some 200 of them, refused to strike with the blacks. When the company brought in blacks to replace the strikers, they refused to go into the plant once they learned of the strike. The company then brought in whites as scabs, including high school football players recruited by their coaches, who wanted them to build their muscles by working in the mill. Instead, several boys lost their fingers and one lost an eye working on the machines, and white IWA members in the plant began to walk out. They still would not join with blacks on the picket line, however, and white scabs refused to listen to black picketers from the IWA. The strike dragged on for ten weeks, and most CIO unions did little to help. Only mass picketing by the NMU, led by Red Davis and Lawrence McGurty, saved the IWA strikers from defeat, as white scabs turned back when confronted by the burly white river workers. Finally, when white rail workers refused to haul materials into the plant, the management agreed to a settlement.[2]

Workers at Nickey Brothers had always been racially divided, with the white sawyers and other skilled workers supporting AFL affiliation and un-skilled blacks joining the IWA during the war. White opposition to the CIO had abated for a time, but like other unions organized primarily as a result of wartime government pressure, the IWA remained vulnerable to union busting once that pressure had dissipated. Concerted struggles against the employer that might have brought the workers together had not occurred, and after the war the left-right split in the international union increasingly diverted its funds and attention from southern organizing. The continued opposition of white males to a union that placed them in a minority to blacks led to the union's steady erosion at Nickey Brothers. Throughout 1948 and 1949 AFL unions used such situations to take whites out of the CIO, while employers increasingly encouraged racial divisions and used scab labor to kill off the unions. When workers at one local linen company tried to organize a union, for example, the employer fired sixteen of them, ten white women and six black women, and replaced them all with black women. Other Memphis employers transferred their work to nonunion bastions in Mississippi. Under these conditions, Lawrence McGurty wrote to a relative, the Nickey Brothers confrontation proved to be "the last successful strike in Memphis for many a year," either in the lumber industry or anywhere else.[3]

The inflamed racism evident at Nickey Brothers also appeared at the new International Harvester plant. There the management set a precedent by hiring blacks (12 percent of the first group of workers hired) with "the same wages for the same work" as whites. White workers had to accept this policy as a condition of employment, but many of them believed they could still keep blacks "in their place." Nor did they necessarily accept the fledgling UAW as a bargaining agent. Many of the incoming workers resembled those who had come into the factories during the war: fresh off the farms with no background in unionism. Workers supported the UAW, however, when they discovered that without a union their $.45 starting wage was a third less than that paid to Harvester workers in the North; without a union, the company could force them to work overtime, make them pay for their own gloves, and even refuse to let production workers use the bathrooms without a supervisor's approval. Crump shook hands at the plant and urged the workers to keep the UAW out, to no avail: they voted 833 to 4 in favor of the UAW in April 1948. White support for CIO unionism did not include any commitment to equality, however, even though the UAW had enshrined this fundamental principle in its contracts. George Holloway, one of the most experienced unionists of the new hires, became one of the keys to building the new UAW. But when he went to the Peabody Hotel for contract negotiations with Harvester, the hotel's management refused to allow him in, claiming that the hotel would never allow a black to dispute a white man's word by participating in negotiations. The union committee and management finally met at the Chisca Hotel, but the owners there only allowed Holloway to come into the hotel by way of the freight elevator, where garbage and wastewater fouled his clothing. None of the local UAW's six white committee members objected to any of these indignities, nor did they object when a company superintendent at the plant insisted on calling Holloway a "nigger" during grievance meetings. Whites also made a point of never seconding a motion by Holloway, the only black on the UAW local executive board.[4]

Despite such damaging racial schisms within the industrial unions, the fall 1948 elections proved that they remained a potentially powerful force. Crump's political associate, Senator McKellar, had always feared that labor would combine its forces with other sectors of the community to defeat the Crump machine. That coalition of forces finally came into being when union, business, and civic reformers handed Crump his first major election defeat since before World War I by putting Estes Kefauver in the Senate over Crump's determined opposition. As Tennessee representative in the House, Kefauver had already taken civil liberties stands, opposing Truman's Loyalty bill, the poll tax, and HUAC. Although he voted against making the Fair Employment Practices Commission a permanent body and opposed other and civil rights measures, he remained remarkably liberal in nonracial concerns. Kefauver had been one of two Tennessee representatives who voted to override the Taft-Hartley Act in Congress. Crump ran vitriolic newspaper ads against Kefauver across the state, calling him a Communist sympathizer. But Crump's red-baiting attacks backfired, only swelling support for Kefauver, who defeated Crump's candidate, John Mitchell, by nearly two to one. Even in Crump's stronghold of Shelby County, Kefauver obtained 27,621 votes to Mitchell's 37,771 votes, and in Memphis, Crump lost forty-six ballot boxes to his opponent. Previous to Kefauver, Crump had not lost a single ballot box in the city since 1926.[5]

The coalition that defeated Crump seemed to represent a sea change in Memphis politics. On one hand, AFL, CIO, and railroad unions joined together based on their opposition to the Taft-Hartley Act, the poll tax, and the conservative policies southern Democrats had followed in regard to labor. At the same time, a handful of business owners concerned about the benighted condition of Memphis and the South formed a citizen's committee for Kefauver. This group included Charles Poe, an official of the Nickey Brothers lumber company; Edmund Orgill, past president of the chamber of commerce; Lucius Burch, an attorney; a paint remover manufacturer; a lumber manufacturer; a doctor; and a paper company executive. This group, with strong support from Edward Meeman, editor of the Memphis

Press-Scimitar, represented "forward-thinking" business owners at odds with some of the city's older plantation-minded leaders. At least one of them had fought in the war and all of them demanded greater democracy in Crump's domain. At least one of them also sought assurances (and got them) from Kefauver that he would not take undue action to overturn the Taft-Hartley Act. Crump for the first time faced a respectable, public opposition from within the business community, one that stirred up support from white lawyers and society women, joined with the power of organized labor. Significant segments of the black community joined the coalition as well, including a number of prominent black business owners, the Urban League's Rev. James McDaniel, who spoke throughout the black community from a CIO sound truck, and black unionists.[6]

After the election, however, Crump primarily blamed the CIO for his defeat, and he was right to do so. Whereas some 7 percent of the population had industrial jobs in 1940, by 1950 some 20 percent had them. With unionization, many factory workers could afford to pay their own poll taxes, unbeholden to Crump. In 1948, they provided an important margin for Kefauver, who carried twenty-two city and four county precincts and 55 percent of the voters in Frayser, a solidly working-class white district. Union campaigning, masterminded by the CIO's Dan Powell, Richard Routon, and Ed McCrea, brought union members out to vote in large numbers, and poll watchers provided by CIO members and middle-class volunteers reduced the typical voting fraud to a minimum. Local 19's door-to-door organizing of the black vote for Kefauver proved especially significant. Much of the black vote, particularly the black labor vote, had shifted against Crump, just as civil rights commentators had suggested it would. According to Clarence Coe, the Freedom Train incident, which had so outraged blacks, had been "the beginning of the end" for Crump. After that incident, black leaders who had cooperated with Crump's version of paternalism no longer found favor with many black voters. In alliance with moderate business owners and middle-class reformers, the black-labor vote finally had the power to bring the Crump regime to an end. "I think he's finished," Kefauver commented after the election. Labor supporters in Tennessee had defeated not only Crump's candidate but the incumbent governor who had supported the state's anti-union "right to work" law.[7]

At the national level, the reelection of Truman (whom Crump had also opposed) in November likewise indicated that labor and liberal voting strength had not been smashed by the cold war. More problematic, however, was the third-party presidential campaign of Henry Wallace. In the

South, Wallace directly challenged segregation in a series of tours, in which he spoke to thousands of people in the largest nonsegregated meetings held since the Reconstruction era. In his first southern tour in late 1947, his support for black civil rights, peace abroad, and a continuation of New Deal social justice at home had been met with great enthusiasm, and Southern Conference for Human Welfare supporters concluded that the South "offers a greater hope for a successful progressive movement than any other section of the United States." For the next year, however, Wallace suffered relentless red-baiting from the liberal Americans for Democratic Action, the Democratic party, the president, and the news media. In his second southern tour, Wallace courageously spoke for integration, traveled with blacks in his entourage, and held unsegregated meetings in seven states and twenty-eight cities. But race hate and anticommunism together poisoned many southern whites. In the mill villages of North Carolina and the steel towns of Alabama, white workers threw garbage on him, mobbed his car, and seemed to be on the verge of killing Wallace, Pete Seeger, and others traveling with him. After one of the more frightening incidents in this tour of "unheard speeches" Wallace commented, "Now I've seen the eyes of fascism."[8]

Despite this terrorism against Wallace and what he stood for, the crusade inspired many. For the first time, a national figure had defied segregation in the South. Southern Conference leaders disbanded the organization in order to work full time for Wallace. Left-wing unionists in the FTA, the NMU, and the International Union of Mine, Mill, and Smelter Workers, as well as blacks such as Daisy Bates, who later led the NAACP's school desegregation fight in Little Rock, played leading roles in Wallace's campaign. Strong-armed NMU members served as guards for Wallace in parts of the deep South, and in Memphis Red Davis chaired the Wallace committee. John Mack Dyson served as an elector, and FTA members provided many of the foot soldiers in the effort to place Wallace on the ballot in the November general election. Black minister D. V. Kyle of the AME Avery Chapel Church, who worked closely with Local 19 in voter registration and other community efforts, ran for state office with a white woman on the Progressive party ticket. In a September rally held in Memphis, over twenty-five hundred blacks and whites turned out in a nonsegregated gathering in Bellevue baseball park to hear Wallace. Perhaps in response to the bad publicity he got during the Freedom Train incident, or perhaps to stir more opposition to Truman, Crump guaranteed the former vice-president a peaceful hearing in Memphis. Except for an incident in which some white youths smashed his car windshield, he got it. Wallace told his audience that "if the United States is to be secure in a world largely populated by men of color, then the end of segregation must come to pass." Clark Foreman came to town a month later with the famed singer and actor Paul Robeson, who made an even more dramatic appeal for black civil rights. Although Crump tried to stop this meeting from taking place, Robeson insisted on going through with it. Introduced by Reverend Kyle at Mason Temple to an interracial audience of some two thousand, Robeson gave a full concert of African-American spirituals and freedom songs and touted the CIO as an opponent of Jim Crow.[9]

The 1948 elections gave leftists hope that Memphis was on the verge of a dramatic movement away from old ways, despite the conformist pressures of the cold war. During the elections, according to McCrea, Local 19 third-party campaigners and poll watchers received civil liberties protections by Kefauver supporters, based on the understanding that they would turn out black votes for Kefauver as a Democrat at the same time they supported Wallace. Memphis CIO leftists did not expect Wallace to get a large vote, however, because the main alternative to Truman in the South was not Wallace but the Dixiecrats. But Wallace's visit to Memphis, as well as those of Robeson and Foreman, struck a blow for civil liberties and set new examples of public support for integration. The Progressive party state ticket received predictably few votes, but the existence of its interracial slate of candidates, including a black man and a white woman, gave many people hope for change. The rhetoric of Reverend Kyle during the campaign contrasted dramatically with the accommodationist black ministers of previous years. Stating "I am for total equality for the Negro" and for "complete integration" of American life, Kyle outpolled Henry Wallace two to one, gaining 3,760 votes—many of them in predominantly white precincts. That Truman won his campaign largely by picking up the economic justice and civil rights themes of the Wallace campaign also convinced some integration supporters in Memphis unions that the Progressive party made a real mark on history.[10]

However, 1948 also proved to be a turning point for the worse. Although Truman got nearly twenty-four thousand votes in Shelby County, Strom Thurmond got over twenty-six thousand, proof that a large hard core of segregationists existed in Memphis. Furthermore, the attacks against "Henry Wallace and his Communists," as President Truman put it, further legitimized the red-baiting rhetoric of both liberals and segregationists. To racially conservative white CIO leaders such as Red Copeland, Wallace's strong stand for integration provided another example of Communist provocation on the race issue and a justification for further attacking the Communist-led unions that supported him. Only five CIO unions supported Wallace, including the FTA and the UFWA. This, plus their opposition to the anticommunist tilt in American foreign policy, set them up for removal from the federation. As confrontations between the United States and the Soviet Union escalated, rational debate in the CIO ended. Van Bittner commented after Truman's election that "a wonderful opportunity lies before us" to organize the South, but the aftermath of 1948 did not lead in that direction.[11]

RED SCARES AND UNION BUSTING

The Truman and Kefauver victories momentarily stemmed the tide of political losses for the union movement, and industrial unions at the end of 1948 won some important representation elections as well, bringing the new Memphis GE plant with more than three hundred workers into the CIO fold. But these hopeful signs did nothing to stop the racial polarization stimulated continually by the Dixiecrats, the news media, and the cold war. The virulent racism and anticommunism so evident during the Wallace campaign created an atmosphere that made it nearly impossible for the CIO to continue to grow, or even to remain stable, in Memphis. At Firestone, according to Richard Routon, even many of the white workers who he thought had become antiracists began openly espousing racist views. In this context, anti-unionism once again became fashionable among the city's business elite, as a number of employers took the offensive and rid themselves of the CIO. As the Memphis Chamber of Commerce launched a new program to promote "Americanism" weeks, it confidently renewed assurances, made to investors since the thirties, that "the large majority of manufacturing plants in Memphis are either open shop or non-union."[12]

The turning point in the CIO's fortunes in Memphis came in 1949 during a bitter strike by the UFWA's largest local, at Memphis Furniture company. The management of Memphis Furniture, always among the most aggressive opponents of the CIO, refused to bargain over Local 282's demand for union dues checkoff, the absence of which had kept the local financially weak and fearful of losing its base in the plant. Dues checkoff represented a recognition by the employer that the union had a legitimate place in the plant, a point Memphis Furniture had never acceded to; so many workers had been fired for belonging to the union in the past that many workers still feared to associate with it.[13] But during the war, black women had become a major part of the work force, remained so afterwards, and became a much more militant force than the men had been in past years.

When negotiations over a new contract came to an impasse, seven hundred workers (out of a total work force of nine hundred), the majority of them African-American women, went out on strike. They began in early January, the coldest month of the year, and continued striking into the summer heat of August. These strikers were truly among the dispossessed, making fifty-five cents an hour and risking eviction and hunger for months on end. As a symbol of the difficulties such desperately poor workers faced in a prolonged strike, the union distributed across the country a picture of a Memphis striker walking the streets with burlap bags on his feet instead of shoes, in the dead of winter.[14]

In contrast to its "friend of labor" image in the war era, the city government now openly took the side of the company. Escorted by as many as seventy city police officers, three eighteen-wheel trucks, patriotically decorated in red, white, and blue and filled with strikebreakers, came into the plant every day; truck drivers sometimes carried pistols, while the company threatened picketers with firing. The police did nothing when strikebreakers carried guns, but made numerous arrests enforcing a strict court injunction that required unionists to picket in such small numbers that they could not possibly halt the introduction of scab workers into the plant. The police frightened strikers by visiting them at their homes after midnight to "question" them and protected company employees as they drove trucks over sidewalks and cordoned off public areas to haul strikebreakers into the plant. According to Copeland, the police even accepted billy clubs made for them by Memphis Furniture scabs.[15]

The scene outside Memphis Furniture very much resembled the violent labor conflicts of the thirties. In an attempt to challenge this open union busting, CIO unions and the CIO Industrial Union Council initially offered strong support to the endangered furniture union. So did the local Urban League and NAACP leaders, for the strike of black women had implications for the economic progress of the entire African-American community. If Memphis Furniture could break up the largest local of black women in the city, what hope would there be for other unorganized workers, many of them female and black, to obtain bargaining rights, better wages, or job security? And if the company could succeed in pitting these workers against each other, what hope would there be for civil rights or labor progress? In appealing for outside support, unionists remained very much aware of the desperate need for work in the African-American community. Black strike activist Rebecca McKinley recalled how one black woman even jumped the fence to get into company premises, after being beaten up by pickets, in order to get a job. Along with the threat of scabs brought in from outside, strikers faced enemies from within the factory. Almost all the white female stitchers, as well as the few white males employed there, refused to join the strike. When the company obtained an injunction from the city courts that limited dramatically the ability of strikers to keep scabs out, the support of other CIO unionists became critical to the strike's outcome.[16]

That support, however, necessarily involved an alliance of right and left in the CIO. CIO area director J. D. Harris told the Memphis Industrial Union Council that it was Red Davis who had won the Nickey Brothers strike by initiating aggressive picket line tactics and that only such an effort would save the Memphis Furniture strike. Accordingly, Harris and Firestone workers beat up scabs several blocks from Memphis Furniture in one incident, and at other points CIO supporters visited scabs at their homes. These men apparently supported IWA organizer George Bentley's conclusion that "the winning of this strike is of paramount importance, not only to us [the woodworkers] but to other CIO unions here in Memphis."[17] Buoyed by CIO support, morale among the strikers remained high three months into the conflict, which cost the UFWA three thousand dollars a week in food and rent costs for the workers. Harris, along with strikers McKinley, Daisy Quiller, Laura Sanders, and Ed McCrea of FTA, joined together in a radio spot appealing for community support, pointing out that black women at Memphis Furniture had poor wages, did not even have privacy in the rest rooms, and suffered other indignities from an employer McCrea called "a shame and disgrace to Memphis." Unionists appeared to be putting up a strong united front against the company. But the strike remained at an impasse. Police continued to escort company vehicles with covered windows that trucked hundreds of blacks as well as some whites into the plant like cattle, making it impossible for picketers to reach strikebreakers with leaflets or to put pressure on them to quit.[18]

In the tenth week of the strike, Memphis business leaders, including Kefauver's key supporters, came up with their own solution to the Memphis labor conflict. Edmund Orgill, along with *Press-Scimitar* editor Edward Meeman, chamber of commerce president Cathy Robinson, and business attorney Lucius Burch formed a citizens' committee that met in mid-March with Bentley, Harris, Earl Crowder of the steelworkers, Douglas Boartfield of the textile workers, and Richard Routon of the rubber workers. Taking their cue from the national hysteria over "communism," the citizens' committee called on the CIO representatives, according to Bentley, to "clean house relative to some left wing representatives sent into Memphis by the Furniture Workers Union," and to "move all left wing elements out of Memphis." In return, they assured the unionists, Memphis

Furniture would be willing to accept a union that complied with the Taft-Hartley Act, namely Bentley's IWA, and bargain with it. The proposal had obvious appeal to the assembled CIO members, none of whom felt sympathetic to the left. On the other hand, the IWA and CIO leaders did not have the strength to defeat the UFWA in the plant; they rejected the offer.[19]

However, in a subtle way the proposal may have had its intended effect of further dividing the CIO from within. After the businessmen's proposal, left and right disputes became increasingly open. Bently expressed disgust with the furniture unionists for not taking the necessary disruptive and illegal actions required to stop scabs from getting into the plant; he complained, "They keep coming to J.D. Harris and myself for advice and would like for us to do their dirty work for them." Furniture unionists and Red Davis, who again played a leading role in strike support, however, blamed union bureaucrats for declining CIO participation in the strike. "Bentley and J. D. Harris weren't going to do anything; we were the ones that saved their asses all of the time, in Nickey Brothers or any other strike that went on," he recalled. "George stayed drunk most of the time and J. D. had a Mississippi mentality and never did get rid of that plantation ideology." Davis, still highly optimistic during the postwar era about the possibility of building an integrated Communist movement based in the working class, saw nothing wrong with using the occasion of a strike to teach courses in black history and Marxism and to recruit black female strikers into the party. Bentley, reporting that "the commies are organizing units among the colored people," saw these activities as provocations and blamed Davis and UFWA organizers Gene Day and David Conner for politicizing the strike.[20]

Under the pressure of the CIO's right-left conflict, working unity in the CIO fell apart. Mainstream CIO unionists had refused the business proposal to "clean house," but now they weren't sure if they really wanted the UFWA to win the strike. At a time when the union's national leadership was fighting to prevent the CIO from purging it for "communist" affiliations, a strike victory would place them back in a position of strength in Memphis.[21] Bentley's international union president recommended "that you do not place yourself in the position 'of pulling the chestnuts out of the fire' for the Furniture Workers leadership and officials," in hopes that the IWA might take over the plant. In mid-April, Bentley ceased his strike support, and other white CIO activists began to do the same. According to UFWA organizer Dave Connor, official CIO support had always been lukewarm, but then it ceased altogether.[22]

As CIO unity fell apart, political conflicts came to be increasingly fought out in racial terms. Left-right conflicts came to a head during the summer of 1949, precipitated in part when FTA business agent Ed McCrea and NMU activist Red Davis offered resolutions before the Industrial Union Council demanding the removal of "white" and "colored" signs from the CIO hall's toilets. "In the council, we had segregated sides in the union hall, and in the rest rooms," recalled Leroy Boyd. "This was white men, white women; that was colored men, colored women. Four different restrooms for the people." According to McCrea, integrationists on the council succeeded several times in having the signs taken down when Copeland was out of town, but Copeland reversed these decisions when he returned. He and others claimed that because city and state ordinances required segregation in public places, the CIO could do nothing but comply. John Mack Dyson, McCrea, and other Local 19 leaders urged the council to go into court to test the laws. Copeland branded such proposals as mere ploys by Communists to use blacks to further their own ulterior aims.[23]

Communists pushed the desegregation issue partly as a means to take the moral high ground as they resisted their growing isolation within the labor movement, but their opposition to segregation was of long standing. Local 19 had followed integrated practices from its inception, held social gatherings on an integrated basis, and since at least the end of the war had opposed segregated seating arrangements at Industrial Union Council meetings. Black and white delegates from the local refused to be separated by color and sat together in the back of the hall. Communists in the CIO had been fighting Jim Crow in various ways since the thirties and in the postwar era believed the time had come to confront racism and segregation directly. But Copeland turned aside the moral question posed by segregation and, in UFWA organizer Conner's words, in its place began "to substitute a campaign to rid the CIO of communism."[24]

With anticommunist hysteria sweeping the United States, Copeland easily defeated the resolution to desegregate the union hall. White "centrists" within the CIO, according to Red Davis, at this point feared to say a word in support of former allies on the left. Ultimately, photos of the "white" and "colored" bathrooms in Memphis appeared in national publications, and the national CIO ordered all southern Industrial Union Councils to integrate their facilities. In the meantime, however, Copeland used the debate as an occasion to escalate his attack on CIO leftists and told UFWA representative Gene Day that unless the union changed its ways it would be "liquidated" in Memphis. At a 31 August CIO staff meeting, Copeland "named names" of suspected Communists and charged a "communist take over" of Local 282. The meeting became an interrogation as to which CIO staff members belonged to the Communist party and, according to Conner, "an occasion for considerable breast-beating" at a time "when every anti-communist must stand up and be counted." The Memphis CIO, like most of the nation, rejected the Bill of Rights as it applied to Communists. Copeland regularly sent out memos alerting CIO members to leftist activities and even notified CIO staff members and local officers that they should get clearance from the CIO Industrial Union Council before going to any nonunion meetings. Once the most advanced force for civil liberties in the city, the CIO became the city's leading force, Copeland would boast, in the crusade to rid Memphis of all radicals or suspected radicals.[25]

The CIO's Industrial Union Council at its 14 September meeting, using as its justification the anticommunist rhetoric of national CIO President Murray, as well as Communist opposition to the American Marshall Plan in Europe and support for Henry Wallace in 1948, branded Communists as "traitors to the United States of America and traitors to the American Labor Movement." Contending that "no loyal American" could be a Communist and that Communists had "infiltrated" local unions, the Industrial Union Council called on local unions to establish vigilance committees to "guard" themselves from the "cancerous growth of the filthy disease of Communism." The resolution, drafted before the meeting by Copeland, Crowder, Bentley, and Harold Marthenke of the textile workers, called on each union local to adopt the Industrial Union Council's resolution on communism as their own statement of policy and established a special committee of the council to make sure that they did so.[26] At the same meeting, the council refused to seat Red Davis of the NMU and Lawrence McGurty, who belonged to the NMU but also worked for FTA Local 19, on charges that they were "party line sympathizers." Only Ed McCrea, apparently allowed to remain because he had quit the party in order to sign the Taft-Hartley Act, and Conner, his affiliations unknown, openly opposed these measures. Copeland attacked them as "red sympathizers" for doing so. No one else had the courage to stand up to such charges: out of some some one hundred union members present at the meeting, no one else openly opposed the expulsions.[27]

Following the meeting, CIO leaders and the newspapers excoriated civil rights activities as the work of Communist "fronts." When UFWA striker McKinley and black union leader James White attended meetings of the Civil Rights Congress in New York and the National Negro Congress in Chicago, the newspapers made a scandal of it, providing Copeland and others with further justification for silencing the left.[28] CIO imposition of a political litmus test on the activities of its member unions became standard procedure. Previously, a certain degree of union autonomy had been regarded by many as a basic measure of self-determination in the industrial federation. Such autonomy no longer appeared to have any place in the CIO. CIO unions apparently could no longer decide what groups to support or meetings to go to, who to support for public office, or what foreign policy positions to take. The Memphis Industrial Union Council banned leftists, many of whom had been key to building the unions, as well as "fellow travelers," which it defined as "those who consistently follow policies" of the Communist party, the Nazis, or the Ku Klux Klan. Such people, as defined by the council, could no longer serve as delegates or as council members. The council went further by beginning an inquisition into the political views of remaining suspected leftists in the CIO, including McCrea and Larry Larsen of FTA and Gene Day and Leonard Ragozin of the UFWA.[29]

The Memphis purges paralleled the CIO's inquisition at the national level. A new provision enacted at the 1949 national CIO convention authorized the CIO Executive Board to investigate and expel unions whose "policies and activities . . . are consistently directed toward the achievement of the program or the purposes of the Communist Party" or of fascists or other presumed totalitarians. CIO "trials" of the political record of various unions ultimately led to the expulsion of eleven unions with nearly one million members, as well as the dissolution of a number of industrial union councils under leftist influence. Numerous CIO unions, once pledged to nondiscrimination against union members because of their political views, began to bar Communists from office, and some went so far as to bar them from union membership, just as the AFL had done many years earlier. Organizational centralization, evident throughout the course of the Operation Dixie campaign, had became political centralization as well. The CIO's actions gave the Memphis Industrial Union Council perfect sanction to expel local leftists and particularly the FTA, whose policies the national CIO claimed "are consistently directed toward the achievement of the program and the purposes of the Communist Party rather than the objectives set forth in the Constitution of the CIO." [30]

In this inquisitorial atmosphere, it remained a short step for the CIO to actively attack left-wing locals. At the Cudahy oil refinery, where Local 19 had fought a difficult battle for recognition during the war, workers in September petitioned the CIO to remove them from FTA jurisdiction. "We do not believe in any form of government except that of the United States of America," they stated and threatened to go to the AFL for support if not taken out of the "Communist" Local 19. That Cudahy workers held their secession meetings at the Rubber Workers hall provided one sign of local CIO support for the renegade movement, but in private an even more duplicitous deal had been cut. CIO Region 8 director Paul Christopher, at the behest of Copeland, had spoken with Van Bittner as early as March 1948 about instigating just such a petition campaign, not only at Cudahy but at Local 19's stronghold in the Buckeye factory. Bittner had even suggested the text of the petition to Christopher, who then told Copeland that "some ground work will have to be done . . . and then the meetings and adoption of the resolutions, copies of which you should have sent to me and Mr. Bittner." The secession movement at Cudahy followed this prescription exactly and included a number of black workers, led by a disgruntled shop steward, while white women in the shop remained supportive of FTA. "The workers themselves are really confused," UFWA representative Gene Day observed. Local 19 lost the plant to the packinghouse workers' union, a surprise to McCrea, the business agent, who blamed himself for being complacent in his expectation of black support.[31] Others blamed the CIO for encouraging the raids on Local 19, however. UFWA director of organization Ernest Marsh commented that "this is about the lowest type of activity that so-called labor leaders could indulge in, and they will eventually destroy the whole labor movement if allowed to continue."[32]

Events proved this observation to be nearly correct. The internecine union conflicts and the failed strike at Memphis Furniture, for example, ultimately led to the almost total collapse of the UFWA in Memphis. Demoralization and blacklisting of union leaders by other companies followed the strike defeat, spreading fear among workers throughout furniture and related industries. At Memphis Furniture Day reported that "the workers are scared to death, and will hardly talk about the Union," and his contacts there dwindled to only one man.[33] At other plants he could hardly get workers to come to meetings and resorted to seeing them privately in their homes. He could not even get a worker to file a grievance, for "the workers are afraid that they will have to strike like the Memphis Furniture Workers." He later observed that "there is the fram[e] of mind on the part of the workers to eccept [*sic*] any offer to avoid a strike."[34] At the national level, pressed by a CIO committee investigating charges of "communism" against the UFWA, which had lost ten thousand members as a result of Taft-Hartley and the red scare, Morris Pizer took over the union and led a purge of its Communist or thought-to-be Communist leadership. Based on the purge, CIO national leaders allowed the union to remain in the CIO. Pizer came down to Memphis in February 1950 to tell one hundred black members of Local 282, "You had a small Iron Curtain here, but it's being pulled back." Earl Crowder and Doyle Dorsey used the occasion to denounce "communism in general and communism in labor unions in particular," according to the newspapers. The union placed the Memphis Furniture local, which had dwindled from 700 to about 250 members, in receivership and replaced a black local president, Rudolph Johnson, with Dorsey, also black. According to Leroy Clark, a black UFWA organizer who came in to do the dirty work, Dorsey was an ineffective leader whose main qualification seemed to be his ability to get along with Copeland. Clark recalled also that Johnson's removal had nothing to do with "communism"; his real problem was his racial militance, which Copeland automatically labeled as communism.[35]

The CIO's postwar hopes of expansion went down to total defeat, as employers emulated Memphis Furniture with a series of attacks against existing CIO unions. UFWA organizer Carl Curtis had observed in 1948 that a "clique of manufacturers in Memphis . . . [had] made up their mind to break the unions in their shops," and in 1950 they began a second round of union busting. "This is our answear [*sic*] to the plea we made for a united front in combating this Union busting machine in Memphis," Gene Day bitterly commented, as billy clubs used against black women and made by scab labor at Memphis Furniture came into play against white women at the American Snuff company.[36] The Condon family, owners of the company and staunch conservatives who later played a prominent role in the John Birch Society, virtually duplicated the patterns tested at Memphis Furniture. The Condons previously had a history of relatively amicable relations with their white female employees, but in 1949 they hired aggressive new managers charged with making the company more profitable. The company refused to bargain for any improvements at contract renewal, provoking another winter strike, in January 1950, of some 350 white women. FTA had first sought to organize this plant before the steelworkers' union, run by arch anticommunist Earl Crowder, gained bargaining rights. The change in union leadership made no difference to the owners, who brought in scab workers by the busload and declared they would rehire strikers only when new jobs became available. The company's refusal to rehire strikers became the major point of conflict for the rest of the strike and represented "the opening wedge in a city-wide campaign to bust the CIO in Memphis," according to a union leaflet.[37]

The snuff strike became the biggest and most violent conflict in the city CIO's history. Beginning in January, it lasted well into July, a total of 185 days, costing the strikers $250,000 in lost wages.[38] Unlike the black women at Memphis Furniture, the white women at American Snuff, most of them older workers, received militant and continuous support from the Memphis CIO, which organized crowds of up to seven hundred outside the plant. After witnessing the near-destruction of the UFWA when it failed to stop scabs from taking their jobs, CIO members from Firestone, International Harvester, and other big plants took direct action early in the strike. But as in the Memphis Furniture strike, city police turned out to protect scabs every day, with forty and fifty and in some instances as many as three hundred on duty. Early in the strike brutal fights reminiscent of the 1930s broke out between female strikers, company managers (including some well-muscled ex-football players), and scabs. Female strikers pulled hair and scratched faces, while one manager pulled out a knife and cut a strike supporter, who received fifteen stitches for the wound. Another fight occurred with over one hundred people milling around watching or participating. Police escorted busload after busload of strikebreakers, some of them newly arrived to the city from rural areas, others recruited on Beale Street.[39]

Strike supporters expressed particular outrage at the company's provocative recruitment of black men and young white women as scabs—a combination clearly aimed at undermining labor solidarity. Early in the strike the company brought fifty black strikebreakers prominently into the plant in an enclosed red truck and after that hauled blacks scabs into the plant at the head of a caravan of buses. Though blacks were also there as strike supporters, the newspapers mentioned that only at the end of the strike, meanwhile giving the impression that blacks had uniformly been scabs.[40] Efforts by the company to stir up racial animosity worked. White strike supporters regularly attacked busloads of black scabs with bricks and other objects. Crowder stirred racial antagonisms further, making the unlikely claim that "our young girls have been subjected [to abuse] by negro strike-breakers, who have called unspeakable insults to them as they walked the picket line." Crowder's willingness to fan the flames of racism indicated the reversion of many CIO activists to the racist practices long followed by AFL conservatives.[41]

The news media uniformly downplayed the provocative role of the police and company managers in favor of sensationalizing labor violence, which worsened throughout the strike. Pickets beat up scabs, overturned cars, and broke out windows on buses, and two anonymously placed bombs exploded in the plant. Predictably, the business community and the Memphis middle class sent dozens of letters to the mayor and to the newspapers condemning the conservative Crowder as a "communist" and praising the city's "neutrality" and support for "law and order." The company's owners believed that "Mr. Crowder had directed his small group of radicals in all the tried methods of the Communistic type of harassment." Other employers wrote that the strike confirmed the need to repeal the Wagner Act, which created "shameful collusion" between unions and the government. Strikers for their part compared the management to fascists and communists overseas and sang "Hail, hail, the scabs all here" outside of the plant.[42]

The American Snuff strike received the longest and certainly the most militant support of the city's working class in CIO history. The battle nearly led to a one-day general strike, with CIO unionists all over the city mobilized to take action. Police arrested dozens of strike supporters, including Red Davis, and the courts imposed thousands of dollars in fines. After nearly two hundred days of conflict, however, it became clear that the company would never give the strikers their jobs back en masse. Picket lines folded, and those who could get back into the plant did so, but without a union contract. The steelworkers' union lost an estimated one hundred thousand dollars on the strike, while the CIO lost a great deal of prestige and influence in the city.[43] After the American Snuff strike, as after the Memphis Furniture strike, many more industrial workers joined the ranks of the fearful and the unorganized.

The pattern of violent confrontation in these two strikes became almost a normal part of labor relations in Memphis and did anything but solidify working-class unity. When a five-hundred-member work force of predominantly white women went on strike at the new General Electric light bulb plant in September 1950, UAW members derailed trainloads of light bulbs and viciously attacked women who refused to strike. Chancellor L. D. Bejach, the same Crump machine judge who had been issuing injunctions since the thirties, once again issued a strict injunction to keep pickets from molesting strikebreakers. UAW members, having witnessed the defeats at Memphis Furniture and the Snuff strike, refused to go along. Bejach ultimately sent twenty-two of them to jail for physically blocking scabs from entering the plant. When workers were well organized, they did not have to resort to physical intimidation, which could easily degenerate into racial violence. During simultaneous strikes in CIO strongholds at Firestone and International Harvester, for example, few if any even attempted to enter the plant as strikebreakers.[44]

Clearly, however, the unions that would survive depended not on sympathetic government boards but on their own ability to keep scabs out of the workplace by whatever means necessary. Anti-union employers meanwhile chipped away at the organized base of labor for the next forty years. Even the building trades unions, which had long monopolized the construction labor market, began to lose their hold, leading to fratricidal violence as workers competed over jobs in a deunionizing industry. AFL ironworkers in 1954 discovered how costly it could be to stop scab labor: scab workers shot down five of the union members at the Memphis Fairgrounds when the unionists attempted to shut down a nonunion construction company. Thirty workers ended up in court, but the nonunion firm prevailed. Such battles between union and nonunion workers became regular occurrences in Memphis, symptomatic of the decline of craft as well as industrial unions. The attacks on southern unions begun with Taft-Hartley and the cold war in 1947 gradually whittled away the base of organized labor, not only in Memphis but throughout the South.[45]

THE COLD WAR AGAINST THE CIO LEFT

By the end of the forties, ideological orthodoxy as well as renewed union busting had descended on the labor movement. Cold war hysteria over internal "subversion," seen in prosecutions of Communist leaders across the United States under the Smith Act and firings of Communists or supposed Communists throughout industry, ran rampant. Members of the National Maritime Union were hit particularly hard. In 1949 a U.S. district court in New Orleans convicted Bob Himmaugh, an early founder of the NMU and the father-in-law of Red Davis, of having falsely told a loyalty board that he had not been a Communist party member. He received three years in prison. NMU president Joe Curran, who originally gained power in the union through the support of the Communists, began sending goons against them. Thugs killed one of McGurty's best friends in South Carolina, prompting McGurty to give a pistol to Red Davis for protection. Unionists in Memphis threw Curran thugs down the stairs of the NMU hall when they attempted to attack Davis, but regardless of rank-and-file support neither Davis nor McGurty could ship out because the Coast Guard would not give them clearance. This effectively blacklisted them from work on the river. In September 1950 the NMU, conducting its own purge of the Left, expelled Red Davis and his brother-in-law McGurty on the vague charge that "by their general conduct and policies they brought the union into ill repute." Contrary to the by-laws of the NMU, the union tried the men outside of their home port because they couldn't get anyone to bring charges against them in Memphis. The NMU expulsions, Copeland announced to the press, "removes the last follower of the Communist Party from the ranks of Memphis CIO." Ominously, he added that "the only Communist-front element still remaining in Memphis organized labor is Local 19."[46]

With NMU leftists detached from their base, the CIO began a campaign to remove Local 19 from its largest stronghold at the Buckeye company. The hot war in Korea provided the rationale for the union's destruction. During the summer of 1950 several Local 19 members circulated the Stockholm Peace Petition, an international appeal to outlaw the stockpiling or use of nuclear weapons. Police arrested a petitioning couple and Red Davis's wife, Carmen, while she pushed their two babies in strollers. In the past, the CIO had supported the right to petition and protest, but now it responded to the arrests by passing a resolution denouncing Communists—presumably the petitioners—as "enemies of America" who "enjoy the freedoms of America while advocating slavery under Communist control." Such petitions, it charged, "should be circulated only behind the Iron Curtain, instead of in peace-loving America," and the CIO called upon the police "to take every possible step to eliminate such subversive and disloyal elements from the City of Memphis." Any notion of the right to dissent had disappeared from the Memphis Industrial Union Council, which held that Communists or their sympathizers should not be allowed to "roam the streets of Memphis." The peace petition had actually been initiated before the Korean War began by notable church and civil liberties leaders concerned about nuclear weapons, and Local 19 president John Mack Dyson pointed out that his local had not even endorsed the petition. The arrested petitioners were not even Local 19 members, but some of the union's members had supported the petition and Dyson declared that the union would "continue to stand by the democratic rights of its membership regardless of race, creed, color, sex or political and religious beliefs."[47]

Though the peace petition ostensibly had little to do with a union of black workers in Memphis, the arrests helped the CIO to focus the red scare on Local 19. In September, a statement of fourteen CIO officials from all the city's major unions called on workers at Buckeye to vote in coming NLRB elections "for a loyal American union," the CIO chemical workers' local, and vote out the "Communist stench" in Local 19. CIO leaders claimed that Local 19 was "not a labor organization as such," and the newspapers began routinely referring to the union as "the Red front group." The Memphis Urban League joined the CIO red-baiting campaign, urging "every Negro member" of Local 19 to take the opportunity to withdraw from the union "for the good of his family and country" and calling on black ministers to speak with black Buckeye workers on the CIO's behalf.[48]

Attacks on Local 19 came at a crucial point in the union's history. Mechanization of cotton processing (including compressing in warehouses as well as the production of cottonseed oil and other by-products) increasingly reduced the number of unskilled jobs and accordingly reduced the number of black workers in some parts of the industry. The Industrial Union Council claimed that the local had a 40 percent decline in membership in 1949, proof that the union "sacrificed the workers' interests for the interests of Communist policies." But mechanization appears to have been the more likely cause for a decline in membership. Communist party members in Local 19 formally dropped out of the party, allowing the union to continue to be represented in NLRB elections, and the union lost few representation elections at a time when many other unions were losing theirs. In the period prior to 1950, the union pointed out that it had negotiated fourteen contracts in Memphis with across-the-board wage increases of five to ten cents an hour, "far better than the CIO has been able to do in a comparable industry." According to UFWA organizer Gene Day in 1949, Local 19 had been "the only union in the area that has consistently got wage increases in their plants," and Ed McCrea many years later still remembered proudly how workers from other plants came to the FTA office to look at their contracts as models for what they too might achieve.[49]

The local remained strong in a period of CIO instability, Ed McCrea insisted, because it had a sizeable core of confident rank-and-file workers and shop stewards who were well versed in all aspects of union politics. Many of them had attended Highlander sessions and had themselves worked out the wording of contracts and the terms of negotiations with employers. With frequent plant-wide meetings at lunch hours and constant steward training, "the union was so organized and structured that no action was taken without the fullest possible participation of its membership," according to McCrea. The Buckeye local had been built along these lines and provided a large membership base for the whole FTA operation in Memphis—one reason that Copeland and other CIO leaders sought to take the plant away from FTA. The union had done especially well at Buckeye, winning time-and-a-half overtime pay and a series of hourly wage increases that benefited skilled and unskilled equally and surpassed wage increases by other unions in similar industries. The Buckeye workers had been first, led by George Isabell, to break down color barriers to black skilled employment and among the first to adopt an antidiscrimination clause in contracts and to implement plant-wide seniority to protect workers from the effects of mechanization and job discrimination. Buckeye black leaders, including Isabell, remained less concerned about charges of "communism" than with the union's record of success in the plant. When Local 19's leadership stated that "our union is not dominated by Communists or anybody else. It is dominated by the membership," Buckeye workers for the most part agreed.[50]

Hence, in an NLRB election in September 1950, Buckeye workers voted to retain Local 19. A considerable number of whites, who made up some 40 percent of the plant's employees, voted for the CIO's competing chemical union. According to George Isabell, these people wanted out of Local 19 not because of communism but because they wanted more white control of the union. Blacks, however, voted almost unanimously for the existing local. For the next year, the CIO focused on changing their minds, led by Henry White of the CIO and Rev. James McDaniel of the Urban League. Adopting a paternalistic tone, McDaniel contended that "the negro worker needs protection and guidance within the labor movement" and "must first learn that there are good and bad labor unions, responsible and irresponsible labor leaders." The CIO itself continued to issue statements and hold meetings denouncing the local as "being led by communistic sympathizers" who posed a "danger of communism spreading in Memphis." But the second campaign to defeat Local 19 at Buckeye, like the first, did no good. By a vote of 216 to 189, black Buckeye workers again defeated the CIO effort to displace the union, in September 1951. At a CIO staff meeting a few days after the balloting, Henry White admitted that "Negro workers [are] sold on FTA." Hoping to coerce the company, which showed no real signs of antagonism to Local 19, into taking a stronger stance against the local, Crowder and another member suggested that the "CIO should nail [the] Company's attitude as being pro-Communist." No such rhetoric seemed to influence blacks at Buckeye, however, and after its second failure to take over the local the CIO chemical union urged an AFL union to organize the whites at Buckeye, a move that could only split the workers into competing racial bargaining units.[51]

Not only did Local 19 weather the CIO effort to undermine its base among blacks but activists in the union took increasingly bold steps in the civil rights struggle emerging in the South. In the spring of 1951, Local 19 shop leader Earl Fisher organized a protest delegation of seventeen Memphians, most of them black workers at Federal Compress, to go to Jackson, Mississippi, to protest the scheduled execution of Willie McGee. The plight of McGee, a black man tried three times on charges of raping a white woman and under threat of death since 1945, had gained national attention as the result of organizing by the leftist Civil Rights Congress. The rape charge, going back to the days of Ida B. Wells, had frequently been the excuse for lynchings of black men. No white man had ever been executed in Mississippi for such a crime; in Memphis, African Americans had been sixteen of the city's eighteen victims of electrocution since 1913. Bea McCrea, Mildred McGurty, Carmen Davis, along with their husbands and the wife of Henderson Davis formed a Save Willie McGee committee in Memphis, while Fisher and other rank-and-file blacks organized foot soldiers for the protest.[52]

Police arrested thirteen of the Memphis protesters at the state capitol building in Jackson before they could even begin participating in a scheduled prayer vigil, organized by Red Davis and an unidentified black man. Leroy Boyd, one of those arrested, apparently on charges of "conspiracy to obstruct justice," recalled how police packed dozens of protesters into jail cells overnight and then threatened to march them to the river to be killed. He and his fellow workers (including his brother) barely escaped Mississippi alive, by having white women drive their cars back to Memphis to divert local vigilantes while the black men left Jackson on a train. "At the train station, they were looking in at us just like cats through a glass at mice. Those peckerwoods wanted to get us, man!" Boyd recalled. "I was prepared to die." It was a fearful and proud moment: their open use of the civil rights style of protest made the workers of Local 19 heroes to many in the Memphis African-American community. "That's what scares the powers, when they see rank-and-file workers doing things like that," Ed McCrea recalled. "I'm not talking about middle-class blacks. I'm talking about workers right out of the plant. That shook the whole town up. That scares the hell out of them. 'Cause that's getting right down to the roots." In the aftermath of the protests, police tightened their surveillance of the Memphis black community and badly beat a *Daily Worker* reporter at the airport.[53]

The state executed McGee in May 1951, with five hundred whooping whites outside. But rather than focusing on the injustices in the McGee trial, the media in the South used the incident to warn of the dangers of "communist agitation" of the race issue. The case prompted Senator James O. Eastland to do likewise. Owner of a five-thousand-acre plantation near Ruleville, Mississippi, populated by black tenants, Eastland made his mark in politics by equating integrationism with communism, opposing Truman's civil rights policies. He later became a key leader of the White Citizens' Council, an organization founded in Memphis and described by many as the "Ku Klux Klan in business suits." In the fall of 1951, Eastland arranged Senate Internal Security Subcommittee (SISS) hearings in Memphis to investigate what the newspapers paraphrased as "a widespread Communist plot to enroll Negroes" in subversive organizations in the mid-South. Eastland's traveling inquisition, conducted in Memphis on 25 and 26 October, occupied the front pages of the Memphis newspapers for the better part of a month, covering the period before and after the second round of elections at the Buckeye plant.[54]

Crowder and Copeland welcomed the hearings, and probably instigated them. There was no indication that employers initiated the hearings and no employers testified. Indeed, Copeland himself later pointed out that the CIO took the lead in instigating the purge of Communists in Memphis. He and Crowder first testified to Eastland in closed session about alleged communists in the southern labor movement and then urged him to hold open hearings to "expose" the "chief promoters of Communism in Memphis." Copeland became so enthusiastic about his mission that he later wrote to SISS attorney Richard Ahrens listing the names of CIO leftists in New Orleans and suggesting others who could inform on remaining leftists in the southern CIO.[55] When Eastland did hold public hearings in Memphis, Copeland and Crowder, along with Rev. James McDaniel of the Urban League, became star witnesses. Eastland's sensationalized proceedings also brought forth a "mysterious" secret witness, who turned out to be the professional informer Paul Crouch. The "mystery witness" pointed out Ed McCrea, business agent of Local 19, as the former "boss of the Communist Party in Tennessee," or, as one newspaper put it in a double four-column headline, a "bigtime red."[56]

The Eastland hearings provided an opportunity for public humiliation and intimidation of Local 19 members, something that CIO leaders had been unable to achieve with their own efforts. Investigators for the security subcommittee "raided" Local 19 offices and took its membership list of 1,100 (a list still in the archives of the U.S. Senate). Eastland subjected McCrea, Local 19 leaders Lee Lashley and Earl Fisher, and union treasurer-secretary A. B. Bartlett, as well as Lawrence McGurty and others, to intensive grillings. In a fashion typical of hunts for "un-Americans" and "subversives," investigators repeatedly asked witnesses whether they were Communists or knew others who were, knowing full well they would refuse to answer. Eastland seemed particularly outraged with the quiet, slow-talking Lashley, whom he threatened with prison and continually called "boy." Eastland badgered Lashley with comments such as "you want to help your country, don't you?" but could never get him or any other "unfriendly witnesses" to name names. His grilling of Earl Fisher proved equally frustrating: Fisher appeared deceptively unaware of his own actions or their meanings. Blinded by his own racism, Eastland concluded that Fisher, a consummate organizer and union leader, was only a "dumb" black who had been deceived by whites; according to the red hunters, McCrea and other white union leaders caused the uppitiness of black workers in Local 19. One newspaper account explained the apparently incomprehensible behavior of African-American workers in a front-page headline, "Union Dupes Negroes to Serve the Reds." [57]

Civil liberties attorney Victor Rabinowitz came to Memphis to give the witnesses advice at the behest of the Distributive, Processing, and Office Workers' Union—now Local 19's parent international, created by a merger of FTA and two other former CIO unions in 1950. But the presence of the New York Jewish lawyer only enraged Eastland, who began grilling Rabinowitz as to whether he too was a Communist, told the lawyer to "shut his mouth" when he tried to answer, and then told marshals "to get that damn scum out of here." The marshalls ejected Rabinowitz unceremoniously and slapped him in the face outside of the hearing room, leaving him with a swollen lip. Appeals to constitutional rights in the midst of such a wholesale assault on the guarantees of witnesses proved futile. Memphis appliance store owner Simon Kaset tried to explain that he was not a member of the Communist party (he had been, but apparently quit) but in solidarity with other victims of the red scare he would take the Fifth Amendment. According to the newspapers, Kaset—like many other witnesses appearing under compulsion who refused to talk—became, in the parlance of the red scare, a "Fifth Amendment Communist." Eastland meanwhile claimed he had proved Local 19 to be "a Communist-controlled organization designed to overthrow the government and promote the interests of the Soviet Union by setting up a negro republic in the South." [58]

If the CIO's raids of Local 19 uniformly failed, the Eastland hearings had much more potent effects. Following the hearings, the CIO filed decertification petitions with the NLRB, claiming the refusal of Local 19 leaders in the hearings to say if they were party members proved that some may have lied in signing the Taft-Hartley anticommunist affidavits—a charge that could send union leaders to prison. As Leroy Boyd observed later, inflammatory publicity produced by the hearings had little effect on blacks. "They didn't pay any attention, because they knew how white men felt about another white man speaking up for the Negro. He was just branded as a Communist." But the hearings did undermine support among white workers, who at Buckeye signed petitions to the NLRB to remove Local 19.

Furthermore, the management at two major cottonseed oil mills (not Buck-eye) refused to bargain with the local, one of them saying, "We should not be forced by the government to do business with persons charged with being Communists."[59]

The hearings made it practically impossible for the local's leadership to carry on their functions. Awarded a Distinguished Flying Cross and a Purple Heart for heroism during World War II, McCrea in particular now became an "un-American," although not to everyone. After the Eastland hearings, white workers asked McCrea to attend a whites-only private gathering, the first time such a meeting had been held in the local. McCrea anticipated trouble, but after some discussion the workers gave him a standing ovation and made speeches praising him for his contributions to the union. This, among other events, convinced McCrea that reactionary union leaders, not white workers, were the real problem during the red scare era. Indeed, McCrea contended that Local 19's membership base in most factories remained solid, even after the Eastland hearings. Nonetheless, the international union's leaders transferred him from Memphis to New York, apparently as a precondition for the union to be reaffiliated to the CIO under a different leadership. The transfer removed one of the CIO's most able organizers from the local labor scene. "It hurt me when he left," Leroy Boyd recalled. "Because he really would speak up for you. He was just as good as an attorney. He was good. He had people behind him, too."[60]

During and after the red scare, Local 19 lost not only McCrea and other white leftist supporters but some of its strongest black leaders. Dyson, one of the CIO's black pioneers, died of a heart attack on 5 August at age fifty-nine. Even the FBI had acknowledged his "tremendous influence" over black Local 19 members. His influence went further than that. Some three thousand mourners overflowed the Mt. Moriah Baptist Church with even more people forced to stand in the streets, indicating the great respect for him in the African-American community. Henderson Davis, also one of the first black leaders of the union and a longtime Communist, died around the same time when a segregated Memphis hospital emergency room refused to take him during a severe illness; by the time union supporters were able to get him to a hospital that would serve blacks, it was too late. Those who survived, such as Earl Fisher, suffered years of harassment by the FBI. In one incident, FBI agents practically tore his house apart looking for Hosea Hudson, a black Communist from Birmingham. In another incident, white CIO members physically attacked Fisher's wife, Ruth, when she catered an event for the steelworkers' union. The FBI repeatedly visited Leroy Boyd,

George Isabell, and other Local 19 members and routinely harassed *Daily Worker* subscribers at their homes. The FBI even investigated Isabell's son years later when he enrolled at the University of Michigan.[61]

Such an intimidating atmosphere made it difficult at best for blacks to play an active public role; some black Local 19 activists to this day will not talk about their experiences. After the Eastland hearings, Local 19 had little choice but to remove itself from the leftist Distributive, Processing, and Office Workers' Union and join the UAW-backed Retail, Wholesale, and Department Store Union. With the local's connections to Communists or suspected Communists removed, in 1953 the Memphis Industrial Union Council allowed it back into the fold. However, Local 19's numbers had dwindled drastically, with only 362 members by the early sixties. Fisher, who became the local's president, pulled the union back together and gained a respected place in the labor movement. The union, however, never regained its former strength.[62]

Similarly, although Local 282 of the UFWA had "cleaned its house" of Communists, the purge left it eviscerated in Memphis for well over a decade. The red scare also drastically changed the union leadership's racial complexion. At one southern regional organizing meeting held by the furniture union in 1950, out of dozens of workers not a single black appeared, one result of what black UFWA organizers derided as the new "lily white" policy in the union. Leroy Clark's widow Alzada recalled with great indignation how in the fifties and sixties her husband could revive the union only by supporting whites for office, when blacks, including Clark himself, could potentially have done a better job. Confronting a weakened and somewhat divided union, furniture employers in Memphis, learning from the Memphis Furniture example, developed anti-union tactics to a fine art throughout the next twenty years. Not until 1978 did the union regain bargaining rights there.[63]

The red scare had other casualties as well. Red Davis recalled that the CIO expulsions not only eliminated white union members who had been the key to building integrated picket lines in many strikes but they also produced a chain reaction of expulsions of leftists from all kinds of organizations. "Our base was destroyed; everyone was afraid to associate with us; few people would even talk to us." Newspaper stories had a particularly potent effect, leading the NAACP and the Urban League, which grew increasingly timid during the red scare, to purge themselves of suspected leftists in order to avoid attack. Banned from employment on the river, his marriage in collapse and soon to come down with cancer, Davis was forced to leave Memphis; so was his brother Mort and other NMU leftists. As had the UFWA and Local 19, the union of riverboat workers went into decline as it lost its key organizers. The purge of leftists by Joe Curran, Davis told workers at the time, "unleashed the worst elements in our Union." Federal corporations since 1947 had refused to bargain with NMU leaders who would not sign the Taft-Hartley oath, and the anticommunists who replaced them began cutting deals with the barge lines up and down the river. At the same time, mechanization by the barge lines as they switched from steam to diesel power eliminated jobs and further weakened the union.[64]

The trials of Communist unionists continued for many more years. The FBI, which had monitored his mail and reading matter and shadowed his every move in Memphis, continued to harass Red Davis in St. Louis. HUAC even brought forward the best man at Davis's wedding to testify against him in hearings, and the blacklisted Davis could not even provide for his children and had to send them away. He survived the FBI, HUAC, and cancer, but blacklisting continued to haunt him. Davis's brother-in-law McGurty, also purged from the NMU, struggled on in Memphis for another six years, never able to hold a steady job. When Memphis police arrested Communist underground leader Junius Scales in Memphis under the Smith Act, party leaders in New York concluded that McGurty was at fault and severed his membership. Regardless of that fact, Eastland's committee, fishing for alleged Communists in the integration movement, called McGurty, summoned as a witness in the first hearing, to another one in 1957. McGurty too finally left town after fruitless efforts to find a liberal organization in which to work. NAACP leaders proved so fearful of associating with McGurty that they even returned donations he sent them through the mail.[65]

On at least the ideological level, the Korean War and the associated cold war, like World War II, had once again brought labor leaders, business leaders, and government together to fight a common enemy. Leftist GI veterans of World War II, such as Red Davis and Ed McCrea, were automatically catalogued as a security risk by the FBI and hounded for resisting the Korean War by American Legion leaders like Henry Loeb, who used anticommunism and patriotism as stepping-stones to public office. Together, the legion, the chamber of commerce, and the CIO cosponsored anticommunist petition drives and "Americanism" months.[66] Crowder and Copeland received the Memphis Veterans of Foreign Wars Award for outstanding citizenship as a result of their "campaign in the interests of true Americanism." The national VFW later gave a similar award to James O. Eastland.[67] The local CIO, which got its start in part as the result of Communist organizing, began quoting FBI director J. Edgar Hoover to the effect that Communists were more "dangerous and fanatical" than Nazis; brought anticommunists sponsored by the U.S. State Department to visit Memphis; and joined together in a luncheon with the AFL and traditionally anti-union businesses such as E. L. Bruce, Anderson-Clayton, Memphis Furniture, and Nickey Brothers in joint support of the Marshall Plan.[68] The American Newspaper Guild's Harry Martin went to work for the Marshall Plan, teaching European workers to emulate American productivity techniques, while Pete Swim, who took over editorship of the national *CIO News* from Len DeCaux during the purge, later worked in a U.S. embassy post in Southeast Asia.[69] Tennessee CIO director Paul Christopher and other unionists joined with business and government in the "Crusade for Freedom," a propaganda campaign headed nationally by General Lucius Clay (the general who later wanted to "bomb Vietnam back into the stone age") that raised money for the Voice of America and Radio Free Europe. Ironically, traditional foes of the union movement began advertising in the *CIO Labor Journal,* one company extolling the "miracle of America" and "how our American System Grew Great" to southern workers, others offering greetings to their "friends in labor." [70]

Both cold and hot wars seemed to turn anticommunism into a substitute for class consciousness for such CIO leaders, some of whom joined with *Press-Scimitar* editor Edward Meeman in promoting a quasi-religious vision of business-labor cooperation called "Moral Re-Armament." This movement convinced John Riffe, director of the national CIO's Operation Dixie after the death of Van Bittner in 1949, of a "comradeship beyond class" that brought him into close friendships with some of the wealthiest men in America. In Memphis, Moral Re-Armament regularly sponsored roundtable discussions with labor and business leaders on the premise that through personal understanding and spiritual regeneration class conflicts could be brought to an end. The members of the steelworkers' union in Memphis even raised one thousand dollars to fly CIO Industrial Union Council president Ray Allen, in his seventh consecutive term of office, to Switzerland for the Moral Re-Armament's world meeting, and the *CIO Labor Journal* played up the fact that in a new era of supposed prosperity for all unionists could "live and play like millionaires." [71]

With leftists and civil rights activists silenced, the CIO's period of growth and innovation ended and its leadership came to act and look more and more like that of the AFL. Accordingly, under the direction of Copeland, the Memphis CIO became the first in the nation to begin merging the two labor federations. Loring's retirement as head of the AFL in 1949, together with the purge of CIO leftists, removed the last obstacles to AFL-

CIO cooperation. By 1955, when AFL and CIO unionists met with the president of the Memphis Chamber of Commerce, Roane Waring (who had declared strikers should be shot during World War II), and other business leaders in a "Labor-Management Group," both labor federations held so closely to the ideology of employers that the *Press-Scimitar* ran the headline "Labor? Management? No One Could Tell Them Apart."[72]

One might think that the severe falling out between employers and the unions in the early fifties would have turned CIO unionists away from corporate-union consensus. Instead, a new kind of compact between labor and segments of business emerged, in implicit alliance with a growing black vote. Legislative and court challenges destroyed the last vestiges of the poll tax by 1953, while Crump's death in 1954 led to the collapse of support for his political machine. Hence, at the same time that the CIO's adoption of cold war imperatives produced a less controversial labor movement, a movement for civic progress and political reform emerged among some business owners. Edmund Orgill, Lucius Burch, and other business leaders initiated a "forward Memphis" campaign, which gained support from both CIO and AFL unions and accelerated registration of the black vote (which increased from 18 percent of the total in 1951 to 31 percent by the end of the decade). This coalition of forces placed Orgill in the mayor's office in 1955, producing an unusual veneer of civility toward blacks and unions by elected officials in Memphis. The fact that blacks could vote in Memphis created a situation quite in contrast to the fascistlike reaction against desegregation and unionism in many parts of the South during the fifties.[73]

*   *   *

If the votes of industrial unionists and African Americans succeeded for a time in realigning Memphis politics, however, the creation of a labor movement more acceptable to business came at a cost. In the name of "fighting communism," the CIO had undermined strong black-led locals almost wherever they existed in the South. In Winston-Salem, the CIO helped to destroy the most significant black-led civil rights union in the South, FTA's Local 22. In Birmingham, CIO leaders cooperated in breaking up integrated and black-led unions in the steel mills and iron ore industries. The CIO even dropped its support for Highlander, the testing ground for integration in the southern labor movement. The silencing of radicals and civil rights unionism undermined the impetus for organizing blacks and poor whites in low-wage industries, and by the time the CIO officially liquidated Operation Dixie in 1953, union organizing in Memphis and elsewhere had come to a standstill. Instead of becoming the dominant force in the South, CIO membership in the region stood at about one-third that of the AFL. In the *CIO Labor Journal* Memphis unionist George Dhuy, noting the retrenchment of anti-unionism, commented that the city seemed "just like it was when CIO first came to Memphis." But rather than battle it out with employers in traditional, low-wage southern industries, the CIO and the strongest of its locals, namely the auto and rubber unions, poured their energies and considerable amounts of money into building new union halls.[74]

Without new organizing, the union movement stagnated, a fact some opponents of the left admitted. Dan Powell, a personal friend of Copeland's, years later acknowledged that the purge of the Communist-led unions left a void in the labor movement. Communist-led unions almost uniformly "did a better job on race relations than the right-wing unions did," said Powell, and leftists generally proved to be better organizers. "I always had a soft spot in my heart for the so-called communists in the labor movement," Powell recalled, "because in most instances they were the ones who wanted to work. The right-wingers, the race-baiters, all they wanted to do was race-bait and they'd use race-baiting as a reason for not doing anything." Many Communist party members may have been blind to the tyranny of Stalinism, but they provided a consistent and vocal force for civil rights and interracialism in the South, especially in contrast to the conservatives who took control in the fifties. Blacks recognized this dynamic. "You're wasting your time in the South if you try to damage somebody by calling them a Communist" among black workers, Powell pointed out. "In fact, you're probably helping them," he thought, by interesting blacks in their program.[75]

However, not only the purges of the McCarthy era but also the 1954 Supreme Court decision outlawing segregation brought chaos to union ranks. Many white workers violently resisted every effort by unions to support desegregation. In Memphis, the misnamed Citizens for Progress launched an all-out defense of segregation, which split the city government and undermined Orgill's reform efforts. Within the factories, according to Powell, from 1955 onward the race issue made it practically "impossible to organize" whites and blacks together. Civil rights unionism lived on among black workers, but in contrast to the period after World War II, almost no white worker dared to speak up for black rights. Whereas workers at Buckeye succeeded in opening up all employment and job classifications to blacks after the war with no violence, such simple acts of change in the fifties could cost you your life. When International Harvester made George

Holloway a machine operator in 1953, whites sabotaged his punch press, which would have killed or maimed him had he turned it on. Racists repeatedly threatened his life off the job, to the point that Clarence Coe's brother Lint had to stand guard over Holloway's home with a shotgun. Vigilantes also shot into the home of Carl Moore, a white UAW representative, as White Citizens' Council members at Harvester attempted to stop integration of the factory and union hall—finally forcing Walter Reuther to lock up the union hall and place the local in receivership for two years. Likewise, when blacks at Firestone sued both the company and the union to force desegregation, whites attempted to kill or maim Clarence Coe on the factory floor several times and made his life and that of many other black workers a living hell for the next decade.[76]

In this context, resegregation occurred in some unions, while others stalled on the issue of equal rights. An apparent step toward progress had occurred in the Memphis CIO in 1950, when photographs of its signs designating segregated rest rooms received national publicity, causing the national CIO to direct that such signs come down all over the South. But by 1954, CIO and AFL unions in Memphis had dropped all but one of their black organizers. With the acceleration of racism after the *Brown v. Board of Education* decision, interracial union efforts floundered. Even the United Packinghouse Workers' Union, which survived the CIO purge with its radical leadership intact and mounted exceptional antidiscrimination programs in Chicago and elsewhere, failed to make much progress in meatpacking and oil plants in places such as Memphis or Birmingham. These plants remained completely segregated, and efforts to change this condition practically tore the union's southern district apart.[77] Meanwhile, many white building trades unions in the AFL continued to ostracize blacks, creating conditions for black artisans perhaps worse than those in the thirties. A black carpenters' union chartered in Memphis in 1936, for example, once had three hundred members, but by 1959 had only fifty left. White carpenters completely refused to work with blacks, who could not get jobs even on federal projects because employers feared the whites would strike. As late as 1965, blacks remained almost completely absent from craft union ranks or apprenticeship programs, and statistics improved only in small increments in the seventies.[78]

The merger of AFL and CIO unions beginning in the midfifties further muted the distinctive interracial presence that industrial unions once provided, placing whites in an increasingly dominant position within the labor movement. At the national level, AFL craft unions took ten of the seventeen Executive Council positions in the new labor federation, and

African Americans had increasing difficulty in making their demands heard within this context. In the Tennessee AFL-CIO and in Memphis, white male dominance of top leadership positions became even more noticeable and the black presence even more diluted than it had been in the CIO. The AFL-CIO's state newspaper, largely edited from Memphis, rarely discussed race, only occasionally showed blacks in pictures, and avoided the major issue confronting the South, desegregation. Women, if they appeared in the paper at all, did so as "bathing beauties." [79] The merger did not seem to help membership enrollment either. In Memphis, the merger of the AFL and CIO created an organization of some forty-two thousand unionists in Shelby County—a far cry from the forty to fifty thousand claimed by the AFL and the thirty thousand claimed by the CIO in 1948—and promised AFL-CIO efforts to renew an "Operation Dixie" type of southern organizing drive did not materialize. By 1961, a smaller percentage of southern workers belonged to unions than in 1950 or 1945, and Memphis AFL-CIO president Prentis Lewis told the newspapers that union growth had stopped altogether.[80]

Despite its failings, the national AFL-CIO remained one of the few institutions that donated significant funds and political support to the civil rights struggle, as did the UAW, the packinghouse union, and a few others. Black disenchantment grew nonetheless, as many craft and industrial unions failed to open up jobs and union hierarchies to people of color and women, and as departmental seniority systems and other discriminatory practices legitimized in union contracts thwarted black advancement.[81] If the national AFL-CIO's commitments on civil rights seemed ambiguous, in Memphis and other southern cities the new federation played a muted role at best in the new struggles to end Jim Crow. As southern unionism declined and the CIO's distinctive interracial presence dissipated, civil rights movements bursting forth in African-American communities, in Memphis as elsewhere, drew their greatest strength from the black churches and a new generation of militant black youth, not the unions. When Martin Luther King, Jr., came to Memphis in 1968, the struggle to unite labor and civil rights efforts still had not prevailed, due in no small part to the postwar failures of southern labor organizing.[82]

Legacies

Black union and civil rights veteran Clarence Coe pointed out that the industrial labor movement left a contradictory legacy in Memphis. "I tell you when both of us get in a ditch together and stay long enough, we'll find the means to get out together, and the CIO was that. But once they got it set up and got that thing working, the white leadership just wasn't going to support you in job equality or equal pay. We had the dirtiest, the cheapest jobs—there was a certain job the white man didn't do, he just didn't do it." Firestone worker Josh Tools similarly recalled that although his union constitution guaranteed equal rights for all, after the 1954 Supreme Court decision in *Brown v. Board of Education,* blacks had to sue both the union and the company to get plant desegregation. Even then, it took until the seventies to finally achieve full desegregation. "Black workers always supported the union, but the union never made a concerted effort to eliminate discrimination," said Tools. He believed that if the union leaders had taken a stand earlier, factory desegregation would have happened far sooner than it did. Most southern whites, said George Holloway, "wanted unions to a certain degree, but they . . . didn't want justice in jobs. Whites still wanted the blacks to be janitors, and they didn't want blacks to advance." Even when Holloway became the first African-American UAW regional representative in the South, white UAW staff members avoided eating lunch with him. For African Americans, racism always remained a problem in the union movement.[1]

Black workers who had been through the industrial union wars necessarily looked back on their lives with a mixture of pride in what they had achieved and bitterness over the humiliations and economic disparities they experienced because of racism. Coe, like many black factory workers, had moved to Memphis from the countryside to get away from the racism and violence of the plantation districts. He discovered that "you come here, and you run into the same damned things." To get your rights in Memphis factories, "you had to fight for every inch. Nobody gave you anything. Nothing." In the depths of the depression "there was just so much pressure to bear on you everywhere you went as a black person," he recalled. "I have seen the time when a young white boy came in and maybe I had been working at the plant longer than he had been living, but if he was white I had to tell him 'yes sir' or 'no sir.' That was degrading as hell. I had to live with it. . . . And you spent all of your good life fooling with petty stuff like this." Even more problematic, during most of the Firestone local's history, blacks remained restricted to laboring jobs; said Coe, "Some of the local whites could move up into higher positions. We were set; couldn't move nowhere." This pattern occurred across the South, according to the historian Gavin Wright: "The typical white unskilled worker could expect to move up over time, the typical black could expect to go nowhere."[2]

Unless it ended job discrimination, unionization could in some ways accentuate the economic effects of racism. At the Firestone plant, for example, the wage gap between blacks in the low-paying jobs and whites in the better-paying jobs increased dramatically after unionization. Coe recalled that "when we first started getting raises, they would give us percentage raises. So if you're making $.87 an hour, and I'm making $.45, hell, you get a percentage rate increase, you see how you're starting to move away from me?" For this very reason, Local 19 after the war negotiated across-the-board wage increases that gave workers in every wage classification the same amount of hourly increase and sought plant-wide seniority rights. But most CIO unions continued percentage increases and did little to overturn departmental seniority, which served to enforce job segregation. As a result, the highest paid of the white workers "just moved plumb out of sight of where we were," Coe remembered. "When I was making $12.00 an hour at the plant, they were making $20.00 on account of those percentage increases over ten or twenty years." Due to the cumulative effects of wage and job discrimination, white workers gained opportunities available to few blacks. Some white workers moved to the suburbs during the "white flight" from the central city in the seventies, put their children in private schools, and moved out of the working class altogether. Richard Routon even set up his own business, importing manufactured parts from abroad. Many black workers also sent their children to college, but few of these workers themselves moved out of factory employment.[3]

The unremitting struggles of Coe and other blacks to gain equality at

Firestone did in the end succeed, but these efforts could not wipe out the economic effects of decades of discrimination. By keeping most blacks in lower-paying jobs, the segregation system placed them at a continued disadvantage to whites throughout the period of southern industrialization. And, the changes finally made came at great personal cost. Said Coe, "Before we left the plant, blacks and whites were virtually equal; if you qualified for something, you could just about get it. But my God, man, when you'd given up thirty years of your life fighting for something that should have been yours to begin with, it's a little bit disheartening." [4]

The outcome of the union struggle proved disheartening in other ways, as devastating structural economic changes undermined the position of the black working class. In the 1940s, the number of black men and women employed as factory operatives nearly doubled in Memphis; during the 1950s, very few additional positions appeared. At the same time, mechanization chased millions off the land, just as the New Deal crop reduction program had in the thirties. The percentage of the cotton crop harvested by machines jumped from 5 percent in 1950 to 50 percent in 1960 and to 90 percent by the seventies. Those who remained in the rural Mississippi Delta suffered unremitting poverty. Those who came into the cities had little education and few saleable skills, at a time when urban industry, prodded by federal minimum wage laws, had also begun to mechanize in order to save on labor costs. In the wood products industries, in cotton processing, in chemicals, in the railroads and other industries, mechanization eliminated tens of thousands of positions normally filled by African Americans. In contrast to the forties, a time of high demand for unskilled and semiskilled factory labor, those without education or skills in the fifties and sixties found increasingly less opportunity for factory employment. For black women, this meant increasing numbers of them would return to domestic work. Meanwhile, patterns of segregation still denied new immigrants access to education, skills, jobs, and hope. With most avenues of advancement closed to them, black migrants rarely moved up economically. At the end of the forties, the median income of blacks in the Tennessee cities (Memphis being the largest one) was only a little more than 46 percent of that for whites, and poverty rather than employment opportunity continued to greet many of the rural migrants to the city. The strike of sanitation workers in 1968 represented a rising of this most dispossessed group of southern workers. But most unskilled laborers never encountered a union; their entrance to the work force coincided not only with the decline of factory employment but the decline of unionized labor in Memphis as well. [5]

These economic shifts wreaked particular havoc on black male workers.

Some 86 percent of black men in Memphis still made their living doing unskilled labor and service work as late as 1969. During the fifties and early sixties, census figures showed that white males and females continued to gain increasing access to professional, managerial, clerical, and skilled employment, while the percentage of black men in such positions remained practically unchanged. Even black women, who typically received the worst jobs at the worst wages, fared better than black men in making their way into some areas of white-collar employment. The major improvement in black male job access occurred at large factories like Firestone and International Harvester, where a number of blacks moved into better-paying production jobs, largely due to the efforts of people like Clarence Coe and George Holloway. But, as in other parts of the country, black men soon lost even this slim hold on the upward mobility ladder. In the fifties and sixties Memphis employment shifted away from heavy industry; in the seventies and eighties, recessions and plant shutdowns gutted the city's unionized industrial jobs—the very jobs that African-American men most depended on for decent-paying employment. Nickey Brothers lumber, which moved much of its operations to the Philippines, was but one of a number of companies that shifted work to poor countries abroad in order to take advantage of even cheaper labor than that available in Memphis. The decline of semiskilled and unskilled occupations undermined thousands of African-American families, as rampant unemployment, unequal education, continuing employment discrimination, and occupational segregation reinforced a long cycle of poverty that kept most African Americans on the bottom tier of the social class system in Memphis.[6]

The impoverishment of the Memphis black community and the resultant disintegration of family units and other social ills, Clarence Coe was quick to point out, did not result simply from impersonal forces such as mechanization, but from the discrimination that employers and most white citizens enforced over the years. City leaders had always relied on influxes of black rural migrants to keep labor cheap. The lack of funds for black education, the existence of segregated housing, media racism, and the suppression of black civil and political rights all were part of a more or less consciously imposed system that furthered the exploitation of black labor and kept wages low in Memphis and the surrounding area. By the sixties, 57 percent of Memphis black families lived below the poverty line.[7] In Coe's view, this remarkable statistic resulted from the systematic exploitation of black labor, which over time had transferred wealth from the black community to the white community and left African Americans mired in poverty. "For not having been fair with me over a period of years and with all the new millionaires being made every year," Coe remarked, "those people have got some of my money in their pockets. Working a guy for three or four dollars an hour, he's got some of the black community's money in his pocket." This transfer of wealth went on not just in the South but all over the United States. "It's no small group of people got that money," Coe concluded.[8]

Given the historic hardships afflicting African Americans, the degree of social vision and effectiveness of unions proved particularly critical to the outcome of African-American struggles for economic justice. Unions in the thirties and forties provided a new frontier for the exercise of rights in the South, as New Deal labor laws and wartime agencies legitimized the right of each individual to vote in representation elections and to be free from various forms of discrimination. After the war, the increasing role (in some shops) of black workers as stewards and committee members, handling grievances of both black and white, reinforced the idea of participation and democracy at the most basic level. Furthermore, blacks in Local 19, the Firestone local, and in other CIO unions also developed as church, lodge, and neighborhood activists in a way that whites often did not. The CIO thus helped blacks to exercise aspirations and dreams the segregation system sought to suppress. The vision of most white workers and union leaders, however, proved unequal to the task of carrying forward the "rights consciousness" that developed among black workers and black southerners generally during the forties. Conservatism in the CIO first of all translated into opposition to black-led, leftist, and rank-and-file movements from below and to civil rights demands, some of the very forces moving industrial unions forward. Mobilization of the kinds of working-class radicalism that existed in the South required a greater degree of confidence in the workers and a broader vision of change than most white CIO leaders possessed. Although the Crump machine charged the CIO with being too radical, in reality it was not radical enough. By the time it merged with the AFL, its ability and willingness to organize the black working class had markedly declined.[9]

The CIO in Memphis and in many other places also failed in most cases to take full advantage of the postwar opportunity to organize women. The activism of "disorderly women" in the sweatshops of Memphis had mobilized unionists at key moments in Memphis labor history, from the Plough women and the garment makers who tore the clothing off scabs in the thirties to the militant women at Memphis Furniture, American Snuff, and General Electric. The infusion of white women into the factory labor force during the war, and increasing numbers of black women after the war, provided an important new constituency that might have bolstered union growth. But while Mary Lou Koger, Mary Lawrence Elkuss, and a few others had pioneered as organizers and educators in the CIO's early days, otherwise women rarely appeared in union leadership. Although CIO unions did organize female telephone and electrical workers after the war, the CIO's lack of female leadership ultimately translated into a failure to organize female service workers, city employees, white-collar workers, and production workers. Unions needed the participation and leadership of women, and particularly black women, who had always participated in the labor market at a far higher rate than white women and whose numbers in hospitals and other growing service sectors continued to increase. Yet most CIO unions in Memphis seemed almost oblivious to their presence.[10]

Did greater possibilities for change during the CIO era exist? Given the almost overwhelming external factors—including structural economic changes and a cold war that allowed segregationists to wrap their opposition to unionism and integration in the flag as part of a worldwide struggle against "communism"—CIO hopes for transforming the postwar South appear in retrospect almost as a mirage. Nonetheless, many union veterans continued to believe that the immediate post–World War II period represented the best opportunity for strong working-class, interracial, and "progressive" alliances in the South. During this era a strong union base and an intermittently expanding economy made union growth possible. But the key factor in union success, some believed, was not external but depended instead upon the extent to which unions fully mobilized and unified their members. The alternative to the top-down, socially conservative unionism that came to dominate the CIO, Ed McCrea believed, could be seen in the organization of Local 19. In his view, "It was the way the local was run and the way it was organized that made it stand up; it depended basically on rank-and-file support and rank-and-file leadership," one that made and implemented decisions collectively, based on a system of shop stewards, mass meetings, and continual education. Like others on the left of the CIO, he condemned the top-down leadership and centralization models of the Operation Dixie campaign and the CIO generally after the war. During his twenty years of organizing, McCrea repeatedly saw that black and white workers "had much in common, much to unite around," but felt that most union leaders often had no confidence in them. The difference between top-down and bottom-up unionism, in his estimation, defined the left-right split in the CIO.[11]

The CIO, like the society generally, remained divided between those who thought in terms of immediate interests and those who sought more long-term and fundamental change. And, as white workers played a larger numerical role in Memphis industry during and after the war than they had previously, the need for CIO leaders to rely on black support decreased. In any case, no one will ever know for certain whether the CIO could have been the vehicle to liberate southern workers, and particularly southern blacks, that leftists and liberals alike had hoped for. Some historians suggest that the industrial unions, as in South Africa, proved to be just one more mechanism for white workers to control blacks within the labor market and to maintain the higher-paying and skilled jobs as a white preserve. They point in particular to the "racialized class consciousness" that caused most whites to seize every opportunity to claim a privileged position in the workplace throughout the history of the labor movement, instead of supporting equality as a basic principle.[12] But despite the disadvantages to blacks in the southern CIO, blacks typically remained the strongest union supporters. In Memphis, African Americans provided the main base for industrial union organizing before, during, and after the war. Why? What did black workers gain from the industrial union experience?

Despite its failures, the CIO offered African Americans at least partial solutions to their oppressed status. The AFL proved it could not build an effective labor movement based on craft exclusionism and segregation; when Thomas Watkins and other blacks attempted to utilize the craft structures, the AFL first isolated and then suppressed them. First and foremost, black workers sought allies. They turned to the CIO because it seemed willing to organize them; it promised equal treatment; and it linked them to white workers, offering them greater potential power in organizing drives and strikes. The CIO policy of biracial organization offered a possible way out of the historical oppression of southern workers and blacks in particular, which hinged on dividing them into competing groups based on skin color, and provided a viable alternative to the AFL.[13] For similar reasons, a number of blacks also turned to the Communist party within the CIO as the most consistent and dedicated group seeking interracial working-class organization and demanding not only union rights but civil rights.

On the broad economic level, biracial industrial unions transformed the seemingly hopeless conditions of the thirties into something far better. The economic improvement in people's lives that began in the forties resulted not just from war and capitalist expansion but from the organized power of labor. As Judge Robert Tillman, among the earliest of CIO supporters in Memphis, recalled in his later years, "Employers in Memphis always opposed improving the conditions of the working people; if they had their way, we'd still be living in slavery."[14] Although blacks usually remained stuck on the bottom tiers of industry, unionization dramatically improved the lives of even those in the lowest-paying jobs. At a place like Firestone, wages for the unskilled went from twenty-eight cents an hour in 1937 to some twelve dollars an hour in the seventies. Vacations, a degree of job security, grievance systems, overtime pay, health insurance, and other benefits raised unionized black and white factory workers from the dregs of society in the thirties to proud holders of the best blue-collar jobs in town in the sixties and early seventies. Before the unions, Hillie Pride remembered, "you were just like mules and hogs; you weren't hardly counted. You had no choice." But by the time the Firestone plant closed, unskilled workers made over one hundred dollars a day. Sometimes through the union and sometimes on their own, blacks eliminated the discriminatory "A, B, C" rates, obtained jobs as supervisors and machinists, and got rid of segregated water fountains, cafeterias, locker rooms, time clocks, and parking lots. Most important, the union finally eliminated seniority by department and put it on a plant-wide basis, allowing blacks to bid for any available job in the plant. Whites resisted, but without the union, said Pride, nothing would have changed: "When it all boiled down . . . the union was a real good thing, 'cause it broke up that mess." [15]

Of course, the industrial unions produced a profound economic change, not only for blacks but even more so for whites. White workers at Firestone and other places discovered rather quickly just how little change they could make through the segregated craft unions and created new biracial industrial structures through the CIO that made it possible for them to bargain effectively. The CIO could not have happened at all if whites had not at some level recognized the need for biracial organization. "We couldn't have organized the South if we hadn't reached that stage," Red Davis pointed out. Simply bringing blacks and whites into the unions together did not eliminate the patterns of segregation that remained a part of daily life in the South, and in the end most white workers continued to defend the racial system. But on an individual level at least, biracial organization opened up new possibilities. Some whites, including the radicals but also people like Richard Routon and many others as well, made rather dramatic changes in their racial attitudes and beliefs. More often, changes came gradually. "It was . . . like calling each other brother or sister, black and white. This was a big step; change came step by step," said Davis. At the very least, most whites in CIO unions came to understand that industrial labor could not succeed with one hand tied behind its back: it needed both its black and its white hand to succeed. Blacks typically understood this from the beginning. It is ironic that whites, often the last to support the CIO, benefited the most from the economic improvements wrought by biracial industrial organization. They did so in some ways at the expense of African Americans, who always provided its bedrock of support.[16]

Biracial industrial organization not only improved the economic position of workers but proved in some ways to be as much a threat to the old order as Boss Crump said it was. At least the power of the union vote and the black vote, allied with some moderating elements of the business class, finally loosened and then broke the power of the Crump machine. In a time of reaction, CIO unions helped to knock down many of the barriers to the exercise of civil liberties erected by segregation, making it possible for the NAACP and other organizations once banned in Memphis to thrive. In the process, they helped elect Kefauver to Congress and relatively progressive people to city hall. Due to CIO voter mobilization and the increase of the voting population in a more prosperous era, the exclusion of working people from political power largely ended. Hence, in the late forties workers not only improved their economic conditions but set the stage for the erosion of the old political order that had kept the South locked into the backward social system of segregation.

Such social and political outcomes of unionization remained as important to African-American workers as their ability to improve wages and working conditions. For them, the CIO was always "a question of freedom," as Ed McCrea put it; "nothing didn't go right, we didn't see freedom until we got that union," black Firestone worker Irene Branch likewise declared. That freedom came in many ways. One one level, freedom came through the activation of the black working class, which allowed people to carry forward a democratic tradition of group-centered leadership and a rich culture rooted in prophetic religion and song. The singing and shouting and collective power so notable in the black freedom movements of the fifties and sixties also animated mass meetings of black sharecroppers in the countryside and black industrial workers in the cities during the thirties and forties. Organizing offered people an opportunity to exercise an oppositional culture and to express the humanity denied to them by segregation. On another level, freedom came in the specific exercise of union power. As they voted in NLRB elections, became union stewards, committee members, organizers, or even union presidents, black unionists gained standing as citizens with legal rights in a society that otherwise denied them such rights. Union veterans like Coe and Holloway even in retirement could quote chapter and verse of union contracts and constitutions. They carried these documents in their pockets and in their heads, ready to use them against supervisors and employers, and sometimes against white unionists, whenever the rights of workers came under attack. These union leaders became exponents and living examples of black freedom and union justice.[17]

Industrial unionism in many ways failed to live up to black expectations in the fight against segregation, but it did help to create a new cadre of black working-class leaders and rank-and-file activists who proved important to its ultimate undoing. Leroy Boyd, Earl Fisher, and other Local 19 activists took the first steps toward direct civil rights protest in the Willie McGee case, when most middle-class elements in the Memphis black community feared to do so. Throughout the fifties and sixties, Matthew Davis, Josh Tools, and other black union veterans provided role models to black youth and helped to build the churches, the NAACP, and voter and other organizations that made civil rights struggles possible. In providing college education for their children, they also produced the foot soldiers for the social movements of the sixties. Evelyn Bates at Firestone as a single parent sent one of her children through the University of Chicago; George Isabell at Buckeye sent his daughter to medical school to ultimately become a cardiologist and assistant dean at UCLA Hospital. He remembered with pride the day he received a call from his daughter at the Memphis police station: she had just been arrested for "integrating" the Memphis Public Library.[18]

Although black ministers, students, and professionals exerted the major leadership in the civil rights movements of the sixties, an earlier generation of unionized blacks made their efforts possible, and not only in Memphis. Union organizational training in the Brotherhood of Sleeping Car Porters allowed E. D. Nixon to mastermind the Montgomery bus boycott and for Asbury Howard from the International Union of Mine, Mill, and Smelter Workers to gain office in the Alabama legislature. In Memphis, union know-how and a lifetime of dedicated service to working people placed Leroy Clark of the Memphis UFWA in the presidency of the Memphis NAACP during the critical period of boycotts, school walkouts, and strikes after the death of Martin Luther King, Jr.[19] However, these black union veterans fought the growing civil rights struggles of the fifties and sixties with tragically few allies from amongst the white working class. The cold war had weakened biracial unionism and in many ways uncoupled it from the civil rights struggle, as unions increasingly became economic pressure groups rather than movements for social transformation. It finally required an independent African-American agenda and community base, and movements quite separate from the unions, to really sunder the police state conditions and the assumptions about black inferiority that afflicted the South for most of its history. Until African Americans as a group gained full exercise of civil rights and civil liberties, there could be no real freedom of speech, thought, and association for white unionists or anyone else in the South. By destroying much of the superstructure of segregation and the debilitating mind-set of white paternalism, black-led movements for social change in the sixties brought forward a new spirit and transforming vision that the labor movement seemed to have lost.

When King came to Memphis in 1968 supporting black sanitation strikers and promoting his national "poor people's campaign," he in a sense picked up where earlier movements for economic justice had left off. He recognized that from the perspective of both civil rights and labor rights advocates, the future belonged to those who could organize broad coalitions around common interests that united people across boundaries of race, gender, or political affiliation. He also recognized that the plight of the sanitation workers—making $1.10 an hour for backbreaking work, with no pensions, vacations, guaranteed hours of work, or adequate health benefits—represented the plight of the working poor of America. Poor people, women, and people of color made up much of the unorganized working class, and neither the civil rights nor the labor movements could make any progress without organizing them. The civil rights movement had opened up new thinking, new politics, new moral standards, and even new possibilities for economic growth in the South; in the person of King, it also opened up the possibility of a reenergized labor–civil rights coalition. In the years after 1968, just such a coalition revitalized unions in hospital, furniture, and a number of other industries in a number of places in the South.[20]

King's death, however, highlighted the tragedy haunting movements for civil rights and economic justice. Society seemed to learn little, even from the most shocking events. After the assassination of King, Clarence Coe and other blacks left work at the Firestone plant expecting the worst. "I told some of the other guys out there that we'd probably never see each other again. That's what I was expecting, you know. . . . They had the National Guard and everything on the streets by that time." Coe had what he described as an "arsenal" in his home and planned to hole up with his weapons in a nearby cemetery. "I just expected to go to war. I mean, that's what I came home for, that's what I was planning on. And I thought that would just happen all over the world." But nothing happened. Instead of war, celebrities poured in from around the country to march in Memphis; the city finally came to the bargaining table; the sanitation workers achieved some of their demands. But many whites, and especially the ruling Memphis families and the business establishment, in Coe's words, "never had thought seriously about what happened." King's death in Memphis not only signified the loss of a prophet but the failure of America's leaders to come to grips with the interrelated problems of economic and racial oppression, war, and greed that he addressed in the last years of his life. "There's going to be a lot more suffering here," Coe predicted in 1988, "because you have white folks who still believe they can make it without us."[21]

In the twenty-five years following King's death, union busting, plant closings, racial polarization, and the federal government's frequent failures to enforce civil rights and labor laws chilled movements for labor unity and social progress. Plagues of unemployment, crime, drugs, and family deterioration swept through poor communities that relied on wage labor to survive. Instead of new economic and social advances for working people, deindustrialization and a drastic shift toward the right politically knocked many of the props from under the hard-won victories of previous generations. These developments devastated many in the post–civil rights generation and plunged much of the African-American community into new depths of economic crisis. Economic decline, coupled with racial divisiveness, earned Memphis the title of the "dark spot in the sunbelt" during the seventies and after. The closing of the Firestone plant and the loss of other major factories in the early eighties hit the black working-class communities of Memphis particularly hard. "Poverty and people's situations are worse now than they were in the depression," Hillie Pride exclaimed. "The Republicans cut all the jobs out and ran all of the best plants away. . . . The jobs people do have, they can't hardly live on them. . . . There's nothing here anymore. . . . At eighty years, I've had experience from a little boy up, and I . . . know what I'm talking about." Even the historic refuge for the down-and-out, Beale Street, provided little solace to the poor, as developers turned it into something resembling a theme park.[22]

However, despite the betrayals of the postindustrial era, for many of the union veterans of the thirties and forties, whites and blacks alike, the positive legacy of the movement for industrial unionism remained clear.[23] Despite their many hardships in the union struggle, they continued to believe that giving service to other people, not gaining wealth and fame, remained the highest calling in life. Black workers particularly stressed how much they had gained and the importance of the union legacy to future generations. "I learned about kindness and fairness in the labor movement," said George Holloway. "I would give my life if every kid when he was seventeen would be guaranteed a job when he reached nineteen." But Holloway also reflected on the hard reality that "people have to fight their own battles," and someone else would have to fight for guaranteed jobs for young people. "The boss have the young people in a trick," Leroy Boyd surmised. "They think they know, but they don't know. Somehow, the experience from the past needs to get passed on to them." Clarence Coe, looking at the dismal state of affairs, still remained hopeful. "I think when people are badly enough oppressed, they'll find a way and do it," he said. "And organizing labor is the only way. It's the only way you can do it. . . . You're going to have to go back to basics, get some of these young whites and young blacks together and start organizing."[24]

Given the legacy of slavery and the persistence of segregation, "race" remained the defining question over which industrial unionism succeeded or perished throughout much of the South. The struggle for labor rights, and in many respects for black freedom as well, could only be fully won by bringing black and white together into common organizations based on equal rights. In the era of industrial decline and social fragmentation at the end of the twentieth century, that lesson remained clearer than ever to many of the South's union veterans. Many have ignored or never knew of the bitter lessons learned at great personal cost by the generations that struggled for change through the labor movement. If we take the time to learn from the past and from those who lived it, the steps they took toward a more just social order can help us to understand what was, what might have been, and what could be. It remains to other generations to take the next steps.

Abbreviations

CA	Memphis *Commercial Appeal*
FBI/FOIA	FBI Investigative Files, Washington, D.C., obtained under the Freedom of Information Act, in author's possession
FEPC	Fair Employment Practices Committee Records, RG 228, National Archives and Records Administration, Washington, D.C., and Suitland, Md.
IWC/DC	Inland Waterways Corporation, Maritime Records of the Department of Commerce, RG 91, National Archives and Records Administration, Washington, D.C., and Suitland, Md.
MID	Military Intelligence Division, War Department General Staff Records, RG 165, National Archives and Records Administration, Washington, D.C., and Suitland, Md.
MLR	*Memphis Labor Review* (affiliated with the Memphis AFL)
MPL	Memphis Public Library
MVC/MSU	Mississippi Valley Collection, Brister Library, Memphis State University
NAACP/LC	National Association for the Advancement of Colored People Papers, Library of Congress, Washington, D.C.
NARA	National Archives and Records Administration, Washington, D.C., and Suitland, Md.
NRA	National Recovery Administration Records, National Archives and Records Administration, Washington, D.C., and Suitland, Md.
NUL/LC	National Urban League Papers, Library of Congress, Washington, D.C.
OD	Operation Dixie Papers, Perkins Library, Special Collections Department, Duke University, Durham, N.C.
P-S	Memphis *Press Scimitar*
SLA/GSU	Southern Labor Archives, Georgia State University, Atlanta
TOC	Tennessee Organizing Committee Files, Operation Dixie Papers, Perkins Library, Special Collections Department, Duke University, Durham, N.C.
UFWA	United Furniture Workers of America Papers, Southern Labor Archives, Georgia State University, Atlanta
UPWA/WHS	United Packinghouse, Food, and Allied Workers' Association Papers, Wisconsin Historical Society, Madison, Wisc.

USDL   U.S. Department of Labor Records, National Archives and Records Administration, Washington, D.C., and Suitland, Md.

USES   United States Employment Service Records, RG 183, National Archives and Records Administration, Washington, D.C., and Suitland, Md.

WDL   Workers' Defense League Files, Walter P. Reuther Library for Labor and Urban Affairs, Wayne State University, Detroit, Mich.

WHS   Wisconsin Historical Society, Madison, Wisc.

WLB   War Labor Board Records, RG 202, National Archives and Records Administration, Washington, D.C., and Suitland, Md.

WPA   Works Progress Administration Records, National Archives and Records Administration, Washington, D.C., and Suitland, Md.

Notes

INTRODUCTION: LABOR AND CIVIL RIGHTS

1. The details related in the Introduction are contained in an affidavit sworn out by Watkins to the FBI on 26 May 1939 and in a letter from Watkins to U.S. Attorney General Frank Murphy, received 31 Aug. 1939, both in File 144-72-0, Criminal Division, Justice Department, RG 60, NARA. FBI agents confirmed the main outlines of Watkins's story after speaking with principals in the case. N. B. Wright report and J. W. Savage report, 27 May 1939, File 16-208-1, Criminal Division, Justice Department, RG 60, NARA.

2. Wright report, 27 May 1939; Watkins to Murphy.

3. A Memphis police blotter dated 23 Aug. 1939, File 144-72-0, Criminal Division, Justice Department, RG 60, NARA, says the army discharged Watkins from Fort Leavenworth, after sentencing him to one year and six months in prison. Several details of this incident were related to me by personal friends of Thomas Watkins, Bertha and Napolean Jilks, interviewed in Portland, Oregon, 13 and 26 Aug. 1989, respectively. Watkins gave his own brief account to the FBI special agent in Portland, SAC to the Director, 25 Aug. 1950, and SAC to the Director, 23 June 1973, FBI/FOIA 250,181-001.

4. Police blotter, 23 Aug. 1939, on arrests; Napolean Jilks interview.

5. W. E. Davis, personal interview, 26 Jan. 1983, St. Louis, Mo.

6. Lucy Randolph Mason to Eleanor Roosevelt, 9 Jan. 1941, related the Cotton case. Mason Papers, OD.

7. Watkins affidavit; Watkins to Murphy.

8. Ibid.; Mason to Roosevelt, 9 Jan. 1941; CA, 14 June 1933.

9. Unless specified otherwise, the rest of this account is taken from the Watkins affidavit.

10. The police blotter showed Watkins was arrested by St. Louis authorities on May 30.

11. E. L. Clark to Attorney General Murphy, received 5 June 1939, File 144-72-0, Criminal Division, Justice Department, RG 60, NARA. Wright report, 27 May and 14 June 1939, on witnesses and medical reports.

12. Newspapers and most whites during most of the time covered by this study refused to capitalize Negro. Throughout this study, the term African American is used to denote nationality and community and is capitalized; black and white are used to denote groups identified by color, but black is also used interchangeably with the term African American.

13. R. G. Draper to the U.S. Attorney General, 3 Aug. 1939, File 144-72-0, Criminal Division, Justice Department, RG 60, NARA. Mason to Roosevelt, 9 Jan. 1941. Reporter quoted in Ralph J. Bunche, *The Political Status of the Negro in the Age of FDR*, Dewey Grantham, ed. (Chicago: University of Chicago Press, 1973), 502. Condemnation of Watkins appeared in the AFL's *MLR*, 14 Apr. 1939.

14. SAC to the Director, 28 Aug. 1973, FBI/FOIA 250,181-001.

15. Bertha Jilks, phone interview, 13 Aug. 1989.

16. Personal interviews with W. E. Davis, 26–28 Jan. 1983; Clarence Coe, 28 and 29 May, 1989, Memphis; Ed McCrea, 6 Mar. and 17 Oct. 1983, Nashville; and George Holloway, 23 Mar. 1990, Baltimore.

17. Most survey treatments of the labor movement place little emphasis on the significance of the CIO's racial policies or on the role of black workers within the CIO. See for example Joseph G. Rayback, *A History of American Labor* (1959; reprint, New York: Free Press, 1966), chap. 25, and Foster Rhea Dulles and Melvin Dubofsky, *Labor in America: A History*, rev. ed. (Arlington Heights, Ill.: Harlan Davidson, 1966), chap. 16. Studies by Philip S. Foner, including *Organized Labor and the Black Worker, 1619–1973* (New York: International Publishers, 1976), F. Ray Marshall, *The Negro and Organized Labor* (New York: John Wiley and Sons, 1965), and by William H. Harris, *The Harder We Run: Black Workers since the Civil War* (New York: Oxford University Press, 1982), are major exceptions. The most thorough treatment of the CIO in the South remains F. Ray Marshall's *Labor in the South* (Cambridge: Harvard University Press, 1967). On southern labor and the CIO, Philip Taft's *Organizing Dixie: Alabama Workers in the Industrial Era*, edited and revised by Gary Fink (Westport, Conn.: Greenwood Press, 1981), provides an overview of one state.

18. See Joe William Trotter, Jr., *Coal, Class, and Color: Blacks in Southern West Virginia, 1915–32* (Urbana: University of Illinois Press, 1990); Robin D. G. Kelley, *Hammer and Hoe: Alabama Communists during the Great Depression* (Chapel Hill: University of North Carolina Press, 1990); Michael Honey, "Labor and Civil Rights in the South: The Industrial Labor Movement and Black Workers in Memphis, 1929–1945" (Ph.D. diss., Northern Illinois University, 1987), and "Industrial Unionism and Racial Justice in Memphis," in *Organized Labor in the Twentieth-Century South*, ed. Robert Zieger (Knoxville: University of Tennessee Press, 1991), 135–57; Robert Rogers Korstad, "Daybreak of Freedom, Tobacco Workers and the CIO, Winston-Salem, North Carolina, 1943–1950" (Ph.D. diss., University of North Carolina–Chapel Hill, 1987); and for a trenchant discussion of the issues raised by black industrial unionism for the civil rights movement, see Robert Rogers Korstad and Nelson Lichtenstein, "Opportunities Found and Lost: Labor, Radicals, and the Early Civil Rights Movement," *Journal of American History* 75 (Dec. 1988): 786–811. On the limits of biracialism, see Robert J. Norrell's case study, "Caste in Steel: Jim Crow Careers in Birmingham, Alabama," *Journal of American History* 73 (Dec. 1986): 669–94.

19. Aldon Morris, in *The Origins of the Civil Rights Movement: Black Communities Organizing for Change* (New York: Free Press, 1985), surveys the various forces leading to the civil rights movement, but confines his treatment to the era from 1953 to 1963 and says little about the role of black workers or the unions prior to that time. William H. Harris, in *The Harder We Run*, concludes that black workers "launched the first wave of the modern civil rights movement" after World War II, and provides

examples in Montgomery and elsewhere, see 124, 144. Foner's *Organized Labor and the Black Worker* likewise makes a strong case for African-American workers as in the vanguard of both labor and civil rights movements. Most civil rights histories, however, take little account of the prior experience of black workers in unions.

20. William Barlow, *"Looking Up at Down": The Emergence of Blues Culture* (Philadelphia: Temple University Press, 1990), 202–29, quote on 223. See also Margaret McKee and Fred Chisenhall, *Beale, Black, and Blue: Life and Music on Black America's Main Street* (Baton Rouge: Louisiana State University Press, 1981).

21. F. Ray Marshall and Arvil Van Adams, "Negro Employment in Memphis," *Industrial Relations* 9, no. 3 (May 1970): 308–23; Arvil Van Adams, *The Memphis Labor Market*, vol. 2 of *Negro Employment in the South* (Washington: U.S. Department of Labor, 1971), 9–11, on poverty statistics.

22. See King's speeches before the AFL-CIO (1961), Hospital Workers Union Local No. 1199 (1965, 1968), District 65 of the UAW (1962, 1963, 1965), the UAW (1961), the Teamsters (1967), the NMU (1962), and the UPWA (1962) in the Martin Luther King, Jr., Papers, Ser. 3, Martin Luther King, Jr., Center for Non-Violent Social Change, Atlanta, Ga.

ONE: SEGREGATION AND SOUTHERN LABOR

1. Barbara J. Fields, "Ideology and Race in American History," in *Region, Race, and Reconstruction,* ed. J. Morgan Kousser and James M. McPherson (New York: Oxford University Press, 1982), 143–77, quote on 159. See Ashley Montague, ed., *The Concept of Race* (New York: Collier Books, 1964), and *Man's Most Dangerous Myth: The Fallacy of Race* (New York: Oxford University Press, 1974), on the fallacy of race as a biological category. On the history of racism and its relationship to the South, see for example George M. Fredrickson, *The Black Image in the White Mind: The Debate on Afro-American Character and Destiny, 1817–1914* (New York: Harper and Row, 1971).

2. For a discussion of the extent of slaveholding and the white South's support for slavery, see Otto H. Olsen, "Historians and the Extent of Slave Ownership in the Southern United States," *Civil War History* 18, no. 2 (June 1972): 101–16, and Eugene D. Genovese, "Yeomen Farmers in a Slaveholder's Democracy," *Agricultural History* 49 (Apr. 1975): 331–42.

3. On slavery and the antebellum Memphis economy, see Gerald M. Capers, *Biography of a River Town* (Chapel Hill: University of North Carolina Press, 1933), 41, 68, 77–79, and Kathleen C. Berkeley, " 'Like a Plague of Locust': Immigration and Social Change in Memphis, Tennessee, 1850–1880" (Ph.D. diss., University of California–Los Angeles, 1980), chap. 1. See also Bette Baird Tilly, "Aspects of Social and Economic Life in West Tennessee before the Civil War" (Ph.D. diss., Memphis State University, 1974).

4. On slavery in Memphis, see James H. Robinson, "A Social History of the Negro in Memphis and in Shelby County" (Ph.D. diss., Yale, 1934), and Charles C. Mooney, "Some Institutional Aspects of Slavery in Tennessee," *Tennessee Historical Quarterly* 1 (Sept. 1942): 195–228. According to Kate Born, in "Organized Labor in Memphis, Tennessee, 1826–1901," *West Tennessee Historical Society Papers* 21 (1967): 60–79, the Memphis Typographical Union was the only existing union before the Civil War. According to Shirley Ayer, in "Labor Is the Community: An Historical Sketch of the

Workingmen in Memphis, Tennessee, 1827 to the First World War" (M.A. thesis, 1967) located in the files of the Memphis AFL-CIO, iron molders and tailors were also organized. On the class dimensions of the secession crisis, see Berkeley, "Plague of Locust," chap. 2.

5. Ayer, "Labor Is the Community," quotes "irrespective of race or color" from the *Memphis Avalanche* in 1877, 29. Born, "Organized Labor in Memphis," lists organized workers, 72–73. Racial conflict and labor solidarity both heightened throughout the South in this period. See Melton McLaurin, "The Racial Policies of the Knights of Labor and the Organization of Southern Black Workers," *Labor History* 17, no. 4 (1976): 568–85; Peter J. Rachleff, *Black Labor in the South: Richmond, Virginia, 1865–1900* (Philadelphia: Temple University Press, 1984); Eric Arnesen, *Waterfront Workers of New Orleans: Race, Class, and Politics* (New York: Oxford University Press, 1991); Daniel Rosenberg, *New Orleans Dockworkers: Race, Labor, and Unionism 1892–1923* (Albany: State University of New York Press, 1988); and Paul B. Worthman, "Black Workers and Labor Unions in Birmingham, Alabama, 1897–1904," *Labor History* 10 (1969): 375–407.

6. On the deadly racial climate in southern cities after the war, see Howard N. Rabinowitz, *Race Relations in the Urban South, 1865–1890* (New York: Oxford University Press, 1978), part 1. On the Memphis riot, see Capers, *Biography of a River Town,* 177; Berkeley, "Plague of Locust," 175–77, 231; Robinson, "Negro in Memphis," 70–76; and Altina L. Waller, "Community, Class, and Race in the Memphis Riot of 1866," *Journal of Social History* 18, no. 2 (Winter 1984): 233–45, which contends that merchants and the middle class played a prominent role in starting the riot. Dennis C. Rousey, "Yellow Fever and Black Policemen in Memphis: A Post-Reconstruction Anomaly," *Journal of Southern History* 51, no. 3 (Aug. 1985): 357–74, gives the 70 percent figure. Census figures show the immigrant population dropping from 30 percent in 1860 to 5 percent at the turn of the century, see Roger Biles, *Memphis in the Great Depression* (Knoxville: University of Tennessee Press, 1986), 13.

7. AFL resolution in *Report of the Thirteenth Annual Convention of the American Federation of Labor,* 11–19 Dec. 1893, Chicago. Born, "Organized Labor in Memphis," 75–79, and Born, "Memphis Negro Workingmen and the NAACP," *West Tennessee Historical Society Papers* 28 (1974): 90–107; and Ayer, "Labor Is the Community," 36, 64, 67. On the AFL unions, see Foner, *Organized Labor and the Black Worker,* chaps. 5, 6, or Harris, *The Harder We Run,* chaps. 3, 4, 5, and Sterling D. Spero and Abraham L. Harris, *The Black Worker: The Negro and the Labor Movement* (New York: Columbia University Press, 1931).

8. On the consolidation of segregation and its effects, see Neil R. McMillen, *Dark Journey: Black Mississippians in the Age of Jim Crow* (Urbana: University of Illinois Press, 1990); and Rabinowitz, *Race Relations in the Urban South,* on the importance of urban segregation to the whole pattern. For an overview, see Arnold H. Taylor, *Travail and Triumph: Black Life and Culture in the South since the Civil War* (Westport, Conn.: Greenwood Press, 1976). C. Vann Woodward's description has been the most influential, see *The Strange Career of Jim Crow* (1955; reprint, New York: Oxford University Press, 1976). On the economic subordination of African-American workers during the construction of Jim Crow, see for example Charles H. Wesley, *Negro Labor in the United States* (New York: Vanguard Press, 1927); Pete Daniel, *The Shadow of Slavery: Peonage in the South, 1901–1969* (New York: Oxford University Press, 1972); and Roger

Ransom and Richard Sutch, *One Kind of Freedom: The Economic Consequences of Emancipation* (New York: Cambridge University Press, 1977).

9. On lower-class agrarian alliances and their destruction, see C. Vann Woodward, *Origins of the New South, 1877–1913* (Baton Rouge: Louisiana State University Press, 1951), and *Tom Watson: Agrarian Rebel,* 4th ed. (New York: Oxford University Press, 1972), and Lawrence Goodwyn, *Democratic Promise: The Populist Moment in America* (New York: Oxford University Press, 1976). On disfranchisement, see J. Morgan Kousser, *The Shaping of Southern Politics: Suffrage Restriction and the Establishment of the One-Party South, 1880–1910* (New Haven: Yale University Press, 1974); V. O. Key, Jr., *Southern Politics* (New York: Random House, 1949); Paul Lewinson, *Race, Class, and Party: A History of Negro Suffrage and White Politics in the South* (1932; reprint, New York: Grosset and Dunlap, 1965), on the one-party South. See Earl Black and Merle Black, *Politics and Society in the South* (Cambridge: Harvard University Press, 1987), 240, on the decline of the Democratic party, which they see beginning in the fifties.

10. The Black leader T. O. Fuller, in *The Inter Racial Blue Book* (Memphis, c. 1925) pointed out some of the newspaper racism of the twenties, and it remains apparent in reading the *Commercial Appeal* in the thirties, forties, and fifties. Billy Hall Wyche, in "Southern Attitudes toward Industrial Unions, 1933–1941" (Ph.D. diss., University of Georgia, 1970), points out examples of the newspaper's antilabor attitude, see especially 75, 76, 83. On Forrest, see Mooney, "Some Institutional Aspects of Slavery in Tennessee," 201. According to John Cimprich and Robert C. Mainfort, Jr., the Fort Pillow massacre was not an exaggeration, as some southerners claimed, "The Fort Pillow Massacre: A Statistical Note," *Journal of American History* 76 (Dec. 1989): 830–37.

11. See Rayford E. Logan, *The Betrayal of the Negro: From Rutherford B. Hayes to Woodrow Wilson* (New York: Macmillan, 1965). *CA,* 5–25 May 1917, covered the Ell Persons lynching, as did *The Crisis* 14, no. 3 (July 1917): 1–4, and see Gloria Brown-Melton, "Blacks in Memphis, Tennessee, 1920–1955: A Historical Study" (Ph.D. diss., Washington State University, 1982), 46. See David M. Tucker, *Memphis since Crump: Bossism, Blacks, and Civic Reformers, 1948–1968* (Knoxville: University of Tennessee Press, 1980), 3–14, and "Miss Ida B. Wells and Memphis Lynching," *Phylon* 32 (Summer 1971): 112–22. See Alfred M. Duster, ed., *Crusade for Justice: The Autobiography of Ida B. Wells* (reprint; Chicago: University of Chicago Press, 1970), 35–66. Paula Giddings also has an account of the significance of Memphis in launching the antilynching crusade, in *When and Where I Enter: The Impact of Black Women on Race and Sex in America* (New York: William Morrow, 1984), chap. 1. Also see "Shelby County's Shame, the Story of the Big Creek Lynching and Trial" (1895), MPL. On Progressivism see William D. Miller, *Memphis during the Progressive Era, 1900–1917* (Memphis: Memphis State University Press, 1957). Sheriff incident in Robert R. Church to James W. Johnson, 5 Sept. 1919, and "Resolution of Memphis Branch NAACP to the Officers and Executive Boards," 5 Sept. 1919, both in Box L-42, Group 2, NAACP/LC.

12. Biles, *Memphis in the Great Depression,* 23–28, and Biles, "The Persistence of the Past: Memphis in the Great Depression," *Journal of Southern History* 52, no. 2 (May 1986): 183–212. See Annette E. Roberta Church, *The Robert R. Churches of Memphis* (Ann Arbor, Mich.: Edwards Brothers, 1974), and the NAACP/LC on Memphis.

13. Richard Wright, *Black Boy* (1937; reprint, New York: Harper and Row, 1966), 245, and see chaps. 11–14 on Memphis.

14. George Holloway, personal interview, 23 Mar. 1990, Baltimore, Md. Clarence Coe recalled the use of veils to separate black and white riders, interview, 29 May 1989, Memphis.

15. See Foner, *Organized Labor and the Black Worker,* 7–8. Ayer, "Labor Is the Community," 81–85, 95, 103–7, 110–13, on Memphis statistics. Railroad worker incidents are described in the *Evening Press,* 6 May 1921, and by Phil Brown, Commissioner of Conciliation, to the Secretary of Labor, 9 May 1921, and related documents, File 8/102f, Division of Negro Economics, USDL, RG 174, NARA. See also Born, "Memphis Negro Workingmen," 98–101; Horace R. Cayton and George S. Mitchell, *Black Workers and the New Unions* (1939; reprint, Westport, Conn.: Negro Universities Press, 1970), 284, 294–97; and Philip S. Foner and Ronald L. Lewis, eds. *The Black Worker: A Documentary History from Colonial Times to the Present,* vol. 4, *The Era of the AFL, the Railroad Brotherhoods, and the UMW, 1800–1903* (Philadelphia: Temple University Press, 1979), 73–114.

16. Thomas L. Dabney report, May 1928, Ser. 6, Box 89, Research Department, NUL/LC; Robert Tillman, personal interview, 24 Feb. 1983, Memphis; George Holloway, personal interview, 23 Mar. 1990, Baltimore, Md., on the AFL quarters.

17. The conditions in Memphis seem to have been typical of the South. On the repressive social climate, see George Brown Tindall, *The Emergence of the New South, 1913–1945* (Baton Rouge: Louisiana State University Press, 1967). For one example of labor repression in the South, among many, see Jeff Ferrell and Kevin Ryan, "The Brotherhood of Timber Workers and the Southern Trust: Legal Repression and Worker Response," *Radical America* 19, no. 4 (1985): 55–73. See also Foner, *Organized Labor and the Black Worker,* chaps. 5–8, for examples of how segregation and racism destroyed labor unity. See Gavin Wright, *Old South, New South: Revolutions in the Southern Economy since the Civil War* (New York: Basic Books, 1986), 183, and chap. 6, and his article "The Economic Revolution in the American South," *Economic Perspectives* 1, no. 1 (Summer 1987): 161–78, on employer's perceived necessity for low wages.

18. According to Robert Higgs, massive wage studies in the thirties by the the federal government found that white and black unskilled workers made about the same wage rates in the North and the South, see "The Persistence of Economic Inequalities," in *The Question of Discrimination: Racial Inequality in the U.S. Labor Market,* ed. Steven Shulman and William Darity, Jr. (Middletown, Conn.: Wesleyan University Press, 1989), 18–19. This pattern is also documented by Wright in *Old South, New South,* 68, 182–83, 201. Statistics on Memphis income and living conditions are presented later in this chapter.

19. Du Bois quoted in David R. Roediger, *The Wages of Whiteness: Race and the Making of the American Working Class* (New York: Verso, 1991), 12, and see Roediger's argument in chap. 1. On settler societies see Marcel van der Linden, ed., *Racism and Power Relations in the Labour Market,* 2 vols. (Leiden, Netherlands: International Institute of Social History, 1993). Higgs, "Persistence," 19–25. On comparisons with South Africa, see John W. Cell, *The Highest Stage of White Supremacy: The Origins of Segregation in South Africa and the American South* (Cambridge: Cambridge University Press, 1982), and George W. Fredrickson, *White Supremacy: A Comparative Study in American and South African History* (New York: Oxford, 1981).

20. Robert A Sigafoos, *Cotton Row to Beale Street: A Business History of Memphis* (Memphis: Memphis State University Press, 1979), 75–76. Rupert B. Vance, *Human*

Geography of the South: A Study in Regional Resources and Human Adequacy (Chapel Hill: University of North Carolina Press, 1932), 194.

21. See Ransom and Sutch, *One Kind of Freedom,* and Wright, *Old South, New South,* on the origins and effects of keeping black wages cheap.

22. Rayburn Whitson Johnson, "Land Utilization in Memphis" (Ph.D. diss., University of Chicago, 1936), 19–25. In table 3, figures for 1929 are drawn from Shelby County, for 1939 from Memphis. Few if any manufacturing plants existed outside of Memphis, however.

23. See Sigafoos, *Cotton Row,* on the nature of the Memphis economy. Paul Barnett, *Industrial Development in Tennessee: Present Status and Suggested Programs,* vol. 2 of the *University of Tennessee Record* (Knoxville, 1941), suggests the weakness of mechanization in the state's four major industrial centers.

24. Sigafoos, *Cotton Row,* 141. On incentives to industry, see Ethel Erickson to Miss Anderson, 8 Feb. 1936, from Memphis, Tennessee, Survey File, 1935, and Hugh Humphries, Tennessee Director of the National Recovery Administration, to John Swepe, 19 Apr. 1934, Compliance Division, Records Relating to Interpretations, Memphis, both in NRA, RG 9, NARA. For similar examples of the southern campaign to attract industry, see James C. Cobb, *The Selling of the South: The Southern Crusade for Industrial Development, 1936–1980* (Baton Rouge: Louisiana State University Press, 1982), chap. 1.

25. *CA,* 15 June 1933. *CA,* 16 June 1933, and see *CA,* 21 June 1933, and *P-S,* 12 Sept. 1933, on the meetings of lumber workers. See Tindall, *The Emergence of the New South,* 442, on the hardwood industry.

26. R. B. Parsons to Hugh Johnson, 12 Dec. 1933, Entry 357, 126—differentials, Henry H. Collins Personal Office Files, Labor Advisory Board, NRA, RG 9, NARA.

27. Emment Norment, manager of the Re-Employment Bureau in Memphis, provided these and other examples of employer cheating of blacks on wage codes, in F. W. Persons, USDL Director of Re-Employment Services in Memphis, to Frances Perkins, 28 Nov. 1933, Office of the Secretary, USDL, RG 174, NARA. This pattern remained common throughout the South, see Classified General Files, Ser. 23, 581—Negroes, NRA, RG 9, NARA. Tindall, in *The Emergence of the New South,* points out that NRA cheating helped set off the 1934 textile strike, see 436–37. See a number of letters by white workers protesting employer noncompliance and cheating on the wage codes, in Classified General Files, Ser. 23, 567—wages, NRA, RG 9, NARA. Hugh Humphries, Tennessee State Director, to Ralph A. Byers, 21 May 1934, on lumber wages, Memphis File, Interpretations, Compliance Division, NRA, RG 9, NARA. On the Buckeye plant, see leaflet in the file of Joe A. Fowler, Chair of the NRA Compliance Board in Memphis, forwarded on 29 Dec. 1933, and see a listing of noncomplying companies in Compliance Division File, Records Relating to Local Compliance Boards, both in Ser. 121, NRA, RG 9, NARA. See J. H. Williams, et al., a group of workers protesting NRA violations at the Federal Barge Line, to John Gilliand, 27 Nov. 1933, Compliance Division File, Records Relating to Local Compliance Boards, Ser. 121, NRA, RG 9, NARA.

28. Katie Hurston to Franklin D. Roosevelt, n.d., and George Isabell to Hugh Johnson, 3 Sept. 1933, both in Classified General Files, Ser. 23, 581—Negroes, NRA, RG 9. NARA.

29. NRA files contain numerous letters of protest on this issue. See Classified General Files, Ser. 23, 581—Negroes, NRA, RG 9, NARA.

30. Harris, *The Harder We Run,* 105. On the NRA's failure to challenge racial wage differentials, see Arthur F. Raper, "The Southern Negro and the NRA," *Georgia Historical Quarterly* 64, no. 2 (Summer 1980): 128–45; Robert C. Weaver, "A Wage Differential Based on Race," *The Crisis* 41 (Aug. 1934): 236–38; John P. Davis, "NRA Codifies Wage Slavery," *The Crisis,* 41 (Oct. 1934): 298–99, 304. Wilkins to Frances Perkins, 2 Aug. 1933, Office of the Secretary, USDL, RG 174, NARA. On Memphis laundry workers, see *MLR,* 1 Dec. 1933, 2 Feb. 1934.

31. Walter White to Hugh Johnson, 28 Sept. 1933, enclosing pamphlet, Classified General Files, Ser. 23, 581—Negroes, NRA, RG 174, NARA. Employers and state officials in the South claimed that paying wages at NRA codes to blacks would lead to a flood of rural migrants to the cities looking for decent paying work and cause "chaos" in the cities. See Arkansas Chamber of Commerce representative Dudley V. Haddock to Hugh Johnson, 29 July 1933, Classified General Files, Ser. 23, 567—labor wages, NRA, RG 9, NARA. Other business owners predicted that NRA codes that required employers to pay blacks the same wages as whites "will cause trouble" and force employers to let their blacks go, *Nashville Banner,* 11 Dec. 1933. Similar arguments appeared in other states, as with Charles L. Kaufman, Attorney in Norfolk, to Leo Wolman, 11 Aug. 1933, in Ser. 357, 126—differentials, Henry H. Collins Personal Office Files, Labor Advisory Board, NRA, RG 9, NARA.

32. Weaver, "A Wage Differential Based on Race," and see similar criticism by the NAACP's Arnold Hill, in *Opportunity* (Sept. 1933).

33. The AFL's John Frey nationally testified against southern wage differentials, but apparently said nothing when it came to blacks, *Blue Eagle,* 8 Feb. 1935. Hughlong Akin, a Trades and Labor Council leader in nearby Jackson, Tennessee, exhibited the same myopia when it came to black workers, in a letter to NRA head Hugh Johnson, 8 Dec. 1933, Henry H. Collins Personal Office Files, Labor Advisory Board, NRA, RG 9, NARA.

34. On negotiations for the new plant, see Raymond C. Firestone to E. H. Crump, 19 Feb. 1937, and Mayor Overton to Crump, 22 Feb. 1937, File 54, Mayor Watkins Overton Papers, MVC/MSU. See also Sigafoos, *Cotton Row,* 191.

35. Personal interviews with Richard Routon, 18 Feb. 1983, Memphis, Forrest Dickenson, 20 Feb. 1983, Memphis, and George Clark, phone interview, 17 Feb. 1983, on wage rates and classifications. More detail on these classifications appears in chapter 7.

36. Chamber of commerce in 1929 quoted in Roger Biles, "Ed Crump Versus the Unions: The Labor Movement in Memphis during the 1930's," *Labor History* 25, no. 4 (Fall 1984): 532–52, and 1936 quote in Memphis Chamber of Commerce, "Factory Facts and Figures, Demonstrating the Superiority of Memphis as a Manufacturing Center" (Memphis, 1936).

37. Dickenson interview. Information on new industries from the *Annual Reports of the Department of Labor, State of Tennessee,* 1930–1935, in the USDL Library, Washington, D.C.

38. Wright, *Old South, New South,* 78–80, chap. 6, and his article "The Economic Revolution in the American South," discusses the failures of the cheap wage system. On continuities between the old ruling class and the new and the analogy to underdeveloped countries, see Jonathan M. Weiner, *Social Origins of the New South: Alabama, 1860–1885* (Baton Rouge: Louisiana State University Press, 1978), and Dwight Billings, Jr.,

Planters and the Making of the "New South": Class, Politics, and the Development of North Carolina, 1865–1900 (Chapel Hill: University of North Carolina Press, 1979).

39. Matthew Davis, personal interview, 30 Oct. 1984, Memphis.

40. Church, *The Robert R. Churches of Memphis;* G. P. Hamilton, *The Bright Side of Memphis* (Memphis: G. P. Hamilton, 1908); Brown-Melton, "Blacks in Memphis," chap. 2 and passim; Barlow, *"Looking Up at Down,"* 205.

41. See David M. Tucker, *Lieutenant Lee of Beale Street* (Nashville: Vanderbilt University Press, 1971), for a glimpse of the black "middle" class in Memphis.

42. This pattern was not unique to Memphis, as numerous accounts disclose. See, for example, Robert C. Weaver, *Negro Labor: A National Problem* (New York: Harcourt, Brace, 1946), 9–14.

43. Personal interviews with Edward Lock, black former sawmill worker, 29 Oct. 1984, Memphis, and black Firestone workers Fred Higgins, Edward Lee Harrel, and Matthew Davis, 30 Oct. 1984, Memphis.

44. See James E. Fickle, *The New South and the "New Competition": Trade Association Development in the Southern Pine Industry* (Urbana: University of Illinois Press, 1980), and Herbert Northrup and Richard Rowan, eds., *Negro Employment in Southern Industry: A Study of Racial Policies in Five Industries* (Philadelphia: Wharton School Industrial Research Unit, University of Pennsylvania, 1970), on the lumber industry.

45. "Report on the Availability of Services to Negro Applicants, of the Tennessee State Employment Service Office," 16 Dec. 1936, Bureau of Employment Security, Division of Negro Labor, USES, USDL, RG 183, NARA.

46. The number of black women in factory jobs in the nation declined from the twenties to the thirties, according to Jacqueline Jones, *Labor of Love, Labor of Sorrow: Black Women, Work, and the Family, from Slavery to the Present* (New York: Random House, 1985), 208–9.

47. Tillman interview. Wage figures in Sigafoos, *Cotton Row,* 192, and Memphis Chamber of Commerce, "Factory Facts and Figures," Memphis Area memo, 13 May 1941, U.S. Bureau of Labor Statistics, USDL, RG 183, NARA; *State of Tennessee Annual Report of the Department of Labor for the Year 1935* (Nashville: State of Tennessee, 1935), 140, 142–46; "Questions and Answers about Tennessee's Women Workers," U.S. Department of Labor Bulletin 149 (Washington, D.C.: Women's Bureau, 1935), Tennessee Survey Files, Women's Bureau, USDL, NARA; Howard A. Hanalong, *Delta Harvest* (Watkins Glen, N.Y., 1966), 352.

48. Sigafoos, *Cotton Row,* 192, and "Union Scales of Wages and Hours in the Building Trades in 70 Cities," U.S. Department of Labor Bulletin 657 (Washington, D.C.: GPO, 1938), 24–25, 28, 46–47. Faith M. Williams and Alice C. Hanson, assisted by Genevieve B. Wimsatt, *Money Disbursements of Employed Wage Earners and Clerical Workers in Twelve Cities of the South, 1934–36,* U.S. Department of Labor Bulletin 640 (Washington, D.C.: GPO, 1941).

49. Notes taken by investigator Ethel Erickson, 1935, Tennessee Survey Files, Women's Bureau, USDL, NARA.

50. Ibid.

51. Johnson, "Land Utilization in Memphis," 50–54, 58, 62.

52. H. B. Griffin, phone interview, 2 Mar. 1983; Sigafoos, *Cotton Row,* 180–84. On

the origins of Pinchgut, see Joe B. Brady, "The Irish Community in Antebellum Memphis," *West Tennessee Historical Society Papers* 40 (1986), courtesy of John Harkins.

TWO: NO BILL OF RIGHTS IN MEMPHIS

1. W. E. B. Du Bois, *The Souls of Black Folk* (New York: Signet Books, 1969), 136. See Clement Eaton, *The Freedom-of-Thought Struggle in the Old South* (1940; reprint, New York: Harper Torchbooks, 1964), and George B. Tindall, *The Emergence of the New South,* chap. 10.

2. See Alfred Steinberg, *The Bosses* (New York: Macmillan, 1972), on Crump's career, and other brief accounts in Tucker, *Memphis since Crump,* and Biles, *Memphis in the Depression.* The lengthiest account, though very uncritical, is William D. Miller, *Mr. Crump of Memphis* (Baton Rouge: Louisiana State University Press, 1964).

3. Brown-Melton, "Blacks in Memphis," 97–106, quote on 106.

4. Steinberg, *The Bosses,* 93–98; *Chicago Tribune,* 2 and 9 Apr. 1937; and Miller, *Mr. Crump.*

5. Steinberg, *The Bosses,* 104–7; Miller, *Mr. Crump,* 204, 212–13, and *Chicago Tribune,* 2 and 9 Apr. 1937; Holloway interview.

6. For the rise of Crump as a controlling figure in state politics in the early thirties, see David D. Lee, *Tennessee in Turmoil: Politics in the Volunteer State, 1920–1932* (Memphis: Memphis State University Press, 1972), 91–92, 140–42, 148–49.

7. Robert Tillman interview, 24 Feb. 1983, Memphis. Miller, *Mr. Crump,* 201. See the *Memphis Social Register and Directory* for some of the city's leading lights (Memphis, 1935). Tucker, *Memphis since Crump,* chap. 1.

8. Miller, *Mr. Crump,* 202, and Firestone to Crump, 19 Feb. 1937, and Overton to Crump, 22 Feb. 1937. See also Sigafoos, *Cotton Row,* 191.

9. John D. Hawkins to author, 22 May 1988.

10. The kinds of alliances between black elites and the black working class suggested by Joe William Trotter, Jr., in his study of West Virginia do not seem to appear in Memphis during this period. *Coal, Class, and Color.* Brown-Melton, "Blacks in Memphis," chap. 2. Armstead L. Robinson details the early class divisions in leadership within the post-emancipation black community, "Plans Dat Comed from God: Institution Building and the Emergence of Black Leadership in Reconstruction Memphis," in *Toward a New South: Studies in Post–Civil War Southern Communities,* ed. Orville V. Burton and Robert C. McMath, Jr. (Westport, Conn.: Greenwood Press, 1982), 71–102. David M. Tucker, *Black Pastors and Leaders: Memphis, 1819–1972* (Memphis: Memphis State University Press, 1975). Steinberg, *The Bosses,* 80–81; Miller, *Mr. Crump,* 103–4. Spero and Harris point out that generally black middle-class leaders and ministers had little sympathy or understanding of the plight of black workers in the thirties, *The Black Worker,* 464–65. Crump's control of black preachers is particularly apparent in Thomas O. Fuller's *The Story of the Church Life among Negroes in Memphis, Tennessee, for Students and Workers, 1900–1938* (Memphs: n.p., 1938), see 19, for example.

11. Ralph McGill, *The South and the Southerner* (1959; reprint, Boston: Little, Brown, 1963), 110. Biles, *Memphis in the Depression,* 96–97.

12. See chap. 6 on Crump's actions against Church, and Brown-Melton, "Blacks in Memphis," 166–69, on the decline of the NAACP the late thirties.

13. Kenneth T. Jackson, *The Ku Klux Klan in the City, 1915–1930* (New York: Oxford University Press, 1967), 51; *P-S*, 3 Dec. 1936, on police wages; Bunche, *Political Status of the Negro,* 102.

14. Tillman interview. Oscar P. Williams, a Carpenters' Union executive, for example, held a job as commissioner of public works, and Sam Campbell, and later Robert Tillman of the printers' union received judicial positions under Boss Crump's regime. Biles, "Boss Crump Versus the Unions," 536–37.

15. Information on wage rates and unionization is taken from *MLR,* 22 Dec. 1933, 6 and 13 Apr. 1934.

16. *MLR,* 15 June, 27 July, and 3 Aug. 1934, and 8 June 1934.

17. *CA,* 10 Mar. 1933, *MLR,* 26 Jan., 4 May, and 11 May 1934.

18. Some of the city's facilities built during the New Deal include the Overton Park orchestra shell, John Gaston Hospital, Crump Stadium, the runways at the city's airport, the city's grain elevator, Dixie Homes, Lauderdale Courts, and other public housing projects, and even Riverside Drive in downtown Memphis. *P-S,* 6 May 1939, and 28 Sept., 16 Oct., and 1 Nov. 1937; and "Index to Reference Cards for Works Projects Administration Project Files, 1935–37," National Archives microfilm T935, roll 65, which lists the projects undertaken in Memphis. See also Biles, *Memphis in the Depression,* 74–84 and chap. 4. Sigafoos, *Cotton Row,* 178–81, 186.

19. For examples of the paternalistic, even feudal, relationship of Crump to his subordinates, see Rev. Ira Cole to Crump, 23 Feb. 1938, D. Edward Stanton to Crump, 10 Nov. 1936, Watkins Overton to Crump, 11 Nov. 1937, all in Box 3, Overton Papers, MVC/MSU. Steinberg, *The Bosses,* 108–10; and *Chicago Tribune,* 2 Apr. 1939.

20. *Chicago Tribune,* 2 Apr. 1939. *P-S,* 12 and 13 May, 7 Apr., and 5 Aug. 1938, and *CA,* 21 May 1938. See Miller's chapter on the Browning campaign in *Mr. Crump,* 242–67.

21. Hosea Hudson, Myles and Zilphia Horton, Claude and Joyce Williams, Owen Whitfield and Howard Kester are the names of just a few of the more well known of such southern radicals from the thirties. On southern radicals, see Nell I. Painter, *The Narrative of Hosea Hudson: His Life as a Negro Communist in the South* (Cambridge: Harvard University Press, 1979); Jim Garland, *Welcome the Traveler Home: Jim Garland's Story of the Southern Mountains* (Lexington: University of Kentucky Press, 1983); Cedric Belfrage, *A Faith to Free the People* (New York: Dryden Press, 1944), on Claude Williams; Junius Scales and Richard Nickson, *Cause at Heart: A Former Communist Remembers* (Athens: University of Georgia Press, 1987); Tom Johnson, "The Reds in Dixie: Who Are the Communists and What Do They Fight For in the South?" 1935 pamphlet in the Louis Slater Memorial Collection, Tammiment Library, New York University; Kelley, *Hammer and Hoe;* and Anthony P. Dunbar, *Against the Grain: Southern Radicals and Prophets, 1932–1959* (Charlottesville: University of Virginia Press, 1981).

22. See note 21 for sources describing repression in the South, and see for example Louise Thompson, "Southern Terror," *The Crisis* 41 (Nov. 1934): 327–28, and Robert Wood, "To Live and Die in Dixie" (1934), pamphlet located in the LC.

23. Horace Davis, "Memoirs of an Ex-Liberal," and Marion Davis Ms., in the possession of their granddaughter Rachel Stocking, Stanford, Calif.

24. Ibid.

25. Quote on "full equality" in Harvey Klehr, *The Heyday of American Commu-*

306 Notes to pp. 54–59

nism: *The Depression Decade* (New York: Basic Books, 1984), 324, and on white workers, Johnson, "The Reds in Dixie." See Kelley, *Hammer and Hoe*. On the appeal of the party's antiracism to whites, see Scales and Nickson, *Cause at Heart;* Steinberg, *The Bosses,* 102, 113; Lee quote in Biles, *Memphis in the Great Depression,* 39.

26. Horace Davis, "Memoirs of an Ex-Liberal," and Marion Davis Ms., and *CA,* 5, 7, and 8 June 1930.

27. Horace Davis, "Memories of an Ex-Liberal," and Marion Davis Ms.

28. *CA,* 8 June 1930, and Marion Davis Ms.

29. *CA,* 8 Oct. 1932, and *P-S,* 8 and 9 Nov. 1932.

30. See Brown-Melton, "Blacks in Memphis," 143–47, on the NAACP. Goldberger's brother Milton, owner and publisher of the *Hebrew Watchman,* had printed Israel's leaflets. *CA,* 14, 15, and 17 June 1933, on the RFC strikes, and 17 June 1933 on the leaflet.

31. Israel worked for the Federated Press in Harlan. Theodore Dreiser, et al., *Harlan Miners Speak: Report on Terrorism in the Kentucky Coal Fields Prepared by Members of the National Committee for the Defense of Political Prisoners* (New York, 1932), 80–82. Coad incident recounted by Hosea Hudson, in Painter, *The Narrative of Hosea Hudson,* 227.

32. See "The Socialist Party and the Negro" resolution in Ser. 3, General Correspondence, Tennessee Socialist Party Papers, MVC/MSU, microfilm; Robert Hyfler, *Prophets on the Left: American Socialist Thought in the Twentieth Century* (Westport, Conn.: Greenwood Press, 1984), 36–37; Harvard Sitkoff, *A New Deal for Blacks: The Emergence of Civil Rights as a National Issue: The Depression Decade* (London: Oxford University Press), 162; H. L. Mitchell, *Mean Things Happening in This Land* (Montclair, N.J.: Allanheld, Osmun, 1979), 32–33; the Socialist Party Scrapbook, Memphis Room, MPL; and Rachelle Saltzman, "Shalom Y'All," *Southern Exposure* 11, no. 5 (Oct.–Nov. 1983): 28–36, on Memphis Jews.

33. See Edward J. Meeman, *The Editorial We: A Posthumous Autobiography* (Memphis: Memphis State University Printing Services, 1976), on Meeman's writings and opposition to Crump. Details of the Norman Thomas campaign and related information in the Socialist Party Scrapbook. See for example *P-S,* 9 Nov. 1932.

34. *P-S,* 28 Dec. 1932, 11 Jan., 3 Mar., 2 Nov. 1933; *CA,* 11 and 16 Jan., 26 and 27 Feb., and 15 and 30 Mar. 1933.

35. Brown-Melton, "Blacks in Memphis," 118–21, chap. 3, and 129. Emmett M. Norment, Manager of the Re-Employment Bureau in Memphis, memo to F. W. Persons, 28 Nov. 1933, details the terrible condition of Memphis blacks in the labor market, Office of the Secretary, USDL, RG 174, NARA. On wages of black domestics, see "Report on the Availability of Services to Negro Applicants, of the Tennessee State Employment Service Office," 16 Dec. 1936, Bureau of Employment Security, Division of Negro Labor, USES, USDL, RG 183, NARA. Hanalong, *Delta Harvest,* 352, cites wage figures for sawmill labor.

36. Sitkoff, *A New Deal for Blacks,* 36, on Atlanta; Harris, *The Harder We Run,* 104, on Negro removal campaigns; Report of Emmett M. Norment to F. W. Persons, on Loewe's theater.

37. On the assassinations, see Cayton and Mitchell, *Black Workers and the New Unions,* 439–45; L. R. Moloy to Oscar DePriest, 17 Feb. 1932, Railway Workers File, Records of the Bureau of Employment Security, Division of Negro Labor, USES, USDL, RG 183, NARA; see also Born, "Memphis Negro Workingmen and the NAACP."

38. Houston, "In re Teague v. Gulf, Mobile & Northern RR. Co.," written from Memphis, 27 June 1940, Box B-188, Group 2, NAACP/LC, courtesy of August Meier. Nationally, the number of black stokers and other railroad workers by 1940 dropped to a fraction of what it had been in 1920. See Foner and Lewis, eds., *The Black Worker*, vol. 7, *From the Founding of the CIO to the AFL-CIO Merger, 1937–55* (Philadelphia: Temple University Press, 1983), 520–21, and see also vol. 6, *The Era of Post-war Prosperity and the Great Depression, 1920 to 1936* (1981), 308–9. The Memphis Negro Chamber of Commerce listed figures in 1941, which showed that only 14 blacks worked as mechanics in railroad and car shops in 1941, while 86 worked as operatives; 431 worked as porters on Memphis railroads, along with 725 in the category of "all other porters"; some 1,200 worked as laborers; 127 blacks still worked as stokers; and 79 worked as brake operators. Negro Chamber of Commerce, "Colored Employment in Memphis," *Classified Directory of Memphis and Shelby County*, 143, Memphis Room, MPL. Cayton and Mitchell, *Black Workers*, 284–309. For other information on black railroad workers see "Preliminary Summary Statement on the Employment of Negroes on Railroads," 21 July 1933, Box 89, Section E, Early Surveys, Ser. 6, Research Dept., NUL/LC.

39. Information on the railroad workers' cases appears in Mediation and Conciliation Service File 165–1438, RG 280, NARA. Karl Phillips to Mr. Kerwin, 23 Jan. 1934, ludicrously, suggested the blacks appeal to the white railroad unions for help; George Washington to Kerwin, 15 Mar. 1935, and to P. W. Chappell, 2 Sept. 1935, contain his protests. See also James A. Cobb to H. L. Kerwin, 8 Jan. 1945, in the same file. See another example of the futility of protest, in the case of H. O. Gair, fired from his job after twenty-three years of service, in Joe Chapman and H. A. Johnson to Lt. Lawrence A. Oxley, 19 Sept. 1934, Brotherhood of Railway Trainmen File 4-A, Box 2, Industrial Relations Department, NUL/LC. Spero and Harris, relate the origins of the black railroad workers' associations, *The Black Worker*, 312–13.

40. Foner and Lewis, eds., *From the Founding of the CIO*, 521. See interviews conducted by Cayton and Mitchell, *Black Workers*, 289–96, on black strikebreaking.

41. George Washington to Kerwin, 15 Mar., and to P. W. Chappell, 2 Sept. 1935.

42. The refusal of contractors and white unions to allow blacks into better-paying positions on WPA jobs, in Memphis and other southern cities, forced New Deal administrator Harold Ickes to back down on his order banning discrimination in WPA programs, while the presence of only eleven blacks among the South's eleven thousand WPA supervisors ensured that the best jobs in the relief programs went to whites. Sitkoff, *New Deal for Blacks*, 47–50. Persons to Perkins, 28 Nov. 1933. See Brown-Melton, "Blacks in Memphis," 150, on the NYA. On the Memphis CCC camp, see *P-S* and *CA*, 7 Sept. 1935. Hostility to black CCC camps occurred in other communities, southern and nonsouthern, according to Henry P. Guzda, in "Francis Perkins' Interest in a New Deal for Blacks," *Monthly Labor Review* 103, no. 4 (Apr. 1980): 34.

43. William McDowell to Harry Hopkins, 28 May 1934, and Cora McKinney to Franklin D. Roosevelt, 21 June 1938. These and other letters complaining of racial discrimination appear in the WPA Correspondence File, Tenn., Ser. 641, RG 69, NARA.

44. Racial segregation and exclusion occurred under the NRA all over the country, according to a 29 Sept. 1933 memo written by Clark Foreman; and Walter White to Frances Perkins, 6 July 1933, and 18 May 1933, both in Negroes, General Subject File, Office of the Secretary, USDL, RG 174, NARA. Sitkoff, *A New Deal for Blacks*, 51.

45. John A. Salmond, *A Southern Rebel: The Life and Times of Aubrey Willis Williams, 1890–1965* (Chapel Hill: University of North Carolina Press, 1983), 57–140.

46. Sitkoff, *A New Deal for Blacks*, 48, 34–57. Leslie Fishel and Benjamin Quarles, "In the New Deal's Wake," in *The Segregation Era, 1863–1954: A Modern Reader*, ed. Allen Weinstein and Frank O. Gatell (London: Oxford University Press, 1970), 219. Biles, *Memphis in the Depression*, 93–96, gives examples of how Crump and local New Deal administrators in Memphis took care to preserve segregation.

47. Racial cartoons and sensationalization can be seen in the *CA*, 14 and 17 June 1930. The killing of the black teenager is in the affidavit of Fannie Henderson, 23 Feb. 1933, Robert Church Papers, MVC/MSU. See also the police clippings file in the Memphis Room, MPL.

48. Laurent Frantz, "People's Rights in Memphis," Box 85, Ralph Bunche Papers, Special Collections, University of California–Los Angeles Library, courtesy of Robin Kelley, and *P-S*, 18 May 1937.

49. *P-S*, 18 May and 17 Aug. 1937, on beatings of suspects, 19 May, 30 and 31 Aug., and 1 Sept. 1937, on the torture chair.

50. E. L. Lung to Attorney General Frank Murphy, 29 May 1939, File 144-72-0, Justice Department, RG 60, NARA.

51. Hatley to the President, 10 Sept. 1939, and T. D. Quinn to Hatley, 20 Sept. 1939. *CA*, 10 Oct. 1936, on the police training academy. E. L. Clark to Frank Murphy, 15 June 1939, all in File 144-72-0, Justice Department, RG 60, NARA. See also Ralph Bunche's references to the Memphis police, *Political Status of the Negro*, 493–501.

52. Deposition of Williams Glover, taken in Cairo, Ill., 23 Jan. 1938, Robert Church Papers, MVC/MSU. George Holloway, whose father was also a member of the Pullman Porters' union, remembered Glover's active role in the union, personal interview, 23 Mar. 1990, Baltimore, Md.

53. See for example Robert P. Ingalls, *Urban Vigilantes in the New South: Tampa, 1882–1936* (Knoxville: University of Tennessee Press, 1988). Or see the section on violence in *Encyclopedia of Southern Culture*, ed. Charles Reagan Wilson and William Ferris (Chapel Hill: University of North Carolina Press, 1989), 1469–1513.

54. Nationally, black employment declined as well. In manufacturing employment, blacks fell from 7.3 percent of the total to 5.1 percent between 1930 and 1940. Arthur M. Ross, "The Negro in the American Economy," in *Employment, Race, and Poverty*, ed. Arthur M. Ross and Herbert Hill (New York: Harcourt, Brace, and World, 1967), 15.

THREE: THE RISE AND REPRESSION OF INDUSTRIAL UNIONISM

1. Rayback, *A History of American Labor*, 327. See Irving Bernstein, *Turbulent Years: A History of the American Worker, 1933–1941* (Boston: Houghton Mifflin, 1970), 40–91 on the upsurge of unionization following enactment of 7(a).

2. Ed McCrea interview. For an account of the industrial conflicts of the thirties, see Bernstein, *The Turbulent Years*. For the difficulties in the South, see Tindall, *The Emergence of the New South*, chap. 10, or part 2 of Marc S. Miller, *Working Lives: The Southern Exposure History of Labor in the South* (New York: Pantheon, 1974), or Painter, *The Narrative of Hosea Hudson*.

3. On the AAA see Tindall, *Emergence of the New South*, chap. 12, and Donald H. Grubbs, *Cry from the Cotton: The Southern Tenant Farmers' Union and the New Deal*

(Chapel Hill: University of North Carolina Press, 1971), 19–25. H. L. Mitchell says the AAA pushed nine hundred thousand tenants off the land, *Mean Things*, 102. Also see Pete Daniel, "The Crossroads of Change: Cotton, Tobacco, and Rice Cultures in the Twentieth-Century South," *Journal of Southern History* 50, no. 3 (1984): 429–56.

4. Howard Kester, *Revolt among the Sharecroppers* (New York: Covici-Friede, 1936), 54–59. Estimates on the number of people killed in the Elaine riot vary; a full account is found in *The Crisis*, Dec. 1919. See George Stith interview in *Southern Exposure* 1, nos. 3–4 (Winter 1974): 18, 19, 29, on race relations in the STFU. Grubbs, *Cry from the Cotton*, 27–28, 66–68.

5. Grubbs, *Cry from the Cotton*, 91. Membership figure from Mitchell, *Mean Things*, 82. Accounts of the atrocities against the tenant farmers are in Dunbar, *Against the Grain*, 110–24, Mitchell, *Mean Things*, 61–74, 87–92, and Grubbs, *Cry from the Cotton*, 88–92 and chap. 4. See Dunbar, 108, 122, and J. R. Butler interview in *Southern Exposure* 1, nos. 3–4 (Winter 1974), on AFL and CIO lack of help, and Grubbs, 36–60, on the weakness of the federal government in the face of plantation Democrats.

6. John Handcox, personal interview, 16 May 1985, Silver Spring, Md. Dunbar, *Against the Grain*, 92, 123–24; Stith and Butler interviews; Foner and Lewis, eds., *The Black Worker*, vol. 5, *From Nineteen Hundred to Nineteen Nineteen* (Philadelphia: Temple University Press, 1980), 176, 628, and John Handcox poem in vol. 7, *From the Founding of the CIO*, 192; Mitchell, *Mean Things*, 91–92.

7. Mitchell, *Mean Things*, 52, 70, 89–90; Clay East in *Southern Exposure* 1, nos. 3–4 (Winter 1974), on Memphis. Grubbs, *Cry from the Cotton*, 57, 98, 118, and Dunbar, *Against the Grain*, 125, 129, on the weakness of federal intervention. Stuart M. Jamieson, *Labor Unionism in American Agriculture*, U.S. Department of Labor Bulletin 836 (Washington, D.C.: GPO, 1945), 312, 322 on the STFU's weakness as a bargaining agent.

8. Butler interview, 15; Clay East interview on the powerful role of blacks in the union, and Grubbs, *Cry from the Cotton*, 67–69, on cultural differences between black and white; Stith interview on the role of the black church and black women.

9. Estimate of 16,000, *MLR*, 22 Dec. 1933, and 20,000, 25 May 1934, and 11 May 1934 cites Googe's southern figure. Broadus Mitchell, in *Depression Decade: From New Era through New Deal, 1929–1941* (1947; reprint, White Plains, N.Y.: M. E. Sharpe, 1975), 273–74, points out the dramatic expansion of company unions under the NRA, covering some 2.5 million workers in 1935.

10. Mitchell, *Depression Decade*, see chap. 7, and 228–31 on the expansion of big business power over the economy. The *Blue Eagle*, organ of the NRA, described the voluntary program of the NRA as business "self-government," 11 June 1934, 2.

11. Therlough Grady to Gen. Hugh Johnson, 19 Sept. 1933, Classified General Files, Ser. 357—labor unions, NRA, RG 9, NARA. Tindall, *Emergence of the New South*, 442–45.

12. Holloway and Tillman interviews.

13. Rayback, *A History of American Labor*, 341.

14. *MLR*, 7 and 14 June 1935, and Brown-Melton, "Blacks in Memphis," 148.

15. *MLR*, 25 Jan., 17 May, and 19 and 23 Nov. 1934, on McCann, and 19 Apr. and 10 May 1934.

16. Rayback, *A History of American Labor*, 342.

17. According to labor educator Lawrence Rogin, the ITU always took a positive stance toward industrial unionism, partly because its members tended to move about

and obtain a wider exposure to trade union issues than most craft unionists. The ITU's president Charles Howard served as first secretary for the CIO. Rogin interview, 11 June 1981, Washington, D.C.

18. *MLR,* 14 June 1935.

19. *MLR,* 2 Aug. and 11 Oct. 1935; J. R. Steelman, "Summary of Final Report of Commissioner of Conciliation," 27 Oct. 1935, Mediation and Conciliation Service File 182–878, RG 280, NARA. Bernstein, *Turbulent Years,* 478–79, on the "Mohawk Valley formula."

20. Mediation and Conciliation Service File 182–878, RG 280, NARA, and *P-S,* 9 Oct. 1935, and final disposition of the case in Steelman, "Summary."

21. Newcomb Barco to H. L. Kerwin, 22 and 30 Jan. 1936, in Mediation and Conciliation Service File 182–878, RG 280, NARA, and *CA,* 16 and 18 Oct. 1935.

22. Allied Printing Trades Council President C. D. Blackney to Overton, 6 Apr. 1935, Drawer 5, Office of the Mayor's Papers, MPL. On the grocery strike and the fire fighter firings, see Newcomb Barco and C. L. Richardson correspondence, Mediation and Conciliation Service File 182-1272, RG 280, NARA. Also see *CA,* 14 and 15 Dec. 1935, *P-S,* 29 and 30 Jan. and 1 Feb. 1936, and Roger Biles, "Ed Crump Versus the Unions," 538–39. *P-S,* 5 Mar. 1936, on the mayor's letter, and H. S. Beverly to Edward S. Ragsdale, 2 Apr. 1936, and C. L. Richardson to Edward S. Ragsdale, 6 Apr. 1936, both in Mediation and Conciliation Service File 179–191, RG 280, NARA, on blacklisting. R. S. McCann to Frances Perkins, 11 Apr. 1936, Tennessee File, Office of the Secretary, USDL, RG 174, NARA, on the city's attacks on public employee unionism.

23. *Decisions and Orders of the NLRB* (Washington, D.C.: GPO, 1937), cases 118 and R-35, 3:28, on Memphis Furniture firings, and Mediation and Conciliation Service File 182-1344, RG 280, NARA, on failure to reinstate.

24. C. L. Richardson to Hugh L. Kerwin, 30 Apr. 1936, Mediation and Conciliation Service File 182-1272, RG 280, NARA.

25. Tillman interview. *P-S,* 15 Oct. 1937, on McCann's ouster; and Louisville *Courier-Journal,* 27 July 1939, on McCann's beating. E. H. Pewett, investigating labor corruption in Memphis, reported on the McCann beating, 8 Aug. 1939, Justice Department Anti-Trust Division File 60-12-47, RG 60, NARA.

26. On the TFL meeting, see James A. Hodges, "The Tennessee Federation of Labor, 1919–1939" (Master's thesis, Vanderbilt University, 1959), 179–87; *MLR,* 28 June, 27 Sept., and 11 Oct. 1935, on the danger of "reds" in the labor movement.

27. Dulles and Dubofsky, *Labor in America,* 279–83.

28. Ibid., 286–300, Rayback, *A History of American Labor,* 348–55, and Robert H. Zieger, *American Workers, American Unions, 1920–1985* (Baltimore: Johns Hopkins University Press, 1986), 46–61. Robert Tillman, in his interview, noted the significance of the Supreme Court decision to southern organizing.

29. Tillman commented on the illusory nature of white-collar privileges, interview; *Labor Journal* (Aug. 1956) gives a short history of the union; for contract terms, see *P-S,* 10 June 1937; Paul R. Coppock to Mayor Watkins Overton, 15 Sept. 1937, Office of the Mayor's Papers, MPL, on terms of unionization.

30. Paul Coppock, *P-S,* 25 Jan. 1976; *CA,* 9 June 1937, on membership in the Trades and Labor Council.

31. Lucy Randolph Mason, *To Win These Rights: A Personal Story of the CIO in the South* (1952; reprint, Westport, Conn.: Greenwood Press, 1972), 106; Tillman interview.

32. Jacquelyn Dowd Hall, "Disorderly Women: Gender and Labor Militancy in the Appalachian South," *Journal of American History* 73 (Sept. 1986): 354–82.

33. ILGWU leader David Dubinsky remained attached to the AFL even after joining in the CIO's formation, and in 1940 brought the union back into the AFL, Bernstein, *Turbulent Years*, 404–5, 708–9. *P-S*, 11 and 24 Mar. 1937, and *CA*, 9 Mar. 1937.

34. *P-S*, 22 Mar. 1937, and *CA*, 21 Mar. 1937.

35. *P-S*, 24 Mar. 1937. See also *P-S*, 26 Mar. 1937, and *CA*, 25 Mar. 1937. Also see Biles, "Ed Crump Versus the Unions," 542.

36. *P-S*, 27 Mar. and 10 Apr. 1937, and *CA*, 6, 14, and 19 Apr. 1937.

37. *CA*, 27 Mar. and 6 Apr. 1937. *P-S*, 27 Apr. 1937.

38. Foner, *Organized Labor and the Black Worker*, 204–12, on the futile efforts to change AFL racial policy.

39. According to F. Ray Marshall, in 1933 blacks accounted for 8.5 percent of all iron and steelworkers, 17 percent of the semiskilled and unskilled workers in slaughter- and packinghouse industries, 68 percent of the tobacco workers of the upper South, and 9.2 percent of the nation's coal miners. *The Negro and Organized Labor*, 35–36. Cayton and Mitchell cite the 60 percent figure in Alabama, *Black Workers*, 323, and see 321–22. Philip Taft, *Organizing Dixie*, 82–95.

40. Tillman interview.

41. *P-S*, 9 and 10 Mar. 1937.

42. *P-S*, 16 Mar. 1937.

43. Mediation and Conciliation Service File 199-1033, RG 280, NARA, on Southern Cotton Oil; *P-S*, 11 Mar. 1937, and Mediation and Conciliation Service File 199-23, RG 280, NARA, on the Chickasaw strike; and *CA*, 22 Mar. 1937.

44. *P-S*, 18 Aug. 1937, and *CA*, 20 Aug. 1937, on the mop and handle workers, and Kate Born, "Memphis Negro Workingmen and the NAACP," 104, on the Kroger incident.

45. Schuyler wrote a series of articles for the Pittsburgh *Courier* on black union organizing, reprinted in *From the Founding of the CIO*, ed. Foner and Lewis, 87–98.

46. Ibid. A. A. Harrison of Painters' Local 49 to N. A. Tolles of the U.S. Labor Department, 28 Jan. 1936, indicates the lowly and disregarded position of black painters within the union. Md-Mz File, 1935–36, Tennessee 641, WPA Correspondence Files, WPA, RG 69, NARA. Born, "Memphis Negro Workingmen and the NAACP," 104, notes the hostility to blacks trying to change the AFL unions.

47. *CA*, 17 Aug. 1937. *CA*, 6 and 11 Aug. 1937.

48. Overton to Crump, 13 Aug. 1937, Box 3, Overton Papers, MVC/MSU. The *P-S* noted the lack of indictments in the McCullough case, 11 Aug. 1937. *P-S*, 17 June 1937.

49. *CA*, 19 Sept. 1937. Davis and Jaspoon statements, *CA*, 20 Sept. 1937. Smith's announcement, *P-S*, 7 Sept. 1937.

50. Tillman interview, whose version of events is consistent with newspaper accounts cited earlier. Bernstein, *The Turbulent Years*, 737.

51. *P-S*, 23 Sept. 1937, *CA*, 30 Sept. 1937; *P-S* and *CA*, 6 Oct. 1937. See also Mason's account, *To Win These Rights*, 104–5. Miller, *Mr. Crump*, 213. J. R. Steelman to Francis Perkins, 8 Oct. 1937, describes the mayor's intransigent attitude. Mediation and Conciliation Service File 199-603, RG 280, NARA. This file also contains the UAW telegrams. Browning to Norman Thomas, 28 Sept. 1937, WDL File 24, Box 39, Reuther Library. Lee quote in *P-S*, 6 Oct. 1937.

52. *P-S,* 9 Nov. 1937.

53. For the Frantz incident see *P-S,* 1 Dec. 1937; John Clarence Petrie, "Memphis Arrests CIO Investigator," *Christian Century* (15 Dec. 1937): 1571–72; Gelders to Harriet Young, 16 Dec. 1937, WDL File 27, Box 39, Reuther Library; Leroy Clark, personal interview, 27 Mar. 1983, Memphis.

54. John Clarence Petrie, *Christian Century* (13 Oct. 1937): 41.

55. Joseph Gelders to Harriet Young, 16 Dec. 1937, and Young to Gardner Jackson, 11 Dec. 1937, both in WDL File 27, Box 39, Reuther Library. Laurent Frantz, "People's Rights in Memphis," Ms., Ralph Bunche Papers, Special Collections, University of California–Los Angeles Library, courtesy of Robin Kelley; Mitchell, *Mean Things,* 78, 199; see also Young to Jackson on Fowler's departure.

56. Mason, *To Win These Rights,* 50–53; *P-S,* 12 July 1937, and *CA,* 13 July 1937.

57. *P-S,* 15, 27, and 28 Sept. 1937; Robert Fox to J. R. Steelman, 29 Apr. 1938, relating the department store organizing, Mediation and Conciliation Service File 199-1284, RG 280, NARA; Tillman interview on the fate of the dress companies; *P-S,* 10 Nov. 1937, on the departure of Ida Sledge.

58. Frantz, "People's Rights."

59. Ibid. Nelson Lichtenstein emphasizes the swing to the right as the result of the 1938 election and the particular role of southern Democrats in weakening congressional liberalism. *Labor's War at Home: The CIO in World War II* (Cambridge: Cambridge University Press, 1982), 19. See also Mike Davis, "The Barren Marriage of American Labour and the Democratic Party," *New Left Review* 124 (Nov.–Dec. 1980): 43–84. Also see David Milton, *The Politics of U.S. Labor from the Great Depression to the New Deal* (New York: Monthly Review Press, 1982), 117–20.

FOUR: BLACK AND WHITE UNITE

1. *City Directory* on union memberships (Memphis: R. L. Polk, 1938); Watkins Overton to Crump, 8 Aug. 1938, Folder 55, Overton Papers, MVC/MSU; Mediation and Conciliation Service File 199-1209 on the Teamsters strike, and File 199-2222 on the Brewery strike, RG 280, NARA.

2. Coe and Holloway interviews.

3. According to one recent article on the 1866 Memphis riot, business owners and the police, not the workers, led the attacks. Altina L. Waller, "Community, Class, and Race in the Memphis Riot of 1866," *Journal of Social History* 18, no. 2 (Winter 1984): 233–46. Black workers in 1877 organized and struck the docks and obtained support on Aug. 3 from two to three hundred workers, "including brickmakers, draymen, and mechanics," according to Shirley Ayer, in "Labor Is the Community," 23. It does not appear that these early organizing efforts survived, however.

4. David Montgomery, *The Fall of the House of Labor: The Workplace, the State, and American Labor Activism, 1865–1925* (New York: Cambridge University Press, 1987), 105–9. Foner, *Organized Labor and the Black Worker,* 66–68; Lester Rubin and William S. Smith, "The Negro in the Longshore Industry," in *Negro Employment in the Maritime Industries,* ed. Lester Rubin, William S. Smith, and Herbert R. Northrup (Philadelphia: Wharton School, University of Pennsylvania, 1974), 15–16, 100, 113, 123, and 101–3, 126, 154; Spero and Harris, *The Black Worker,* 183–86, 191–92. And see Eric Arnesen's deeply textured account, *Waterfront Workers of New Orleans.*

5. Material on the 1939 strike is drawn largely from various files of the IWC/DC, mostly in Boxes 6 and 7, RG 91, NARA. "Report," 20 May 1939, Reports File, Box 7, IWC/DC, RG 91, NARA, says the Memphis terminal was one of its largest. See also "Port of Memphis on the Mississippi River" (Memphis: Harbor Commission, Memphis Chamber of Commerce, 1939), MPL.

6. On wages, see "Report," n.d., Reports File, Box 7; "Report," 20 May 1938 on Memphis; Felix Siren to David Niles, 21 June 1939 and "Extracts from Circular Letters" enclosed in the Wages and Hours File, Box 7; "Barge Line Arbitration, April 1938" Arbitration File, Box 6, all in IWC/DC, RG 91, NARA.

7. Felix Siren to David Niles, 21 June 1939, enclosing a list of wages, Wages and Hours File, Box 7, IWC/DC, RG 91, NARA; *The Pilot,* 19 May 1939, on long hours; and the East St. Louis *Journal,* 27 Apr. 1939, on eight cents an hour; Leonard W. Arthur and Pat Matthews to Franklin Roosevelt, 12 May 1939, Contracts File, Box 6, IWC/DC, RG 91, NARA; W. E. Davis interview; and " 'Federal Barge Lines' Using Scab Herding," leaflet in File 1602-8-1, Justice Department, RG 60, NARA, on bad conditions.

8. Siren to Niles; W. E. Davis, phone interview, 17 June 1984; *Chicago Tribune,* 4 May 1939.

9. Memo, "Barge Line Arbitration, April 1938," Arbitration File, Box 6, IWC/DC, RG 91, NARA, suggests the IBU's development of shoreside interracial unions in Baton Rouge, New Orleans, Vicksburg, and Helena. W. E. Davis and Morton Davis both related the difficulties in opening up all jobs on the boats to blacks, W. E. Davis interview, and Morton Davis interview, 26 Jan. 1983, St. Louis. *Chicago Tribune,* 4 May 1939. "Barge Line Arbitration, April, 1938," Arbitration File, Box 6, IWC/DC, RG 91, NARA.

10. Petition of Fifty-three Memphis dockworkers, 7 July 1937, Mediation and Conciliation Service File 199/95, RG 280, NARA.

11. *Strike Bulletin,* 4 May 1939, Folder 25, Box 39, WDL, Reuther Library. Both the IBU and the ILA called for removal of Major General T. Q. Ashburn, head of the Federal Barge Line, as well as General Superintendent of Terminals Glenn E. Taylor, New Orleans District Superintendent L. E. Barry, and Superintendent of Transportation C. E. Patton in Memphis. Felix Siren and Harold Spies public letter to Louis Johnson, Assistant Secretary of War, 24 Apr. 1939, File 16-208-1, IWC/DC, RG 91, NARA. On FBL expansion, see *CA,* 26 May 1937.

12. W. E. Davis interview. J. W. Savage report, 16 May 1939, File 16-208-1, Criminal Division, Justice Department, RG 60, NARA. Mason to Roosevelt, 9 Jan. 1941, relates Warner and Tamble's reputations as whiskey runners. Their firm first dominated the river, after a fire wrecked the Hanrahan Bridge, for a time leaving their tow boats as the only transportation across the river to Arkansas, *P-S,* 2 June 1973, and *CA,* 28 Feb. 1974. Tamble killed Everett Jackson in a gunfight in the De Soto Hotel, which Tamble owned, according to the *CA,* 14 June 1933.

13. "Annual Report of the Inland Waterways Corporation, 1937," Reference Material, Box 2, IWC/DC, RG 91, NARA. Thomas Watkins to U.S. Attorney General Frank Murphy, 12 Aug. 1939, File 144-72-0, Criminal Division, Justice Department, RG 60, NARA. On the July strike, see *CA,* 11 and 14 July 1937, *P-S,* 10 July 1937, and Mediation Conciliation Service File 199-95, RG 280, NARA.

14. "Annual Report"; Savage report; *P-S,* 26 and 27 Oct. 1937.

15. Hugh Friel, "Progress Report," 16 Dec. 1937, Mediation and Conciliation Ser-

vice File 199-979, RG 280, NARA. *P-S,* 2 Dec. 1937, and *CA,* 16 Dec. 1937; reports of the federal mediator in Mediation and Conciliation Service File 199-979; Savage report.

16. See the rather complicated history of the longshore and maritime organizational efforts from 1935 to 1938, in Bernstein, *The Turbulent Years,* 572–89. Ferdinand Smith addressed NMU efforts to deal with the racial problem in *The Pilot,* 3 Mar. 1939; Bridges and others in the ILWU also attempted to fight racial discrimination on the waterfronts, though with less success, according to Rubin and Swift, "The Negro in the Longshore Industry," 141, 104, 115; Marshall, *The Negro and Organized Labor,* 99–100; W. E. Davis, phone interview, 17 June 1984; on the 1938 strike see Annual Report of the Inland Waterways Corporation, 1938, Reference Material, Box 2, IWC/DC, RG 91, NARA.

17. Watkins described the various roles he played on the waterfront to FBI agent Scott Alden, who reported to his superior J. Edgar Hoover on 24 May 1939, in Classified Subject Correspondence File 16-208-1, Department of Justice, RG 60, NARA. The ILA listed locals 1506, 1539, 1549, and 1595 in Memphis, but did not list local 1490. *Proceedings,* ILA Thirty-second Convention, New York, 10–14 July 1939, in UDSL Library.

18. Descriptions of Watkins vary, but he clearly was a powerfully built man with great energy. SAC in Portland to the Director, 25 and 28 Aug. and 2 Oct. 1950, FBI/ *FOIA* 250,181-001, provides background on Watkins's life history. Napolean Jilks and friend Luke, personal interview, 16 Aug. 1989, Portland, Ore. Oregon State Health Division Certificate of Death, 16 May 1989, lists Watkins's birth as 5 June 1904, contrary to FBI reports of a 1910 birth date. Other details from Portland SA to the Director, 28 Aug. 1973, FBI/FOIA 250,181-001, and police blotter, dated 23 Aug. 1939, File 144-72-0, Criminal Division, Justice Department, RG 60, NARA. Russell Warner mentioned the police beating, Savage report, 17. The Memphis *City Directory* (Memphis: R. L. Polk, 1939) for 1939 lists Watkins as a laborer at 69 W. De Soto, and in 1944 lists ILA Locals 1490 and 1549 at 27 W. De Soto. The IBU Hall was located at 279 W. California.

19. The quote from Warner is in the words of Savage; see Savage report, 4, 7, 8, 17.

20. Nebraska Jones to Lt. Oxley, 27 June 1939, and related correspondence, Conciliation Service File, Division of Negro Labor, USDL, RG 183, NARA. Jones is also quoted in Bunche, *Political Status of the Negro,* 52. Searcy wrote about the "Americanism" committee to John Beecher, who related the incident in his 1942 report, "Training and Employment of Negroes in Memphis, Tennessee," John Beecher Files, FEPC, RG 228, NARA. Herbert Northrup related threats against the Urban League by the AFL in *Organized Labor and the Negro* (1944; reprint, New York: Harper and Row, 1976), 44–45. And see Brown-Melton, "Blacks in Memphis," 155–56.

21. Watkins to Attorney General Frank Murphy, on his version of events, 31 Aug. 1939, File 144-72-0, Justice Department, RG 60, NARA; J. C. Howard "Final Report," 14 Mar. 1939, on the dangerous situation and Watkins to R. A. Walton and Joseph Ryan, 28 Feb. 1939, opposing Loring's settlement, both in Mediation and Conciliation Service File 199-3247, RG 280, NARA.

22. "Affidavit," Thomas Watkinz [*sic*], n.d., File 144-72-0, Justice Department, RG 60, NARA, and *CA,* 15 Apr. 1939.

23. *CA,* 15 Apr. 1939, *P-S,* 21 Apr. 1939; police blotter, 23 Aug. 1939; *MLR,* 14 Apr. 1939.

24. *CA,* 15 Apr. 1939, and *MLR,* 14 Apr. 1939.

25. Davis interviews, Notes in Arbitration File, Box 6, and Reports File, Box 7; and

Siren to David Niles, Assistant to the Secretary of Commerce, 9 June 1939, Wages and Hours File, Box 7, all in IWC/DC, RG 91, NARA.

26. "Strike Bulletin," 4 May 1939, File 25, Box 39, WDL, Reuther Library. Petition of strikers to the Secretary of Commerce and Secretary of War, n.d., Petition File, Box 7, IWC/DC, RG 91, NARA, on declaration of war; East St. Louis *Journal,* 25 Apr. 1939; Felix Siren and Harold Spies to Louis Johnson, Assistant Secretary of War, 24 Apr. 1939, Contracts File, Box 6, IWC/DC, RG 91, NARA. *The Pilot,* 5 and 19 May 1939, and Felix Siren, secretary-treasurer of the IBU, charged that the refusal of shippers to make settlements was designed to break the unions, Siren and Spies to Johnson, 24 Apr. 1939; *The Pilot,* 5 May 1939; East St. Louis *Journal,* 27 and 28 Apr. 1939, on the numbers of strikers.

27. General Council of Riverworkers letterhead, Felix Siren and Harold Spies to Louis Johnson, 24 Apr. 1939, and East St. Louis *Journal* 27 and 28 Apr. 1938.

28. Loring quoted in Watkins FBI affidavit. *MLR,* 12 May 1939. Scott Alden report, 24 May 1939, File 16-208-1, Justice Department, RG 60, NARA. A *CA* press account of 28 Apr. 1939 confirms that the ILA's Memphis walkout came after orders from the Chicago headquarters of the ILA. Loring's version and Googe's telegram are in Savage report, 14; comments on the role of Googe, Savage report, 9; Police Chief Lee, like Patton, believed that Watkins wanted to lead his local into the CIO, and had made a trip to St. Louis in 1938 for that purpose, Savage report, 21.

29. Bruno quoted in Savage report, 3. Smith to David Clendenin, 2 May 1939, Folder 25, Box 39, WDL, Reuther Library. Patton comments from SA Matthew McGuire to J. E. Hoover, 8 May 1939, File 16-208-1, Justice Department, RG 60, NARA; FBL ad in *CA,* 9 May 1939; Patton request and Watkins response in *CA,* 6 May 1939; Googe effort mentioned by SA McGuire to Hoover, 8 May 1939, File 16-208-1, Justice Department, RG 60, NARA, and Savage tells of response, Savage report, 14.

30. *CA,* 6 May 1939. Details on the guard's story are in Savage report, 10–11, 15–16, 19. J. Edgar Hoover to Assistant Attorney General Matthew McGuire, 29 May 1939, relates the anonymous phone call claiming Watkins cut the barges loose. H. R. Odell to Major General T. Q. Ashburn, 6 May 1939, confirmed the original story that the masked men were white, both in File 16-208-1, Justice Department, RG 60, NARA.

31. Smith to David Clendenin, 9 May 1939, Folder 25, Box 39, WDL, Reuther Library; telegram from the "Memphis Council for Freedom and Democracy," numerous postcards to Attorney General Frank Murphy from dockworkers asking for the removal of Barge Line officials, and numerous other letters in File 16-208-1, Justice Department, RG 60, NARA, indicate the concerted effort made to enforce civil liberties during the 1939 strike; *P-S,* 10 May 1939; U.S. Attorney Toxey Hall to Brien McMahon, Assistant U.S. Attorney, 9 May 1939, also in File 16-208-1. On white picketers, see Savage report, 13.

32. Savage report on Loring's use of scab labor, which was well under way by May 9, see 15, 19; L. H. Barnard report, 18 May 1939, tells of the recruitment of the *Vicksburg* crew, 23–25; J. Edgar Hoover Memorandum, 9 May 1939, reports on the same incident, and also confirms the use of scab labor by Loring in Memphis; and U.S. Attorney Henry C. Blanton memo, 3 May 1939, reported the story of five hundred workers; Brien McMahon to Mr. McGuire, 4 May 1939, passed on the report that workers threw the captain overboard. A picture of the *Vicksburg* crew shows five black and thirteen white workers, all in File 16-208-1, Justice Department, RG 60, NARA.

33. M. R. Wilson affidavit, 29 May 1939, and corroborated by H. H. Duke affidavit, 29 May 1939, both in Affidavits File, Box 6, IWC/DC, RG 91, NARA. *CA*, 9 May 1939; see also Felix Siren to David K. Niles, 19 May 1939, File 16-208-1, Justice Department, RG 60, NARA, and Barnard report, 28.

34. Mobile incident detailed in affidavits by Herman Wonzy, Cora Lee Jones, John Kewley, M. M. Pearson, et al., and A. B. Kendricks, 9 May 1939, Affidavits File, Box 6, IWC/DC, RG 91, NARA. See materials on the same incidents in File 16-208-1, Justice Department, RG 60, NARA. On New Orleans incident, see J. Edgar Hoover to Acting Assistant Attorney General Matthew McGuire, 9 May 1939, in same file. Siren to All Agents and Members, 9 June 1939, Contract File, Box 6, IWC/DC, RG 91, NARA.

35. *Chicago Tribune*, 5 May 1939. See also the complaints of pilot C. S. Hamilton on the Steamer Cairo to Maj. T. Q. Ashburn, and H. R. Odell to Ashburn, both on 3 May 1939, IWC/DC, RG 91, NARA. An earlier strike in 1935 had been plagued by violence. See Wood, "To Live and Die in Dixie," 10. Also see a series of memos from the FBL superintendent in New Orleans, L. E. Berry, about the 1935 strike, in File 16-208-1, Justice Department, RG 60, NARA.

36. See Brien McMahon, Assistant Attorney, to Harry C. Blanton, 3 May 1939, File 16-208-1, Justice Department, RG 60, NARA. Barnard report, 25–26.

37. The FBI rejected the appeals of Superintendent Patton of Memphis for protection for scab laborers on the boats, Barnard report, 25. *Chicago Tribune*, 4 May 1939.

38. *The Pilot*, 12 May and 2 June 1939.

39. W. E. Davis, phone interview, 14 Jan. 1986. Siren to All Agents and Members, 9 June 1939, emphasized the importance of the Memphis ILA's steady support for the strike despite the AFL's effort to crush it.

40. Watkins to Murphy, and Watkins affidavit. Watkins was consistent and meticulous in his accounts of the events of 1939 in both documents. His version of events is verified by N. B. Wright report, 27 May 1939, File 16-208-1, Justice Department, RG 60, NARA. See also the *CA* account, 13 May 1939.

41. Siren to All Agents and Members; comments at the second national convention, *Proceedings*, 244. And see the agreements signed by Siren and G. E. Taylor, General Superintendent of FBL, Contracts File, Box 6, IWC/DC, RG 91, NARA.

42. Watkins to Murphy, 15 Aug. 1939, File 144-72-0, Justice Department, RG 60, NARA, and Alden report quoting Watkins, 2.

43. Accounts of the attempted murder include Watkins to Murphy, received 12 Aug. 1939, File 144-72-0, Justice Department, RG 60, NARA; Watkins affidavit; and Wright report; see Wright report on witnesses, 14 June 1939, and on medical examination, 27 May 1939; R. G. Draper to Murphy, 3 Aug. 1939, File 144-72-0, Justice Department, RG 60, NARA.

44. Watkins did not know why Taylor, who knew him as an AFL leader, described him as a CIO man. Watkins to Murphy, July 1939, Ms. 265, Watkins, Tom, Subject File, Folder 13, Box 76, Highlander Folk School records, WHS. Msgr. Francis J. Haas verified the attempts of officials, especially in New Orleans, to sabotage the strike settlement by discriminating against union workers during hiring, see his reports in Box 6, and Felix Siren to Major General T. Q. Ashburn, 27 June 1939, L File, Box 6; G. E. Taylor to Ashburn, 7 July 1939, on Orleans and Mobile, Box 6; Siren to David K. Niles, 15 July 1939, Violations File, Box 7, on commanders and mates; Arthur E. Phillips, IBU Assistant

Secretary-Treasurer, to Ashburn, 17 June 1939, Arbitration File, Box 6, on Henderson, all in IWC/DC, RG 91, NARA.

45. Watkins to Murphy, 31 Aug. 1939; affidavits of George V. Harrison, 30 June, and William Carter, 26 June 1939, Affidavits File, Box 6, IWC/DC, RG 91, NARA. See File 16-208-1, Justice Department, RG 60, NARA, for various allegations of civil liberties violations brought to the FBI. While all allegations are not verified, reports of agents J. C. Strikland, 11 May 1939, and C. W. Dunker, 8 May 1939, both from New Orleans, substantiate many of the reports of company-inspired violence, as do a number of accounts of the post-strike events cited in the next several paragraphs. See File 16-208-1, Justice Department, RG 60, NARA. The NMU's local in Baytown, Texas, came under attacks by vigilantes, while one of the union leaders in the Gulf district disappeared, with members sure he had been thrown into the Mississippi. *The Pilot*, 23 and 30 June 1939.

46. *IBU News*, 21 June 1939. Memo of IWC official enclosed with W. C. Carter, IBU Gulf organizer, to Niles, Assistant Secretary of Commerce, 12 July 1939, Violations File, Box 7, and note enclosed with affidavit of Cora Lee Jones, Arbitration File, Box 6, on official responses to the Scott and Wonzy incidents. Handwritten note of Ashburn on Siren to Ashburn, 27 June 1939, L File, Box 6, all in IWC/DC, RG 91, NARA.

47. Johnson to Ashburn, 19 Sept. 1939, calling for an end to anti-union activities, and Johnson to L. W. Childress, 5 May 1940, Thompson File, Box 13; St. Louis report, 22 Aug. 1939, Reports File, Box 7, on lack of wage increases; "Resolution of the Gulf District," IBU Division of the NMU, St. Louis, 10 Aug. 1939, to David K. Niles, Assistant to the Secretary of Commerce, Box 6, on long hours, all in IWC/DC, RG 91, NARA. Drew Pearson, "Washington Merry-Go-Round," *Times Herald*, 22 Nov. 1939, on the Ashburn scandals.

48. Address of Thompson to Twenty-third Annual Convention of the Mississippi Valley Association, 28 Oct. 1941, St. Louis, Thompson Speech File, Box 8, IWC/DC, RG 91, NARA, on modernization.

49. Contract, enclosed in Thompson to Niles, 18 May 1939, on Memphis locals; Thompson to Sec. of Commerce, 20 Dec. 1940, on 1940–41 wage increases; "Annual Report of the Inland Waterways Corporation, 1940," Reference Material, all in Box 2, IWC/DC, RG 91, NARA.

50. Ibid. on ILA contracts; and Memo of phone conversation, M. C. Foster and C. C. Thompson, 21 Dec. 1940, Thompson File, Box 8, and Thompson to the Sec. of Commerce, 20 Dec. 1940, Labor File, Box 13, on long hours; C. S. Murray Memo, 3 Aug. 1942, Labor File, Box 13, all in IWC/DC, RG 91, NARA, on improvements under the War Labor Board.

51. W. E. Davis interview and Lawrence McGurty, personal interview, 17 Jan. 1983, Hometown, Ill.

52. In 1983 I attempted to interview one of the ILA local leaders, but he so feared to speak of the union's current conditions or its past that I could never arrange a meeting. ILA president Joseph Ryan was "elected" to a life term presidency in 1943, and the ILA in New York under his tutelage became "steeped in crime and corruption," according to Rubin and Swift, in "The Negro in the Longshore Industry," 21–22.

53. Chester C. Thompson to the Secretary of Commerce, 18 Oct. 1940, Thompson Speech File, Box 8. And see C. C. Thompson to M. Kerlin, 17 July 1941, Thompson File,

Box 13, both in IWC/DC, RG 91, NARA, on modernization in Helena and St. Louis. Technological change in longshore work generally tended to displace black workers, see Rubin and Swift, "The Negro in the Longshore Industry."

54. Mason to Attorney General Robert Jackson, 16 Oct. 1940, and Mason to Roosevelt, 14 Oct. and 9 Jan. 1941, all in Mason Papers, OD. Superintendent for thirty years, John Murphy took over the Warner-Tamble operations in 1973. These then included a fleet of sixteen towboats, one of the largest operations on the river, and still nonunion. *CA*, 3 June 1973.

55. On Thomas Watkins, File 10104-1570/125, Frank Bruno, Correspondence 1917– 41, MID, RG 165, NARA; FBI file on Watkins, FOIA 250,181-001; and personal interviews, Bertha and Napolean Jilks, 14 Aug. 1989, and Luke, 17 Aug. 1989, Portland, Ore. Napolean, a dockworker, knew Watkins since 1942 and Luke roomed with him during his later years. Watkins died of congestive heart failure on 5 Apr. 1988, Oregon State Health Division Certificate of Death, 16 May 1989.

FIVE: RACE, RADICALISM, AND THE CIO

1. See Dunbar on southern radicals, in *Against the Grain,* and Sitkoff on the growth of antifascism and antiracism, in *A New Deal for Blacks,* chaps. 6 and 7.

2. Johnson, "The Reds in Dixie," 32, on social equality. Painter, *The Narrative of Hosea Hudson;* Kelley, *Hammer and Hoe;* Bert Cochran contends "politicized" Communist-led strikes in the South were a disaster for workers in *Labor and Communism: The Conflict That Shaped American Unions* (Princeton: Princeton University Press, 1977), 53. But Jim Garland, who was intimately involved in the Harlan County strike, points out that despite frequently incompetent leadership, Communists were the only ones who would support Harlan workers, see *Welcome the Traveler Home,* chaps. 15 and 16. Also see Tindall, *The Emergence of the New South,* 383–86, Fred A. Beal, *Proletarian Journey: New England, Gastonia, Moscow* (New York: 1937), and Theodore Rosengarten, *All God's Dangers: The Life of Nat Shaw* (New York: Avon Books, 1974), for accounts of Communist labor organizing in the South. Also very useful as a general framework is Mark Naison, *Communists in Harlem during the Great Depression* (New York: Grove Press, 1983).

3. The Socialist party's Clarence Senior, after a tour of the South, felt that even in industrial Birmingham the party's situation seemed "hopeless," and apparently only the branches in Memphis and Knoxville remained viable. "Notes on Southern Tour of Paul Porter and Clarence Senior, May 1935," File 7, William Amberson Papers, MVC/ MSU. Party membership did not significantly revive after this. Dunbar, *Against the Grain,* chap. 3; Kester, *Revolt among the Sharecroppers. Recent History of the Labor Movement in the United States, 1918–1939* (Moscow: Progress Publishers, 1977), 274– 86, provides some of the history of Communist party/Socialist party cooperation. See Sitkoff on growing interest in the Socialist party left in racial discrimination, *A New Deal for Blacks,* 140–63. Horton was an executive member of the Tennessee Socialist party, which held its state convention at Monteagle in 1932, and most of Highlander's staff held explicitly socialist views. Ser. 3, General Correspondence, Tennessee Socialist Party Papers, MVC/MSU, microfilm. See Frank Adams, *Unearthing Seeds of Fire: The Idea of Highlander* (Charlotte, N.C.: n.p., 1975). Useful dissertations on Highlander

have been written by Anne Petty, Amy Horton, and see John Glen, *Highlander: No Ordinary School, 1931–1962* (Lexington: University Press of Kentucky, 1988).

4. According to Myles Horton the primary purpose of the Southern Conference was to involve southern liberals in support of the CIO and later the civil rights movement, personal interview, 1 June 1983, New Market, Tenn. See Clark Foreman's account, "The Decade of Hope," in *The Negro in Depression and War: Prelude to Revolution, 1930–1945*, ed. Bernard Sternsher (Chicago: Quadrangle Books, 1969), 150–65; Thomas A. Krueger, *And Promises to Keep: The Southern Conference for Human Welfare, 1938–1948* (Nashville: Vanderbilt University Press, 1967); and see Robin Kelley's discussion of the SNYC, *Hammer and Hoe*, chap. 11. For a somewhat cynical account of the Communist party in the thirties, see Harvey Klehr, *The Heyday of American Communism: The Depression Decade* (New York: Basic Books, 1984), and likewise Bert Cochran, *Labor and Communism: The Conflict That Shaped American Unionism* (Princeton: Princeton University Press, 1977). A more balanced account is Harvey Levenstein, *Communism, Anti-Communism, and the CIO* (Westport, Conn.: Greenwood Press, 1981).

5. See Marshall's discussion of the various forces influencing CIO policies, *The Negro and Organized Labor*, 34–40.

6. See Foner, *Organized Labor and the Black Worker*, 229–30, and see 215–30, and Marshall, *The Negro and Organized Labor*, 35–37, on the relationship between black workers, the Left, and the CIO. See also August Meier and Elliott Rudwick, *Black Detroit and the Rise of the UAW* (New York: Oxford University Press, 1979).

7. Red Davis's father had begun working on the rivers at age thirteen. He eventually became a pilot and then a captain, and ended up in Memphis. McGurty (brother-in-law of Red Davis) interview. W. E. Davis interview.

8. W. E. Davis interview.

9. Ibid.

10. On NMU anti-discrimination policy, see the National Council resolution printed in *The Pilot*, 1 Apr. 1939; Ferdinand Smith's articles, *The Pilot*, 21 and 31 Mar. 1939, and in *Opportunity*, Apr. 1940, reprinted in *From the Founding of the CIO*, ed. Foner and Lewis, 135–38. See also Foner, *Organized Labor and the Black Worker*, 226–27, 458. Resolutions of the NMU, 1940–41, in Foner, *Organized Labor and the Black Worker*, 458, and "Resolutions of IBD" enclosed in Felix Siren to All Inland Boatmen, 10 Sept. 1940, *NMU Proceedings*, USDL Library.

11. W. E. Davis interview.

12. W. E. Davis and McGurty interviews.

13. Bruno became port agent in St. Louis, left the party in the late forties, and died at age sixty-five. Himmaugh and Despaux worked out of New Orleans and Louisville, respectively. Interviews with W. E. Davis, Ed McCrea, and McGurty.

14. W. E. Davis and McGurty interviews, and Morton Davis interview.

15. Ed McCrea interview; Harry Koger deposition, 2 Sept. 1941, FBI/FOIA 100-33752-1.

16. Koger worked in Memphis, Texas, Arkansas, and in other parts of the South for UCAPAWA, eventually resettling in Texas, where his daughter Mary Lou Ford continued to live after his death. Harry Koger deposition, 2 Sept. 1941, Memphis, enclosed in an FBI report dated 15 Oct. 1941, FBI/FOIA 100-33752-1, and correspondence between Williams and Koger in the Claude Williams Papers, Reuther Library.

17. W. E. Davis interview.

18. Ed McCrea interview. In contrast with McCrea's estimate, Harvey Klehr cites a Tennessee membership of ninety-nine in June 1937, based on a national membership report of the party. *Heyday*, 380. The *Labor Journal* (Aug. 1956) discussion of the history of the CIO in Memphis acknowledges the early role of UCAPAWA and the NMU.

19. W. E. Davis interview on Dyson. Ed McCrea remembered a young Communist at the Wabash company who helped to build the local on the basis of his ability to make rousing speeches. Roy Pierson described the establishment of the local there to the Highlander School in 1940. Whether he is the character McCrea recalled or had anything to do with the Communist party is unknown. Frames 27–28, Reel 32, "The Life of a Free Lance Organizer," Highlander Folk School Newsletter, Fall Term 1940, OD microfilm.

20. Ed McCrea interview. The anticommunist consensus of the fifties and sixties denigrated the Left's strongest contributions to the labor and reform movements of the depression era, including its antiracist emphasis. See for example Hubert Humphrey's introduction and Max Kampleman's book, *The Communist Party Vs. the C.I.O.: A Study in Power Politics* (New York: Frederick A. Praeger, 1957), and Wilson Record for the consensus treatment of the Communists and the racial issue, in *The Negro and the Communist Party* (1951; reprint, New York: Atheneum, 1971), and *Race and Radicalism: The NAACP and the Communist Party in Conflict* (Ithaca: Cornell University Press, 1964). For a review of literature on anticommunism as it relates to the CIO, see James R. Prickett, "Anti-Communism and Labor History," *Industrial Relations* 13 (1974): 219–27, and "Communists and the Communist Issue in the American Labor Movement, 1920–1950" (Ph.D. diss., University of California–Los Angeles, 1975).

21. Ed McCrea interview. W. E. Davis, like McCrea, understood Lynch to have been a member of the Communist party, a fact no one can verify since Lynch himself is dead. W. E. Davis interview.

22. Ed McCrea recalled this red-baiting going back to his days as a child in Cambridge, Maryland, but felt it accelerated after the formation of the Dies Committee. Personal interview.

23. Morton Davis interview. Cash quoted in Foner, *Organized Labor and the Black Worker*, 230. FBI Special Agent on Harry Koger, FBI/FOIA 100-33752-1. Horton interview. Harvey Levenstein, like Myles Horton, concluded that workers "were not particularly anti-Communist. . . . If Communist leaders could achieve these [union] objectives as well or better than others, they would support them." *Communism, Anti-Communism, and the CIO*, 30.

24. Ed McCrea interview.

25. Dan Powell personal interview, 1 Feb. 1983, Memphis. "Proceedings," UCAPAWA Third Annual Convention, Chicago, 61, brochure, WHS.

26. Mitchell interviewed by the Institute for Southern Studies, in *Southern Exposure* 1, nos. 3–4 (Winter 1974): 28. *P-S*, 29 Sept. 1937, reported on this meeting. NAACP traveler report in Born, "Memphis Negro Workingmen and the NAACP," 106.

27. See Bernstein, *The Turbulent Years*, 143–70, and Kelley, *Hammer and Hoe*, especially chap. 2, on repression of organizers. For greater detail on the falling out between the STFU and the CIO, see Honey, "Labor and Civil Rights in the South," 219–23, 249–50; H. L. Mitchell's comments in *Mean Things*, 153–63, 164–73; Grubbs, *Cry from the Cotton*, 81–84 and 163–72; Mark Naison, "The Southern Tenant Farmer's Union

and the CIO," in *American Labor Radicalism: Testimonies and Interpretations*, ed. Staughton Lund (New York: John Wiley and Sons, 1973); issues of *STFU News*, especially May 1938; Dunbar, *Against the Grain*, 164–85; Jamieson, *Labor Unionism*, 315.

28. *Official Proceedings*, UCAPAWA First National Convention, July 9–12, 1937, Denver, and *Official Proceedings*, UCAPAWA Third Annual Convention, Chicago, Dec. 1940, WHS. *UCAPAWA News*, 1940.

29. "Employment and Wage Data," 1939, *Annual Report of the Tennessee Department of Labor, for the Fiscal Year Ending June 30, 1939* (Nashville: 1939), 12–31, USDL Library.

30. *UCAPAWA News*, July and Oct. 1939 and Feb. 1940. Koger deposition, FBI/FOIA 100-33752-1. Jamieson, *Labor Unionism*, 322–23.

31. *UCAPAWA News*, July-Aug. 1940, and notes on the Memphis school in Folders 28 and 29, Claude Williams Papers, Reuther Library. *CA*, 16 Aug. 1940.

32. *UCAPAWA News*, Sept.–Oct. 1940.

33. Ibid. Figures are also given in the *Proceedings*, UCAPAWA Third Annual Convention. Ed McCrea interview.

34. *UCAPAWA News*, May-June, 1940. Morton Davis interview. Henderson Organizer's Reports, TOC, OD.

35. *Proceedings*, UCAPAWA Third Annual Convention, and *UCAPAWA News*, Oct. 1940.

36. Mason to Mrs. Roosevelt, 28 Nov. 1940, and to Allan S. Haywood, 5 Oct. 1940, in Mason Papers, OD; and Mason, *To Win These Rights*, 30.

37. Roger Keeran, *The Communist Party and the Auto Workers' Unions* (New York: International Publishers, 1980).

38. Mason to Roosevelt, 28 Nov. 1940.

39. Mason, *To Win These Rights*, 108, and Mason to Roosevelt, Apr. 1941; Mason Papers, OD.

40. Mason, *To Win These Rights*, 108.

41. Ibid.

42. Ibid., 109.

43. Ed McCrea interview. Mike Ross, an organizer of mine and steelworkers in Tennessee, Georgia, and Alabama in the early CIO days, also emphasized the importance of whites speaking out for black freedom in building the CIO movement among blacks. Personal interview, 6 Nov. 1982, Chapel Hill, N.C. Tillman interview. Clarence Coe remembered a meeting down at the river that resulted in beatings, which may have been the same one referred to by McCrea, interview.

44. John Handcox wrote powerful poems and songs, a number of them produced in Alan Lomax, Pete Seeger, and Woody Guthrie's *Hard Hitting Songs for Hard-Hit People* (New York: Oak Publications, 1967). Handcox interview. Claude Williams to Harry and Grace Koger, n.d., Folder 6, Box 15, Claude Williams Papers, Reuther Library. Folklorist and musician Pete Seeger confirmed the accuracy of Williams's account of the origins of "Union Train," personal interview, 19 Jan. 1986, Washington, D.C.

45. W. E. Davis interview.

46. Cayton and Mitchell, *Black Workers and the New Unions*, 348, 353–54, 366.

47. Ibid., 350–53, and W. E. Davis interview. Morton Sosna, *In Search of the Silent South* (New York: Columbia University Press, 1977), 78.

48. Cayton and Mitchell, *Black Workers and the New Unions*, 345.

49. Ibid., 354–55, and W. E. Davis and Holloway personal interviews.

50. Communists during the popular front had already dissolved their shop papers and concentrated more on building the CIO than determining American foreign policy; they had little control over the top decisions in the CIO under Lewis or his successors. Levenstein, *Communism, Anti-Communism, and the CIO,* 79–84, 86–92, 94. Rayback, *A History of American Labor,* 367.

51. Zieger, *American Workers,* 74. A Military Intelligence Report in 1941 alleges that Communist party members of the CIO in Chicago even feared to challenge their exclusion from a city group organized by CIO leaders, thinking this would lead to a total purge of the Left. File 10110-2666, 369, MID, War Department General Staff, RG 165, NARA.

52. *Constitution of the Tennessee Industrial Union Council, Affiliated with the CIO,* 5 Feb. 1941, USDL Library. *Labor Journal* (Aug. 1956), history of the Memphis council. Paul R. Coppock, *Memphis Memoirs* (Memphis: Memphis State University Press, 1980), 248; and *Proceedings of the Seventh Annual Convention of the American Newspaper Guild,* 8–12 July 1940, Memphis, Tennessee, USDL Library, 187, 169, 189, 191–94.

53. FBI/FOIA 100-523, on Copeland. The FBI began its security check in the fall of 1941.

54. See for example statements by Noel Beddow of the Steelworkers in Birmingham, Foner and Lewis, eds. *From the Founding of the CIO,* 104–5.

55. Ed McCrea interview.

SIX: BLACK SCARES AND RED SCARES

1. Zieger, *American Workers,* 62–69, 69–74. Foner, *Organized Labor and the Black Worker,* 239–42.

2. Mason quotes and quotes from the *Atlanta Constitution,* May 1941, in Mason to Ralph Jones, 16 May 1941, Mason Papers, OD. On anti-labor laws, see C. H. Gillman to Hon. Eugene Talmadge in Georgia, Mason Papers, OD. Rayback, *A History of American Labor,* 342, 373.

3. Files 10110-1581 (22) and 10104-1570 (125), MID, RG 165, NARA.

4. Koger to Claude Williams, 28 May 1940, File 5, Williams Papers, Reuther Library. CIO regional director Paul Christopher described the close collaboration of the authorities in South Carolina to break textile unions to Mason, 5 Mar. 1940, Mason Papers, OD. Franz Daniel told the 1939 textile convention of the CIO that the revival of the Klan was the primary reason textile drives had been defeated, cited in Wyche, "Southern Attitudes," 161. Kelley, *Hammer and Hoe,* 186, 190, 214. Numerous letters in the Mason Papers, OD, document the role of the the KKK as an anti-union weapon in 1940 and 1941. Mason to Mrs. Roosevelt, 28 May 1940, described the "hysterical campaign," giving Georgia as an example.

5. Bunche, *Political Status of the Negro,* on fears of black voting, xxiii–xxv; Painter, *Narrative of Hosea Hudson,* chap. 15; Gilbert Osofsky, *The Burden of Race: A Documentary History of Negro-White Relations in America* (New York: Harper and Row, 1967), details the rumors about the "Eleanor Clubs" in the South, 401–8.

6. See the details on this atrocity in Brownsville in the El Williams File, Box A-375, Group 2, NAACP/LC.

7. Mason to John L. Lewis, 26 Sept. 1940, to Mrs. Roosevelt, 9 Jan. 1941, Mason Papers, OD.

8. Lee quoted in Bunche, *Political Status of the Negro,* 500–501. For an assessment of the role of black preachers in Memphis, see Tucker, *Black Pastors and Leaders,* and Bunche, *Political Status of the Negro,* 499–500. See also Brown-Melton, "Blacks in Memphis," on the weakness of black protest organizations in Memphis, for example, 140–51, passim, and Cayton and Mitchell, *Black Workers,* 372–83.

9. Williams quoted in Brown-Melton, "Blacks in Memphis," 187. Leigh D. Fraser, "A Demographic Analysis of Memphis and Shelby County, Tennessee, 1820–1973" (Master's thesis, Memphis State University, 1974).

10. See Steinberg, *The Bosses,* chapter on Crump.

11. Bunche, *Political Status of the Negro,* 494–99. Webb and Miller to Frank Murphy, n.d.; Anna Damon, of International Labor Defense, to Murphy, 24 May 1939; R.G. Draper to Murphy, 3 Aug. 1939; U.S. Attorney John Rogge to Webb and Miller, 28 Aug. 1939, all in File 144-72-0, Justice Department, RG 60, NARA.

12. *Southern Worker,* June 1937, quoting Googe speech in Anniston, Alabama, and see Marshall, *Labor in the South,* 221, on the AFL Southern Conference. On the national AFL, see Bernstein, *The Turbulent Years,* 688–703, 666. Wyche, "Southern Attitudes," 158–59; Foner, *Organized Labor and the Black Worker,* 230; and Zieger, *American Workers,* 60, on the AFL versus the CIO.

13. Reports and agreements forwarded by V. C. Finch, Mediation and Conciliation Service File 199-6483, RG 280, NARA. Rebecca McKinley, phone interview, 27 Mar. 1983, Memphis. *CA* and *P-S,* 18 Feb. 1941. Mediation and Conciliation Service File 199-1242, RG 280, NARA.

14. AFL unionists did strike the Dixie-Burton cotton batten plant in December, where about one-third of the seventy workers were black. *P-S,* 2 Dec. 1940. Local 255 struck Belz Furniture for five days in February, but all twenty upholsterers seem to have been white. See Mediation and Conciliation Service File 199-1242 and 196-6298 on Hartwell Brothers handle company "preferential" shop agreement, File 196-6329 on U.S. Bedding, and File 196-4996 on Gates Lumber, RG 280, NARA. The hod carriers' and common laborers' union was so undemocratic that its 1944 convention in St. Louis was the first one held by the union in twenty years. Mitchell, *Mean Things,* 189.

15. Daniel Nelson, "The Rubber Worker's Southern Strategy: Labor Organizing in the New Deal South, 1933–43," *The Historian* 46, no. 3 (May 1984): 336. Harold Selig Roberts, *The Rubber Workers: Labor Organization and Collective Bargaining in the Rubber Industry* (New York: Harper and Bros., 1944), chaps. 2–5, Bernstein, *The Turbulent Years,* 589–602, and Marshall, *Labor in the South,* 190.

16. Dickenson interview; Matthew Davis interview; Edward Lee Harrel and Fred Higgins, personal interviews, 30 Oct. 1984, Memphis.

17. Hillie Pride, personal interview, 26 May 1989, Memphis. Coe and Davis interviews.

18. Dickinson and Routon interviews.

19. George Clark and W. E. Davis interviews.

20. Routon interview.

21. Routon, George Clark, and W. E. Davis interviews.

22. Ibid. Harrel and Hillie Pride interviews.

23. Griffin interview.

24. I. J. Bedgood, "The Attempt to Organize Firestone," Reel 32, Highlander Folk School Newsletter, Fall 1940, OD microfilm.

25. Nearly 10 percent of the workers at Goodyear in Akron in 1929 came from Tennessee. Roberts, *The Rubber Workers,* 19. Routon interview.

26. Holloway interview.

27. *P-S,* 24 Aug. 1940. "Transcript of Statements Made in the Office of the United States Attorney's Office, Federal Building, Memphis, 27 August 1940," File 134-72-0, Justice Department, RG 60, NARA. This document provides the basis for the Bass narrative that follows, unless otherwise noted.

28. *P-S,* 24 Aug. 1940. Bass affidavit and George Clark interview.

29. *CA,* 25 Aug. 1940.

30. Ibid. Bass affidavit. "Firestone Workers!" leaflet, File 134-72-0, Justice Department, RG 60, NARA. Charles H. Martin, "Southern Labor Relations in Transition: Gadsden, Alabama, 1930–1943," *Review of Radical Political Economics* 10 (Fall 1978): 559.

31. Griffin interview; Bass affidavit.

32. Bass affidavit.

33. Pierson, "Life of a Free Lance Organizer"; Routon interview.

34. Routon interview, Bass affidavit, and *CA,* 30 Aug. 1940.

35. Bass affidavit and Frank McCallister to Henry Schweinhaut, 11 Sept. 1940, File 134-72-0, Justice Department, RG 60, NARA, on suspicions about Ford agents. Routon, in his interview, said Ford was not implicated. W. E. Davis interview.

36. Chandler quote from Justice Department attorney Stanley Denlinger to U.S. Attorney John Rogge, 10 Sept. 1940, and McCallister to Schweinhaut, both in File 134-72-0, Justice Department, RG 60, NARA.

37. W. R. Henderson to Lee Pressman, n.d., and Federated Press Release, 5 Sept. 1940, Folder 21, Box 39, WDL, Reuther Library, on the Democratic National Committee, and Rogge to Mason, 6 Dec. 1940, File 134-72-0, Justice Department, RG 60, NARA.

38. Holloway interview.

39. Clark to Clendenin, 20 Sept. 1940, Folder 20, Box 39, WDL, Reuther Library.

40. Carroll quoted in *P-S,* 30 Aug. 1940. Routon interview.

41. Dickenson interview. Clark to Clendenin, 20 Sept. 1940. Nelson, "The Rubber Worker's Southern Strategy," 322–25. George Clark interview; Mason to Eleanor Roosevelt, 29 Nov. 1940, Mason Papers, OD.

42. Clark interview. Griffen interview. Marshall, *Labor in the South,* 190. Roberts, *The Rubber Workers,* 181–85, 187. *P-S,* 30 Aug. 1940.

43. Mason, *To Win These Rights,* 111.

44. Dickenson interview. Holloway interview.

45. Collins George to Daisy Lampkin, Memphis Reign of Terror File, Box A-391, Group 2, NAACP/LC.

46. Mason to Justice Department Criminal Division Director John Rogge, 6 Oct. 1940, to Attorney General Robert Jackson, 16 Oct. 1940, and to Eleanor Roosevelt, 28 Nov. 1940, Mason Papers, OD. Williams to Harry and Grace Koger, n.d., Folder 6, Box 14, Williams Papers, Reuther Library. Edward Strong of SNYC to Roosevelt, 28 Dec. 1940, Memphis Reign of Terror File, Box A-391, Group 2, NAACP/LC.

47. *P-S*, 11 June 1940, *CA*, 12 Oct. and 18 Dec. 1940.

48. *Pittsburgh Press*, 7 Dec. 1940. *Time* quoted in Brown-Melton, "Blacks in Memphis," 194. El Williams File, Box A-375, Group 2, NAACP/LC. Mason to Roosevelt, 28 Nov. 1940.

49. Brown-Melton, "Blacks in Memphis," 188–90, 195. Police stakeout story in the *Pittsburgh Press*, 7 Dec. 1940. On Beale Street raids, see *CA*, 14 Nov. 1940, *P-S*, 15 Nov. 1940, and see *CA*, 30 Oct. 1940.

50. The *CA*, 5 Dec. 1940, carried the entire text of Boyle's statement. Boyle's second statement was in *P-S*, 11 Dec. 1940, and Crump's statement in *P-S*, 6 Dec. 1940. Brown-Melton, "Blacks in Memphis," 192–98, and Memphis Reign of Terror File, Box A-391, Group 2, NAACP/LC.

51. Howard Lee's comments in Lee to President Roosevelt, 21 Dec. 1940. Mason to Roosevelt, 9 Jan. 1941, Mason Papers, OD. "NAACP Asks Justice Department to Stop Terror in Memphis," press release, 27 Dec. 1940, both in Memphis Reign of Terror File, Box A-391, Group 2, NAACP/LC.

52. Brown-Melton, "Blacks in Memphis," 192–95. Memphis Reign of Terror File, Box A-391, Group 2, NAACP/LC.

53. The Interracial Commission was a joint effort by the city's two associations of white and black ministers, led by James McDaniel (black) and Samuel Howie (white), and had some fifty members in 1940. According to Brown-Melton, Wingfield stated in private that after the meeting with Boyle, "two opposite philosophies of the treatment of the Negro were [evident] and some of the members had a feeling of hopelessness in making the Commission's viewpoint and purpose understood," "Blacks in Memphis," 199–200, see also 196, 234–35. *CA*, 30 and 31 Jan. 1941.

54. Carter to Marshall, 11 and 8 Jan. 1941, Memphis Reign of Terror File, Box A-391, Group 2, NAACP/LC.

55. Woodcock report cited in *P-S*, 10 Jan. 1941; Marshall to Hon. Robert H. Jackson, 20 Jan. 1941, and Wendell Berge to Marshall, 4 Feb. 1941, both in Memphis Reign of Terror File, Box A-391, Group 2, NAACP/LC.

56. Crump statement, 9 Jan., quoted in Brown-Melton, "Blacks in Memphis," 199. Boyle quoted in *CA*, 16 Jan. 1941. George to White, 1 Feb. 1941, Memphis Reign of Terror File, Box A-391, Group 2, NAACP/LC.

57. Saunders Redding, *No Day of Triumph* (New York: Harper and Row, 1942), 178, 180. *CA*, 16 Dec. 1940.

58. Williams to Harry and Grace Koger. Mason to Roosevelt, 9 Jan. 1941. Routon interview.

59. Routon interview. Final Report of V. C. Finch, 30 Dec. 1940; and Stanley Denlinger, General Counsel for the United Rubberworkers (CIO) to Sherman Dalrymple, URW President, 11 Dec. 1940, both in Mediation and Conciliation Service File 199-6048, RG 280, NARA.

60. Ibid. Holloway interview.

61. Boyle quoted in *CA*, 19 Jan. 1941. Streetcar and trash fire incidents reported in the *CA*, 16 and 19 Jan. 1941. Brown-Melton documents the increased controversy over segregated street cars, "Blacks in Memphis," 197, 202, 205, 217.

SEVEN: WAR IN THE FACTORIES

1. Mason to Haywood, 4 June 1941, Mason Papers, OD. *P-S*, 26 Jan. 1945.

2. *P-S*, 3 Jan. 1941, 5, 28, and 31 Jan. 1942, and 8 Jan. 1943. Figure of forty thousand from "Memphis, Tennessee" report in Racial Tension Files, FEPC, RG 228, NARA. Records of USES, USDL, RG 183, NARA, and the "Labor, 1943" File, Office of the Mayor's Papers, MPL, report similar statistics.

3. Mason to Roosevelt, 5 Oct. 1940, and 5 Mar. 1941, and to Allan Haywood, 5 May 1941, Mason Papers, OD.

4. J. R. Watkins Co., Mediation and Conciliation Service File 196-2236, RG 280, NARA; Mason to Roosevelt, 5 Mar. 1941, and to Haywood, 4 June and 16 Oct. 1941, Mason Papers, OD.

5. Mississippi Valley Hardwood, Mediation and Conciliation Service File 199-6700, RG 280, NARA. *P-S*, 12 Sept. 1941.

6. Nickey Brothers, Mediation and Conciliation Service Files 196-7118, 196-7119, and 209-1471, RG 280, NARA.

7. The IWA won elections at Gooch Lumber, with seventy-one workers, and Turner, Day, and Woolworth handle company, the latter with about sixty workers, for example. For Gooch Lumber see Mediation and Conciliation Service File 7518-13, RG 280, NARA, and *The Timberworker*, Aug. 1941. Sixty shops reportedly were covered by Henderson, *P-S*, 27 Sept. 1941.

8. For Memphis Cotton Oil see Mediation and Conciliation Service File 199–7468 and for Wabash Screen Door see File 199-6714, RG 280, NARA.

9. For Claridge Hotel see Mediation and Conciliation Service Files 199-5465 and 199-6661, RG 280, NARA, and *CA*, 25 May and 26 July 1941, and *P-S*, 14 July and 1 Aug. 1941.

10. Mediation and Conciliation Service Files 199-7432 and 209-3424, and Brown-Melton, "Blacks in Memphis," 211, on the laundry workers; File 199-7108 on Allied Feed Mills; Files 209-5049 and 464-1446 on American Snuff, all in RG 280, NARA, and Northrup, *Organized Labor and the Negro*, 112; *P-S*, 11 Aug. 1941, showed the AFL organizing white clerks and stockers as well. See *P-S*, 1 and 2 Aug. 1941, and *CA*, 1 Aug. and 24 Sept. 1941, on the hod carriers; FEPC administrators to the President of Hencke Construction, 24 Sept. 1942, and related material on discrimination, in "Labor, 1942" File, Office of the Mayor's Papers, MPL.

11. On Lane and Bowler see Mediation and Conciliation Service File 196-3481 and *P-S*, 2 Oct. 1941; U.S. Bedding, File 196-6298; Gates Lumber, File 196-4996; Humphries Mills, File 196-7035, all files in RG 280, NARA.

12. At Anderson-Tulley the AFL represented 12 white employees out of nearly 500 workers, at Humko cottonseed oil represented 5 of 180 workers, and similarly represented a handful at Chickasaw Wood Products. See Mediation and Conciliation Service Files 196-4827 (Anderson-Tulley), 452–469 (Humko), and 452–309 (Chickasaw), RG 280, NARA.

13. Mary Lawrence Elkuss, personal interview, 27 Jan. 1983, St. Louis, Mo. Mason said that Tennessee had "more violations of labor's rights than any other state," Mason to Malcolm Ross, 20 Oct. 1941, Mason Papers, OD. Henderson's Organizer's Reports, 1941–42, TOC, OD.

14. Harry Lasker weekly reports, 25 Oct. to 16 Nov. 1941, "Labor Extension: Mem-

phis CIO, 1941–42," 1947 Folder, Highlander Files, WHS. Dickenson interview, on illiteracy, and see also Lasker weekly reports. Elkuss interview.

15. Elkuss interview. Mason to Haywood, 10 Sept., 28 Mar., and 6 June 1941, Mason Papers, OD; and "The Year 1941," Frames 91–92, Reel 32, Ninth Annual Report of the Highlander Folk School, OD microfilm; and Lasker weekly reports. See Frank Adams and Myles Horton, *Unearthing Seeds of Fire: The Idea of Highlander* (Winston-Salem, N.C.: John F. Blair, 1975).

16. Lasker weekly report, 24 Nov. to 1 Dec. 1941, and other material in "Labor Extension" Folder; Christopher to Haywood, 2 Oct. 1941, Mason Papers, OD.

17. Dickenson and Routon interviews.

18. Ibid.

19. On Firestone see Mediation and Conciliation Service File 209-4516, RG 280, NARA; Routon and Holloway interviews.

20. Mason to Philip Murray, 17 Mar. 1942, Mason Papers, OD; Copeland to Christopher, 9 Sept. 1943, TOC, OD; Copeland to Allan Haywood, 6 June 1945, Region 8 Files, SLA/GSU; employment figures in Mayor Walter Chandler to E. H. Crump, 26 May 1943, "Labor, 1943" File, Office of the Mayor's Papers, MPL; War Manpower Commission Program Planning and Review Division report, 1 July 1943, Reports and Analysis Unit, Region 4, USES, USDL, RG 183, NARA; and "Memphis, Tennessee" report, Racial Tension Files, FEPC, RG 228, NARA.

21. See Lichtenstein, *Labor's War at Home*, 66–72.

22. Chandler statement, *P-S*, 6 June 1942. CIO representative unionist quote in *P-S*, 8 June 1942. 1945 statement in Chandler to Tom Simmons of *Labor Review*, 26 July 1945, "Labor, 1945" File, Office of the Mayor's Papers, MPL.

23. C.H. Williams Special Report, 14 Mar. 1940, Mediation and Conciliation Service File 195-1240, RG 280, NARA, on the Tennessee Industrial Personnel Conference; and Memphis Chamber of Commerce, Documents of the Committee for Economic Development, 1 and 23 July memos, and "Interview" memo, n.d., 1943, Economic Development File, Office of the Mayor's Papers, MPL.

24. Wassell Randolph to Truman, 21 Mar. 1942, and Adie Russell to Truman, 21 Mar. 1942, and see other letters enclosed in National Defense Committee File, Office of the Mayor's Papers, MPL. Waring quoted in *Southern Patriot*, 16 Oct. 1942.

25. War Labor Board Case 111-1951-D, Cudahy, 23 July 1943 and Sept. 1943, Reports and Dissenting Opinions, and Elizabeth Sasuly to W. B. Shirer, WLB Appeal Agent, 10 July 1944, Regional War Labor Board, Region 4, all in RG 202, NARA.

26. Mississippi Valley Hardwood, Mediation and Conciliation Service File 301-471; William Botkin to J. R. Steelman; Anderson-Tulley, Mediation and Conciliation Service File 301-2997, all in RG 280, NARA. *War Labor Reports* (Washington, D.C.: GPO, 1945), 22:785–88.

27. On Memphis Furniture see Mediation and Conciliation Service Files 301-6897, 199-6483, 452-171, 464-125, and 474-1577, RG 280, NARA, and *CA*, 18 Feb. 1941, and *P-S*, 18 Feb. and 26 Apr. 1941. SAC report on Local 282, 22 Nov. 1943, FBI/FOIA 100-7002-159.

28. William Eaves to John R. Steelman, 7 Sept. 1942, describes the STFU Memphis Conference and the terrible conditions in the countryside, File 195-2004, STFU Files, RG 280, NARA. On the Memphis area labor market, see "Demand Supply Supplement for Balance of Memphis Administrative Area" and "Demand-Supply Supplement," May

1944, Memphis Files, USES, USDL, RG 183, NARA. And see "Re-survey of the Labor Market Situation in the Memphis, Tennessee Area," USES, 19 Mar. 1943, "Labor, 1943" File, Office of the Mayor's Papers, MPL.

29. "Survey of the Employment Situation in the Memphis Area," June 1942, USES, "Labor, 1943" File, Office of the Mayor's Papers, MPL. See office files of John Beecher, and his report on 11 Apr. 1942, "Training, General" File, FEPC, RG 228, NARA. "Protest Telegrams," 24 Jan. 1941, "FEPC, Tennessee, 1941" File, General Office Files, Box A-271, Group 2, NAACP/LC. Mississippi situation detailed in Flora, Ms., File, John Beecher Files, FEPC, RG 228, NARA. Statistics taken from "Labor Market Developments Report," c. 15 Oct. 1943, Memphis Files, USES, USDL, RG 183, NARA. Bruce Nelson, "Mobile during World War II: Organized Labor and the Struggle for Equality in a 'City That's Been Taken by Storm,'" paper given at the Southern Labor Studies Conference, 11 Oct. 1991, 10–13, Atlanta, Ga.

30. Beecher report, 11 Apr. 1942, Training File, FEPC, RG 228, NARA. Data on training programs in "Negro Composition of Placements," Dec. 1941 to Feb. 1942, Negroes File, Division of Negro Labor, USES, USDL, RG 183, NARA; Cy Record to Robert Weaver, n.d., John Beecher Files, FEPC, RG 183, NARA; and Beecher memos in "Memphis, Tenn." File, FEPC, RG 228, NARA. Also "Labor Market Development Reports," 15 June 1943, USES, USDL, RG 183, NARA. And see John Beecher to Eugene Glazier, 11 Apr. 1942 and 20 Jan. 1944, in Racial Tension Files, Division of Review and Analysis, both in FEPC, RG 228, NARA. Merl E. Reed, "FEPC and the Federal Agencies in the South," *Journal of Negro History* 54, no. 1 (Winter 1980): 43–56, and see 49–50. Bruce Hunt to Will Maslow, 18 Mar. 1944, Weekly Reports, FEPC, RG 183, NARA.

31. Lois Ruchames, *Race, Jobs, and Politics: The Story of the FEPC* (New York: Columbia University Press, 1953), 148–49, 190. Also see Carl L. Brown and George R. Leighton, *The Negro and the War* (New York: AMS Press, 1942), and Robert C. Weaver, *Negro Labor: A National Problem* (New York: Harcourt, Brace, 1946).

32. "Labor Market Report," USES, Nov. 1942, "Labor, 1942" File, Office of the Mayor's Papers, MPL. "Survey of the Employment Situation." Beecher report, "Millington, Tenn.," n.d., John Beecher Files, FEPC, RG 228, NARA.

33. Beecher to Lawrence Cramer, 30 Apr. 1942, and to Will Alexander, 27 Feb. 1942, John Beecher Files, FEPC, RG 228, NARA. White to Roosevelt, 5 Feb. 1942, Negro File, General Subject Files, Office of the Secretary, USDL, RG 174, NARA. AFL representative George Googe claimed the "Fourth Regional War Labor Board is made up overwhelmingly of anti-union employers." *Southern Patriot,* Dec. 1943. FEPC was first under the authority of the Office of the War Manpower Commission, Reed, "FEPC and the Federal Agencies in the South," 43–44. Witherspoon Dodge reported on the sexual harassment case at the VA Hospital, Memphis, File 7-GR-601, Active Cases, FEPC, RG 228, NARA.

34. Cliff Davis to Mayor Walter Chandler, 1 Dec. 1943, and 11 Apr. 1944, "Labor, 1944" File, Office of the Mayor's Papers, MPL. *War Labor Reports* (Washington, D.C.: GPO, 1944), 15:636–43 and 799. Hand-written reports of Cy Record and J. L. Searcy, n.d., "Memphis, Tenn." File, on complaints against the AFL iron workers' union and the plumbers' union, John Beecher Files, FEPC, RG 228, NARA.

35. On the Buckeye and Forest Products plants see Memphis File, 2 June 1942, John

Beecher Files, FEPC, RG 228, NARA. Dupree Davis to Walter White, 7 July 1941, "FEPC, Tennessee, 1941," General Office Files, Box A-271, Group 2, NAACP/LC. "Labor Market Report," Nov. 1942," Office of the Mayor's Papers, MPL.

36. On Firestone see Beecher report, headed "Millington, Tenn.," and on the Fisher situation, see Mar. 1942 report, both in FECP, RG 228, NARA. *P-S*, 18 Feb. 1943, on Fisher.

37. Coe interview.

38. "Re-survey of the Labor Market Situation"; "Labor Market Report," Nov. 1942; "Labor Market Development Report," 15 Oct. 1943, both in "Labor, 1942" File, Office of the Mayor's Papers, MPL.

39. See "wage rates" for January 1945 in "A Brief Survey of Industrial Facilities and Cost Factors in Memphis" (Memphis: Memphis Chamber of Commerce, 1945), MPL, 18. For Firestone wages, see "Piecework Classifications," 5 June 1945, Firestone Rubber case 111-14975-D, Dispute Case Files, NWLB Records, Region 4, WLB, RG 202, NARA.

40. Ibid.

41. Ruth Milkman, in *Gender at Work: The Dynamics of Job Segregation by Sex during World War II* (Urbana: University of Illinois Press, 1987), 54, points out the exclusion of black women in northern industry. Mary Martha Thomas, in *Riveting and Rationing in Dixie: Alabama Women and the Second World War* (Tuscaloosa: University of Alabama Press, 1987), notes the same pattern in Alabama. See also Jones, *Labor of Love*, 238–40 and 236. On Memphis statistics, see Memphis Negro Chamber of Commerce, *A Classified Directory of Memphis and Shelby County* (Memphis, 1941), 143–44, Memphis Room, MPL.

42. Evelyn Bates, personal interview, 25 May 1989, Memphis.

43. Bates interview and Irene Branch, personal interview, 25 May 1989, Memphis. See Jones, *Labor of Love*, 252–53, on the general lack of interracial female solidarity during the war.

44. Johnson to Mrs. Roosevelt, 13 May 1942, Mediation and Conciliation Service File 196-8955, RG 280, NARA. John Mack Dyson to Phil Murray, 2 July 1942, UCAPAWA Records, TOC, OD. Henderson Organizer's Report, 14 Mar. 1942, TOC, OD. On the Buckeye disputes see Mediation and Conciliation Service Files 196-8955, 209-6926, 301-574, 300-2855, RG 280, NARA; *War Labor Reports* (Washington, D.C.: GPO, 1943) 2:145–50, and *P-S* accounts, 26, 27, 28 Feb. 1942, 1 Aug. 1942, and 3 Mar. and 20 May 1943. See also *CA*, 21 Feb. 1943; on the laundry workers walkout, *P-S*, 24 and 26 Feb. 1943, and on another strike they held, *P-S*, 21 July 1943; on Chapman-Dewey see Mediation and Conciliation Service File 209-1207, RG 280, NARA.

45. On Firestone see Mediation and Conciliation Service Files 209-4516, 199-9202, 199-9626, RG 280, NARA, and *CA*, 30 and 31 Jan., 1, 2, and 11 Feb., 20 and 21 Apr. 1943. The FBI investigated this case on suspicion of sabotage of war production by the workers, Special Agent Percy Wylie to J. Edgar Hoover, 23 Apr. 1943, FBI/FOIA materials on Firestone.

46. *War Labor Reports* (Washington, D.C.: GPO, 1944), 9:729, 731, 735; and contract, contained in "Progress Report," 5 Jan. 1944, Mediation and Conciliation Service File 302-829, RG 280, NARA, and Routon interview. See Mediation and Conciliation Service File 452-1596, RG 280, NARA, on 1–5 June 1945 strike.

47. Mediation and Conciliation Service Files on Buckeye, 301-574, 300-6436, 209-8766, 301-3446, 442-572; the five-day strike came in September 1944, File 442-2182; and unrest continued, Files 442-1668 and 442-1696, all in RG 280, NARA.

48. Harold J. Lane to Locals, 21 Dec. 1944, Region 8 Files, SLA/GSU. Mediation and Conciliation Service Files 301-574, 301-3446, 442-572, 442-620, RG 280, NARA; and see War Labor Board case 111-4847-D, Records of the Dispute Division, RG 202, NARA.

49. Griffin interview. Military intelligence and the FBI kept the events at Firestone under close surveillance, according to FOIA documents, including Wylie to Hoover, 23 Apr. 1943. J. T. Bissell, War Department Military Intelligence Service, to J. Edgar Hoover, 9 Feb. 1943, enclosing reports on strikers at Memphis Firestone, and 1 Jan. 1944 report on the Banbury incident, received from Thomas Conley, Department of the Army, 13 June 1985, in author's possession.

50. *War Labor Reports,* 9:733–36. "Piecework Classifications," 5 June 1945; and "Confidential Wage Analysis," 2 Aug. 1945, and "Memorandum to the Board, Reconsideration," 22 Oct. 1945, all in Case 111-14975-D, Dispute Case Files, NWLB Records, Region 4, WLB, RG 202, NARA.

51. On Firestone employment, Weekly Reports, FECP, RG 228, NARA. Regarding the national situation, Will Maslow, "Strikes Involving Inter-racial Issues," 14 Feb. 1945, Field Letter No. 47, FECP Field Letters, 47–54, CIO Secretary-Treasurer's Files, Reuther Library. Also see Racial Tension Files, typewritten notes, and Will Maslow report, 28 Oct. 1944, Weekly Reports, all in FECP, RG 228, NARA. Mike Ross report related in William Henderson to Paul Christopher, 4 Aug. 1942, TOC, OD. Stanfield letter, Economic Development, 1943 and B Files, Office of the Mayor's Papers, MPL. On conflicts in Birmingham, Mike Ross interview, and Hosea Hudson, personal interview, 29 May 1985, Takoma Park, Md. On the Detroit riot, John Hope Franklin, *From Slavery to Freedom: A History of Negro Americans,* 4th ed. (New York: Alfred A. Knopf, 1974), 454–55. Nelson, "Mobile during World War II," 35.

52. Pete Daniel, "Going among Strangers: Southern Reactions to World War II," *Journal of American History* 77, no. 3 (Dec. 1990): 886–911. Brown-Melton, "Blacks in Memphis," on "Eleanor Clubs," and see also *Memphis World,* 29 Jan. 1943. See O. D. Bratton, Memphis Veneer Company to Mayor Chandler, 7 June 1944, T. J. Malone to the Mayor, 18 May 1944, Chandler to Bratton, 26 June 1944, *CA,* 5 Aug. 1944, and WHBQ script, all in "Labor, 1944" and "Negroes, 1944" Files, Office of the Mayor's Papers, MPL. "A Monthly Summary of Events and Trends in Race Relations," Fisk University Institute on Race Relations, Mar. 1945, on the planters.

53. Brown-Melton, "Blacks in Memphis," 201–5. Willie Hall, personal interview, 29 Oct. 1984, Memphis, and Coe interview, 29 Feb. 1989.

54. Negro People of the U.S.A. to Mr. F. D. Roosevelt, Memphis, 1940, File 144-72-0, Justice Department, RG 60, NARA. Quote on blacks in film from Brown-Melton, "Blacks in Memphis," 202. Poll cited in Thomas F. Pettigrew, *A Profile of the Negro American* (Princeton, N.J.: D. Van Nostrand, 1964), 50. On conditions, also see Walter White, et al., to Franklin D. Roosevelt, 5 Feb. 1942, Negro File, General Subject Files, Office of the Secretary, RG 174, NARA. Examples of the terrible treatment of black soldiers in the South can be found in Phillip McGuire, *Taps for a Jim Crow Army: Letters from Black Soldiers in World War II* (Santa Barbara, Calif.: ABC-CLIO, 1983). Morton Sosna offers some revealing examples of this treatment in "The GI's South," in

Developing Dixie: Modernization in a Traditional Society, ed. Winfred B. Moore, Jr., Joseph F. Tripp, and Lyon C. Tyler, Jr. (Westport, Conn.: Greenwood Press, 1988), see especially 320–21.

55. Coe interview. Brown-Melton, "Blacks in Memphis," 201–5. Holloway interview.

56. Articles by and about Bell in the *Chicago Defender,* 22 and 29 Jan. 1944. Brown-Melton, "Blacks in Memphis," 215–17; and Jesse Thomas Moore, Jr., *A Search for Equality: The National Urban League, 1910–1961* (University Park: Pennsylvania State University Press, 1981), 153–54.

57. *Chicago Sun,* 20 Nov. 1943, and *CA,* 14 Nov. 1943.

58. Long quoted in *P-S,* 9 Mar. 1944, and *CA,* 7 Mar. 1944. Documentation of the Randolph incidents are in Folder 21, WDL, Reuther Library. *Labor Review,* 10 Mar. 1944.

59. Cornelius Maiden to Morris Milgram, 10 and 19 June 1944, along with Benjamin Bell to Morris Milgram, 18 June 1944, File 22, WDL, Reuther Library. Tucker, *Black Pastors and Leaders,* 104. See also *Chicago Defender,* and *Michigan Chronicle,* 29 Jan. 1944, and *P-S,* 27 May, 10 June 1944. Tucker, *Lieutenant Lee,* 142–43.

60. On the Banbury incident, "Special Report," 12 Jan. 1944, Mediation and Conciliation Service File 302-829, and FBI report, 1 Jan. 1944, on Firestone Tire and Rubber, FBI/FOIA 100-7002-159.

61. Mediation and Conciliation Service File 442-1796, "Special Report," 17 June 1944, and Firestone File 442-134.

62. Coe and Routon interviews, and *Chicago Defender,* 3 Mar. 1945.

63. Routon interview, and W. A. Copeland to Paul Christopher, 31 Mar. 1945, Region 8 Files, SLA/GSU.

64. Copeland to Christopher, 31 Mar. 1945, and Routon interview. On southern efforts to dump Henry Wallace, see *New York Times,* 14 June 1944.

65. The CIO Executive Board Minutes for 1944 and 1945, Reuther Library, reflect these concerns, as does the correspondence of George Weaver, who directed the CIO's antidiscrimination committee along with James B. Carey, CIO Secretary-Treasurer's Files, Reuther Library. W. H. Harris, *The Harder We Run,* 118. The seventh CIO convention passed the antidiscrimination provision, George Weaver to All Internationals, 27 Feb. 1945, Box 203, George Weaver Files, Part 2 of CIO Secretary-Treasurer's Files, Reuther Library.

66. Swim to Carey, 26 May 1944, Industrial Union Councils, Miscellaneous Correspondence, George Weaver Files, Part 2 of CIO Secretary-Treasurer's Files, Reuther Library.

67. Dennis Dickerson notes the same lack of educational preparation of white union members in the Pittsburgh steel industry, in "Fighting on the Domestic Front: Black Steelworkers during World War Two," in *Life and Labor: Dimensions of American Working-Class History,* ed. Charles Stephenson and Robert Asher (Albany, N.Y.: SUNY Press, 1986), 224–36, 234–35.

68. Mason to Christopher, 5 Oct. 1940, Mason Papers, OD; see Copeland to Christopher, 23 Dec. 1942, William A. Copeland Files, on Left-Right splits, and Mary Lawrence to Christopher, 31 July 1944, Lawrence File, both in TOC, OD; Dan Powell, personal interview, 1 Feb. 1983, Memphis, and Elkuss, W. E. Davis, and Leroy Clark interviews on Copeland.

69. Secondary accounts by Marshall, *The Negro and Organized Labor,* and *Labor in the South,* as well as Sumner Rosen, in "The CIO Era," in *The Negro and the American Labor Movement,* ed. Julius Jacobsen (Garden City, N.J.: Doubleday, 1968), 195–97, suggest an abandonment of equal rights by leftist unions during the war. But this is not borne out in Memphis or in Winston-Salem. Korstad, "Daybreak of Freedom." *FTA News* shows significant black-led gains in other southern locales during the war.

70. Memphis Staff Meeting Minutes, 19 Oct. 1944, CIO Industrial Union Council, TOC, OD.

71. Henderson quoted in Christopher to Copeland, 30 Sept. 1944, Copeland Files, TOC, OD. See this letter also for other details and see Memphis Staff Meeting Minutes, 19 Oct. 1944.

72. Beddow quoted by Beecher in confidential memo of John Beecher to Lawrence Cramer, 23 Apr. 1942, John Beecher Files, FECP, RG 228, NARA. E. L. Sandefeur to Christopher, 9 Mar. 1945, and related letters in Region 8 Files, SLA/GSU, on the Highlander school; and see Christopher to Carey Haigler, 28 Apr. 1945, Region 8 Files, SLA/GSU. Routon interview on Henry White, and Christopher to Haywood, 9 June 1945, Region 8 Files, SLA/GSU. Beddow disclaimed any intention to disturb segregation, see Beddow in *From the Founding of the CIO,* ed. Foner and Lewis, 104–5, as did W. H. Crawford, quoted in Robin Kelley, *Hammer and Hoe,* 60, 68;

73. *P-S,* 26 Jan. 1945 and 19 Sept. 1945.

74. Coe interview.

EIGHT: THE CIO AT THE CROSSROADS

1. On membership figures, Marshall, *Labor in the South,* 225–27, Zieger, *American Workers,* 101, 114–16, and Fickle, *The New South and the "New Competition,"* 316. In 1948, the AFL would claim forty to fifty thousand members in Memphis, but it does not appear that its membership during the war surpassed that of the CIO. *MLR,* 19 Mar. 1948.

2. John A. Salmond, *Miss Lucy of the CIO: The Life and Times of Lucy Randolph Mason* (Athens: University of Georgia Press, 1988), 124–25. Lucy Randolph Mason, "The CIO in the South," in *The South and World Affairs* (Chapel Hill, April 1944).

3. Nelson Lichtenstein, "The Unions' Retreat in the Postwar Era," in *Major Problems in the History of American Workers,* ed. Nelson Lichtenstein and Eileen Boris (Lexington, Mass: D.C. Heath, 1991), 530. Jack M. Bloom, *Class, Race, and the Civil Rights Movement* (Bloomington: Indiana University Press, 1987), 66–69.

4. *Southern Patriot,* on Athens, Aug. 1946. James C. Cobb, *Industrialization and Southern Society, 1877–1984* (Chicago: Dorsey Press, 1984), notes GI revolts in Arkansas, Georgia, and Louisiana, 102. Brown-Melton, "Blacks in Memphis," 244, and W. E. Davis interview.

5. Eleanor Roosevelt, "The South in Postwar America," *Southern Patriot,* June 1944; Mason, "The CIO in the South."

6. *Southern Patriot,* May and June 1946.

7. *Proceedings,* CIO International Executive Board, 16–19 and 25 Nov. 1944, 183–207, 308–12, quote on 246, Reuther Library. Krueger, *And Promises to Keep,* 124–26.

8. On 1946 numbers, *The Carolinian,* 28 Dec. 1946; for examples of Tennessee

graduates, see *CIO News*, 16 June 1941 and 4 Nov. 1940; see also the *Chattanooga Times*, 23 Nov. 1940 and 18 June 1945; *UAW*, 15 July 1942.

9. Will Alexander quoted in *Southern Patriot*, Nov. 1943. *Harper's*, Jan. 1945. And see Mason, "The CIO in the South." "Petition to Kill the Poll Tax Now," *Southern Patriot*, Feb. 1944. Sosna, in *In Search of the Silent South*, points out the conference's earlier emphasis on economic improvement instead of protest as the solution to the race problem, 93; Krueger, *And Promises to Keep*, 150–51; and *Southern Patriot*, Dec. 1946, on New Orleans conference.

10. The Tennessee CIO recommended that "the precedent set by the inter-racial UAW Summer School at Highlander be followed by other unions holding residence sessions," *Highlander Fling*, July 1944, and see also the Nov. 1945 issue. Dorothy McDade to Paul Christopher, 21 June 1945 on the UAW 1945 summer school, Box 33, Region 8 Files, SLA/GSU; the International Union of Mine, Mill, and Smelter Workers asked Highlander to conduct classes for its members on CIO nondiscrimination policy in the areas surrounding the Columbia, Tennessee, race riot, *Highlander Fling*, Jan. 1947; see also Glen, *Highlander*, 95–99, on CIO schools, and 101–3 on interracialism after war; and *The Carolinian*, 28 Dec. 1946, on postwar interracial programs.

11. Haywood quote, *CIO News*, 18 June 1945. Murray article enclosed by Len DeCaux to CIO Editors and Educational Directors, *CIO News*, 27 Aug. 1945, Box 33, DeCaux File, Region 8 Files, SLA/GSU, and see *CIO News*, 17 June 1946. Murray's longer quote in Marshall, *Labor in the South*, 254.

12. Haywood statement in *CIO News*, 18 June 1945; F. Ray Marshall and Virgil L. Christian, Jr., eds., *Employment of Blacks in the South: A Perspective on the 1960s* (Austin: University of Texas Press, 1978), 42, on CIO racial advantage over AFL; Rosen, "The CIO Era," 189, on CIO anti-discrimination. "CIO," pamphlet of the CIO Department of Education and Research, Sept. 1945.

13. *Southern Patriot*, Mar. 1946, and Apr. 1947 on Willie Earle. Prominent civil rights supporters formed the National Committee for Justice in Columbia, Tennessee, after the incident, Folder 28, Box 39, WDL, Reuther Library. "Report to the National CIO Committee to Abolish Discrimination," Nov. 1946, enclosed in CIO Committee to Abolish Discrimination Folder, OD. Also see Dorothy Beeler, "Race Riot in Columbia, Tennessee, February 25–27, 1946," *Tennessee Historical Quarterly* 39, no. 1 (Spring 1980): 49–61. Lynching statistic from Brown-Melton, "Blacks in Memphis," 244, and see Stetson Kennedy, *Southern Exposure* (New York: Doubleday, 1946), 162–86, on the KKK.

14. See Robert J. Norrell's "Labor at the Ballot Box: Alabama Politics from the New Deal to the Dixiecrat Movement," *Journal of Southern History* 42, no. 2 (May 1991): 201–34.

15. Morton Sosna speculates that whites experienced some racial liberalization during the war, in "More Important than the Civil War?: The Impact of World War II on the South," in *Perspectives on the American South*, ed. James C. Cobb and Charles R. Wilson (New York: Gordon and Breach Science Publishers, 1987), 145–61. On the other hand, the sociologist Howard Odum thought race relations reached a new low during the war, see David R. Goldfield, *Promised Land: The South since 1945* (Arlington Heights, Ill.: Harlan Davidson, 1987), 19.

16. Elkuss interview. Mason, *To Win These Rights*, 107.

17. Routon interview.

18. Ibid.

19. Mason, "The CIO in the South."

20. Karl Korstad, personal interview, 20 May 1981, Greensboro, N.C., and interviews with W. E. Davis, Morton Davis, Ed McCrea, and McGurty.

21. Elkuss interview.

22. W. E. Davis interview. The UFWA may have had a black president, but I have not found documents to this effect. James White was one of the union's early black leaders, *Tri-State Defender,* 11 Feb. 1989. Ed McCrea interview. In the AFL unions, even the president of the hod carriers' union, an all-black unit, was white, according to Clark Porteous, phone interview, 11 Feb. 1983. Cayton and Mitchell, *Black Workers and the New Unions,* 354–55.

23. The highest paid worker in one organized woodworking shop in 1947, for example, made $1.02, while the lowest paid semiskilled worker made $.71 an hour. Unskilled workers made considerably less than that. "Job Classifications and Rates for Memphis, Tennessee Works Effective May 15, 1947," Turner, Day Handle Company, in IWA Folder on American Fork and Hoe Company, TOC, OD. Lichtenstein, "The Unions' Retreat," 526.

24. Marsh quoted in General Executive Board Minutes, 6–8 May 1945, 56, UFWA, SLA/GSU. Coe, Ed McCrea, and Korstad interviews on attitudes of employers and black workers and negotiating difficulties over race.

25. Federated Press release, 10 Aug. 1945, microfilm, Highlander News Clippings File, WHS.

26. Area Employment Summary, Memphis and Shelby County, Oct. 1946, Tennessee Department of Employment Security, USES, USDL, "Labor, 1946" File, Office of the Mayor's Papers, MPL. David Tucker, *Memphis since Crump,* 54, on the 1940 to 1950 increase in industrial employment.

27. Sigafoos, *Cotton Row,* 210–14; USES figure, *CA,* 2 Feb. 1946, and on housing patterns, 3 Apr. 1946; Brown-Melton, "Blacks in Memphis," 245–50, on the black economic crisis.

28. Brown-Melton, "Blacks in Memphis," 256–58, on police brutality; Crump called the CIO's Political Action Committee "communistic" and even claimed the mild-mannered League of Women Voters had been "hatched by CIO sympathizers," *CA,* 6 June 1946, and on League of Women Voters, Miller, *Mr. Crump,* 312. Weaks to Senator McKellar, 14 June 1947, Letters File, Kenneth McKellar Papers, MPL.

29. W. A. Copeland to Paul Christopher, 30 Jan. 1946, Reel 28, TOC, OD microfilm. *MLR,* 1946–47, shows little in the way of new AFL organizing. Loring began his tenth term in 1946 and finished his eleventh term in 1947, *MLR,* 15 Feb. 1946 and 14 Mar. 1947.

30. Copeland to Christopher, 9 Sept. 1943, Reel 25, TOC, OD microfilm. Examples of minimum wage workers noted by H. White Organizer's Report, 5 and 7 July 46, Reel 52, TOC, OD microfilm; wage levels noted by the USES, in A Brief Survey, 1946, and "Labor Market Development Report," Memphis Labor Market Area, July 1946, also by the USES, both in Box 357, USES, USDL, RG 183, NARA. "Wage Survey of CIO Plants in Memphis," compiled 1 Jan. 1947, based on contracts in 162 plants, Reel 28, Copeland Files, TOC, OD microfilm.

31. Tennessee Department of Employment Security, *The Labor Market,* Oct. 1947; and *General Industrial Survey* (Memphis, 1948); *The Labor Market,* July 1947, shows

women at 34 percent, and in 1948 at 33.1 percent of the working population, all in Labor Market Report File, Memphis Area, Box 353, USES, USDL, RG 183, NARA.

32. Women comprised 63 percent, 51 percent, and 28 percent, respectively, of the state's workers in service, trade, and government employment. *Annual Report,* Memphis Labor Market, June 1949, Box 353, USES, USDL, RG 183, NARA. Brown-Melton, "Blacks in Memphis," 295.

33. See George I. Whitlach, ed., *Industrial Resources of Tennessee, Revised Edition, 1948–49* (Nashville: Tennessee State Planning Commission, 1949), table 62; and table 9 of *Subsidies for Industries in Tennessee* (Nashville: Tennessee State Planning Commission, 1947).

34. According to the USDL, by March the real wages of the average factory worker had dropped 10 percent from the previous year, Strikes and Lockouts File, General Subject File, Office of the Secretary, USDL, RG 174, NARA; Barbara S. Griffiths gives a figure of 15 percent wage decline, *The Crisis of American Labor: Operation Dixie and the Defeat of the CIO* (Philadelphia: Temple University Press, 1988), 15. Memphis food and other costs in Whitlach, *Industrial Resources of Tennessee,* 24. On skyrocketing profit levels, *MLR,* 28 Feb. 1947; Rayback, *A History of American Labor,* 393; Cochran, *Labor and Communism,* 248. On price controls, *P-S,* 8 June 1946; on PAC efforts, *P-S,* 5 May 1945, 29 Jan 1946, 23 Feb 1946, 5 June 1946; *CIO News,* 18 June, 20 Aug. 1945; and the poll tax, *P-S,* 23 Feb. 1946.

35. Rayback, *A History of American Labor,* 390–93, 395; *CIO News,* 17 June 1946, on opposition to the Truman-Case antilabor bills.

36. "Labor Market Report," July 1947, on east-west industrialization, Box 353, USES, USDL, RG 183, NARA; and Whitlach, *Industrial Resources of Tennessee.* Powell interview. Griffiths, *The Crisis of American Labor,* 5–11, 25–28, and Marshall, *Labor in the South,* 256, on southern strategy.

37. See for example the 1 Mar. and 15 Mar. 1947 articles "When Employees Organize" in the *Southern Lumberman,* enclosed in George Bentley to Paul Christopher, 19 Mar. 1947, Bentley 1946–47, IWA File, TOC, OD.

38. See Organizer's Reports and correspondence from Copeland to Paul Christopher, Jan. to Oct. 1946, and 6 Jan. 1946, and Organizer's Report, 25 May 1946, Reel 28, TOC, OD microfilm. Henry White led the red caps into the CIO from an AFL union established for forty years, Copeland Organizer's Report, 6 Jan. 1946; the USWA won a shop away from the IAM that had established a closed shop five years earlier, Organizer's Report, 25 Apr. 1946; the UFWA won Southern Central away from an AFL union in the shop for six years, Organizer's Report, 19 Oct. 1946, TOC, OD

39. Fickle, *The New South and the "New Competition,"* 317. Copeland to Paul Christopher, 1 Feb. 1947, Reel 28, Copeland Files, TOC, OD microfilm. *CA,* 6 June 1946. For a listing of the impressive SOC victories in Memphis, see NLRB Docket Sheets, Box 57, Region 8 Files, SLA/GSU.

40. "The Southern Organizing Drive," Recommendations of the Executive Officers to the meeting of the CIO Executive Board, 30–31 Aug. 1948, Ralph Helstein Files, Box 50, UPWA/WHS. Joseph Yates Garrison, "Paul Revere Christopher: Southern Labor Leader, 1919–1974" (Ph.D. diss., Georgia State University, 1976), 161, on Tennessee locals; Marshall, *Labor in the South,* 258, 264–66. *CIO News,* 30 Dec. 1946, on NLRB elections.

41. Mary Frekerickson gives the women's statistics in Operation Dixie, in " 'I Know Which Side I'm On': Southern Women in the Labor Movement in the Twentieth Century," in *Women, Work and Protest: A Century of U.S. Women's Labor History,* ed. Ruth Milkman (1985; reprint, New York: Routledge and Kegan Paul, 1987), 173. Philip Murray gave the figures listed here in the 1947 CIO convention report, cited by Donald Henderson in his testimony before the CIO committee, FTA Hearings File, CIO Secretary-Treasurer's Files, Reuther Library. Korstad and Ed McCrea interviews. Paul Christopher's correspondence, Region 8 Files, SLA/GSU, bears out FTA's role in Memphis in listings of CIO election returns.

42. Marshall, *Labor in the South,* 246–54, Meany quote on 247.

43. Eugene Albert Roper, Jr., "The CIO Organizing Committee in Mississippi: June, 1946–January, 1949" (Master's thesis, University of Mississippi, 1949), 19–26. New members listed in *MLR,* 14 Feb. 1947; and Marshall, *Labor in the South,* 247, 253; on number of black AFL members, Marshall, *The Negro and Organized Labor,* 43, and on Laurel situation, 44. *MLR* "communist" charge, 24 May and 15 Nov. 1946; all white AFL officers in *MLR,* 1 Mar. 1946. Copeland statement on no strikes, *P-S,* 10 Jan. 1946, and to Lillian Lane, 14 Jan. 1945, Copeland Files, TOC, OD; Ed McCrea interview; *MLR,* Feb.–June 1946, on the Greyhound strike. *MLR* from 1946 to 1950 shows little evidence of any AFL organizing in Memphis.

44. Griffiths, *Crisis of American Labor,* 30–36, 42.

45. Copeland to Van Bittner on IAM competition, 20 Aug. 1946. The FTA lost an election at Humko, in a "pretty vicious pre-election campaign," Copeland Organizer's Report, 19 Jan. 1946; and the UAW lost an election 68–51, Organizer's Report, 21 Sept. 1946; and Copeland to Christopher, 25 Sept. 1946, on illnesses, Christopher to Copeland, 20 Sept. 1946, all in Reel 28, Copeland Files, TOC, OD microfilm.

46. Copeland to Christopher, 28 May 1946, and 2 July 1946, on AFL organizers; to Bittner, 6 July 1946, on petitions; and to Christopher, 25 July 1946, discussing the SOC lines of authority, all in Reel 28, Copeland Files, TOC, OD microfilm.

47. Griffiths, *Crisis of American Labor,* 67–68. Glen, *Highlander,* 101; Horton interview. Rev. L. F. Sledge to Christopher, 15 June 1946, Copeland recommending Dorothy Daniel to Christopher, 27 May 1946, and Christopher to Copeland, 28 May 1946, all in Reel 27, Copeland Files, TOC, OD microfilm. Mareda Holloway, a black women, a teacher, a graduate of Fisk, and a Southern Conference member thought working for the CIO would be the most effective route to equality, but she was apparently wrong. Holloway to Louis Krainock, 15 Aug. 1947, and Christopher to Weaver, 3 Sept. 1947, Reel 50, Christopher Correspondence, TOC, OD microfilm.

48. Bittner quoted in Krueger, *And Promises to Keep,* 142. *Richmond Times,* 10 May 1946, and *News Sentinel,* 15 May 1946, in Region 8 News Clippings File, SLA/GSU.

49. Bilbo quoted in *Southern Patriot,* Jan. 1946; on the CIO's role in the Southern Conference's demise, see Krueger, *And Promises to Keep,* 142–43; on CIO hostility to the Left, see David Oshinsky, "Labor's Cold War: The CIO and the Communists," in *The Specter: Original Essays on the Cold War and the Origins of McCarthyism,* ed. Robert Griffith and Athan Theoharis (New York: New Viewpoints, 1974), 118–51.

50. Griffiths, *The Crisis of American Labor,* 30–36, 42, 57, and chap. 4 on textile failures. Suspicions against the Left are apparent in letters between Christopher, Copeland, and Allan Haywood, TOC, OD. Ross, Ed McCrea, Korstad, Routon, and Powell interviews on left-wing union organizing.

51. Carson to Morris Muster, 6 Apr. 1946, Organizer's Reports, UFWA, SLA/GSU. Copeland to Christopher, 31 July 1946, on White resignation; and to Haywood, 27 Oct. 1946, on wage discrimination, both in Reel 28, Copeland Files, TOC, OD microfilm.

52. Resignation of Richard White, Copeland to Christopher, 31 July 1946; Copeland to Bittner, 7 Nov. 1946, and to Christopher, 9 Nov. 1946. Months later, Copeland was still trying to replace Routon. McGurty to Bittner, 17 Oct. 1946, all in Reel 28, Copeland Files, TOC, OD microfilm, and McGurty interview.

53. On the CIO-PAC and Routon, *P-S*, 5 July and 20 May; and see *CIO News*, 17 June and 15 July 1946, and *CA*, 6 June 1946, on electoral politics.

54. Copeland to Christopher, 16, 18 (quote), and 19 Oct. 1946, Reel 28, Copeland Files, TOC, OD microfilm. On the Buckeye strike, Mediation and Conciliation Service File 464-1458, RG 280, NARA. Van Bittner sent Copeland's correspondence on the National Negro Congress incident to FTA president Donald Henderson and told him to stop such political activities, Bittner to Henderson, 18 Oct. 1946, Philip Murray Papers, Catholic University, courtesy of Robert Korstad.

55. Typed manuscript written in 1957, in the personal collection of Lawrence McGurty, and McGurty interview.

56. Karl Korstad, "An Account of the 'Left-Led' CIO Unions' Efforts to Build Unity among the Workers in Southern Factories during the 1940's," paper given at the Southern Labor Studies Conference, Oct. 1982, Atlanta, Georgia, and Korstad interview.

57. Korstad and Ed McCrea interviews, and Boyd interview, 6 Feb. 1983, Memphis; Aptheker to Honey, 23 Nov. 1982, in author's possession, and Korstad to McGurty, 11 Mar. 1947, McGurty personal collection.

58. "Reports of General Executive Officers to FTA 6th National Convention," 13–17 Jan. 1947, WHS, on 1946 membership figures; *CA*, 17 Oct. 1946, on Cornith and Montgomery strikes; wage figure in "Summary of Proceedings of the Mississippi Delta Regional Council Conference," 24–25 Aug. 1946, Region 8 Files, SLA/GSU; and Ed McCrea Notes, 31 Mar. 1990, in author's possession. On continued FTA election wins, although mostly at small shops, NLRB Docket Sheets, c. 1946–49, Region 8 Files, SLA/GSU. *FTA News* also notes various election victories in the Deep South, for example in Port Gibson, Leland, Greenville, Mississippi, and in Helena, Arkansas, 1 Nov. 1946, and the establishment of organizing committee, 1 Dec. 1946; 15 Oct. 1947 and 1 Apr. 1947 on continued FTA organizing successes.

59. Lane comments in "Summary of Proceedings," 10.

60. Of seventy Democratic representatives who voted for HUAC in 1945, all but seven came from the South, while 80 percent of the Republicans voted for it, *Southern Patriot*, Jan. 1945. On "Militant Truth" antilabor campaign, *Southern Patriot*, May 1946, and on the KKK, May and July 1946; on Christian America financial backers, Aug. 1944; Christian fundamentalist Searcy College put out a steady barrage of anti-union propaganda, June 1946. A black FTA member was even murdered in the Southern Cotton Oil strike in Arkansas, while the state arrested strikers instead of their attackers; see an "An Appeal to Union Members and Friends," 18 Jan. 1946, and FTA letter to staff, 23 Jan. 1947, both in Folder 23, Box 201, WDL, Reuther Library.

61. Hoover letter, 12 Nov. 1946, Memphis Room, MPL. Green, *World of the Worker*, 197, on corporate anti-communism. See virulent attacks on the CIO from Representative Howard Smith of Virginia in a 1946 speech, in Barton J. Bernstein and Allen J. Matusow, *The Truman Administration: A Documentary History* (New York: Harper and Row,

1968), 123. *MLR*, various issues, 1946–50. The *CA* reprinted its series of articles on communism in a pamphlet titled "Listen Closely," MPL. McGurty to Loretto, 16 Apr. 1946, started noticing his letters being opened, McGurty personal collection and interview. File on Davis, FBI/FOIA 250,326.

62. Copeland to Christopher, 30 Nov. 1946, and Christopher to Copeland, 3 Dec. 1946, on Operation Dixie cuts; and Christopher to Copeland, 2 and 3 Mar. 1947, on east Tennessee defeats, all in Reel 28, Copeland Files, TOC, OD microfilm.

63. Copeland to Christopher, 20 Mar. 1945. Copeland to Christopher, 7 Sept. 1947, both in Reel 28, Copeland Files, TOC, OD microfilm. Jones to Lucy Mason, 2 Nov. 1948, Mason Papers, OD. Horton interview on the textile organizer's claim; Copeland to Christopher, 5 Nov. 1946, on SNYC; 2 Jan. 1947 on Highlander graduates; Copeland to Haywood, 31 Mar. 1947; to Milton Murray, president of the Newspaper Guild, 31 Mar. 1947, objecting to Carl Haesler's presence at Highlander; to Christopher, 25 Mar. 1947, all in Reel 28, Copeland Files, TOC, OD microfilm. Boyd Payton, regional director of the Textile Workers Union of America, wrote to Lucy Mason about Copeland's information on various people he thought were "commies," 21 Dec. 1948, Mason Papers, OD. See other letters about Copeland's red-baiting, which he denied, 1948–49, Mason Papers, OD. Powell interview, on Copeland and the FBI.

64. See correspondence of Copeland, Christopher, and J. D. Harris, on elections in early 1947, and, for example, Christopher to Harris, 30 June 1947, on wins in a number of small shops, in their correspondence files, TOC, OD.

65. Denunciations of labor "reds": Orgill statement in *MLR*, 30 Aug. 1946; KKK announcing its top priority is "reds," blacks taking second place, *Knoxville Journal*, 17 May 1946; "Bittner Denies Communist Tag Applies to CIO," *Atlanta Journal*, 29 Aug. 1946. Rayback, *A History of American Labor*, 395–400, on Taft-Hartley and state laws; note on Tennessee law in memo to Grover Hathaway, 21 July 1947, Ms. 118. District 9 File 2, Box 42, 1947, Office of the President, UPWA/WHS.

66. J. R. Haas, of U.S. Bedding, to McKellar, 4 and 26 June 1947. E. A. Sparrow to McKellar, 28 May 1947, both in L File, McKellar Papers, MPL. Rayback, in *A History of American Labor*, 398, points out the bill was essentially drafted by the National Association of Manufacturers. Supporters for it in Tennessee included, for example, Edgar McHenry of Bess and Bess supplies, Germantown, to McKellar, 5 May 1947, claiming unionists were dictators like those fought in World War II, and W. W. Simmons of Broadway Coal in Memphis, 30 June 1947. Quote from J. L. Boyd, 8 May 1947, and the CIO's B. R. Allen was among Memphis unionists who wrote McKellar in opposition, 13 June 1947, L File, McKellar Papers, MPL; Chamber of Commerce "Resolution," 1947 Files, Office of the Mayor's Papers, MPL. On the Landis bill for higher wages and a forty-hour week, Douglas Heruer, National Lumber Exporters Association in Memphis, to McKellar, 7 July 1947; Henry Fisher, Southern Laundry Owners Association in Memphis, 2 Jan. 1947; and Howard Powell of Brownsville, 7 July 1947, all in L File, McKellar Papers, MPL.

67. McDonald quoted in *CA*, 2 Sept. 1947, and *P-S*, 1 Sept. 1947; Brown-Melton, "Blacks in Memphis," 278; *MLR*, 29 Sept. 1947; Hollis Reid to Memphis workers, 5 Apr. 1947, Copeland Files, TOC, OD.

68. Paul Christopher to J. D. Harris, 14 and 18 July 1947; on the FTA strikes, Harris to Christopher, 10 Oct. 1947; on Willard Battery and Watkins, Harris to Christopher, 11 Dec. 1947, and Christopher to Harris, 17 Dec. 1947, in Harris Files, TOC, OD.

69. Christopher to Harris, 17 Dec. 1947, on two successes in Memphis.

70. Christopher "Tennessee Staff Notes," 29 July 1948, on the incredible maze of Taft-Hartley bureaucracy, in Folder 12, Christopher Files, TOC, OD. Garrison, "Paul Revere Christopher," 166–68, on statistics. Christopher to R. C. Thomas, 14 Nov. 1947, on the Vultee strike, Region 8 Files, SLA/GSU; on East Tennessee, Copeland to Christopher, 26 Aug., 8 Sept. 1947, and other letters in Copeland Files, TOC, OD. Christopher pointed out later that under Taft-Hartley "it takes an average of 1 ½ years to process an unfair labor practice charge," in "Tennessee CIO" newsletter, 13 Mar. 1951, Folder 13, Christopher Files, TOC, OD. Grover Hathaway to Frank Ellis, 18 Aug. 1947, Folder 2, Box 42, District 9 Files, UPWA/WHS. Rayback, *A History of American Labor,* 409–10, on strike decline and cost of living increases.

71. Rayback, *A History of American Labor,* 407–8; Green, *World of the Worker,* 199–201; debate in *Proceedings,* CIO International Executive Board, 8–11 Aug. 1947, 61–68, Reuther Library; see also Martin Halpern, "The Disintegration of the Left-Center Coalition in the UAW, 1945–1950" (Ph.D. diss., University of Missouri, 1982).

72. General Executive Board Minutes, 30 June to 1 July 1947, 11, and listing of organized shops, "Prepared for Southern Organizing Committee by the United Furniture Workers of America," May 1946, UFWA, SLA/GSU.

73. General Executive Board Minutes, 6–8 May 1945, 37 passim; 21–22 Nov. 1947, 22, and related minutes; 26–27 May 1949, 12–13 ff., and "Statement on Compliance"; and 6–9 Dec. 1949, 434–38, UFWA, SLA/GSU.

74. General Executive Board Minutes, 26–27 May 1949, 16, UFWA, SLA/GSU.

75. Copeland to Christopher, 22 Aug. 1947, and J. D. Harris to Copeland, 28 Aug. 1947, Copeland Files, TOC, OD.

76. Copeland to Christopher, 25 Jan. 1947, Harris to Copeland, 29 July 1947, Christopher to Harris, 31 July 1947, and Harris to Christopher, 7 Aug. 1947, Harris Files, 1946–47, TOC, OD.

77. "Election Results" in J. D. Harris Organizer's Report, 13 Dec. 1946, Harris Files, TOC, OD.

78. Boyd interview, 6 Feb. 1983.

79. Ibid. W. E. Davis interview. According to Robert Korstad, the Communist party in the South had two thousand members in 1947 and aggressively recruited black workers, paper given at the Southern Historical Association, and comments by Junius Scales, panel on the Communist party in the South, Southern Historical Association Meeting, Norfolk, Virginia, 11 Nov. 1988. Boyd, Ed McCrea, and Powell interviews. On the Communist party and the CIO generally, see Levenstein, *Communism, Anti-Communism, and the CIO,* chaps. 9–11.

80. Boyd and W. E. Davis interviews.

81. W. E. Davis interview. George L. Edwards, Assistant Southern Field Director, to Nelson Jackson, Field Director, National Urban League Southern Regional Office, 27 Apr. 1951, NUL General Office Files, Manuscripts Division, LC.

82. Ed McCrea and Korstad interviews. An FBI document on Local 19, n.d., FBI/FOIA 85-1714, reports that in late 1949 or early 1950 all Local 19 leaders who also belonged to the Communist party, including John Mack Dyson, left the party in order to sign the Taft-Hartley provision. One Communist party organizer without warning announced the membership of Local 22 members in front of a mass meeting, when their membership had not been previously known, causing embarrassment and hard feelings. Korstad paper.

83. W. E. Davis interview.

NINE: THE COLD WAR AGAINST LABOR AND CIVIL RIGHTS

1. Bilbo quoted in *Southern Patriot*, June 1946. Crump quoted in *P-S*, 25 Nov. 1947. Pleasants quoted in *P-S*, 27 Nov. 1947. Miller, *Mr. Crump*, 323; *P-S*, 3 Mar. 1947; *P-S* articles on the Freedom Train, 19, 21, and 25 Nov., 1 Dec. 1947.

2. J. D. Harris to Christopher, 24, 27 Apr., 15, 21, and 28 May, 17, 24, and 26 June 1948, Harris File, TOC, OD. *P-S*, 24 and 25 June 1943 and 18 Dec. 1947. Other details in reports by William Whorton, June 1948, in Mediation and Conciliation Service File 474-657, RG 280, NARA, and George Bentley Organizer's Reports, File 1949–50, UFWA, SLA/GSU.

3. McGurty to Palazzi, 14 Jan. 1983, McGurty personal collection. Copeland to Christopher, 16 Mar. 1948, and to Joseph Froesch, 21 Jan. 1948, and to Harry Sayre, 6 Mar. 1948, all in Copeland Files, TOC, OD, and "Tennessee CIO Staff Notes," 29 July 1948, Christopher Files, TOC, OD. IWA Local 332 in Memphis had sided with the IWA Left and was purged in 1946. Jerry Lembcke, "Social Structure and Southern Unions: A Case Study of the International Woodworkers of America," 20–23, n.d., ms. in author's possession.

4. Robert Ozanne, *A Century of Labor-Management Relations at McCormick and International Harvester* (Madison: University of Wisconsin Press, 1967), 189. Holloway interview.

5. On CIO vote potential, Brown-Melton, "Blacks in Memphis," 155, and McKellar to Crump, 4 Apr. 1938, and Hargrove to McKellar, 6 Apr. 1938, in Crump-McKellar Correspondence, McKellar Papers, MPL; Allen H. Kitchens, "Political Upheaval in Tennessee: Boss Crump and the Senatorial Election of 1948," *West Tennessee Historical Society Papers* 16 (1962): 104–26; Miller, *Mr. Crump*, 331; and Joseph Bruce Gorman, *Kefauver: A Political Biography* (New York: Oxford University Press, 1971), 51–59, voting tabulations on 59. For a general treatment, see Charles L. Fontenay, *Estes Kefauver: A Biography* (Knoxville: University of Tennessee Press, 1980), 145–52. Tucker, *Lieutenant Lee*, 146.

6. Meeman, *The Editorial We*, 99–105. Meeman stressed the influence of the war on the support for democracy by anti-Crump people, 100, 109. Tucker, *Lieutenant Lee*, 146.

7. Kefauver quoted in *Washington Post*, 7 Aug. 1948; Copeland to Bittner, 9 Aug. 1948, 1948 Folder, Copeland Files, TOC, OD. *P-S*, 8 Aug. 1949; Lucius Burch, phone interview, 25 May 1989. Holloway, Powell, and Ed McCrea interviews. See also Tucker, *Memphis since Crump*, statistics on 54 and 56–59.

8. Southern Conference supporters quoted in *Southern Patriot*, Nov. 1947. Wallace quoted in Patricia Sullivan, "Gideon's Southern Soldiers: New Deal Politics and Civil Rights Reform, 1933–1948" (Ph.D. diss., Emory University, 1983), 223–30, 246–331, quote on 331; and see also Curtis MacDougall, *Gideon's Army* (New York: Marzani and Munsell, 1965), 3:707–44.

9. Sullivan, "Gideon's Southern Soldiers," 247, 340, 347–48, and the *Memphis World*, 7 and 14 Sept. and 5 Oct. 1948. MacDougall, *Gideon's Army*, 3:676. Tucker, *Lieutenant Lee*, 147. Personal interviews, Ken and Nona Clark, 5 Dec. 1982, New York City, and Clara Vincent, Jan. 1983, Livonia, Michigan. All three worked on the Wallace campaign in Tennessee.

10. Kyle quoted in Tucker, *Black Pastors and Leaders*, 106, and *Lieutenant Lee*, 147. Brown-Melton, "Blacks in Memphis," 269, 287; Sullivan, "Gideon's Southern Soldiers," 358–60; Ed McCrea interview; MacDougall, *Gideon's Army*, 3:735.

11. Bittner quoted in Virginia State CIO Committee reprint, 9 Nov. 1948, 1948 Organizing Committee Folder, CIO Secretary-Treasurer Files, Reuther Library. Levenstein, *Communism, Anti-Communism, and the CIO*, 217–18; for examples of racist demagoguery, see the *Southern Patriot*, 1948–55; Mary Sperling McAuliffe, *Crisis on the Left: Cold War Politics and American Liberals, 1947–1954* (Amherst: University of Massachusetts Press, 1978), 38–47.

12. "General Industrial Survey of Memphis, Tennessee, 1948." Minutes, Memphis Chamber of Commerce meeting, 18 Mar. 1948, and Warren Cruzen to Mayor James Pleasants, 1 Mar. 1948, all in Chamber of Commerce, 1948 File, Office of the Mayor's Papers, MPL. The IBEW won the GE plant, M. E. Duncan to Christopher, 7 Sept. 1948, Memphis Lamp Works File, TOC, OD.

13. Organizers commented on the fear and weak leadership base at Memphis Furniture, Director of Organization Ernest Marsh to organizer Gene Day, 18 Nov. 1948, in Day correspondence; and Carl Curtis Organizer's Report, 15 May 1948, UFW, SLA/GSU.

14. McKinley phone interview; *United Furniture Worker News,* Jan.–Aug. 1949.

15. Copeland to Watkins Overton, 2 Mar. 1949, File 26, Box 2, Overton Papers, MVC/MSU.

16. *Furniture Workers Press,* Feb. 1949; McKinley phone interview.

17. Bentley Organizer's Report, 12 Mar. 1949, File 185/21, IWA District 4, SLA/GSU. Day to Marsh, 10 Mar. 1949, in Day Organizer's Reports, UFWA, SLA/GSU; Harris Organizer's Report, 16 Apr. 1949, TOC, OD, on beatings.

18. Bentley Weekly Report, 5 Mar. 1949, gives the three-thousand-dollar figure, IWA Papers, SLA/GSU; script for radio program, in possession of Bea McCrea; Day to Marsh, 15 Mar. 1949, UFWA, SLA/GSU; and McKinley phone interview on the inability to stop scabs.

19. Bentley Weekly Report, 19 Mar. 1949, IWA Papers, SLA/GSU.

20. Bentley Weekly Reports, 16 Apr. 1949, 14 and 28 May 1949, IWA Papers, SLA/GSU; W. E. Davis interview.

21. David Conner to Ernest Marsh, 1 Sept. 1949, District 9 File, Local 282, UFWA, SLA/GSU.

22. J. E. Fadling, International President, to Bentley, 28 Apr. 1949, in Bentley Weekly Reports, IWA Papers, SLA/GSU; after Fadling's letter on April 28, Bentley reported no further strike support work at Memphis Furniture. Conner to Marsh, 1 Sept. 1949, noted the lack of IWA and CIO support, District 9 Files, UFWA, SLA/GSU.

23. Boyd and Ed McCrea interviews.

24. Conner to Marsh, 1 Sept. 1949, UFWA, SLA/GSU. Korstad, "An Account"; Junius Scales, in *Cause at Heart,* makes the point that much of his own attraction to the Communist party was its open opposition to Jim Crow, in contrast to southern liberals who feared to confront the system.

25. Conner to Marsh, 1 Sept. 1949; *P-S,* 19 Sept. 1949; Copeland to All Staff, June 8 and 20 Sept. 1949, 1949 Folder, Copeland Files, TOC, OD. Brown-Melton, "Blacks in Memphis," 349n11.

26. Day to Marsh, 2 Sept. 1949, District 9 Files, UFWA, SLA/GSU, and Bentley Weekly Report, 30 July 1949, IWA Papers, SLA/GSU. "Resolution on Communism," District 9 File, Local 282, UFWA, SLA/GSU.

27. *P-S,* 19 Sept. 1949. Ed McCrea recalled that "Copeland opened the meeting with his usual anti-communist tirade and went on at length to describe some mysterious

unknown communist who had gotten onto the organizing staff of some unnamed international union in the south. His name was Tietlebaum and if anyone knew or came across such a man he should let him know." Conners and McCrea privately shared the joke that the former was the mysterious Teitlebaum, a pseudonym McCrea had once used. McCrea notes, 31 Mar. 1990, to the author.

28. Conner to Marsh, 1 Sept. 1949; McKinley interview; *P-S,* 19 Sept. 1949.

29. *P-S,* 21 Sept. 1949.

30. On the CIO's internal purge, "Statement of Allan S. Haywood on Behalf of the Congress of Industrial Organizations with Regard to Communist Dominated Unions before the Subcommittee on Labor and Labor Management Relations, United States Senate, June 17 1952." On Memphis FTA expulsion, *P-S,* 23 Sept. 1950, and "Resolution Expelling the Food, Tobacco, Agricultural and Allied Workers Union of America," 15 Feb. 1950, all in FTA Investigation Folder, TOC, OD.

31. Petition attached to W. A. Copeland to Paul Christopher, 20 Apr. 1948, Folder 134, Copeland Files, TOC, OD. Christopher to Copeland, 11 Mar. 1949, 1948 Folder, Copeland Files, TOC, OD. Day to Marsh, 12 Aug. 1949, District 9 Files, UFWA, SLA/GSU. On the Cudahy secession, *P-S,* 19 Sept. 1949; see John Mack Dyson to B. R. Allen, Memphis CIO President, n.d., forwarded by Allan S. Haywood to Ralph Helstein, 6 Sept. 1949, Ms. 118, A. S. Haywood File, Office of the President, UPWA/WHS; McCrea notes.

32. Marsh to Day, 30 Dec. 1949, District 9 Files, UFWA, SLA/GSU.

33. Day to Marsh, 22 Oct. 1949. Day to Marsh, 20 Sept. 1949, on blacklisting, both in District 9 Files, UFWA, SLA/GSU.

34. Day to Marsh, 12 Aug. 1949. Day to Marsh, 25 Apr. 1950, both in District 9 Files, UFWA, SLA/GSU.

35. *P-S,* 19 Feb., no year, quote on Pizer meeting, District 9 Files, UFWA, SLA/GSU. George Clark interview. See "Report of the Committee to Investigate Charges against the United Furniture Workers of America," Internationals File, UFWA, SLA/GSU.

36. Curtis Organizer's Report, week ending 17 Apr. 1948, UFWA, SLA/GSU. Day to Marsh, 7 and 31 Mar. 1950, District 9 Files, UFWA, SLA/GSU, on billy clubs.

37. "CIO Call to Action," Memphis CIO Strike Committee leaflet, 8 May 1950, enclosed in the American Snuff Company Strike Files, Overton Papers, MVC/MSU. William Ross, active in the Memphis AFL-CIO for many years, phone interview on the Condon family, 2 Mar. 1983. The description of the strike comes from dozens of press clippings in the strike file, many of which do not have dates. The women originally were represented by an AFL union, Copeland to Christopher, 15 Aug. 1949, 1949 Folder, Copeland Files, TOC, OD.

38. *P-S,* 17 July 1950.

39. Report of W. H. Crawford to 8th Annual District Conference USWA, Memphis, 23–24 Sept. 1950, Overton Papers, MVC/MSU, on numbers of police involved; Chief of Police Claude Armour to Overton, 7 June 1950, on recruitment procedures, in American Snuff File, Overton Papers, MVC/MSU.

40. *P-S,* 7 Mar. 1950, on the red truck, 29 Mar. 1950, on caravan, 17 July 1950, on black strike supporters.

41. *P-S,* 31 Mar. 1950. See 6 Mar. 1950 and other articles in the *P-S* on bus incidents.

42. W. J. Condon to M. J. Condon, 22 Feb. 1950, on Crowder; Fred Peoples to Overton, enclosed letter to employees dated 1 Mar. 1949; "CIO Call to Action" and leaflet,

22 Mar. 1950, American Snuff Company Strike Files, Overton Papers, MVC/MSU. See *P-S* on striker activity and comments.

43. *CA*, 15 Mar. 1950, and *P-S*, 8 May 1950, on calls for general strike; $2,625 in fines were levied by the courts as of 31 Mar., and see *CA*, 18 July 1950, on union funds lost.

44. *P-S*, 13, 19, 20, 25, 26 Sept., 6, 16, 18 Oct. 1950, 11 Jan. 1952.

45. On construction shootings, *P-S* and *CA*, 27 Aug. and 6 Sept. 1954, and see files of both papers on the building trades strikes in MVC/MSU.

46. Quotes in *P-S*, 10 Sept. 1950. *P-S*, 25 July 1949 and 10 Sept. 1950, on Himmaugh; "Maritime Protest to CIO Council," *CA*, n.d.; W. E. Davis and McGurty interviews.

47. *P-S*, 27 July 1950, attacks on Local 19, and 29 July 1950, response by Dyson. Al Greenburg and his wife were the couple arrested. Greenburg personal interview, 14 Nov. 1987, Larchmont, N.Y.

48. *P-S*, 19 Sept. 1950. *P-S*, 10 Sept. 1950. *P-S*, 21 Sept. 1950. *CA*, 11 Sept. 1950. On black ministers, Staff Meeting Minutes, 24 Sept. 1951, Memphis File, TOC, OD.

49. *P-S*, 23 Feb. 1950, on reported FTA decline, and *P-S*, 19 Sept. 1950, on FTA contracts. Day to Marsh, 12 Aug. 1949, UFWA, SLA/GSU. Copeland to FTA Acting President John Tisa, 7 Nov. 1949, 1949 Folder, Copeland Files, TOC, OD. Ed McCrea interview. On FTA's five hundred new members, Copeland to Christopher, 7 Apr. 1948, 1948 Folder, Copeland Files, TOC, OD. Paul Christopher's Region 8 Files on Memphis indicate that Local 19 had a consistent record of success in representation elections, SLA/GSU. FBI memo 100-100713, FBI/FOIA 85-1714, on Local 19 members dropping out of the Communist party.

50. *P-S*, 19 Sept. 1950. Ed McCrea interview and notes; Isabell interview; "Food, Tobacco, and Allied Workers Institutes, 1946–1947," Folder 7, Box 60, and "Labor Extension: FTA Workers, 1946 and 1948," Folder 3, Box 59, Highlander Files, WHS.

51. Isabell interview; *P-S*, 11 Sept. 1951; *CA*, 21 Sept. 1951, on Buckeye vote; Memphis Staff Meeting notes, 24 Sept. 1951, Industrial Union Council File, and Copeland to Christopher, 22 Nov. 1952, 1952 Folder, Copeland Files, TOC, OD. *P-S*, 25 Oct. 1952, on the AFL union.

52. *Memphis World*, 6 Apr. 1951; Brown-Melton, "Blacks in Memphis," 258, on electrocutions; Boyd interview

53. Boyd interview; Ed McCrea interview. *Southern Patriot*, June 1951; Red Davis recalled FBI agents as well as police swarming all over town and thought that as many as seventy-five ended up in jail, interview. FBI File 100-347485, FBI/FOIA 250,326, on "conspiracy charges."

54. Mitchell, *Mean Things*. Eastland background in the *CA*, 28 Oct. 1951, and 5 Feb. 1956.

55. *Labor Journal*, Aug. 1956. Copeland to Richard Arens, SISS attorney, 14 Nov. 1951, Distributive, Processing, and Office Workers Union, Internal Security Subcommittee, Subject File, Records of the U.S. Senate, RG 46, NARA.

56. *CA*, 24 Oct. 1951. *P-S*, 17 Oct. 1951. *P-S*, 26 Oct. 1951. Ed McCrea interview.

57. *P-S*, 26 Oct. 1951. *P-S*, 4 Sept. 1952. See the 26 Oct. 1951 issue also for the hearings on Fisher. The Local 19 membership list is still in the Distributive, Processing, and Office Workers Union subject file. Subcommittee to Investigate the Administration of the Internal Security Act and Other Internal Security Laws, *Hearings on "Subversive Control of Distributive, Processing, and Office Workers of America"* (Washington, D.C.: GPO, 1952), 146.

58. The quote by Eastland is paraphrased by reporter Clark Porteous, *P-S*, 28 Oct. 1951. *P-S*, 25, 26, and 27 Oct. 1951 on the Rabinowitz expulsion.

59. Boyd interview. *P-S*, 2 Dec. 1951. *P-S*, 2 Nov. 1951, 1 Jan. 1952.

60. Boyd interview. *P-S*, 2 and 24 Dec. 1951, on McCrea war record; *CIO Labor Journal*, Mar. 1952; W. E. Davis and Ed McCrea interviews and McCrea notes.

61. *Memphis Review*, 12 Aug. 1950, on Dyson funeral; J. S. Hostetler, Agent in Charge, 26 Apr. 1948 Report, File 100-2165, FBI/FOIA 250,185 and FBI File 100-341531, in author's possession, on Dyson; Ed McCrea interview on Davis's death and Fisher's harassment; Hudson interview on his escape from the FBI in Memphis; W. E. Davis, Ed McCrea, Leroy Clark, and Hudson all mentioned the assault on Fisher's wife; Isabell and Boyd interviews on FBI harassment; FBI Files 100-2589 on Earl Fisher, FBI/FOIA 250,182, and File 100-459 on FTA, FBI/FOIA 250,193; Powell interview.

62. Attempted interviews in 1983, 1985, and 1990 with shop leader William Lynn; *Southern Patriot*, Oct. 1972, interview with Fisher.

63. Leroy Clark interview; Lost Shops File, District 9, particularly the file on Sam Belz Manufacturing, a company that engaged the union in a running battle for ten years, UFWA, SLA/GSU. The *Furniture Workers Press*, 1949–55 and Nov. 1950, on the southern meeting; see 1952 and 1953 correspondence in Leroy Clark, Organizer's Files, UFWA, SLA/GSU, on the "lily white" policy and black staff members objections to it; Alzada Clark, personal interview, 24 May 1989, Memphis. Daniel B. Cornfield, *Becoming a Mighty Voice: Conflict and Change in the United Furniture Workers of America* (New York: Russell Sage Foundation, 1989), 171.

64. W. E. Davis interview. "To All NMU River Members," leaflet, n.d., McGurty personal collection. Assistant Secretary of Commerce South Trimble, Jr., to Ralph D. Hetzel, 19 Jan. 1949; group letter from the crew of the St. Wake Island, 6 July 1949, enclosed in a series of telegrams for workers in St. Louis and Memphis complaining about layoffs to Secretary of Commerce Charles Sawyer, both in Labor File, Box 37, IWC/DC, RG 91, NARA. FBI File 100-347485, FBI/FOIA 250,326 on Davis.

65. McGurty interview, and McGurty to Al Greenberg, 27 Nov. 1955, and to Vince, 6 Nov. 1955, McGurty personal collection

66. Democratic Governor Frank Clement, as well as Loeb, became well known in part through their American Legion leadership. *CA*, 23 Aug. 1949, 27 July 1949; *P-S*, 30 July 1952, on Henry Loeb. SAC Memphist to Director, 7 June 1948, notes security index on Davis, and 23 Aug. 1950 suggests that all Communist party vets should be considered armed and potentially dangerous. FBI File, FBI/FOIA 261,129, on Red Davis.

67. *CIO Labor Journal*, Jan. 1952. Memphis Chamber of Commerce to Board of Directors, enclosing national chamber pamphlet on socialism, 20 Mar. 1950, Overton Files, MVC/MSU; *CA*, 9 Nov. 1952, on cosponsorship; *CA*, 30 June 1960, on Eastland award.

68. Hoover quoted in *CIO Labor Journal*, June 1951. See *CIO Labor Journal*, Oct. 1951 and Feb. 1952, on State Department visits; Economic Cooperation Administration File, 1951, Office of the Mayor's Papers, MPL.

69. Swim worked in Thailand and Pakistan, *CIO Labor Journal*, Jan. 1954.

70. *CIO Labor Journal*, Jan. 1952; *P-S*, 13 Nov. 1950 and 38 Apr. 1949, 6 May 1952, on Swim and Martin; "Crusade for Freedom" letterhead, 17 Oct. 1950, Christopher on the Advisory Committee, TOC, OD; *P-S*, 12 Sept. 1950, 11 Sept. 1951, on "Crusade";

CIO Labor Journal, Oct. and Nov. 1951; "Crusade for Freedom," Office of the Mayor's Papers, MPL; *Labor Journal,* Sept. 1951, and numerous business ads to "their friends in labor," Jan. 1952.

71. *CIO Labor Journal,* Jan. 1957. *P-S,* 7 Dec. 1954; William Grogan, *John Riffe of the Steelworkers: American Labor Statesman* (Coward-McCann, 1959); *CIO Labor Journal,* Sept. 1953, on Allen trip.

72. Explorations for negotiating peace between AFL and CIO unions at the national level coincided almost exactly with the purge of the left-led unions, see Philip Murray to William Green, 6 June 1950, 85–87, and AFL-CIO Unity Talks, 29 Aug. 1950, 76–85, in *Proceedings,* CIO International Executive Board. *P-S,* 21 June 1950, on AFL changes. *P-S,* 8 Jan. 1955, on labor's meeting with business.

73. For examples of racial violence from this period, see the United Electrical Workers union pamphlet, "Terror in the South," c. 1955, Louis Slater Collection, Tammiment Library, New York University. Tucker, *Memphis since Crump,* 77, 87–99. Brown-Melton, "Blacks in Memphis," 313–16, 330–32. *P-S,* 22 Nov. 1954. Tucker, *Lieutenant Lee,* 170, and Tucker, *Memphis since Crump,* 77 passim.

74. Dhuy quoted in *CIO Labor Journal,* July 1953. Total AFL membership in the South stood at 1,148,100 compared with 362,200 southern CIO members in 1953, Marshall, *Labor in the South,* 268–69. *P-S,* 22 Nov. 1954, on labor cooperation, and 20 May 1955, and B. R. Allen to Ralph Helstein, 2 May 1949, Office of the President, UPWA/WHS, on CIO buildings. Korstad, "Daybreak of Freedom," and see Foner, *Organized Labor and the Black Worker,* 281–82; Horace Huntley, "Iron Ore Miners and Mine Mill in Alabama: 1933–1952" (Ph.D. diss., University of Pittsburgh, 1977); Horton interview, and Horton to J. Lewis Henderson, 25 Feb. 1950, and related materials in Group 2, Ser. 1, Highlander Research and Education Center Library, New Market, Tenn.

75. Powell interview.

76. Powell, Holloway, Carl Moore, and Coe interviews. Record Books, Minutes, UAW Local 988, UAW Records, Reuther Library. Tucker, *Memphis since Crump,* 83–99. Ozanne, "A Century of Labor-Management Relations," 188–92.

77. Les Orear, personal interview, 1 Aug. 1981, Chicago. District 9 Files of the UPWA have a great deal of material on the antidiscrimination fight in the South, which met with both success and failure. On the Memphis plants, A. T. Stephens to Dick Durham, 6 Oct. 1954, Folder 15, and see Survey, Folder 18, both in Box 357, Program Department, UPWA/WHS. On the remarkable civil rights struggle within the CIO packinghouse union, see Moses Adedeji, "Crossing the Color Line: Three Decades of the UPWA's Crusade against Racism" (Ph.D. diss., North Texas State University, 1978); Eric Brian Halpern, "Black and White Unite and Fight: Race and Labor in Meatpacking, 1904–1948" (Ph.D. diss., University of Pennsylvania, 1989), and "Interracial Unionism in the Southwest: Fort Worth's Packinghouse Workers, 1937–1954," in *Organized Labor in the Twentieth-Century South,* 158–82; and Roger Horowitz, "The Path Not Taken: A Social History of Industrial Unionism in Meatpacking, 1930–1960" (Ph.D. diss., University of Wisconsin, 1990).

78. J. Carlton Yeldell, UL Labor Relations Secretary, to M. A. Hutcheson, National President of the Carpenters' Union, 9 July 1959, Affiliates, Dept. D, Industrial Relations, Ser. 4, NUL Papers, LC. Harry Alston, Southern Field Director, to Nelson Jackson, Director of Community Services, 19 May 1954; and "Twenty-two Years of Progress with

the Memphis Urban League in Human Relations and General Welfare, 1932–1954"; and Nelson Jackson to Lester Granger, 27 Nov. 1950, both in Ser. 4, NUL Papers, LC. *CA,* 29 May 1965 and 8 Jan. 1978.

79. The *CIO Labor Journal,* May 1951 to June 1957, figures from June 1957 issue, and pin-ups; see Marshall, *The Negro and Organized Labor,* on the effects of the AFL-CIO merger.

80. *MLR,* 19 Mar. 1948. "There are 40,000 unionized workers in Memphis, but this number is not increasing," said Lewis. Anti-unionism and automation, he concluded—ignoring the race question—were killing the union movement. *P-S,* 4 Sept. 1961. Marshall, *Labor in the South,* 271–76.

81. David Brody points out that the AFL-CIO supported a job discrimination ban in the 1964 Civil Rights Act that would apply to unions as well as employers, *Workers in Industrial America: Essays on the Twentieth Century Struggle* (New York: Oxford University Press, 1980), 223. But see Zieger, *American Workers,* 174–82, for a detailed account of the reasons for black discontent, and Marshall, *The Negro and Organized Labor,* 53–85.

82. Marshall, *Unions in the South,* 266. Michael Goldfield, *The Decline of Organized Labor in the United States* (Chicago: University of Chicago Press, 1987), on the secular decline of organized labor, and see his paper "The Failure of Operation Dixie," Southern Labor Studies Conference, 12 Oct. 1991, Atlanta. See also Honey, "Operation Dixie: The CIO's Fast Organizing Drive," paper presented at the Southern Labor Studies Conference, Oct. 1993, Atlanta, and Griffith, *The Crisis of American Labor.*

CONCLUSION: LEGACIES

1. Coe interview. Josh Tools, phone interview, 3 Mar. 1983. Holloway interview.

2. Wright, *Old South, New South,* 186. Coe interview.

3. "White flight" coincided with school busing and plant closings in Memphis. Sandra Vaughn, "Memphis: Heart of the Mid-South," in *In Search of the New South: The Black Urban Experience in the 1970's and 1980's,* ed. Robert D. Bullard (Tuscaloosa: University of Alabama Press, 1989), 104. Coe, Isabell, Ed McCrea, and Routon interviews, and McCrea notes.

4. Coe interview.

5. There were 7,372 black male and 1,866 black female operatives in 1940; 13,239 and 3,561, respectively, in 1950; and 14,070 and 3,253 in 1960 in the Memphis metropolitan area. In contrast, the number of private household workers declined between 1940 and 1950 in Memphis, but in 1960 returned to about the same number as in 1940. Brown-Melton, "Blacks in Memphis," 293. F. Ray Marshall says black median income in the South declined relative to whites by 10 percentage points in the fifties, "Industrialization and Race Relations in the Southern United States," in *Industrialization and Race Relations: A Symposium,* ed. Guy Hunter (New York: Oxford University Press, 1965), 91. Wright, *Old South, New South,* 243, on cotton percentages, and 247, 255, on mechanization of industry. F. Ray Marshall and Arvil Van Adams, "Negro Employment in Memphis," *Industrial Relations: A Journal of Economy and Society* 9, no. 3 (May 1970): 308–23, on the structural economic problems of the black community in the sixties. John M. Brewster, *Labor and Power Utilization at Cotton Seed Oil Mills,* U.S. Department of Agriculture Marketing Research Report no. 218 (Washington, D.C.: GPO,

1958), 3, points out that the upward trend in wages caused cottonseed oil producers to introduce labor-saving devices. Fickle, in *The New South and the "New Competition,"* 314–15, points out a similar trend in lumbering. Black entrance into southern industry, however, had always been premised on low skill and wage requirements. Northrup and Rowan, *Negro Employment in Southern Industry.* "General Characteristics" of urban population, 1949, in *Census of Population: 1950* (Washington, D.C.: GPO, 1952), vol. 5, part 2, pp. 42–51. Donald D. Stewart, "Poverty in Memphis: Report of a Preliminary Study," Memphis State University Department of Sociology and Anthropology printed report, 1964.

6. *P-S*, 17 Feb. 1960, on Nickey Brothers. Marshall, "Industrialization and Race Relations," 91. On the educational and employment patterns keeping Memphis blacks at the bottom of the social system, see Arvil Van Adams, "The Memphis Labor Market," in *Negro Employment in the South*, vol. 2, Manpower Research Monograph no. 23, ed. F. Ray Marshall (Washington, D.C.: GPO, 1971), 9–18.

7. Marshall and Van Adams, "Negro Employment in Memphis," 310. Coe interview.

8. Coe interview.

9. See Robin D. G. Kelley, "'We Are Not What We Seem': Towards a Black Working-Class Infrapolitics in the Twentieth Century South," paper presented at the Seventh Annual Southern Labor Studies Conference, 10–13 Oct. 1991, Atlanta, Ga. Robert Korstad and Nelson Lichtenstein discuss the rise of "rights consciousness" among black workers as a direct outgrowth of principles they established by their struggles to implement 1930s labor laws and the directives of federal agencies during the war. Korstad and Lichtenstein, "Opportunities Found and Lost," and see Korstad, "Daybreak of Freedom."

10. See Van Adams, "The Memphis Labor Market," 15–19.

11. Ed McCrea interview.

12. F. Ray Marshall and Virgil L. Christian point out that unions helped to formalize job segregation through contracts which restricted black mobility, "The Old South and the New," in *Employment of Blacks in the South*, ed. Marshall and Christian, 6. See various accounts of white union racism by Herbert Hill, for example, "Race and Ethnicity in Organized Labor: The Historical Sources of Resistance to Affirmative Action," *Journal of Intergroup Relations* 12, no. 4 (Winter 1984): 5–50, and "Black Labor and Affirmative Action: An Historical Perspective," in *The Question of Discrimination*, ed. Shulman and Darity, 190–267. Norrell, "Caste in Steel." The "racialized class consciousness" phrase is from Robin Kelley, "'We Are Not What We Seem," 31, 35–36. And see the discussion by Edna Bonacich, "Capitalism and Racial Oppression: In Search of Class Consciousness," in *Research in Urban Sociology: Race, Class, and Urban Change*, ed. Herry Lembcke (Greenwich, Conn.: JAI Press, 1989), 181–94 and especially 187.

13. Herbert Northrup, surveying the unions in 1944, found more than a score of AFL unions that specifically excluded African Americans by provision, ritual, or tacit agreement. He could find no CIO unions that excluded blacks or segregated them into Jim Crow locals, although he noted that occupational segregation and departmental seniority remained major black grievances. *Organized Labor and the Negro* (1944; reprint, New York: Harper and Brothers, 1976), 2–6, 14–16.

14. Tillman interview.

15. Hillie Pride, George Clark, and Coe interviews.

16. W. E. Davis interview.

17. Ed McCrea interview. Branch interview. Coe and Holloway interviews. Kelley, " 'We Are Not What We Seem,' " provides a wonderful analysis of the oppositional culture carried by the black working class. See also his specific treatment of how this culture emerged in Birmingham, in *Hammer and Hoe*.

18. Davis, Tools, Bates, and Isabell interviews.

19. Leroy Clark and Alzada Clark interviews.

20. See Leon Fink and Brian Greenberg, *Upheaval in the Quiet Zone: A History of Hospital Workers' Union, Local 1199* (Urbana: University of Illinois Press, 1989), 129–58, on the strike of hospital workers led in part by the Southern Christian Leadership Conference in Charleston, South Carolina. See also Carl E. Farris, "The Steelworkers' Strike in South Carolina," SCLC Press, n.d., on the efforts to forge a labor–civil rights coalition. In the UFWA, a revitalizing force emerged of women and people of color, Cornfield, *Becoming a Mighty Voice*, chap. 5. On the 1968 strike, see Joan Beifuss; F. Ray Marshall, and Arvil Van Adams, "Negro Employment in Memphis," *Industrial Relations* 9, no. 3 (May 1970): 308–23; and Thomas W. Collins, "Unionization in a Secondary Labor Market," *Human Organization* 36, no. 2 (Summer 1977): 135–41.

21. Coe interview.

22. Pride interview. Vaughn, "Memphis: Heart of the Mid-South," 111.

23. Bates, Boyd, Branch, Alzada Clark, George Clark, Leroy Clark, Coe, Matthew Davis, W. E. Davis, Dickenson, Griffen, Handcox, Holloway, Horton, Korstad, Bea McCrea, Ed McCrea, McGurty, McKinley, Powell, Routon, and Tillman interviews. .

24. Holloway interview. Boyd phone interview, 3 July 1991. Coe interview.

Primary Sources Consulted

ARCHIVES AND LIBRARIES

Federal Bureau of Investigation
   FBI investigative files, Washington, D.C., obtained under the Freedom of
      Information Act, in author's possession.
   Subject files:
      William A. Copeland
      W. E. Davis
      John Mack Dyson
      Firestone Tire and Rubber Co.
      Local 282, United Furniture Workers' Union
      Earl Fisher
      Harry Koger
      Local 19, Food, Tobacco, and Agricultural Workers
      Thomas Watkins
Highlander Research and Education Center Library, New Market, Tenn.
Library of Congress, Washington, D.C.
   National Urban League Papers
   National Association for the Advancement of Colored People Papers
Martin Luther King, Jr., Center for Non-Violent Social Change, Atlanta, Ga.
   Papers of Dr. Martin Luther King, Jr.
Memphis Public Library
   Office of the Mayor's Papers (Cossitt Branch Archives)
   Kenneth McKellar Papers (Cossitt Branch Archives)
   Socialist Party Scrapbook (Peabody Main Library)
Mississippi Valley Collection, Brister Library, Memphis State University
   Mayor Watkins Overton Papers
   Robert Church Papers
   William Amberson Papers
   Socialist Party Papers (microfilm)
National Archives and Records Administration, Washington, D.C., and Suitland, Md.
   Records of the U.S. Justice Department
      Includes Classified Subject and Correspondence and Investigative Files,
         Criminal Division, RG 60
   U.S. Department of Labor Records
      Office of the Secretary, RG 174
      United States Employment Service, Division of Negro Labor, RG 183

Records of the National Recovery Administration
    Classified General Files, Compliance Division Records, Labor Advisory Board
        Records, RG 9
Works Progress Administration
    Correspondence Files, RG 69
Fair Employment Practices Committee, RG 228
    John Beecher Files
    Weekly Reports
    Racial Tension Files
Inland Waterways Corporation, Department of Commerce, RG 91
Military Intelligence Division, War Department General Staff, RG 165
Records of the Federal Mediation and Conciliation Service, RG 280, Suitland, Md.
War Labor Board Records, RG 202, Suitland, Md.
Decisions and Orders of the National Labor Relations Board (bound volumes,
    Suitland, Md.)
War Labor Reports (bound volumes, Suitland, Md.)
Special Collections Department, Perkins Library, Duke University, Durham, N.C.
    Operation Dixie Papers
        Lucy Randolph Mason Papers (correspondence)
            Tennessee Organizing Committee Files
            William A. Copeland Files
            Paul Christopher Files
            William R. Henderson Files
            various records, by name of international union
        microfilm (same records, on microfilm)
Southern Labor Archives, Georgia State University, Atlanta
    Region 8 Files (Paul Christopher Papers)
    United Furniture Workers of America Papers
    International Woodworkers' Association District 4 Files
    Stetson Kennedy Papers
Tammiment Library, New York University
    Louis Slater Memorial Collection
Walter P. Reuther Library for Labor and Urban Affairs, Wayne State University,
        Detroit, Mich.
    Claude Williams Papers
    Workers' Defense League Files
    CIO Secretary-Treasurer's Files
        Part 2. George Weaver Files
    CIO Executive Board Meetings, Minutes
    Walther P. Reuther Records (UAW)
    UAW Local Unions, Local 988, Memphis
Wisconsin Historical Society, Madison, Wisc.
    United Packinghouse, Food, and Allied Workers of America
    Highlander Research and Education Center Files
    Highlander news clippings (microfilm)

NEWSPAPERS

Chattanooga Times
CIO Labor Journal (Tennessee, 1950s)
CIO News Tennessee edition
Memphis *Commercial Appeal*
FTA News
Highlander Fling (newsletter, Highlander Folk School)
Memphis Labor Review (affiliated with the Memphis AFL)
Memphis World (Memphis African-American paper)
The Pilot (NMU) Memphis *Press Scimitar*
Southern Patriot (Southern Conference Educational Fund)
Southern Worker (Communist party)
UCAPAWA News

PERSONAL INTERVIEWS

Evelyn Bates, 25 May 1989, Memphis
Leroy Boyd, 6 Feb. 1983, Memphis, and phone interview, 3 July 1991
Irene Branch, 25 May 1989, Memphis
Lucius Burch, 25 May 1989, phone interview
Alzada Clark, 24 May 1989, Memphis
George Clark, 30 Oct. 1984, Memphis, and phone interview, 17 Feb. 1983
Leroy Clark, 27 Mar. 1983, Memphis
Ken Clark, 5 Dec. 1982, New York City
Nona Clark, 5 Dec. 1982, New York City
Clarence Coe, 28 May 1989, Memphis, and phone interview, 28 May 1989
Danny Davis, 26 May 1989, Memphis
Matthew Davis, 30 Oct. 1984, Memphis
Morton Davis, 28 Jan. 1983, St. Louis
W. E. (Red) Davis, 26–28 Jan. 1983, St. Louis, and phone interviews, 17 June 1984, and
    14 Jan. 1986
Forrest Dickenson, 20 Feb. 1983, Memphis
Mary Lawrence Elkuss, 27 Jan. 1983, St. Louis
Rozelle Fields, 29 Oct. 1984, phone interview
Al Greenburg, 14 Nov. 1987, Larchmont, N.Y.
H. B. Griffin, 30 Oct. 1984, Memphis, and phone interview, 2 Mar. 1983
Willie Hall, 29 Oct. 1984, Memphis
John Handcox, 16 May 1985, Silver Spring, Md.
Edward Lee Harrel, 30 Oct. 1984 and 26 May 1989, Memphis
Fred Higgins, 30 Oct. 1984, Memphis
George Holloway, 23 Mar. 1990, Baltimore, Md.
Myles Horton, 1 and 2 June 1981, New Market, Tenn.
Hosea Hudson, 28 May 1985, Takoma Park, Md.
George Isabell, 7 Feb. 1983, Memphis
Bertha Jilks, 13 Aug. 1989, phone interview
Napolean Jilks, 26 Aug. 1989, Portland, Ore.

George King, 24 May 1989, Memphis
Karl Korstad, 20 May 1981, Greensboro, N.C.
Mose Lewis, 17 Feb. 1983, phone interview
Edward Lindsey, 27 May 1989, Memphis
Edward Lock, 29 Oct. 1984, Memphis
Bea McCrea, 6 Mar. and 17 Oct. 1983, Nashville, Tenn.
Ed McCrea, 6 Mar. and 17 Oct. 1983, 28 Oct. 1984, and 25 May 1988, Nashville, Tenn.
Lawrence McGurty, 17 Jan. 1983, Hometown, Ill.
Rebecca McKinley, 27 Mar. 1983, phone interview
Robert Matthews, 26 May 1989, Memphis
James Mitchell, 26 May 1989, Memphis
Fred Montgomery, 4 Mar. 1983, Henning, Tenn.
Carl Moore, 7 Feb. 1983, phone interview
Les Orear, 1 Aug. 1981, Chicago
Frances Owens, 2 Feb. 1983, Memphis
Clark Porteous, 11 Feb. 1983, phone interview
Dan Powell, 1 Feb. 1983, Memphis
Hillie Pride, 26 May 1983, Memphis
Laura Pride, 26 May 1983, Memphis
Cleveland Robinson, 15 Oct. 1983, phone interview
Lawrence Rogin, 11 June 1981, Washington, D.C.
Lonnie Roland, 1 Nov. 1984, Memphis
Mike Ross, 6 Nov. 1982, Chapel Hill, N.C.
William Ross, 2 Mar. 1983, phone interview
Richard Routon, 18 Feb. 1983, Memphis
Junius Scales, 3 Apr. 1987, Philadelphia, Pa.
Carl Scarborough, 8 Oct. 1982, Nashville, Tenn.
Pete Seeger, 19 Jan. 1986, Washington, D.C.
Robert Tillman, 24 Feb. 1983, Memphis
Josh Tools, 3 Mar. 1983, phone interview
Clara Vincent, 10 Jan. 1983, Livonia, Michigan
Susie Wade, 27 May 1987, phone interview
Johnny Williamson, 26 May 1989, Memphis

Index

NOTE ON THE AUTHOR

Michael K. Honey was an organizer for the Southern Conference Educational Fund and southern director for the National Committee against Repressive Legislation. He received his Ph.D. from Northern Illinois University in 1988 and his M.A. from Howard University. He was a fellow at the Stanford Humanities Center, has taught at Wesleyan University and the University of Puget Sound, and is presently an assistant professor at the University of Washington–Tacoma.